SACRED SCHISMS

Schism (from the Greek "to split") refers to a group that breaks away from another, usually larger organization and forms a new organization. Though the term is typically confined to religious schisms, it can be extended to other kinds of breakaway groups. Because schisms emerge out of controversies, the term has negative connotations. Though they are an important component of many analyses, schisms in general have not been subjected to systematic analysis.

This volume provides the first book-length study of religious schisms as a general phenomenon. Some chapters examine specific case studies while others provide surveys of the history of schisms within larger religious traditions, such as Islam and Buddhism. Other chapters are more theoretically focused. Examples are drawn from a wide variety of different traditions and geographical areas, from early Mediterranean Christianity to modern Japanese new religions, and from the Jehovah's Witnesses to Neopagans.

JAMES R. LEWIS is Lecturer in Philosophy at the University of Wisconsin, Stevens Point. He is editor of a number of collected works including *The Invention of Sacred Tradition* (2007) with Olav Hammer, and author of numerous books and articles, including *Legitimating New Religions* (2003).

SARAH M. LEWIS is Lecturer in Religious Studies in the Department of Theology and Religious Studies, University of Wales, Lampeter.

SACRED SCHISMS

How Religions Divide

EDITED BY

JAMES R. LEWIS AND SARAH M. LEWIS

CAMBRIDGE
UNIVERSITY PRESS

CAMBRIDGE UNIVERSITY PRESS
Cambridge, New York, Melbourne, Madrid, Cape Town, Singapore, São Paulo, Delhi

Cambridge University Press
The Edinburgh Building, Cambridge CB2 8RU, UK

Published in the United States of America by Cambridge University Press, New York

www.cambridge.org
Information on this title: www.cambridge.org/9780521881470

First published 2009

Printed in the United Kingdom at the University Press, Cambridge

A catalogue record for this publication is available from the British Library

Library of Congress Cataloguing in Publication data
Sacred schisms : how religions divide / [edited by] James R. Lewis, Sarah M. Lewis.
p.   cm.
Includes bibliographical references and index.
ISBN 978-0-521-88147-0 (hardback)
1. Religion–History.   2. Schism.   I. Lewis, James R.   II. Lewis, Sarah M.
BL65.H5S33 2009
209–dc22   2009000048

ISBN 978-0-521-88147-0 hardback

Contents

v

Figures

Notes on contributors

MICHAEL ABRAVANEL is currently pursuing an MA in Human Systems Intervention at Concordia University where he is a research and teaching assistant. He has a BA Honours in Religion and has developed a special focus on the history and philosophy of Church Universal and Triumphant and an interest in theosophy and other related NRMs.

RACHEL S. BOBBITT is a graduate student in the Sociology Program in the Wilder School of Government and Public Affairs at Virginia Commonwealth University in Richmond, Virginia. Her current research involves studying the development of religious movements emanating out of Marian apparitions and the role of religion in the public sphere.

DAVID G. BROMLEY is Professor of Religious Studies and Sociology in the School of World Studies at Virginia Commonwealth University. His most recent books are *Teaching New Religious Movements* (2007) and, with Douglas Cowan, *Cults and New Religious Movements: A Brief History* (2007). He is past president of the Association for the Sociology of Religion, former editor of the *Journal for the Scientific Study of Religion*, and founding editor of the series Religion and the Social Order.

JOSEPH M. BRYANT holds a cross-appointment in the Department for the Study of Religion and the Department of Sociology at the University of Toronto. He is the author of *Moral Codes and Social Structure in Ancient Greece: A Sociology of Greek Ethics from Homer to the Epicureans and Stoics* (1996), and co-editor, with John Hall, of *Historical Methods in the Social Sciences* (2005), a four-volume set in the series Benchmarks in Social Research Methods.

GEORGE D. CHRYSSIDES is Head of Religious Studies at the University of Wolverhampton. He has taught in several British universities. His publications include *The Advent of Sun Myung Moon* (1991), *Exploring New Religions* (1999), and *Historical Dictionary of New Religious Movements* (2001), as well as numerous journal articles and contributions to anthologies on new religions.

ALAN COLE is full professor at Lewis & Clark College where he teaches in the Religious Studies department and in the East Asian Studies program. He recently published *Text as Father: Paternal Seductions in Early Mahayana Literature* (2005), and is currently finishing a book on early Chan (Zen) entitled *Fathering Your Father: The Zen of Fabrication in Tang-Era Chinese Literature.*

ROGER FINKE is Professor of Sociology and Religious Studies at the Pennsylvania State University and is Director of the Association of Religion Data Archives (www.theARDA.com). He is the co-author (with Rodney Stark) of *The Churching of America, 1776–2005* (2005) and *Acts of Faith: Explaining the Human Side of Religion* (2000) as well as scores of research articles. He is now completing cross-national research on religious regulation and persecution, with a recent article (with Brian Grim) appearing in the *American Sociological Review.*

RON GEAVES is Professor of Religious Studies and Chair at the Liverpool Hope University. He is the author of *Sectarian Influences in British Islam* (1996), *Sufis of Britain: An Exploration of Muslim Identity* (2000), *Aspects of Islam* (2005), and *Key Words in Islam* (2006), and joint editor of *Islam and the West: Post-September 11th* (2004) as well as having written journal articles and contributions to edited works. His research interests are the diversity of Islam and the reproduction of such diversity in the West.

OLAV HAMMER is Professor of History of Religions at the University of Southern Denmark. He has published extensively on New Age religion, Western esotericism and new religious movements. He is, inter alia, the author of *Claiming Knowledge: Strategies of Epistemology from Theosophy to the New Age* (2001) and, together with James Lewis, editor of *The Invention of Sacred Tradition* (2008).

CYNTHIA HUMES is Associate Professor of Religious Studies, as well as Chief Technology Officer and Executive Director of Information Technology Services at Claremont McKenna College. She is co-editor with Bradley R. Hertel of *Living Banaras: Religion in Cultural Context* (1993; 1998), and with Thomas A. Forsthoefel of *Gurus in America* (2005). Recently, she has co-written a book on the history of the Transcendental Meditation movement in the United States, with Dana Sawyer.

ROBERT KISALA is Fellow at the Nanzan Institute for Religion and Culture and Professor of Religious Studies at Nanzan University, Nagoya. His publications include *Prophets of Peace: Pacifism and Cultural Identity in Japan's New Religions* (1999) and *Religion and Social Crisis in Japan: Understanding Japanese Society through the Aum Affair* (co-edited with Mark Mullins, 2001).

SUSAN J. PALMER teaches in Religious Studies at Concordia University where she is a Research Associate and Lecturer, and Dawson College, both in Montreal. She has written four books on new religious movements, notably *Aliens Adored: Rael's UFO Religion* (2004), *AIDS as an Apocalyptic Metaphor* (1997), and *Moon Sisters, Krishna Mothers, Rajneesh Lovers: Women's Roles in New Religion* (1994), and co-edited three volumes: *Children in New Religions* (1999), *Millennium, Messiahs and Mayhem* (1998), and *The Rajneesh Papers* (1993). Her next two books, *Black Gnosis* and *The New Heretics of France*, will appear in 2009.

CHRISTOPHER PARTRIDGE is Professor of Religion at the University of Lancaster. He is co-editor of the journal *Fieldwork in Religion*, and author of *The Re-enchantment of the West*, 2 volumes (2004–6) and of *H. H. Farmer's Theological Interpretation of Religion* (1998). He is the editor of several volumes on religious belief in the contemporary world, including *The World's Religions* (2005), *Encyclopedia of New Religions* (2004), *Finding and Losing Faith: Studies in Conversion* (with Helen Reid, 2006), *UFO Religions* (2003), *Mysticisms East and West* (with Theodore Gabriel, 2003), and *Fundamentalisms* (2001).

JESPER AAGAARD PETERSEN is PhD Fellow/Doctoral Candidate at the Norwegian University of Science and Technology. He is the co-editor of *The Encyclopedic Sourcebook of Satanism* (2008) and *Controversial New Religions* (2005) with James R. Lewis, and is currently editing *Embracing Satan: Contemporary Religious Satanism*.

MURPHY PIZZA is a PhD candidate in Anthropology and Comparative Religions at the University of Wisconsin-Milwaukee. Through the Ethnic Studies department at UWM, she has taught courses on Wicca and Neopaganism and Western occult traditions. She is co-editor of the forthcoming *Handbook of Contemporary Paganism* and a frequent book reviewer for *The Pomegranate: The International Journal of Pagan Studies*.

E. BURKE ROCHFORD is Professor of Sociology and Religion at Middlebury College. He has studied the Hare Krishna movement over the past thirty years and has published numerous articles on the movement's development. In addition to his book *Hare Krishna in America* (1985) he has a forthcoming book, *Hare Krishna Transformed*.

CHRISTOPHER P. SCHEITLE is a doctoral candidate in the Department of Sociology at the Pennsylvania State University. His research examines the organizational structure and dynamics of religion in the United States. He has previously published on such issues as denominational growth, financial contributions to congregations, and religious organizations' social networks. His dissertation uses original data on over 1,900 of the largest Christian non-profit organizations in the United States to understand their history, role, and operations.

Acknowledgments

In the process of compiling this book, we have incurred debts of gratitude to numerous people, not all of whom we can acknowledge here without generating a chapter-length document.

James Lewis owes a debt of gratitude to Evelyn Oliver, wife and partner of two decades, who supported him during this project in ways too numerous to mention.

Thanks are especially due to the contributors. We anticipate this will become an important collection – one to which all future scholars writing on schisms will refer – because of the high-quality chapters these individuals have contributed.

We thank Kate Brett, our acquisitions editor, who took interest in the initial proposal and supported it through the approval process at Cambridge University Press. Also, thanks to the manuscript's anonymous reviewers whose feedback led to improvements in the final product.

Introduction

James R. Lewis and Sarah M. Lewis

Three decades ago, James Lewis was a student at a regional university in the mountains of western North Carolina. As part of his financial aid package, he worked for an oral history project housed on the university campus. His interest in religion prompted him to seek interviews with local ministers – mostly elderly Baptist ministers who rejected affiliation with the Southern Baptist Convention because the SBC was too "liberal."

One of the more amusing stories he heard during those years was about a small Baptist church that began holding ice cream socials on Sunday afternoons following services. It was apparently a popular innovation. As long as the weather was mild, it was possible to hold the gatherings outside on the church lawn. However, as winter approached, these picnic-like social events became progressively problematic. Lacking other facilities, part of the congregation favored holding the gatherings inside the sanctuary. This proposal was opposed by another segment of the congregation who felt the sanctuary should be reserved for worship services. The dispute escalated until the congregation finally split over the issue.

We might humorously refer to the two churches emerging from this schism as the Ice-Cream-in-the-Sanctuary Baptists and the Anti-Ice-Cream-in-the-Sanctuary Baptists, as if the ice cream issue was a quasi-theological dispute causing the breakup. In actuality, however, it is unlikely that a disagreement over where to hold Sunday afternoon socials was the sole factor – or even the primary factor – behind the split. Rather, it is more probable that there were preexisting tensions within the congregation, and the ice cream issue was merely a flashpoint leading to an eruption of latent hostilities.

Lacking more detailed information about this schism, we can only speculate about other factors: perhaps there were non-ice-cream-related theological disputes feeding the conflict. Or maybe people within the church had previously disagreed over the manner in which worship services should be conducted, and the ice cream dispute merely reignited old tensions. It could also have been the case that an assistant pastor felt inclined to lead a breakaway group so he could occupy the top position in a new congregation, and the ice cream issue provided an opportunity to bring his inclinations into reality. To generalize from this example, we can say that the overt phase of a conflict can sometimes obscure other – often more important – factors paving the way for a schism.

The present collection brings together various treatments of schisms. Some chapters examine specific conflicts. Others provide surveys of the history of schisms within larger religious traditions. And a few are theoretically focused. In addition to this diversity of approaches, examples are drawn from different traditions.

SOURCES OF SCHISMS

Schism ('to split') refers to a group that breaks away from a (typically, but not invariably) larger organization and forms a new organization. Though the term is usually confined to religious contexts, it can be extended to other kinds of breakaway groups. Schisms arise out of conflict; a group that splits from its parent organization amicably would not normally be labelled a "schism." Because schisms emerge out of controversies, the term has a negative connotation – though less so than related terms like "heresy." Because of this connotation, breakaway groups do not typically refer to themselves as *schisms*.

In the pluralistic context of the contemporary world (as opposed to the comparatively monolithic religious environment of medieval Europe, for example) an individual who leaves one church and starts another church is not schismatic in the proper sense. Rather, a schism involves a *group* of people who leave a parent body and form a new organization. Thus, for instance, Eckankar is not a schism of Ruhani Satsang because only Paul Twitchell and his spouse left Ruhani Satsang to found Eckankar. Ruhani Satsang, on the other hand, *is* a schism of Sawan Singh's Radhasoami organization because Kirpal Singh left that movement along with a group of former members to found Ruhani Satsang.

Though they are an important component of many analyses (e.g., Neibuhr's *Social Sources of Denominationalism*), schisms in general have not been subjected to systematic analysis in recent years (a series of articles by Roger Finke, a contributor to the present collection, being a notable exception). Given the general poverty of current "schism theory," it will be useful to lay out a preliminary typology of schisms delineating the various factors that prompt splits.

The literature has identified a number of different factors contributing to schisms. These factors – which are not mutually exclusive – can be roughly classified into five groups:

Membership subgroupings. Splits can take place along economic, ethnic, racial, national, or other fault lines.

Personal ambition; personality conflicts. Schisms can be set in motion by individuals with leadership ambitions, or arise as a result of personality conflicts among the leadership.

Doctrinal/liturgical/behavioral norm disagreements. Though schismatic disagreements can take place at any point in a group's organizational life, they often occur in response to changes in a group's doctrines, liturgy and/or degree of strictness (e.g. the sectarian schisms resulting from the liberalization of mainstream denominations that are the focus of Neibuhr's work).

Death of a charismatic founder. A juncture at which schism frequently occurs is upon the death of the charismatic founder. Analyses of this category of institutional crisis go back at least as far as Max Weber's discussion of the "institutionalization of charisma."

Availability of alternative means of legitimation. Roy Wallis noted organizations that were "pluralistically legitimate" (e.g. the revelational authority available to multiple mediums in a Spiritualist church) were more likely to experience schisms than groups that were "uniquely legitimate." Wallis's more general point was that schismatics must find ways of legitimating their schisms.

Though an analysis of the various factors that play into schisms is useful, it is also static. In addition to referring to a group that has splintered off from another body, "schism" is a verb referring to the *process* of splitting. The actual dividing of an organization is usually only the final stage in a conflict that has been taking place for some time. It should be possible to analyze specific schisms in terms of the various stages leading to a split, such as identifying the stage at which the "point of no return" had been reached. Additionally, it should be possible to apply the same sort of analysis to similar organizational conflicts that do not result in schisms.

The factors that feed into a schism can also develop in dynamic ways. For example, a relatively minor doctrinal disagreement can lead to personal animosities that in turn exacerbate previously minor tensions between a regional association and a national denomination. Perhaps there had been festering tensions over the allocation of resources, such as a regional association of mostly rural churches upset over denominational funds being spent disproportionately in urban areas. An ambitious individual or individuals on the losing end of a doctrinal disagreement who also happened to belong to this hypothetical rural association could be offended enough by the doctrinal dispute to exploit prior tensions over funding and lead a schism of regional churches from the denomination.

Analysts should also be sensitive to differences among religious traditions, though these may be differences of emphasis rather than of substance. In the South Asian context, for example, schisms often arise out of disputed successorships – as in the earlier example of Kirpal Singh, whose claim to guruship following Sawan Singh's death was rejected by the Radhasoami organization. Though splits over successorship can be found in some Western religious organizations, more often the issues that divide Christian groups are (at least at the overt level) disagreement over proper doctrine and practice (which is not to say that these types of disagreements are confined to Christianity). As another example, Muslims of every persuasion go on the Hajj and otherwise cooperate in ways that have no exact parallel among, for instance, Christian sects.

Roger Finke is one of the few contemporary scholars writing on schisms. His and Christopher Scheitle's chapter "Understanding schisms: theoretical explanations for their origins" builds on organizational and religious economy theories to explain the social context and organizational dynamics involved in schisms. Their chapter begins by examining religious markets that promote or deter schisms. The authors then analyze how relationships between denominations, congregations, and clergy contribute to schisms. The chapter concludes with a brief discussion of the consequences of schism.

Chapters 2–4 present overviews of schisms in different major religious traditions. In "Charismatic authority in Islam: an analysis of the cause of schisms in the *ummah*," Ron Geaves puts forward an analytical framework for understanding schisms within Islam, focusing on types of authority and legitimacy. In the first section, Geaves places the initial schisms following Muhammad's death in the context of contemporary charismatic leadership debates and the need to remain authentic to the primal message. He then explores Shi'a and Sunni Islam, seeking to understand alternative patterns of schism in each main branch. Later schisms within each branch are related back to the initial causes of division and the competing theologies that developed out of these schisms.

In similar mode, Alan Cole's "Schisms in Buddhism" presents a sweeping overview of schisms within another major world religious tradition. In sharp contrast to Western stereotypes of Buddhism as static and unchanging, Buddhism has been characterized by dynamic change and innovation. As Cole points out, it would not be an exaggeration to characterize the entire twenty-five-century history of Buddhism as a series of schismatic developments – and he proceeds to do just this, starting from Gautama's original split with the Indian religious tradition of his day to contemporary forms of Buddhism that emerged out of Asia's confrontation with Western colonialism.

'New Religion' is a direct translation of *Shin Shukyo*, the expression coined by Japanese sociologists to describe the explosion of innovative religious movements that emerged in the wake of the Second World War. However, instead of dissipating after the initial cycle of innovation, the impulse to create new religions remained strong beyond the post-war period, leading to newer organizations that emerged from schisms with the original new religions. In "Schisms in Japanese new religion movements," Robert Kisala surveys this line of development, focusing on the history of three of the older new religions – Tenrikyo, Omotokyo, and Reiyukai – and the newer schismatic groups that have emerged from them.

One ordinarily thinks of schismatic groups as introducing doctrinal and organizational innovations following their secession from parent religious bodies, while the parent group remains relatively unchanged. In "Finishing the *Mystery* – the Watch Tower and 'The 1917 Schism'," George D. Chryssides examines the transition from Charles Taze Russell, founder of the original Watch Tower Society, to the new leader, Joseph Franklin Rutherford. In this case, one of the principal factors prompting schism was the doctrinal and organizational innovations introduced by Rutherford – innovations that reshaped the Watch Tower into what would become a very different kind of movement.

David G. Bromley has written extensively on the dynamics of contemporary religious movements and the social conflicts in which they have been involved. In "Challenges to charismatic authority in the Unificationist Movement," he and Rachel S. Bobbitt argue that emergent segments of a developing movement – the inner circle, administrative and mission-oriented organizations, and the grassroots membership base – can each become a power base from which challenges to movement leadership potentially originate (i.e. each component is a source of potential schisms). The authors utilize examples from the Unificationist Movement to illustrate the points of their analysis.

We also usually think of schisms as weakening the parent body. This is not, however, invariably the case, as discussed by Joseph M. Bryant in his chapter, "Persecution and schismogenesis: how a penitential crisis over mass apostasy facilitated the triumph of Catholic Christianity in the Roman Empire." Following a persecution during which numerous Christians had renounced the faith rather than suffer martyrdom, a debate over whether or not such apostasy could be forgiven led what became the Church of the Katharoi (Novationists) to a split from the Catholic Church. Following the exodus of hardliners, the Catholic leadership was free to pursue a less severe approach better suited to attracting new converts.

The example of the Katharoi schism should not, however, blind us to the fact that schisms often do lead to a weakening of the parent body. Susan J. Palmer and Michael Abravanel's "Church Universal and Triumphant: shelter, succession and schism" presents an almost textbook case of how not to treat potential schismatics in the wake of the death (in this case, the "social death") of the charismatic leader. Though the Board of Directors was not solely responsible for defections from the Church Universal and Triumphant, their moves to assert total control over the organization managed to alienate the majority of Teaching Centres outside of Montana, resulting in the exodus of numerous centers and individuals, and a subsequent weakening of the church.

In his chapter on "Schism and consolidation: the case of the theosophical movement," Olav Hammer examines a particularly schism-prone tradition, the Theosophical Society and its numerous splinter groups. Drawing on the plentiful history of organizational splits within the theosophical movement for illustrations, the analysis focuses on the identity politics that take place as new schisms seek to distinguish themselves from their parent body while maintaining enough of a family resemblance with the original organization to seem familiar – and, more importantly, legitimate – in the eyes of potential converts. Hammer discusses the forging of new groups in terms of the *branding* of distinctive new religious products. He also brings up Colin Campbell's notion of the "cultic milieu," and mentions how the theosophical movement functions as its own distinct milieu, sharing certain critical characteristics with the larger cultic milieu. This notion is further developed in Petersen's chapter.

Jesper Aagaard Petersen's "Satanists and nuts: the role of schisms in modern Satanism" is a rich piece that is much more than a discussion of contemporary Satanism and the construction of Satanic identity. Among Petersen's insights is his extension of Campbell's cultic milieu to encompass certain sub-milieus, such as the phenomenon he dubs the

"Satanic milieu." Though he does not explicitly discuss this point, one issue developed in subsequent chapters is that, though schisms may weaken specific organizations, they can contribute to the expansion of a particular subculture – in this case, to the expansion of the Satanic milieu. This milieu initially came into existence as a consequence of schisms from the original Church of Satan. Similar observations apply to sub-milieus arising from other kinds of schisms, such as those that have arisen in the wake of schisms within the Pagan movement and the Hare Krishna movement.

Though she does not refer to Campbell, Murphy Pizza's "Schism as midwife: how conflict aided the birth of a contemporary Pagan community" discusses the larger Neopagan community in terms that resonate with Campbell's characterization of the cultic milieu. Like the Satanic milieu, contemporary Paganism is a sub-milieu within the larger cultic milieu that could be termed – extending Petersen's terminology – the Pagan milieu. In terms of this theme, Pizza's chapter on the Twin Cities Pagan milieu is important for its highlighting of what was implicit in Petersen's chapter, namely that, instead of viewing a schism as a failure, a schism can instead be "a catalyst for growth and for the rethinking of community." But, assuming this observation is correct, can it be extended to other milieus?

In "Succession, religious switching, and schism in the Hare Krishna movement," E. Burke Rochford recounts the many institutional woes and attendant dramas of schisms within this movement. He also points out that Hare Krishna schisms tend to be expressed in terms of the quest for doctrinal purity, but the underlying conflicts are often matters of contested religious authority. One consequence of these frequent conflicts is that many people who have defected from the warring organizations continue to participate in a larger Hare Krishna milieu. As with Pizza's discussion of the Pagan milieu, Rochford argues that institutional failures are not the same as movement failure. Instead, it seems that the emergence of a de-institutionalized movement has actually served to spread the original teachings into new settings.

Cynthia Ann Humes's chapter, "Schisms within Hindu Guru groups: the Transcendental Meditation movement in North America," presents a somewhat different case study. Humes examines three distinct splinters from TM: Robin Carlsen's World Teach Movement; Ravi Shankar's quasi-independent following, which remained nominally within the TM fold; and Deepak Chopra, who was ejected from TM as a potential threat to the Maharishi's authority. Though it could be said that a TM milieu constituted in part by non-affiliated TMers emerged in the vicinity of the Maharishi International University, the TM situation differs from the Hare Krishna movement. Instead of staying within the TM milieu, the majority of defectors from the TM organization subsequently became involved in other neo-Hindu groups – groups that share certain basic beliefs with TM.

Christopher Partridge's "Schism in Babylon: colonialism, Afro-Christianity and Rastafari" shifts the discussion of schisms into a significantly different cultural context. This chapter provides a concise overview of the history and ideology of the Rastafarian movement. Like a number of other contributors to this volume, Partridge explicitly invokes Campbell's idea of "cultic milieu" (the basis for his notion of "occulture") to describe the emergent spiritual subculture in Jamaica. He also argues that within what we might term the Rastafarian milieu schisms are less of a specific event and more of a process in which "schism and syncretism sometimes overlap and problematise easy definition." In this sense, the Rastafarian milieu is more similar to the Pagan milieu than it is to some of the other sub-milieus we have mentioned.

The milieu discussion which began with the overview of Hammer's chapter should serve to make us attentive to the possibility of other, comparable milieus or sub-milieus beyond the ones mentioned above. In Western countries – and particularly in the US – there is a Christian milieu that extends well beyond the boundaries of organized Christianity (not to mention certain sub-milieus, such as the Mormon milieu). Christian denominations can splinter and new denominations arise. Alternatively, organizationally alienated Christians can pray at home or form their own home churches. But, as Philip Jenkins forcefully demonstrates in *The Next Christendom*, Christianity continues to grow, demonstrating once again that organizational failure does not equate to the failure of a religious movement.

PART I

Theoretical overview

CHAPTER I

Understanding schisms: theoretical explanations for their origins

Roger Finke and Christopher P. Scheitle

Since the dawn of the social sciences, scholars have written at length on the topic of schisms. The rich descriptions of Weber and Troeltsch, in particular, offered contrasts between the established churches and the sects they spawned. Each scholar pointed out stark differences in charismatic leadership, social class, asceticism, and soteriology. H. Richard Niebuhr (1929), though, was the first to inject theoretical life to the process of schism formation, explaining that sects arise to meet the religious needs of the "masses." Niebuhr went on to explain that over time the more successful sects tend to be taken over by the privileged and are transformed into churches that no longer adequately serve the needs and tastes of the proletariat. Consequently, dissidents break away and yet another schism occurs. This gives rise to an endless cycle of transformations and schisms.

But a serious limitation of Niebuhr's model was that it relied almost entirely on class interests to explain schisms. There is no doubt that social class dynamics have contributed to many schisms, but an abundance of recent research has shown that social class differences are often not a motivating factor behind them. In fact, many of the most historically significant schisms, such as those producing the Essenes (Baumgarten 1997), the Christians (Stark 1996), and the Waldensians (Lambert 1977), were not based on the proletariat. A second limitation is that Niebuhr's model offers little explanation of the organizational dynamics underlying schisms or the larger context in which this process occurs. Because attention is focused so narrowly on social class, all other factors fade away.

Building on organizational and religious economy theories, this chapter will explain the social context and organizational dynamics involved in schisms. We begin by looking at the religious markets and ecological spaces that promote or deter schisms. How does the state's regulation of religion and the existing supply of religion open the door for schisms? Next we look within religious organizations. How do the relationships between denominations, congregations, and clergy contribute to schisms? Finally, we briefly discuss the consequences of schisms. How do they change the organizations involved and how do they contribute to larger religious change?

CLARIFYING THE CAUSES

The drama and turmoil of a marital divorce is often interpreted as the source of the relationship's demise. The fighting between the couple becomes seen as the reason for their inevitable failure and is used to explain larger trends in divorce. Such an interpretation may be accurate in some cases, but for most it is an error in attribution. As most sociologists would argue, relationships often end for reasons that have little to do with the personality dynamics between partners. It is unlikely that the rise in the twentieth-century divorce rate is simply because couples disliked each other more then than they did in the nineteenth century. The real causes are to be found in larger structural and historical forces. Increases in life expectancy, social expectations of gender roles, economic downturns, changes in the legal system, and many other forces can be the hidden source of the drama that surrounds separations.

Similar descriptions can be given for divorces within religious groups. The same heightened emotions and drama can be found in schisms. Arguments about theology, leadership, and actions can often find parallels in arguments between two individuals about neglect, infidelity, and abuse. As with separations of individuals, we must be careful not to let the manifest drama of a schism distract us from its latent causes (Blasi 1989: 311). Instead of looking to the surface phenomena that occur during schisms, we must examine the deeper social and organizational contexts that give rise to schisms. We begin by examining the role of national context in creating an environment that spawns or suppresses schisms.

Country context and schisms

When Swiss-born, German-educated Philip Schaff wrote one of the first surveys of American religion, he explained to his European audience that the religious freedoms of the new voluntary system in America resulted in increased levels of religious zeal and commitment. But he also cautioned that the new sect system had a "shady side" that "changes the peaceful kingdom of God into a battle-field" (Schaff 1855: 99, 102). What Schaff and a host of other nineteenth-century European visitors were observing was that schisms occurred with increasing regularity when sects could compete on equal footing with the established churches. A starting point for identifying the origins of schisms is understanding the freedom, or lack thereof, that sects have in splitting from existing churches. In other words, what are the start-up costs for a new group?

When considering a schism, the potential costs for new religious groups are many and they vary widely across countries. In nineteenth-century America new sects flourished because they could. Once a new religion split from the parent group it could immediately compete for adherents without any limitations or sanctions. Unlike the churches so familiar to Europeans, schism did not result in a loss of subsidy. To the contrary, no religion was favored by the state. This lack of state inter-ference also allowed schisms to form without facing state penalties. Religions were not required to register and young sects held the same freedoms as the groups from which they split (Finke 1990). As Schaff noted, this resulted in a highly competitive battlefield, with new legions (i.e. sects resulting from schisms) entering the field each year.

But the effects of regulation are not confined to one nation or time period. Japan serves as one of many examples. Before the end of World War II, the government strictly controlled religious activity in Japan. The state subsidized Shinto shrines and participation in ceremonies was a matter of civic duty. Alternative religions required government recognition legally to exist and, once recognized, they faced interference, suppression, and persecution from the state (McFarland 1967; Hardacre 1989). But the Japanese defeat and the Allied Occupation in 1945 led to the immediate repeal of all laws controlling religion, disestablished the Shinto religion, and granted unprecedented religious freedom (Nakano 1987).

The response was overwhelming. The period immediately following 1945 is called *kamigami no rasshu awa*, the "rush hour of the gods." It was said that "New Religions rose like mushrooms after a rainfall" (quoted in McFarland 1967: 4). By 1949, 403 new religious groups had been founded, and 1,546 other groups had established independence through secession from the shrines, temples, or churches to which they had pre-viously belonged. In contrast, only thirty-one religious groups had received official recognition in the decades before 1945 – thirteen Shinto sects, twenty-eight Buddhist denominations, and two Christian groups (Nakano 1987: 131). Like nineteenth-century America, schisms flourished once the start-up costs were reduced.

Moving into the contemporary period, we see the same trend around the globe. Anthony Gill (1994), Andrew Chesnut (2003), and others have documented the surge in schisms and religious competition in Latin America following a lifting of regulations on the new sects. After four centuries of a monopoly religion, evangelical Christians burst onto the scene as regulations were lifted in the latter half of the twentieth century, with the percentage of evangelicals in the population doubling and tripling since the 1970s. The lifting of regulations in Taiwan has been more recent, but no less dramatic. Yunfeng Lu (2008) reports that after the 1989 Law on Civic Organizations allowed all religions to exist and removed multiple prohibitions there was a twelvefold increase in the number of different religious groups in Taiwan (from 83 in 1990 to 1,062 in 2004) and the total number of temples and churches more than doubled.

To summarize, the first step in identifying the origin of schisms is to understand the barriers potential new groups face. Will they lose subsidies and do they face penalties from the state or larger culture once they are formed? But even when sects can compete on equal footing with the dominant religions, the call for schisms will vary. Our next step is to identify when there is "ecological space" or a "market opening" for new religions to arise from schisms.

Ecological space and schisms

After Niebuhr's promising work on explaining the process of schism, much of the work that followed returned to the task of specifying the differences between churches and sects. Multiple types and subtypes of sects were soon identified and all were described in detail (see Wilson 1959). In 1963, however, Benton Johnson laid the conceptual groundwork for future theoretical work by explaining that churches and sects were religious organizations located at opposing ends of the same continuum. Churches accepted their social environment while sects rejected it. Rather than placing groups within different categories of a typology, where each group was defined by different qualities, Johnson placed the groups on a conceptual continuum. The abstractness and parsimony of this continuum allowed it to be applied to other world religions and provided a conceptual clarity for explaining sect movement across the continuum to become more church-like. Johnson's work has served as a theoretical starting point for a large body of theoretical work that followed (Stark and Bainbridge 1985; Iannaccone 1988; Finke and Stark 1992).

For understanding schisms, however, we want to identify why religious groups are scattered across this continuum and how movement on the

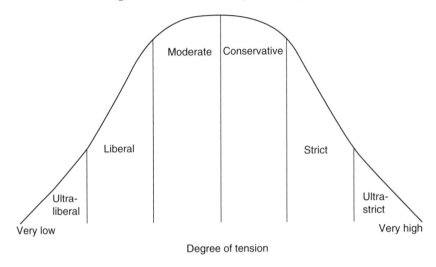

1.1 A hypothetical distribution of religious niches

continuum increases or decreases the chance of schism. To do so, we focus less on the religious groups for a moment and more on the demand underlying their diversity. Suppose we ranked people according to their preference for intense religion. Previous work has shown that the results approximate a bell-shaped curve where people cluster toward the center of the axis in the area of medium tension, as shown in Figure 1.1 (Stark and Finke 2000). Few want a religion that forces complete submission, requiring a life of isolation from the secular society. Likewise, few want a religion whose god is so distant and powerless as to offer little assistance in daily living and few promises for the life hereafter. To the extent people seek religion, and not all do, the demand is the highest for religions that offer close relations with the supernatural and distinctive demands for membership, without isolating individuals from the culture around them. As Weber (1946; 1993) noted and a host of anthropologists have shown, people differ in how much religious intensity they prefer, regardless of the society.

This variation in demand is obvious in an unregulated religious economy where the supply of religions becomes a reflection of religious demand. It is less obvious in highly regulated and monopolized religious economies where the preferences of many niches go unmet. But even in these societies the existence of groups wishing higher- and lower-tension options shows up as the never-ending line of heretical challengers to the monopoly, some offering higher-tension faith and some proposing more worldly faiths. This ever present diversity of demand has resulted in "religious niches" that are important for understanding the origins of schisms (Stark and Finke 2000).

The idea of niches and the importance of understanding niches is not new in the social sciences. Recent work has shown that there are many similarities between research on religious markets and organizational ecology (Scheitle 2007). As its name might suggest, organizational ecology has its roots in animal and plant ecology. The basic premise is that organizations are much like species of plants or animals in that each species (e.g. a denomination) consists of a population of organizations (e.g. congregations). All individuals within this population are relying on a particular type of resource in the environment. A species of animal relies on a particular food source and/or a particular location to survive, while a species of organization relies on a particular demographic, such as a specific gender, age, race, income, or other niche.

Because an organization's niche is where it looks to acquire resources, it has important implications for growth. If niche size is stable and a religious group has exhausted the existing resources in the niche by converting all who are willing to join, a group can only grow through expanding its niche outwards. For groups on the tails of the distribution, this can be done either by moving entirely toward the middle, or by stretching its niche toward the middle while attempting to hold its appeal to its current fringe niche. The former strategy can be called niche shifting while the latter can be called niche stretching. A group already in the middle can also attempt to stretch its niche outwards while trying to hold on to its current position.

It is easy to see how the church–sect literature maps on to this framework. Sects tend to have very narrow niches that usually focus on the segment of the population that is interested in a highly demanding religion. When a sect becomes more church-like by stretching its niche to appeal to those wanting a less demanding religion, it increases the size of the niche to which it appeals. This may or may not be an intentional growth strategy, but the consequences are the same regardless.

But if niche expansion offers the potential for growth, it also offers the threat of schism.[1] Attempts to expand a niche result in conflict and

---

[1] Simply shifting a niche is not necessarily easy to do either, but, for reasons that will be discussed, it is easier than holding on to a niche while simultaneously moving into another.

schisms due to both cultural and material issues. Stretching a niche into new demographic or religious populations means that an organization will try to incorporate individuals who have different social, political, and theological attitudes and expectations. Satisfying such heterogeneous interests is a naturally difficult task and an easy source of conflict. For religious groups it is nearly impossible to claim the exclusive divine authority that appeals to some individuals and simultaneously to appeal to the relativistic and humanistic interests of other individuals. Even if the group were somehow able to create religious services and products that superficially fulfilled the demands of both segments, the attempt to straddle both niches would entirely void the group's authority in each part of the market. The group's legitimacy in each segment of the market would be questioned.

Beyond the issues of legitimacy, expanding a niche so that it includes multiple segments of the population creates the potential for conflicts about the economic and material resources of the group. For example, minority[2] groups within the organization's stretched niche may feel that they are not fully represented in leadership positions or seminaries. At the very least this can lead to conflict within the group, and often it can lead to the minority group deciding they would be better off on their own or by joining a more like-minded group.

The Methodists of the nineteenth century serve as one of many examples. When the lay-led, holiness-seeking, camp-meeting Methodists of the early nineteenth century began to include more middle-class congregations with seminary trained clergy at the end of the nineteenth century, a series of schisms began. One of the first started with an outspoken group of clergy from the Genesee Conference in the 1850s. Following the lead of the Reverend Benjamin Titus Roberts, they objected to doctrines they described as "liberal to the point of Unitarianism" and to lifestyles that departed from "nonconformity to the world." They were especially critical of the introduction of "pew rentals" as abandoning the poor and of the growing centralization and excess of "executive power and ecclesiastical machinery" (Bureau of the Census 1910: II, 487). Later "read out" of the larger denomination and eventually forming the Free Methodists, their departure was little noticed. Yet, it was an omen for what was to come.

---

[2] Minority here refers to a racial, economic, theological, or other social minority within a religious group.

By the close of the nineteenth century the "ecclesiastical machinery" attacked by Roberts was struggling to control a rapidly growing holiness movement. Supported by forty-one periodicals, four publishing houses, and a growing number of holiness evangelists, the movement was calling for a return to the holiness emphasis of Methodist founders. In response, the Methodist bishops launched an attack on Methodist clergy participating in the movement and denied holiness evangelists the right to preach in local churches without the permission of the local pastor (Peters 1985). More than ever, the Methodist church was struggling in an attempt to be both sect and church. With the bishops clamping down on the holiness evangelists and clergy, holiness spokesmen began to call "all true holiness Christians to come out of Methodism's church of mammon" (Melton 1989). And out they came.

Similar struggles with niche stretching can also be observed in local congregations (Christerson and Emerson 2003). In her study of a Korean congregation trying to incorporate other races and ethnicities, Dhingra (2004) observed a variety of problems resulting from the presence of the new members. These problems ranged from the type of food to serve to the congregation, the type of ministries to offer, and the use of the Korean language in the congregation. Because there was still a clear majority in the congregation, it was often easier to serve that "core" membership than it was to change everything the congregation was used to doing. If the congregation does serve the minority members, it might do so at the expense of alienating its current majority. Furthermore, because there are other congregations "specializing" in their own ethnicity, many of those minority members will feel both a push and a pull pressure to leave the congregation.

In empirical studies of schisms (e.g. Liebman, Sutton, and Wuthnow 1988; Sutton and Chaves 2004), one of the more consistent findings is that group size increases the likelihood of schism. This may seem ironic in that size is usually seen as a sign of group success, and therefore one might expect a reduced risk of conflict and schism in such organizations. However, when taking into account the idea of niche stretching, it becomes clear that size is often a proxy for an over-stretched niche.

Resource dependence and schisms

The first two sources of schism emphasized the social context and the larger religious markets of denominations. Now we turn our attention to the religious organization. Rather than looking at market regulation or niches, we look at the internal operations of the organization and how it contributes to schism. In particular, we will focus on the exchange of resources that occur between congregations and the larger denominational structure. How do these relationships serve to increase or decrease the propensity to schism?

Speaking of "religious groups" or "denominations" has the consequence of projecting a false sense of unity. The reality is that instead of being a single organic being, a religious group or denomination is a heterogeneous collective of different organizations and individuals all connected by various networks of social ties. Congregations, denominational agencies, seminaries, ministers, members, and central authorities are some of the most common, although not all, of the nodes within this web that makes up our perception of a single organization.

Each tie between these units consists of resource exchanges between actors (Pfeffer and Salancik 1978). Some of these resources may be tangible, such as money, land for buildings, and worship materials. Other resources, such as legitimacy and authority, are less visible but just as important. These ties vary in the balance of their exchanges. Some may be an equal exchange of resources, but many are unequal exchanges where one actor depends on the other more than the reverse. When one party's dependence does not equal the other's, then there is a power imbalance where the latter holds power over the former (Emerson 1962).

While all denominations are made up of these ties and their resource exchanges, each denomination varies greatly in the balance and direction of the exchanges that occur within its "web." Consider the pattern and balance of exchanges within a highly centralized, bureaucratic, or rational–legal denomination, as illustrated in Figure 1.2. In such denominations the central office of the denomination provides resources and/or legitimacy to seminaries. These seminaries in turn provide the professional credentials and create capital for the ministers (Finke and Dougherty 2002). The central office also provides direct resources to ministers through placement, professional development training, and possibly even retirement benefits. Congregations also receive "official" worship materials and other assistance from the central offices, not to mention the "brand name" and religious history of the denomination. Of course, the seminaries, congregations, and ministers provide some resources back to the denomination, including the money from congregations to the denominational offices. However, the overall patterns of direct and indirect exchanges in such a denomination are in the favor of the denominational office. The seminaries would struggle without the

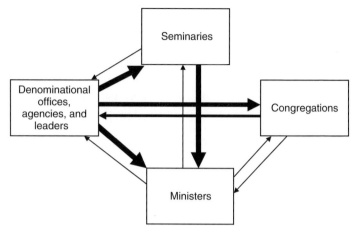

***Weight of line represents amount of resources given from actor to recipient. Thicker lines mean the recipient is more dependent on the giver.

1.2 Exchange and power dynamics in a centralized denomination

money and legitimacy provided, ministers would struggle if they lost their professional identity and credentials, and congregations define themselves by the religious tradition of the denomination.

We can contrast this to the exchanges that occur in a decentralized or "charismatic" denomination.[3] Denominations such as this often favor lay ministers. This eliminates the influence of seminaries. Similarly, because the independence of congregations is often emphasized, the central office provides few worship resources and little religious capital to congregations. Instead, the denomination is taking more from the congregations and ministers, as it relies on them not only to expand the denomination but to support the denominational offices. There is a heavy but balanced exchange between minister and congregation. The former is at the mercy of the congregation's favor, while the latter is invested in the personality of the minister. In short, the exchange dynamics in denominations such as this favor ministers and

---

[3] It is debatable whether the terms rational–legal and charismatic describe the same concepts as centralized and decentralized. However, they are often used to describe the same phenomena, so we simply treat them as equivalents here.

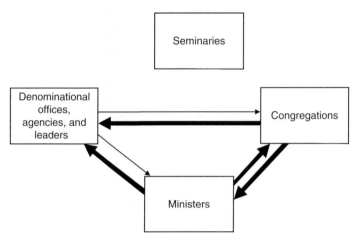

***Weight of line represents amount of resources given from actor to recipient.
Thicker lines mean the recipient is more dependent on the giver.

1.3 Exchange and power dynamics in a decentralized/charismatic denomination

congregations, and the most important tie is between those two actors (Figure 1.3).

We can easily parallel this to other types of organizations. When an individual purchases a franchise from a recognized national restaurant chain, the individual knows that success depends on the larger brand. Because the customers are coming for the reputation of the larger chain, not the individual owner, the balance of power is in the favor of the organization. The brand has given the owner the training, credentials, and perceived authenticity with customers. If the owner has a dispute with the organization, she cannot simply change the name, symbols, or procedures of her restaurant without losing the benefits of affiliating with the larger organization. The owner may be providing a franchise fee to the central office, but this fee is much less important to it than what it provides to the individual owner.

When there is a grievance with a centralized organization, the actors know that they are not the power holders. Hence, they are more invested in working out the problem, which usually means going through the "system" provided by the central office. This results in a series of committee hearings, resolutions, formal debates, and votes that may or may not actually solve the original grievance, but frequently succeed in delaying the issue until it goes away or at least providing the aggrieved a sense of being heard.

Recent history has seen many denominations going through these steps to prevent a schism. Groups such as the Episcopal Church and the United Methodist Church have been faced with potential schisms over homosexuality that have, as of now, been largely delayed through the mechanisms of their organizational structure[4] (Banerjee 2006; Vegh 2006). Conflicts in decentralized (or "charismatic") denominations are more likely to end in schism and that result is likely to occur more quickly. The power lies in the hands of the congregations and ministers, so the central office has little ability to delay and/or prevent splits. This helps to explain why over the last two hundred years Catholics have spawned only a few sects and Baptists have generated scores of new groups (Melton 2003).

We should also mention that organizational relationships, like niche positioning, are not static. Like other organizations, religious organizations will tend to become more centralized and support increasingly large administrative staffs as they increase in size (Blau 1970; 1972; Stark and Finke 2000: 162–3). In the Methodist example offered earlier, the Genesee Conference and the holiness movements that followed objected to the increasing administrative authority. Whereas the local congregation once had substantial freedom in selecting local clergy and class leaders, the new bishops were now ruling on who could preach and how clergy would be trained and placed. This resulted in less independence for the local congregations and gave increased powers to the bishops. Southern Baptists have historically been offered as a model for decentralization, with local congregations that were highly independent and only loosely affiliated in their efforts to support missions. But since the middle of the twentieth century local churches have become increasingly dependent on the services of their state associations and the larger denominational structure. Not surprisingly the national organization has also sought to exert more control over the local churches (Finke and Stark 1992). To the extent that denominations can increase congregational dependency on their services, we expect this to reduce schisms.

Inimitability and schisms

To the extent that a denomination holds claim to an exclusive truth, prophet, historical tradition, or ecclesiastical office, the chance of schism

---

[4] Some individual or small groups of congregations have left their denomination over these issues, but a larger schism has not occurred yet.

will also be reduced. In the parlance of organizational theory, the organization holds a competitive advantage because it provides an inimitable good or service. From the perspective of potential sect movements, the option for schism is reduced because leaving the denomination would result in the loss of both legitimacy and a host of unique resources. Thus, inimitability increases congregations' dependency on the denomination and offers yet another organizational deterrent against schism.

The sources of this inimitability can be many, but one of the most obvious is the unique histories of religious groups that imbue them with ecclesiastical offices, services, and traditions that are unique to their group. Dissidents are forced either to remain or to lose part of their religious heritage. Whereas some Protestant sects feel that a return to the teachings of Christ and the apostles requires them to depart from their existing denomination in protest, Catholic movements seeking such a return are compelled by their very belief structure to remain within the church. For example, conservative Catholic movements seeking to restore previous traditions are compelled by their very beliefs to remain within the church. Splitting from the formal structure of the Roman Catholic Church would mean abandoning the church they define as the "one true church" and nearly two millennia of church tradition. For those calling for a revival of past traditions, any attempts to split from the church would deny them the very traditions they seek to restore (Finke and Stark 1992: 273; Dinges 1995: 252–8; Finke and Wittberg 2000). This is clearly evident in Orthodoxy as well. Bumper stickers such as "Orthodoxy: Proclaiming the Truth since A.D. 33" illustrate the importance of history for claiming legitimacy. Even when movements within these groups fail to win over the church authorities, schism is seldom an attractive option.

Closely related to the unique histories of the religious groups are the unique prophets and ecclesiastical offices that are tied to the group. Once again, the Catholic Church serves as an example with the papacy. Splitting from the formal structure of the Roman Catholic Church would mean losing the institutional source for Apostolic Succession and ignoring the Vicar of Christ. Potential sect movements within the Church of Jesus Christ of the Latter-Day Saints (Mormons) face a similar decision. Because the Mormon President is a modern-day prophet, any schisms lose the historical legitimacy of this position and the institutional supports tied to this office.

Along with the unique religious qualities and resources, groups are often interwoven with unique social qualities. None has been more prominent than ethnicity. American religious history is filled with examples of religious groups offering a unique combination of religion and ethnicity. Whether the groups were Greek Orthodox or Swedish Lutherans, the worship life and institutions were infused with language, rituals, songs, and saints that were specific to a group. For first-generation immigrants schism was seldom attractive because the other local congregations could offer few or none of these options.[5]

The examples just given all illustrate how the inimitable qualities of a group increase the congregations' dependency on the larger denomination for legitimacy. Like the resource dependency discussed earlier, the inimitable qualities of a denomination discourage schism. Unable to find suitable substitutes for the unique histories, prophets, and cultural assets of their current denominations, potential sect movements choose to remain within the fold.

Religious professionals and schisms

The final source of schism moves from the organization to emphasize a group of key actors in the organization: the clergy. Next to the church–sect explanation of schisms, one of the most common is that schisms result from charismatic leaders who are able to garner support from a group sizeable enough to break from the larger group. But this raises questions about why charismatic leaders arise in some denominations and not others. Does this mean that schismless groups have fewer dynamic individuals than schism-prone groups? Furthermore, this suggests that schisms are chaotic and random events driven by the circumstantial presence or non-presence of a personality type, à la Gabriel Tarde. We realize that charismatic leaders can make a difference, but we turn our attention to the larger clergy community and the relationships they hold with their congregations and denominations.

One of the keys to understanding clergy's relationship with the larger denomination is the degree to which they are professionalized (Finke and Dougherty 2002). Perhaps the central debate of nineteenth-century American religion was whether seminary education was either necessary or desirable. For clergy from the colonial mainline, the thought of abandoning such training was absurd. At the opening of Andover Seminary, Timothy Dwight complained the sectarian groups where "under

---

[5] Although we use American examples, international examples abound on the durability and intensity of the overlap between religion and ethnicity (e.g. the Middle East, Africa, and eastern Europe).

the guidance of quackery" (as quoted in Hatch 1989: 19). Lyman Beecher, another leader of the old colonial mainline, referred to sectarian clergy as "ignorant" and "unlettered" (Beecher and Nettleton 1828: 99). But the sectarian clergy were unrepentant, noting that "God never called an unprepared man to preach."[6] The upstart sects not only admired their untrained clergy; they also feared the clergyman produced by the seminaries. The Baptists prided themselves on local autonomy, fearing any change suggesting centralized control or a professional priesthood. The Methodists were hierarchical in organizational design, but the first American bishop, Francis Asbury, feared that a seminary-trained clergy would lose touch with the people. He explained: "[w]e must suffer with if we labor for the poor" (as quoted in Coleman 1954: 214–15). In short, both groups feared the trappings of making the ministry a profession.

Organizational theory supports what the nineteenth-century clergy suspected: professionalization changes the loyalties of the clergy (DiMaggio and Powell 1983). To the extent that religious organizations rely on professional clergy, clergy will be more restrained by the norms of the larger organization than those of the local congregation. Because the professional clergy and the larger denomination will attempt to standardize educational criteria and provide increased professional support, the clergy's allegiance will increasingly shift to professional networks and the larger denomination (Stark and Finke 2000; Finke and Dougherty 2002). Likewise, congregations will become ever more dependent on denominations for setting clergy standards and making clergy appointments.

The Southern Baptist Convention offers a recent example of how quickly this transition can take place. It took nearly a century for the Convention's seminaries to furnish their first 10,000 graduates (9,946 from 1859 to 1950), but the next 10,000 arrived in less than a decade (11,627 from 1951 to 1960). From 1951 to 1990, enough time to furnish one generation of church professionals, the seminaries produced over 60,000 graduates (Finke 1994). The Southern Baptist Convention underwent a "quiet transformation" in the mid twentieth century as the once loosely affiliated, small fellowships with part-time bi-vocational clergy became large congregations served by seminary-trained professionals closely linked to the larger Convention (Finke 1994). Nancy Ammerman (1990: 158) reports that by the late twentieth century seminary training was the "union card" needed to demonstrate credentials and served to introduce

---

[6] The 1871 *Baptist Quarterly* provides a survey of Baptist opinion on an educated clergy (see Finke and Stark 1992: 76).

clergy and their congregations "to programs and networks that frame their church lives." She noted that when controversy emerged in the 1980s and a schism seemed imminent, the running joke was that the "clergy would go with whichever side took the Annuity Board" (1990: 258). Prior to the professionalization of the clergy, the Annuity Board and many other clergy services would have never been a concern for clergy anticipating a schism.

Despite the Baptists' switch to seminary education, and similar changes by other sects from the nineteenth century (e.g. Methodists and Disciples of Christ), the use of professionalized clergy is still far from a consensus. The most rapidly growing segment of organized Christianity in America, the independent congregations, largely relies on clergy without seminary training or extensive professional networks. With many of the megachurches falling into this category, these large independents are becoming highly visible. Likewise, two rapidly growing new movements formed in the latter half of the twentieth century, the Vineyard Christian Fellowship and Calvary Chapel, approach seminary education with caution. Though not prohibiting seminary training, they tend to emphasize classes combined with hands-on training from a pastor at the local church – a program that roughly resembles the apprentice program of early nineteenth-century Methodist itinerants. Sounding remarkably similar to the Baptists of the nineteenth century, the founder of Calvary Chapel, Chuck Smith, states that "God does not call the qualified, but instead qualifies the called" (Miller 1997: 141).[7] Like the upstart sects before them, leaders of the Calvary Chapel and the Vineyard Christian Fellowship have expressed concerns that when pastors become seminary-trained professionals the "fellow seminarians become the person's peer group, rather than the congregation, and this creates a distance that is difficult to bridge" (Miller 1997: 166). When clergy are embedded in professional networks and the larger organization, their conformity to the demands of the larger organization will increase. Conforming to these demands also serves to block many forms of organizational change, including schisms.

Once again this illustrates how a congregation's dependency on the larger denomination deters schism. When clergy rely on the denomination for job placement, seminary training, annuity accounts, and professional

---

[7] Donald E. Miller (1997: 166) reports that Smith could also be sharply critical of seminary education. When several pastors of expanding mega-churches were pursuing doctorate of ministry degrees, Smith was quoted as saying, "If they get enough education, maybe they'll bring their congregations down to a manageable size."

networks, splitting from the denomination becomes increasingly more costly for the clergy and their congregations. Rather than leading a call for schism, they are more likely to call for reforms from within.

Throughout American history the marginal minority faiths of one era have become the prominent mainline religions of the next. From the first sects immigrating to America (e.g. the Puritans, Baptists, and Methodists) to those born on American soil (e.g. the Disciples, Assemblies of God, and Jehovah's Witnesses), the upstarts have charted the most dramatic growth throughout American history (Finke and Stark 1992). Thus, the small seemingly powerless sects that result from schisms can have powerful consequences on the larger religious market.

We recognize, of course, that the vast majority of sectarian groups show little potential for growth.[8] Only one of the many Bible student groups that formed in response to the teachings of Charles Taze Russell went on to become the Jehovah's Witnesses, and of the scores of sects spawned by the Baptists and Pentecostals only a handful have been able to support sustained growth. Yet, when start-up costs are low, schisms quickly fill new openings in the religious market and a handful succeed at generating a broad appeal. Without these schisms, large segments of the religious demand would go unmet and overall levels of religious involvement would be far lower.

But schisms do more than fill market openings, they also serve as a source for organizational innovation. Despite Ernst Troeltsch's open disdain for the sects, and his convictions that their "primitive," "naïve," and "non-reflective" religious teachings could only appeal to the lower classes, he acknowledged that it was the sects that "do the really creative work" (Troeltsch 1911: 44–5). He credited sects with serving as the initial foundation for all great religious movements. Sects continue to provide "creative" innovations. Just as the Catholic counter-reformation borrowed innovations from the schismatic movements, mainstream churches continue to borrow from small upstart sects.

The sects spawned by schisms hold a couple of key advantages in generating innovations. First, because their congregations are frequently less dependent on a centralized administrative structure, they face fewer

---

[8] After collecting data on 417 American-born sects, Stark and Bainbridge (1985: 134) report that "nearly a third of all sects (32 percent) reached their high-water mark on the day they began."

roadblocks when attempting to introduce innovations or start new organizations. For example, how and when new churches can be started is often heavily regulated by the larger organization. Mainline denominations will typically provide financial support for congregations that receive approval from the local district, presbytery, diocese, or conference.[9] Yet this approval relies on congregations meeting a wide range of criteria, typically including: support of surrounding congregations, increasing need due to population growth, the leadership of an ordained pastor, grassroots support, and a financial plan for support after the subsidy has ended. If churches shun the financial support and begin without the approval of surrounding congregations, they can still be denied admission into the denomination. Whereas the Jehovah's Witnesses, Assemblies of God, and Mormons annually start more than twenty new churches per thousand existing churches, the United Methodists, the United Presbyterian Church (USA), and the Evangelical Lutheran Church of America start fewer than five (Stark and Finke 2000: 153). The formal controls that denominations place on the formation of new congregations are only one example of the many internal regulations that restrict organizational innovation.

But the internal regulations that curb innovations are not always formal controls imposed by a central office; they are often informal expectations imposed on the local clergy. To the extent that schisms result in sectarian groups with a decentralized structure and a less professionalized clergy, efforts to mimic and conform to peer institutions are also reduced. This follows directly from a key insight of new institutional theory: organizations' efforts to conform to the norms, traditions, and social influences of peer organizations result in a homogeneity or isomorphism among the organizations (DiMaggio and Powell 1983; Powell and DiMaggio 1991). This tendency to conform to existing standards and to mimic the actions of peer institutions will curb innovations that depart too far from existing solutions. Whether at the level of the congregation or the larger denomination, the informal controls of fellow professional clergy can serve to curb innovations.

Finally, schisms often serve to mobilize the most committed. Although our attention has been on the organizational structure and vitality of the sects formed, we should also note that, because sects tend to hold higher

---

[9] This varies from one denomination to the next, but the most typical plan is 100 percent support for the first year, 80 percent for the second, and so on until they are receiving no support at the end of five years.

levels of member commitment and are in tension with the larger culture, they are able to generate substantial social change. In his classic *Religious Outsiders and the Making of Americans*, R. Laurence Moore (1986) demonstrates that religious outsiders helped to define a new brand of Americanism and showed the flaws of existing definitions. Despite their small size and marginal status these groups helped to reshape American culture. One obvious example is the Jehovah's Witnesses. They have been described as a small religious group that "has no political power and reaches for none" (Fowler and Hertzke 1995: 196), yet owing to their strong, uncompromising beliefs they have done more to extend religious civil liberties than perhaps any other religious group in the nation (Reichley 1985). Refusing to pledge allegiance to the flag and relentless in their pursuit of new converts, Jehovah's Witnesses have tested and retested the boundaries of religious freedom in most nations around the globe. During the early 1940s alone Jehovah's Witnesses made frequent visits to the US Supreme Court, shaping the contours of religious freedom. Yet most refused to vote.

CONCLUSION

Because there are rarely "bloodless" schisms, it is easy to be distracted by the acrimony and drama that occurs. We have attempted to uncover the underlying forces leading to schism rather than focusing on tensions at the surface. We have pointed to forces both internal and external to religious groups that affect a group's susceptibility to schisms.

At the macro level, environmental contexts vary in how they feed or suppress schisms. In particular, state regulation or interference can create an environment that is hostile to new religious groups and therefore lowers the likelihood of schisms. At the meso or organizational level, resource exchanges between denominations, congregations, and other religious organizations create power imbalances that increase the cost of schism for some groups. Groups that offer exclusive or inimitable religious goods are also at a lower risk of schism because potential sects know that they would be giving up irreplaceable resources. Similar dynamics occur between groups with professionalized clergy. Professionalized leaders know that their material and professional interests rest with the larger organization, so they are less likely to break with it.

Schisms have been seen as the primary way religious innovation and groups are introduced into the environment. While this is true, changes in the religious landscape of the United States raise interesting questions for future studies of schisms. Maybe most significant has been the growth of "independent" or "non-denominational" congregations and identities. At first glance, it may seem that schisms are a non-issue with such congregations since they lack a larger organization from which to split. More likely, though, is that schisms occur but in a less visible manner. It is difficult for a congregation to be an "island," and many independent congregations form networks with other congregations and parachurch organizations. Grievances between factions could just as easily lead to a schism between these groups, but this may not produce the organizational fireworks and paper-trails that usually serve as a sign of schism. Furthermore, schisms within independent congregations could simply produce a new independent congregation and therefore not look like a split at all. Despite the challenges these new religious forms present for research from a practical standpoint, we believe the theoretical dynamics presented concerning environmental contexts and resource dependencies still apply. While research methods may need to adapt, good theories are flexible.

REFERENCES

Ammerman, Nancy Tatom. 1990. *Baptist Battles: Social Change and Religious Conflict in the Southern Baptist Convention*. New Brunswick, NJ: Rutgers University Press.

Banerjee, Neela. 2006. "Church Urges Its Dioceses Not To Elect Gay Bishops." *The New York Times*, June 22, A18.

Baumgarten, Albert I. 1997. *The Flourishing Jewish Sects in the Maccabean Era: An Interpretation*. New York: Brill.

Beecher, Lyman and Asahel Nettleton. 1828. *Letters of the Rev. Dr. Beecher and Rev. Mr. Nettleton on the "New Measures" in Conducting Revivals of Religion*. New York: C. & G. Carvill.

Blasi, Anthony J. 1989. "Sociological Implications of the Great Western Schism." *Social Compass* 36: 311–25.

Blau, Peter M. 1970. "A Formal Theory of Differentiation in Organizations." *American Sociological Review* 35: 201–18.

   1972. "Size and the Structure of Organizations: A Causal Analysis." *American Sociological Review* 37: 434–40.

Bureau of the Census. 1910. *Religious Bodies: 1906*, vols. I and II. Washington, DC: Government Printing Office.

Chesnut, R. Andrew. 2003. *Competitive Spirits: Latin America's New Religious Economy*. Oxford: Oxford University Press.

Christerson, Brad and Michael Emerson. 2003. "The Costs of Diversity in Religious Organizations: An In-depth Case Study." *Sociology of Religion* 64: 163–81.

Coleman, Robert Emerson. 1954. "Factors in the Expansion of the Methodist Episcopal Church from 1784 to 1812." Unpublished PhD dissertation, University of Iowa.

Dhingra, Pawan. 2004. " 'We're Not a Korean American Church Any More': Dilemmas in Constructing a Multi-Racial Church Identity." *Social Compass* 51: 367–79.

DiMaggio, Paul J. and Walter W. Powell. 1983. "The Iron Cage Revisited: Institutional Isomorphism and Collective Rationality in Organizational Fields." *American Sociological Review* 48: 147–60.

Dinges, William D. 1995. " 'We Are What You Were': Roman Catholic Traditionalism in America," in Mary Jo Weaver and R. Scott Appleby (eds.), *Being Right: Conservative Catholics in America* (pp. 241–69). Bloomington: Indiana University Press.

Emerson, Richard M. 1962. "Power–dependence Relations." *American Sociological Review* 27: 31–41.

Finke, Roger. 1990. "Religious Deregulation: Origins and Consequences." *Journal of Church and State* 32: 609–26.

1994. "The Quiet Transformation: Changes in Size and Leadership of Southern Baptist Churches." *Review of Religious Research* 36: 3–22.

Finke, Roger and Kevin D. Dougherty. 2002. "The Effects of Professional Training: The Social and Religious Capital Acquired in Seminaries." *Journal for the Scientific Study of Religion* 41: 103–20.

Finke, Roger and Rodney Stark. 1992. *The Churching of America 1776–1990: Winners and Losers in our Religious Economy.* New Brunswick, NJ: Rutgers University Press.

Finke, Roger and Patricia Wittberg. 2000. "Organizational Revival from Within: Explaining Revivalism and Reform in the Roman Catholic Church." *Journal for the Scientific Study of Religion* 39: 154–70.

Fowler, Robert Booth and Allen D. Hertzke. 1995. *Religion and Politics in America: Faith, Culture, and Strategic Choices.* Boulder, CO: Westview Press.

Gill, Anthony J. 1994. *Rendering unto Caesar: The Catholic Church and the State in Latin America.* Chicago: University of Chicago Press.

Hardacre, Helen. 1989. *Shinto and the State, 1868–1988.* Princeton: Princeton University Press.

Hatch, Nathan O. 1989. *The Democratization of American Christianity.* New Haven: Yale University Press.

Iannaccone, Laurence R. 1988. "A Formal Model of Church and Sect." *American Journal of Sociology* 94: S241–268.

Johnson, Benton. 1963. "On Church and Sect." *American Sociological Review* 28: 539–49.

Lambert, Malcolm D. 1977. *Medieval Heresy: Popular Movements from Bogomil to Hus.* New York: Holmes and Meier Publishers.

Liebman, Robert C., John R. Sutton, and Robert Wuthnow. 1988. "Exploring the Social Sources of Denominationalism: Schisms in American Protestant Denominations, 1890–1980." *American Sociological Review* 53: 343–52.

Lu, Yunfeng. 2008. *The Transformation of Yignan Dao in Taiwan: Adapting to a Changing Religious Economy*. Lanham, MD: Lexington Books.

McFarland, H. Neill. 1967. *The Rush Hour of the Gods: A Study of New Religious Movements in Japan*. New York: Macmillan.

Melton, J. Gordon. 1989. *The Encyclopedia of American Religions* (3rd edn). Detroit: Gale Research Inc.

2003. *Encyclopedia of American Religions* (7th edn). Farmington Hills, MI: Gale Group Inc.

Miller, Donald E. 1997. *Reinventing American Protestantism: Christianity in the New Millennium*. Berkeley: University of California Press.

Moore, R. Laurence. 1986. *Religious Outsiders and the Making of Americans*. New York: Oxford University Press.

Nakano, Tsuyoshi. 1987. "The American Occupation and Reform of Japan's Religious System: A Few Notes on the Secularization Process in Postwar Japan." *Journal of Oriental Studies* 26(1): 124–38.

Niebuhr, H. Richard. 1929. *The Social Sources of Denominationalism*. New York: H. Holt and Company.

Peters, John Leland. 1985 [1956]. *Christian Perfection and American Methodism*. Grand Rapids, MI: Francis Asbury Press.

Pfeffer, Jeffrey and Gerald R. Salancik. 1978. *The External Control of Organizations: A Resource Dependence Perspective*. New York: Harper and Row.

Powell, Walter W. and Paul J. DiMaggio. 1991. *The New Institutionalism in Organizational Analysis*. Chicago: University of Chicago Press.

Reichley, James. 1985. *Religion in American Public Life*. Washington, DC: Brookings Institution.

Schaff, Philip. 1855. *America: A Sketch of Its Political, Social, and Religious Character*. Cambridge, MA: The Belknap Press.

Scheitle, Christopher P. 2007. "Organizational Niches and Religious Markets: Uniting Two Literatures." *Interdisciplinary Journal of Research on Religion* 3: Article 2: www.religjournal.com.

Stark, Rodney. 1996. *The Rise of Christianity: A Sociologist Reconsiders History*. Princeton: Princeton University Press.

Stark, Rodney and William Sims Bainbridge. 1985. *The Future of Religion: Secularization, Revival, and Cult Formation*. Berkeley: University of California Press.

Stark, Rodney and Roger Finke. 2000. *Acts of Faith: Explaining the Human Side of Religion*. Berkeley: University of California Press.

Sutton, John R. and Mark Chaves. 2004. "Explaining Schism in American Protestant Denominations, 1890–1990." *Journal for the Scientific Study of Religion* 43: 171–90.

Troeltsch, Ernst. 1960 [1911] . *The Social Teaching of the Christian Churches* (2 vols.). New York: Harper Torchbooks.

Vegh, Steven G. 2006. "United, but not of the Same Mind." *The Virginian-Pilot*. June 13, B3.

Weber, Max. 1946. *From Max Weber: Essays in Sociology.* Ed. H. H. Gerth and C. Wright Mills. New York: Oxford University Press.

The Sociology of Religion. Trans. Ephraim Fischoff. Boston: Beacon Press, 1993.

Wilson, Bryan R. 1959. "An Analysis of Sect Development." *American Sociological Review* 24: 3–15.

PART II

Survey of schisms in selected traditions

CHAPTER 2

Charismatic authority in Islam: an analysis of the cause of schisms in the ummah

Ron Geaves

Any attempt to explore the causes of schism within Islam has first to acknowledge the powerful rhetoric of unity that is constructed upon the ideal of *ummah* (the universal community of believers). So successful is the rhetoric that a general perception of Islam is one of a monolithic religious entity that overrides the diversity of nationalities and ethnicities that form the whole. This ideal is maintained by Muslims themselves, who though aware of the diversity of religious positions across the Islamic spectrum still persist in presenting the ideal of a single community of believers in the one God to outsiders.[1] So successful is this strategy, arising from a powerful sense of an imagined community, that few outside the knowledgeable are likely to know more than the fact that Islam has two main branches, the dominant Sunnis and the minority Shi'as. Even between these two, differences are likely to be played down in spite of centuries of conflict.

The ideal of the *ummah* has supplied a rationale for political and moral activism. Guided by the word of God and the actions of the Prophet Muhammad, the *ummah* is believed to possess a moral mission to create a new social order based on faith and obedience to the revelation. It is reasonable to argue that it is this ideal of the solidarity of the *ummah*, or threats to its apparent unity, that has been Islam's major contribution to the political sphere. The *ummah* is held together not by any formal

---

[1] Muslims are not the only voices that proclaim the solidarity of the *ummah*. Several Western orientalists also describe Muslims in such terms. For example Montgomery Watt (1961: 174) states that "the Islamic state had gone a long way towards becoming a genuine community" (Watt 1961 *Islam and the Integration of Society*. London: Routledge and Kegan Paul). Charles Adams insists that "Islamic society is held together by ideological harmony, composed of individuals with various ethnic-linguistic backgrounds" (Adams 1983: 120). Finally, Hamilton Gibb claims that "it consists of the totality of individuals bound to one another by ties, not of kinship or race, but of religion in that all of its members profess their belief in one God, and in the mission of the Prophet Muhammad. Before God and in their relation to Him, all are equal, without distinction of rank, class or race" (Gibb 1963: 173).

organization but by a collective act of will, inspired by personal conviction and embodied in the ritual duty of daily prayer, the month-long fast
of Ramadan and the annual pilgrimage to Mecca. Five times a day,
millions of Muslims face Mecca all at the same time to observe the same
ritual prayers. This core of shared ritual practices combined with observances of the *shari'a* is integral to Muslim life and creates the bonds that
tie the *ummah* together.

Despite the ideal held by many Muslims of a single, divinely revealed
and united Islam, there have been and continue to be diverse interpretations of Islam. It is a historical fact that the community was already torn
by dissent and split into factions within the lifetime of the first generation
of believers. The Qur'an acknowledges the existence of the sects (*ta'ifa*),
signifying a smaller group that has broken away from a larger whole but
which has also developed a discrete and coherent religious worldview of
its own. As stated by Khuri (1990: 28), *ta'ifa* indicates a "split-off group
possessing a religiously autonomous character." Khuri also refers to al-
Baghdadi's use of *firqa* (team) and al-Shahrastani's use of *nihla* (religious
order).[2] *Firqa* can be understood to mean a number of sub-divisions or
groups within one *ta'ifa*, for example the various movements within
Shi'ism. However, *nihla* provides a different understanding of sectarianism that is more pertinent to divisions within the Sunni mainstream.
Shahrastani uses the term in opposition to *milla* (a nation ruled over by a
body of religious law). Thus the nation of Israel, for example, is ruled
over by one law revealed by God but may contain many religions or even
different interpretations of the law.

The initial division occurred over the issue of the leadership of the
ummah. Other divisions were created concerning the nature and shape of
the community itself. Major stress was also placed on the *ummah* by the
spread of the Arab empire and its attendant rapid incorporation of older,
more sophisticated cultures brought into the fold of Islam. Any attempt
to formulate an overriding theory of schisms in Islam would need to take
account of these factors and also acknowledge both religious and political
tensions. It is also important to note that the original schism that produced Sunni and Shi'a Islam set up divergent patterns for future divisions
in the *ummah*. Sunni sectarianism will take place within a different
context to Shi'a. The various Shi'a movements, some of which have
developed into separate religions outside the fold of Islam, would appear

---

[2] Khuri 1990: 27–8. Khuri cites from al-Shahrastani's *al-milal wa al-nihal* and al-Baghdadi's *al-farq bain al-firaq*.

to have been formed over disagreements around leadership, often at a juncture occurring upon the death of the charismatic founder. It would be tempting to analyze this category of schism within the framework of the relationship between institution and charisma classically provided by Max Weber. Sunnis, on the other hand, have tended to disagree on matters of interpretation of law or of changes in a group's doctrines and/or degree of strictness arising out of such processes of legal/religious interpretation. Yet caution needs to be observed in either of these analyses, as splits can also be driven by ethnic, tribal, racial, or national fault lines.

THE ORIGINAL SCHISM

Heinz Halm makes the point that the original community founded by Muhammad had to find a way to absorb various social groups with different traditions and interests. He argues that integration was never completely successful and that the "points of fracture" were there from the very beginnings of Islam (Halm 1991: 5). Thus Halm sees the first and unhealed division as being caused by social oppositions and tensions which characterized the first community of Muslims. In such an analysis one would need to assess the impact of the various tribes that provided membership to the fledgling Muslim community and the competition for resources and personal feuds that existed between them; the differences in lifestyle that were developing between the desert Arab and the city dwellers of Makkah and Madina and the relationship between Muhammad's first supporters from Makkah, the "emigrants" or "exiles," and the settled tribes of Madina who provided hospitality and shelter to the former founder members. If Halm is right, then the first causes of Muslim schism can be located in social differentiation giving rise to divergence of interest along the lines identified by Niebuhr (1957: 6). Zald and Ash (1966: 327–40) argue that such "heterogeneity of social base" is one of the two major preconditions for factionalism and schism in social movements. Halm identifies two further social factors that came about as a result of the immediate expansion of the Arab empire after Muhammad's death. Arab tribal warriors settled and were assimilated into the conquered territories, but perhaps more significantly Mesopotamians, Iranians, Egyptians, Syrians, and Berbers who had been subjugated gradually converted to Islam. Known as *mawali* (clients), these groups undermined the religious doctrines of the equality of believers as they were treated as second-class Muslims by the dominant Arabs (Halm 1991: 6).

However, social groups are not religious groups, or at least, to avoid arguments as to whether religion exists as an entity *sui generis*, religious groups must be identified as a unique sub-category of social groups where reference is made to the supernatural. Although Halm is right that such tensions existed, any analysis would need to consider the strength of religious conviction and the effect that the new worldview incorporating powerful unifying rituals and divinely legitimated codes of behavior would have in uniting various levels of social differentiation. In this respect, the key to understanding schism would need to be sought between those who fully accepted the religious nature of the message and its ability to transform both individual and group lives, and those who joined the ranks of the new religion because of the benefits that it brought, such as protection, status, power, or wealth. Although it might be argued that the early Makkan and Madinan converts had little advantage in joining Muhammad, this would not have been true for later Arabian tribes who flocked in traditional style to offer fealty to a powerful man. A part of the exchange of fealty was conversion to the new religion that replaced the Arab desert custom of finding protection with a more powerful tribe. This dilemma of motivation is acknowledged by the Qur'an in its condemnation of hypocrites (*al-munafiqun*). After the death of Muhammad the first civil war between Muslims came about as various tribes who had joined the religious community rebelled and attempted to break away.

This problem of mixed motivation was also found amongst the inhabitants of Makkah and particularly focused upon the Banu Umayya, a wealthy clan of the Quraysh tribe. As the dominant group amongst the Makkan merchants, it had been the Quraysh who had most to lose from Muhammad's preaching on social justice. In addition they feared the loss of income associated with the tribal pilgrimages into Makkah to worship the gods and goddesses installed in the ancient Ka'aba. Many of the most aggressive opponents of the new religion and its leader were members of the Quraysh and had fought against the Muslims in the battles that took place before Muhammad's victorious entry into Makkah. Muhammad's victory brought many of his enemies into the fold of Islam, where they quickly established their position amongst the elite of Arab society.

By the time of the third Caliph, Uthman elected in 644 CE, the Arabs had expanded their territory to include much of Persia, Byzantine Syria, Egypt, North Africa, and Jerusalem. Uthman belonged to the Banu Umayya and favored his relatives and supporters, appointing them to positions of authority throughout the expanding empire. In Damascus, Mu'awiyya ibn Abi Sufyan became the most powerful of the Umayyad rulers, governing Syria. Ironically much of the Muslim world was now ruled over by representatives of the old ruling Makkan clans that had for years opposed Muhammad and his message. After Uthman's assassination in 656 CE, Muhammad's cousin and son-in-law, Ali ibn Abi Talib, succeeded to the Caliphate. However, this was disputed by the supporters of the Umayya clan who increasingly departed from Madina and took up residence in their power base of Damascus. After Ali's death at the hands of an assassin in 661 CE, Mu'awiyya took control of the Caliphate, turning it into the first dynastic Muslim empire commonly known as the Umayyad era.

The succession of Mu'awiyya was to have two repercussions. First, no longer could the Caliphate be considered a religious institution, a fact recognized by Sunni Muslims who declare only the first four Caliphs to have been divinely guided. The apparent loss of the Prophet's and his Companions' asceticism and religiosity amongst the new rulers led to many of the devout separating themselves from the activities of the court and living in semi-retreat in Madina, where they attempted to recreate the lifestyles of the first Muslims. To this development can be traced the first roots of Sufism or Islamic mysticism.

Any analysis of these divisions would need to take account of mixed motivation between those who paid nominal allegiance to Islam and those who espoused piety and commitment to the faith. Such an analysis would lead to the post-Weberian sociologists Thomas O'Dea and Peter Berger. The important point in O'Dea's argument is that in taming the charismatic, there occurs a distortion. There is a constant or recurring tension between the forces which work for stability, even at the risk of distortion, and the forces which work for a truer realization of the initial charismatic moment. Berger is also indebted to Weber's ideas on the routinization of charisma. In an article published in 1974, he writes:

Religious institutions assign the potentially disruptive manifestations of the other reality (as opposed to the reality of the ordinary, everyday world) to carefully circumscribed times and places in society. They domesticate the ecstasies, channel them into socially acceptable and useful activity (such as moral conduct), and even manage to convert the religious definition of reality into legitimations of the sociopolitical order. (Berger 1974: 132)

O'Dea looked at this process in greater detail and divided it into five dilemmas.[3] The first one he identified is particularly useful for the arguments presented here. In the dilemma of mixed motivation, O'Dea

---

[3] The five dilemmas are the dilemma of mixed motivation, the symbolic dilemma, the dilemma of administrative order, the dilemma of delimitation and the dilemma of power. These are all fully developed by O'Dea (1964: 71–89) and reproduced by Foy (1978: 298).

argued that the only motivation of the founder-innovator is communicating his or her message, but that successors will have additional motivations, such as personal power, prestige, status, and influence (Foy 1978: 300–1). Greenslade also examines the motivations of the leaders of schismatic factions. In a fashion similar to O'Dea's argument of mixed motivation he also notes that ambition or personal antipathy have often had an important part as stimulating factors. However, Greenslade (1953: 55) suggests that it is rare for such personal factors to be the sole cause of schism, although they may be the main cause.

Clearly we can see that politics and leadership were to play a role from the very beginning. But the death of Muhammad was to be the catalyst for the first main schism in Islam. Wallis argues that new religious movements are marked by unstable authority and can be destabilized by the death of a charismatic leader, although he admits that where processes are put into place to prepare for the transfer of authority at death, the impact of such destabilization can be negated and legitimacy can be smoothly passed from one kind of leadership to another with little disruption from competing claims (Wallis 1979: 188). The Prophet left no son to be his heir or to take his place, nor is it certain that primogeniture was observed in Arabian culture. The election of the aged Abu Bakr as the first Caliph (632–634 CE) would appear to have marked a return to the traditional tribal method of choosing a leader and could be said to mark a move away from the type of charisma represented by the Prophet to a more institutional form of leadership based on political authority.

If this is an accurate estimation of the change of leadership brought about by the demise of the Prophet, then the first schism of Islam could be attributed to a straightforward Weberian analysis of charisma and institutionalization followed by attempts to restore charismatic leadership. According to Shi'a narratives, the origins of the division go back to an incident that took place not long before Muhammad's death, when he was returning to Medina from his farewell pilgrimage to Makkah. The Prophet and his Companions stopped near a pool called Ghadir Khumm. It is said that after asking them if it was true that he was closer to them than they were to themselves, he said something of major significance for the succession. It is believed by the Shi'a that Muhammad took his son-in-law and cousin, Ali, and said, "He, of whom I am the patron, of Him Ali is also the patron." To many this signified that Ali was Muhammad's chosen successor (Brown 2004: 101).

Ali was married to the Prophet's daughter, Fatima, and was the father of Muhammad's grandchildren. Even the Qur'an appeared to endorse the specialness of Muhammad's family and direct bloodline. "And Allah only wishes to remove all abomination from you, Ye Members of the Family, and to make you pure and spotless."[4] In Shi'a conviction, Ali was blessed with a charisma similar to Muhammad's own: one who shone with Allah's light on his countenance. Shi'a tradition states that Muhammad came to know that Ali was his successor when it was revealed to him on the Night Journey, the mystical ascension to the divine presence (Brown 2004: 101).

However, the Shi'a religious sensibility was to be based on a cult of suffering which began with this first moment of error and deprivation. They came to believe that on the Prophet's deathbed, when his family were gathered around him and thereafter performing the rites of death, the elders of the tribes met and chose Abu Bakr. Yet there were those who never accepted the decision, believing it to be in opposition to the Prophet's wishes and these people became known as the Party of Ali – Shi'at Ali or Shi'a.

Whatever the historical events may have been surrounding Ali, there is no doubt that for the Shi'a he and the surviving direct descendants of Muhammad, the *ahl al-Bait*, the people of the household, all become significant figures of their religious imagination, doomed to suffer on behalf of their community and deprived of true recognition by the majority of Muslims who had cast their lot with the Sunni Caliphate. The Shi'a developed the theological and political position that Ali should by right have been the first Caliph, handing on to the "people of the household," the Prophet's direct family descendants, thus giving the leadership of the Muslims over to a rule of the bloodline which mysteriously contained some of Muhammad's spiritual power and authority. In many ways, what took place was a classic sociological dilemma that occurs at the death of a founder and the loss of charismatic leadership. The Umayyads were content to accept the more institutional leadership of the community, begun with the more rational choice of Abu Bakr. The shift from charismatic leadership to a fully institutional leadership takes place gradually for most Sunnis with the first four Caliphs providing a bridge between the two types of authority. As we shall see later, not all Sunnis, felt this way and some were able to resurrect charismatic leadership through the institution of sainthood. The Shi'a, on the other hand,

---

[4] *The Holy Qur'an* (1405 AH, revised Abdullah Yusef Ali English translation), The Presidency of Islamic Researches, Mushaf Al-Madinah An-Nabawiyah: King Fahd Holy Qur'an Printing Complex, Sura 33:33.

utilized the doctrines of the pure and unsullied "people of the household" to retain charismatic leadership and resist the dominant institutional power established by the Umayyads.

After Ali's death, the Shi'a may have been inclined to accept pragmatically the reality of Umayyad power but only with the retention of a sense of grievance. It is a central belief that Ali and Mu'awiyya made a sacred pact after the battle between their forces, in which Ali agreed to Mu'awiyya's succession to the Caliphate, but only if he renounced the right of his son Yazid to follow him. On Mu'awiyya's death, the leadership of the Muslims was to revert to the grandsons of Muhammad, Hassan and Hussain.

Whatever the truth, it is believed that Hassan, the elder of the two grandsons, was persuaded to relinquish his claim to the Caliphate, and retired into exile in Madina, where he died in strange circumstances. According to the Shi'ite version of the tale, he was poisoned by the Umayyad leadership. Thus the tale of the woes of the family continues: destined to be martyred and deprived of their birthright as the Sunnis grew from strength to strength. But the real fateful story that grips the Shi'ite religious imagination, in effect marking out their differences from the Sunnis and providing the myth for a theology of patient suffering, is discovered in the tragic circumstances of the death of Hussain, the Prophet's sole surviving grandson.

After the death of Mu'awiyya in 680 CE, his son Yazid inherited the Caliphate, thus beginning a hereditary dynasty. The details vary according to which side is telling it. One version states that Yazid placed a repressive general to subdue Ali's stronghold in Kufa. It is said that the Kufans called for Hussain to liberate them, promising to support his right to the Caliphate. Hussain was intercepted on his way to the rescue by forces loyal to Yazid and persuaded to move in another direction. He then departed for Karbala, where he set up camp on October 2, 680 (the second day of Muharram). Other accounts claim that Hussain marched on Damascus from his father's old stronghold in Kufa with a force of seventy-two loyal followers, believing implicitly in Allah's promise to bring victory to the righteous, even by miraculous means as described in the Qur'an after the defeat at Uhud. After arrival in Karbala, he was trapped by the Umayyad armies of Yazid under the command of Umar ibn Sa'ad, who insisted Hussain could not leave unless he submitted to the authority of Yazid.

Whatever the truth, Hussain's small force was attacked in Karbala on the tenth day of the Muslim month of Muharram by an overwhelmingly superior army comprising five thousand armed troops. In Shi'a accounts, the fighting raged all day on the tenth day of Muharram, a day to be known henceforth by the Shi'a as Ashura. By the afternoon, Hussain remained defiant, cradling his own dead son in his arms, only to be cut down with his last surviving companions. Those who survived were beheaded. Hussain's widow, Zaynab and his surviving son, Ali, were brought in chains to Yazid, who gloated over his victory for days over the decapitated head of Hussain. Eventually the widow and her son were released.

Thus it is believed that a wicked and ruthless tyrant came to usurp the Caliphate that rightfully belonged to the family of the Prophet. This motif would run throughout Shi'a interpretations of history. Henceforth the Shi'a would view the mainstream of Sunni Islam, although ostensibly successful and the majority of Muslims, as representative of an illegitimate and degenerate empire that could never be the true people of God. The escape of Hussain's son, Ali, from the slaughter ensured the survival of the true inheritors of Islam, the direct line of the Prophet, replete with their special powers inherited through his bloodline that permitted them to know the inner secrets of the Qur'an, and thus qualified them to lead the faithful. For the Shi'a these were the true leaders of the community, known as the Imams and differentiated from the Sunni imams who are merely leaders of the prayer.

Amongst the Ithna'ashariyya, the Twelver Shi'as as they are known, still the dominant group in Iran and Iraq, there are believed to have been twelve Imams beginning with Ali. But all Shi'a groups are united in acceptance of the first six Imams: Ali ibn Talib, the cousin and son-in-law of Muhammad; Hasan ibn Ali (d.669), the son of Ali and brother of Hussain; al-Hussain ibn Ali (d.680), the son of Ali, the *Sayyid ash-Shuhada*, the "Prince of Martyrs"; Ali Zayn al-Abidin (d.713), the son of Hussain, and supposedly quiescent in the struggles between Shi'a and Sunni; Muhammad al-Baqir (d.731), the son of Ali Zayn al-Abidin, a significant scholar, attributed with the development of Shi'a laws and doctrines; and finally Ja'far al-Sadiq (d.765), the son of al-Baqir, also quietist and scholarly in his approach to the Caliphate. It was during his period that the Shi'a doctrine of the infallibility of the Imams was developed. Fuad Khuri makes the observation that the choice of the title "Imam" used in opposition to "Caliph" by all Shi'a groups is intentional and indicates how such sectarian movements utilize moral authority as a means of legitimacy (Khuri 1990: 105). The Qur'an is regarded as the ultimate exoteric authority, but it is the Imam who governs the esoteric realm which holds sway over the exoteric realm. The Imam is both exemplar, the perfect religious model to be followed, and a visible salvationary symbol of the hidden realms, the completion or embodiment of religion. According to Khuri (1990: 107), the Sunnis perceive the sects as a natural product of historical processes whereas the Shi'a sects see themselves as expressions of divine will.

SCHISMS AMONGST THE SHI'A

Momen reminds us that when the Arabs expanded into territories that lay within the Fertile Crescent they were to meet with ancient civilizations that had already developed complex religious systems. Zoroastrianism, Mazdakism, Manichaeism, Judaism and various sects of Christianity all rivaled each other and added practices and doctrines to the worldview of the area. These prevalent ideas such as transmigration of souls, occultation, descent of the spirit of God into man, divinely inspired guidance, and delegation of God's powers became jointly known as *ghulat* or extremist by the orthodox amongst Muslims (Momen 1985: 66). Momen suggests that the converts to Islam from this region adopted Ali and his successors as an embodiment of the above religious speculation, providing a hero-martyr and a priestly succession (1985: 66). When Ali moved his headquarters to Iraq it was natural that he would gain loyalty from the local populace. The death of Hussain and the second-class status attributed to the non-Arab Muslims of this area provided political aspirations to overcome the Syrian Umayyad hegemony.

Thus it is difficult to assess the historical accuracy of the various Shi'a accounts of the Imams. The prototypical Shi'a certainly took time to develop the full salvationary narrative around the Imams, and in particular the role of the final Imam or *Mahdi*. Shi'a writers tend to depict the Imams as quasi-legendary figures rather than historical. These hagiographical accounts come complete with wondrous birth stories, performance of miracles, possession of supernatural knowledge, and authentication tales to legitimize their succession. Consequently it is difficult to ascertain whether they had the qualities of charismatic leadership. Even Shi'a texts describe Ali as corpulent, short-sighted and balding, hardly the epitome of charismatic appearance. The focus is on his heroic traits, and popular depictions show him wielding a two-pronged sword, fighting against the opponents of Islam or wild animals (Halm 1991: 12). He is also considered to be eloquent. However, Halm notes that the collection entitled "The Path of Eloquence" (*Nahj al-balagha*), describing his speeches in classical Arabic, did not appear until the eleventh century (1991: 13). Thus it would seem that the Imams can be defined as possessing a constructed charisma rather than actual personality or character traits. This constructed charisma needs to be explored within the context of its role in the theoretical "invented tradition" first developed by Eric Hobsbawm (1992). Invented traditions form a set of practices and organizational structures which are heavily dependent on continuity with a historic past: a reference to old situations which consist not only of tacitly accepted rules and rituals and norms of behavior heavily reinforced by repetition, but also of historic relationships with rival Muslim movements.

A mention has to be made to the final Imam or the doctrine of the *Mahdi* that has become central to Shi'a movements. The classic model is found amongst the Twelver Shi'a. The Shi'a's embracing of a cult of suffering, based upon their sense of being Allah's righteous minority struggling against the sins of the world, would be reinforced by their conviction that all their infallible Imams, the true servants of Allah from Ali to the eleventh Imam, were victims of violence by their enemies. The sense of being under continuous threat led to the practice of *taqiyya* (dissimulation), whereby Shi'a leaders and their followers could conceal their true beliefs to avoid persecution by their enemies. However, this pragmatic decision was deemed insufficient to avoid martyrdom, and when the twelfth Imam provided no direct progeny the significant doctrine of *ghayba* (occultation) appeared, in which Allah protected his last Imam by taking him to a special place of concealment. This event is supposed to have occurred in 874 CE, and after this date a succession of official representatives known as *babs* intermediated mystically between the Imam and the faithful. In 941 CE, the period of the greater *ghayba* began, where the Imam is incommunicado until his return as the *Mahdi* at the end of time to bring final vindication.

It is the belief concerning the occultation of the Imam and when it occurred that generally marks out different Shi'a sects. The Zaydiyya or Zaidis believe that the son of the fourth Imam was the true successor, based on his argument that the Imamate can be claimed by any descendant of Ali and Fatima who is pious and learned, and who comes out openly to make his bid. Zaid and his half brother, the fifth Imam Muhammad al-Baqir, disagreed over several points of doctrine. After his death in battle, several Zaidi imams rose in rebellion. On several occasions various groups of supporters claimed they were the final Imam and in occultation. Subgroups of the Zaidis are the Jarudiyya, the Jaririyya, and the Butriyya.

The death of Ja'far al-Sadiq, the sixth Imam, resulted in one of the most notable fragmentations of the Shi'a community. Ja'far appointed his son Isma'il to succeed him, but he died. The community experienced another major division. The Twelvers believed that his death annulled his Imamate and moved on to another branch of the family, but another group came to believe that the Imamate ended with Isma'il. The Isma'ilis are therefore known as the "Seveners." The pure Isma'ilis believe that he did not die but was taken into occultation. Other groups were to follow the descendants of Isma'il. In Shi'a circles, the many sub-groups, some of whom are no longer in existence, are divided into three categories:

1 *Ghulat* (the extremists) are those groups who hold to beliefs that assert that there are prophets after Muhammad or who believe that God can incarnate as a person. They may also believe in the transmigration of souls.
2 *Waqifa* (those who hesitate or stop) applies to groups who deny or hesitate over the death of a particular Imam and refuse to acknowledge any further Imams.
3 *Qat'iyya* (those who are certain) applies to groups who are sure about the death of an Imam and go on to the next Imam (Momen 1985: 45).

However, it is not only differences over the Imam that can create divisions amongst the Shi'a. There are also eschatological groups that appear from time to time announcing an imminent end to the world and following a leader who is proclaimed to be the *Mahdi*. Even *babs*, the mystical intermediaries between the Imam and the faithful once he has entered occultation, can cause new sects to arise. The most notable example would be the Baha'i, who went on to become a separate world religion. The Baha'i's origins lie in the life and teachings of Sayyid Ali Muhammad Shirazi (1819–50), who first claimed to be the Bab or Gate to the Imam but who went on to assert that he was the returned twelfth Imam and that the Islamic dispensation or revelation was abrogated in favour of a new prophetic cycle.

Another independent religious group to emerge from the Shi'a accused of *ghulat* doctrines was the Druze. Located today in Israel, Syria, Lebanon, and Jordan, the Druze originally emerged as a breakaway from the Isma'ilis. According to Robert Betts, Druzism appeared as a reaction to the failure of the Isma'ilis to create a messianic kingdom out of their Fatimid dynasty with its capital in Cairo (Betts 1988: 8). In reality, the state was little different from that of the Abbasids or Byzantine enemies.

Saviour figures began to emerge, and one such was the Fatimid Caliph al-Hakim. Around 1009 CE several leaders in Cairo began to proclaim al-Hakim as the fulfillment of scriptural promises and to acknowledge his divinity. Al-Hakim is a contested figure judged by Western historical scholarship to be a megalomaniac. Certainly some of his actions are not what is normally expected of a religious founder, albeit one of his foremost followers, Hamza ibn Ali ibn Ahmad al-Zuzani, a Persian Isma'ili theologian, was able to spread the religion successfully throughout the Fatimid empire. After al-Hakim's probable assassination in 1021 CE, the usual myth of the hidden Imam in occultation emerged. However, Betts (1988: 9) argues that, even in its early stages, Druzism saw itself as a new religion aiming to establish a new world order.

SUNNI SCHISMS

It would be difficult to get Sunnis to admit that there are schisms in Islam's dominant grouping. It is here that the myths of the *ummah*'s unity are found in their strongest expressions. Unlike the Shi'a, the Sunnis have been the dominant group and historically the rulers of the Muslim world, with a few exceptions such as Iran and the Fatimid dynasty. As rulers they were able to utilize the state as the main means of organizing religious life. Indeed, Fuad Khuri (1990: 99) goes as far as to state that Sunnis feel "lost" when deprived of centralized power. The Caliph or Sultan has ideally embodied both governance and piety, but ruling through the implementation and execution of *shari'a*, the divine law. Ideally he is not there to create laws as these have already been given in entirety by Allah. Any difficulties of interpretation are resolved by bodies of *ulama* or religious scholars, experts in jurisprudence. The situation in contemporary Muslim states is diverse, depending upon the form of government, but most religious Muslims would still consider that it is the role of the state not to create law but rather to implement God's law. Whereas the Shi'a are more likely to speak of justice, oppression, and expected salvation, the Sunnis are more likely to speak of consensus and unity. Khuri goes as far as to argue that the Shi'a sects have historically been the refuge of the oppressed and underprivileged and that sects are a means to reject the centralized authority of the Muslim state (1990: 40–1).

A number of elements can contrive to form separatist or rebellious movements against the unity of state and religion within Sunni Islam. The degree to which Islam is actually practiced by Muslims can be controversial, and even a cause of political rebellion. The question of whether nominal Muslims were within the fold of Islam arose early in Islam's development and is a continuation of the hypocrite concerns that arose in Madina. The first movements to declare war against the Umayyad state were the Kharijites, who were unequivocal that the defining feature of Muslim identity was piety and who controversially claimed the right to declare *jihad* against nominal Muslims, stating they were *kufr* or unbelievers. The state was quick to recognize that such a position led to unrest, civil wars, and anarchy, and adopted the Asharite position that only God could judge the condition of *iman* (faith). Nevertheless, the Kharijite position has never disappeared and it has re-emerged dramatically in the twentieth century amongst various *jihad* movements.

Similar to the Kharijite position on individual allegiance to Islam is the issue of state loyalty to the religion. In practice the union of revelation and governance has not always been watertight. Many rulers have been at odds with the *ulama* with regard to authority, and not all have implemented the *shari'a*. Most of today's Muslim states have either discarded *shari'a* law or mix it in varying degrees with legal systems adapted from various European codes. It is only family law that has remained sacrosanct. The compromise with the political union of *din* (religion) and *dunya* (world) has led to some movements and organizations that condemn the state and seek to implement an Islamic revolution, sometimes through violent overthrow.

The justification for such movements in Sunni Islam is to reform or revitalize Islam, and they base it, as did the Kharijites, on verse 3: 104 in the Qur'an. "Let there arise out of you a band of people inviting to all that is good, enjoining what is right, and forbidding what is wrong. They are the ones to attain felicity." Originally revealed in Madina, probably as a reaction to the recruiting of various tribes whose religious motives were suspect, the political and religious significance of this verse can be highly subversive for Muslim states who are seen by the devout to have compromised God's revelation. In the twentieth century, a number of revivalist movements have set themselves up as a righteous vanguard to renew Islam and purge the community of anything that is perceived to be a threat to the religion.

Whereas, in previous eras, the revival and reform of Islam had appeared in localized contexts, responding to local crises, the eighteenth century witnessed Muslim revivals along similar lines across the gamut of the Muslim world. From South-East Asia, through Arabia to Africa, significant Muslim figures created movements to reform Islam. Out of these simultaneous revolutionary responses, perhaps influencing each other through significant meetings at the Hajj, the most important has to be the radical attempt to reform the original heartlands of Islam – Arabia – by Muhammad ibn al-Wahhab. The successful cleansing of Arabia of its countless shrines, tombs, and sacred objects associated with popular Sufism was linked to the Prophet's cleansing of the pagan gods from the Ka'aba and was achieved by joining the religious zeal of Muhammad Wahhab with the temporal power of Muhammad ibn Saud, a local tribal chieftain. The combination was to create the first modern Islamic state, to be known henceforth as Saudi Arabia, but more significantly a global religious movement that to this day remains influential as it promotes the ideals of its founder throughout the Muslim world as the "authentic" and "pure" version of Islam.

The third factor to impact on the appearance of Sunni radical or revolutionary reform movements is the complete or partial loss of state power, especially to a non-Muslim invader. The doctrine of Manifest Success provides an underlying pattern that repeats itself throughout Sunni Muslim history. Arising out of the Qur'an's response to the two battles of Badr and Uhud, Manifest Success provides a theology that is linked to worldly success and failure. The doctrine asserts that the evidence of divine favor is found in political success, expansion, or prosperity. In this context, Malise Ruthwen (2004: 39) refers to Islam being "programmed for victory" and argues that it is a "triumphalist faith." From this date forward (624 CE) the majority of Muslims would regard victory and success in the world as proof that they were God's final community of revelation. Material misfortune raises the specter of the withdrawal of God's favor. The only reasonable response for the believers is to seek reparation, the means to restore divine favor, but the logic of the theological position insists that the only evidence of the return of God's favor will be a restoration of material well-being. Thus the theology of manifest success demands that all future failure be seen either as a test of God's faithful in adversity or as a sign that in some way the believers were lacking in the required submission, faith, or obedience.

In these two battles, Sunni Muslims found a pattern that was to re-emerge again and again throughout history. When confronted with political setbacks and military failure, the *ulama* or religious reformers demanded religious revival as an attempt to regain God's favor. Significantly there was no challenge to the doctrine of Manifest Success until the invasion of the Mongols in the thirteenth century destroyed the centers of

Arab Muslim civilization. The shock to the Sunni mentality resulted in self-reflection, the religious seeing the downfall of the dynasty as caused by its profligate behavior and departure from the ways of the Prophet and the first Muslims. They called for religious revival to revitalize Muslim fortunes and return the community to its supremacy. Yet the fall from power that resulted from European colonialism was to be the biggest shock of all – for the new imperial powers brought before Sunni Muslims the vision of a revival of Christian authority – a religion which God was supposed to have supplanted by Islam as his new community of salvation. The response throughout the eighteenth and nineteenth centuries was a succession of regional religious revivals, for defeat could only be interpreted as a sign of God's disfavor. To restore favor to his last community it was necessary to be self-critical, and seek revival and the reform of Islam.

CHARISMATIC LEADERSHIP IN SUNNI ISLAM

It would be a mistake to assume that charismatic leadership does not occur amongst Sunnis. Sufism provides many examples of such and deserves to be treated separately as a unique form of *ta'ifa* consisting of many *firqa*. Yet Sufism is not the only manifestation of charismatic leadership. However, if Sufism follows more closely the Shi'a pattern of charisma, the concept of a renewer of Islam, a *mujaddid*, follows on from Sunni ideas of rejuvenation of the *ummah*.

As we have seen, the doctrine of Manifest Success leads to a pattern of religious revival as a response to external crises. In addition, the Muslim worldview of Islam as the final revelation gives an urgent need to protect the "purity" of God's revealed practices and beliefs. For Muslims there can be no replacement of their revelation, as they believe happened to Judaism and Christianity (the revelations that were given before the advent of Muhammad and the Qur'an), for it is believed that Muhammad was the "seal of the Prophets" and the Qur'an is the co-eternal Word of God in its entirety. Thus it has come to be a part of traditional Muslim belief that Allah sends a reformer every hundred years to maintain the revelation and destroy any innovatory departure from it. Any movement with a new charismatic leader endowed with personal piety and the energy to impact on the world around him can claim that their leader is the *mujaddid*. A special *mujaddid* is also believed to appear every thousand years. The followers of such a personality are likely to become subdivisions of the Sunni community.

SUFISM

Sufism, sometime defined as Islamic mysticism, probably began as an ascetic reaction to Umayyad worldliness. The proto-Shi'a and Kharijites reacted with armed insurrection but others retreated to Madina to live a semi-reclusive life, attempting to protect the piety they deemed to be central to the Prophet and his community. From these early examples of asceticism and withdrawal appeared a variety of movements composed of disciples to various spiritual guides who taught paths to self-purification based on the remembrance of Allah's names.

As Sufism formalized itself under the guidance of a number of skilled exponents of its disciplines, a variety of "maps" appeared that are identified as "stages" (*maqamat*) and "states" (*ahwal*) on the progress within the path to self-annihilation in God. Each of these variations on a theme became a distinct order of Sufism, each with a founding master (*shaikh*) and a lineage of masters that succeeded him. These orders are known as *tariqa* and are considered by most Sufis to complement the outer practices of Islam (*shari'a*). Discipleship is therefore central to Sufism, to provide guidance to the *murid* (student) along the way of transformation from a self-centered existence to one which is God-centered (Geaves 2005: 124).

These mystical doctrines and practices developed into a cult of saint-hood in which a hierarchy of deceased saints who are believed to maintain the spiritual well-being of the world from outside time combined with popular belief and dependence upon living *shaikhs* to create the doctrine of *karamat* or special favor that was bestowed upon the saint to perform miracles and even intercede on behalf of those requiring Allah's mercy and assistance. This belief in miracles caught the imagination of the populace and led to extravagant and fantastic stories of the deeds of Sufis. When the *shaikhs* died the religious piety of their followers turned to the graves, which would then develop as important shrine centers and the focus of the continuing development of the *tariqa*. It was believed that the power to intercede and perform miracles was contained within the remains of the saint, who was in some way still alive awaiting Judgment Day. Similar to the Shi'a belief concerning their Imams, it was also believed that the Sufi's power was retained in his bloodline and it was usually his immediate remaining family who would take over the religious functions and administration of the shrine. The proliferation of shrines of deceased saints brought a new dynamic into Muslim belief and practices as millions of rural adherents of the faith concentrated their devotional practices and petitions around the tombs (Geaves 2000: 18).

The rapid expansion of Sufi teachings infiltrated the Islamic consciousness as the *tariqa* networks spread throughout the Muslim world in a spider-web pattern. Although the *silsila* (lineage) chains functioned to ensure the legitimacy of the individual *shaikh* and the teachings that he promoted, time and distance enabled many teachers to attract followers with less credulous claims of authority linking them back to the eminent *awliya* (lit. friends of God) and eventually the Prophet himself. As thousands of *shaikhs* and *pirs* across the Muslim world taught their individual methods of self-purification they attracted groups of followers of varying sizes, and it was not surprising that a cult of saints began to develop in the Muslim tradition. This cult of sainthood took on several recognizable features that arose out of the organization of the *tariqas*, the doctrines of Sufism, the credulous imagination of increasing populations of rural followers, and even blatant manipulation and false claims on the part of less reputable *shaikhs* (Geaves 2000: 17).

Although Ibn Arabi (1165–1240) would argue that there is no contradiction with conventional Islamic doctrine, as it would not be possible for the man of self-knowledge to contradict the revelation brought to the messenger of God, such a doctrine is open to abuse by charlatans and religious impostors claiming to be such elevated beings. Indeed, there were Sufis who insisted that they were not required to follow the externals of Islam as their experience of immediacy made redundant the ritual life of the religion or its encompassing framework of laws and ethics. At best, this led to heterodox interpretations of Islam freed from the confines of obedience to the outer disciplines; at worst, it led to sexual impropriety, abuses of power, and misappropriation of funds. Although, for most, the inner path complemented the outer, for others the experience of God's presence within supplied an authority that overrode the historical revelation. Some were to claim the elitist position that the revelation and its outer strictures were given to the ordinary masses, whereas the inner truths of the mystical journey were the only guidance required for a spiritual minority.

The loosely organized localized structures of the *tariqas* around an individual *shaikh* and his followers allowed for no central control of either doctrine or practices. Even reputable *shaikhs* had little control over belief and practice outside the inner circle of his followers. The classic pattern of Sufi allegiance, which still exists to the present day, consisted of an inner circle of initiates who resided with the *shaikh* and an outer circle who still maintained the *shaikh*'s teachings but also had other more worldly priorities. The *shaikh* could exercise a considerable degree of control over these two groups of followers. However, outside of these groups of loyal and committed disciples there was a wider circle that took *bai'at* (initiation) with the *shaikh* as a means of acquiring status and prestige in their social milieu. Over this group the *shaikh* would have little control, either for their behavior or for the way in which they promoted his teachings and spiritual prowess. The more they communicated stories of miraculous powers to the credulous, the more their own reputations soared through vicarious holiness or sanctity. Outside these three groups of followers there would be an even larger group of the general populace who would use the *shaikh* to resolve a whole range of medical, social, and psychological problems through access to his spiritual counsel or belief in his miraculous powers based on his proximity to Allah. Finally, an even more nebulous connection to the *shaikh* existed in the wider population, based on pride or status in having such an elevated figure in their locality (Geaves 2000: 17–18).

The development of a fully fledged theosophy of sainthood, both living and in the tomb, troubled many orthodox Muslims, especially amongst the ranks of the *ulama*. There was considerable criticism of the need to submit to the authority of charismatic men who claimed a special relationship to Allah through ecstasy. Some believed that Islam was being subverted through vicarious holiness arising out of dependence on holy men, pilgrimage to their shrines, adoration of their relics, and total commitment of physical and mental resources to their service (Nicholson 1989: 146). Arberry (1956: 119) suggests that the cult of miracles led to the incredulous masses allowing themselves to be duped by impostors and that the Sufism represented by illustrious figures such as ibn Arabi and al-Farid fell into decay caused by superstition and ignorance.

The other major criticism of Sufism appeared from both outside and within its own ranks. As observed above, some Sufis began to assert that the intimate relationship with Allah which is enjoyed by the *wali* (friend of God) negates the requirement of obedience to the outer laws of Islam, i.e. the *shari'a*. Some suggested that obedience to the exoteric laws and requirements of Islam was a duty required only during the early stages of spiritual development. It was inevitable that a dichotomy should arise between the experience of those who claimed direct inner access to the divine, and therefore felt themselves to be completely surrendered to the divine will, and those who dutifully followed the external requirements of the *shari'a*. As a corollary of the view that the outer requirements of Islam contained in the revelation were only for the masses and were not binding on the spiritually elect, some, like Niffari, claimed that the inner knower of truth only had to follow the outer requirements of Islam if they were in accordance with his vision of reality (Nicholson 1989: 72).

If such sentiments are followed through to their ultimate logical conclusion, Sufism can be completely disconnected from its Islamic roots and perceived as a form of universal mysticism. Haeri (1995: 41 ff), along with many other Muslims including those from within the *tariqas*, finds this view extremely problematic and labels it as "pseudo-Sufism." It is important to acknowledge that the emphasis on such extreme viewpoints among Sufis usually originates from members of the Muslim reform and revivalist movements who often blame Sufism for the decline of the *ummah*. However, most Sufis have been equally critical of those who have departed from obedience to the *shari'a*. The vast majority of the *tariqas* teach that inner development is not possible without the exoteric demands of Islam contained in the final Revelation to humankind from Allah, delivered to and fully manifested in the behavior of Muhammad, the final Prophet of God.

Sufism came to be regarded as the traditional enemy of the neo-orthodox movements long before they perceived the West as a threat. Before the domination of Muslim territory by European powers, any sign of decline in the Muslim community was blamed on inner lapses within the *ummah* and often laid at the door of Sufism by its critics. With the belief that they were the custodians of the final revelation for humankind from God, the representatives of Islam zealously guarded the community from deviation or innovation. Either of these could lead the community from the straight path and result in a failure to protect the revelation in the original purity of its genesis. Internal political failure or conquest by non-Muslims were both likely to be interpreted as punishment for failing to maintain pristine Islam. Events such as the invasion of the Mongols, which destroyed the Abbasid empire, or the rise of European domination from the eighteenth century onwards, drove Muslims in upon themselves to examine their own religious belief and practice. As a consequence, a number of neo-orthodox movements were born that puritanically tried to purge the Muslim community of religious and cultural accretions said to be the influence of foreign cultures or other religions. Such movements were highly critical of Sufism and attempted to present it as a corrupted form of Islam influenced by Buddhists, neo-Platonists, Hindus or Christian mystics, depending on the prevalent traditions within a given geographical region. For the neo-orthodox reformers, Sufism was the cause of Islam's decline and to be eliminated.

CONCLUSION

The division of Islam into sects is implicit in the saying attributed to the Prophet, where it is stated that his community would divide into seventy-two sects, with only one maintaining the true Islam. Obviously each movement feels itself to be that one and its competitors to be the heretical remainder. Yet, the saying itself provides the stimulus for sectarian movements to appear as each new reformer and his followers see them-selves as the one that maintains true Islam. The analyses of divisions tends to fall into two categories: those that seek political causes and those that explore theological or religious differences. Most commentators agree that the major schism in Islam is that between Sunni and Shi'a, and writers on Shi'a are aware of the propensity of Shi'a Islam to sub-divide apparently over issues of charismatic leadership and disputes concerning the Imamate. Fewer commentators are prepared to acknowledge that there are schisms amongst the dominant Sunnis, despite the fact that for centuries various movements have appeared and utilized the vehicle of the *fatwa* (declarations made by legal scholars interpreting Islamic jurispru-dence) to declare their religious opponents as non-Muslim (*kufr*).

Typically most scholars indicate that the first divide in Islam occurred with the death of the Prophet and disputes over who should succeed Muhammad as temporal and spiritual leader of the *ummah*.[5] The temptation here would be to analyze the schism through the application of classical Weberian theories of charismatic leadership. However, two problems occur in such an approach. The first concerns the linearity of simplistic approaches to charisma and institutionalization. Although several scholars have noted the cyclical pattern of such developments throughout history, there is also the problem of when such shifts began to occur. There were difficulties of motivation in the fledgling Muslim

[5] Typical examples would be Cole and Keddie (1986) and Momen (1985). The former states: "Two major branches of the Islamic religion predominate. Both had their origins in disputes within the early Muslim community over who should succeed the Prophet Muhammad as temporal and spiritual leader. The majority Sunni branch, with over 90 per cent of Muslims, hold that after the passing of Muhammad four rightly guided caliphs were elected by the community leaders, after which less revered Muslim dynasties were established. At the opposite pole, Shi'a emerged as the partisans of Ali, the Prophet's cousin and son-in-law, holding that he and his descendents should rule the realms of Islam and serve as spiritual guides" (*Shi'ism and Social Protest*. Newhaven and London: Yale University Press, pp. 1–2). The latter similarly follows suit: "The succession of Muhammad is clearly the key question in Shi'i Islam and the principal factor separating Shi'is from the Sunni majority. The question is not only who was the successor of Muhammad but also the nature of the role of this successor, for it is on both these points that Shi'is and Sunnis disagree" (*An Introduction to Shi'i Islam*. Newhaven and London: Yale University Press, p. 11).

community even when the Prophet was alive, and a recent thesis written by Ruth Bradby (2007) suggests that institutionalization processes begin even under the guidance and direction of the charismatic leader.[6] Of more concern is the fact that charisma can often be invented later than the actual lifetime of the leader and developed by generations of followers living against a background of social, economic, political, and religious upheaval. If charisma is an aspect of the phenonemon of "invented traditions" and develops after the historic event of "schism," then in itself it cannot be the singular cause of the division. That is not to say that "invented charisma" cannot play a part in schismatic conflicts over leadership. The emphasis on the charismatic element of Shi'a leadership that focuses on the original division is likely to lead to a primordial understanding of Shi'a identity that ignores the diversity of the tradition. As stated by Juan Cole (2002: 3), Shi'a tends to express diverse manifestations of the religion depending on whether it is practiced in feudal, semi-feudal, pre-modern or capitalist dictatorships or in democracies. Any attempt to discover the causes of schism in the early community of Muslims would need to take account of the expansion of the Arab empire and the absorption of a variety of social groups into the religio-political entity (*ummah*). The issue here is not only political and economic, in as much as the *mawali* (non-Arab Muslims) felt themselves to be second-class citizens and were able to turn to Islam's strong call to justice as a rallying cry for equality, but that such communities also had long and enduring theological traditions that pre-dated Islam. The parallels between such beliefs and the doctrinal narratives of Shi'a movements are striking, to the point that some sets of beliefs are so heterodox that, when adopted as a set, they led to the exclusion of the movement from the world of Islam. The situation is complex and probably results from a series of factors occurring within a particular milieu to create new movements. The important point is not to think of Shi'a schisms as occurring from a series of breakaways from a true or original position that existed from the beginning and remained unchanged as deviants broke away (Halm 1991: 2). Such an emic position would not do justice to the complexity of sect formation.

It has to be remembered that the religion of Islam was to turn into a body politic in a very short number of years. Tensions between the religious worldview of the pious and their rulers, between those who

---

[6] Ruth Bradby demonstrates in her thesis how institutionalization processes began amongst the founders shortly after the Course in Miracles was channelled to them.

offered their loyalty to the revelation and those who gave it primarily to the state, were endemic. The link between religion and state was so powerful that those who broke away from the religion or deviated from orthodoxy were likely to be seen as traitors, punishable by legal codes. If Shi'a Muslims were to become a despised minority, never being able to celebrate Manifest Success as did their Sunni compatriots, the majority were able to celebrate overwhelming victory. But it came at a cost to religious life and caused dreadful soul searching when territory was lost to non-Muslim forces. Khuri looks at Sunni sectarian formation and assesses it in the context of state structures, centralized authority, the resort to coercive measures and the tendency to standardize. A "fabric fitted together by the logic of power and conquest," he argues (1990: 19). The logic of Khuri's analysis leads to a conclusion that sectarianism within the Muslim world can be explained as instruments of moral control operating outside the heartlands of the Arab empire, either outside the arena of state authority or consciously resisting it for either political or religious reasons. In Khuri's argument (1990: 17–18), sects and state stand in opposition to one another. Such an analysis would help to explain the "invented charisma" of Imams, Sufis, and the hundred-year renewers of the faith (*mujaddid*). Their miraculous powers, heroic personalities, and hagiographies functioned to provide an authority different from that of the bureaucratic state, a resistance to the state monopoly of religion, all legimitimized by an immediate access to the divine providing the means to negate all-powerful human authorities by the display of supernatural powers that even overturned the laws of nature. To such figures, invented or otherwise, flocked the dispossessed, the powerless, the seekers of justice, ethnic and tribal minorities, the searchers for God, or merely those who were too far from the centers of power to feel its influence.

REFERENCES

Adams, Charles. 1983. "Mawdudi and the Islamic State." in John Esposito (ed.), *Voices of Resurgent Islam*. Oxford and New York: Oxford University Press.
Arberry, A. J. 1956. *Sufism*. London: George Allen & Unwin.
Betts, Robert Brenton. 1988. *The Druze*. New Haven: Yale University Press.
Berger, Peter. 1974. "Some Second Thoughts on Substantive versus Functional Definitions of Religion." *Journal for the Scientific Study of Religion* 13(2).
Bradby, Ruth. 2007. *A Better Way, A Course in Miracles: The Development and Legitimation of a new Religious Discourse and Its Diffusion through Spiritual Self-Help Literature*. Chester: University of Chester.

Brown, Daniel. 2004. *A New Introduction to Islam*. Oxford: Blackwell.
Cole, Juan. 2002. *Sacred Space and Holy War*. London: I.B. Tauris.
Cole, Juan and Nikki Keddie. 1986. *Shi'ism and Social Protest*. Newhaven and London: Yale University Press.
Foy, Whitfield (ed.). 1978. *Man's Religious Quest*. Milton Keynes: Open University Press.
Geaves, R. A. 2000. *Sufis of Britain*. Cardiff: Cardiff Academic Press.
    2005. *Aspects of Islam*. London: Darton, Longman & Todd and Washington, DC: Georgetown University Press.
Gibb, Hamilton. 1963. "The Community in Islamic History." *Proceedings of the American Philosophical Society* 107 (2): 173.
Greenslade, S. L. 1953. *Schism in the Early Church*. London: SCM Press.
Haeri, S. F. 1995. *The Elements of Sufism*. Shaftesbury: Element Books.
Halm, Heinz. 1991. *Shiism*. Edinburgh: Edinburgh University Press.
Hobsbawm, Eric and Terence Ranger. Eds. 1992. *The Invention of Tradition*. Cambridge: Cambridge University Press.
Khuri, Fuad. 1990. *Imams and Emirs*. London: Saqi Books.
Momen, Moojan. 1985. *An Introduction to Shi'i Islam*. New Haven: Yale University Press.
Neibuhr, H. Richard. 1957. *The Social Sources of Denominationalism*. New York: Meridian Books (originally published 1929).
Nicholson, R. 1989. *The Mystics of Islam* (4th edn). Harmondsworth: Arkana.
O'Dea, T. F. 1964. "Sociological Dilemmas: Five Paradoxes of Institutionalisation." In E. A. Tiryakian, (ed.), *Sociological Theory, Values, and Socio-Cultural Change* (pp. 71–89). New York: The Free Press of Glencoe.
Ruthwen, Malise. 2004. *Fundamentalism*. Oxford: Oxford University Press.
Wallis, Roy. 1979. *Salvation and Protest: Studies of Social and Religious Movements*. New York: St. Martin's Press.
Watt, Montgomery. 1961. *Islam and the Integration of Society*. London: Routledge and Kegan Paul.
Zald, Mayer and Roberta Ash. 1966. "Social Movement Organizations: Growth, Decay and Change." *Social Forces* 44: 327–40.

CHAPTER 3

Schisms in Buddhism

Alan Cole

While popular notions of Buddhism in the twentieth and twenty-first centuries have often assumed that Buddhism is, and was, as poised, polished, and monochromatic as those charming jade Buddha-statues found in Asian-American restaurants, a bit of familiarity with Buddhist history suggests otherwise. In fact, it would probably be no exaggeration to say that the history of Buddhism, in the twenty-five centuries since the Buddha's death, could be told as a series of schismatic developments. To make sense of this fractious history, this chapter will present a thumbnail account of the evolution of Buddhism in India, Tibet, and East Asia, along with some brief comments about Buddhism in the Occident. In offering this historical overview of Buddhist schisms, which will be by definition partial and minimalist, I have selected particular developments based on whether they either add something to our appreciation of the vicissitudes of the Buddhist tradition, or provide potentially useful information for comparative reflections.

In light of the material found in the Buddhist tradition, I believe we will do fine defining "schism" simply as "a publicly recognized division within a religious group." As in any tradition, such a division could emerge from disagreements over doctrine, history, leadership, practices, or institutional arrangements. In defining "schism" in this broad manner, the point is not just that schisms result from differences of opinion over an issue, but also that these differences have been elevated into "identity-producing" divides. That is, in any religious community, there will normally be all sorts of fissures in the group, and yet the language of "schism" only begins to be meaningful when a particular divide or difference is taken up as a means to define a new group's identity.

Putting matters this way works well to get started, but we also need to be careful with what we mean by "group." In the above paragraph it seems like a rather uncomplicated entity in which a dividing line might emerge and threaten the integrity of the group. But are there not other ways that schisms form? For instance, in many social settings there will be a group of people who consciously know themselves to represent a mini-group within the larger group, with distinct interests that are often at odds with those of the larger group. Should we say that this represents a schismatic, or, at least, proto-schismatic situation? At first one might say no, especially since it does not fulfill the above definition of making the line-of-difference publicly known. But what if this internal group were rather stable, had a coherent body of ideas and/or practices, worked to recruit members, and in general were very aware of itself and the per-imeter that divided its clandestine members from the larger group? In this case, it would seem that we have a schism of sorts, since clearly there is a break in the social whole, and, though the reality of this divide is not fully public, it is nonetheless *public within the dissident mini-group* whose members know very well about the divide and what lies on either side of the line. Thus, I believe that we can speak of these situations as schismatic as long as the clandestine group within the larger group has a certain cohesion and self-awareness, and, most importantly, polices the border between itself and the larger "parent group" to which it nominally belongs.

Clarifying such clandestine schisms helps in profiling the vast number of secret societies that have flourished throughout history, as well as the cliques that form in practically any situation – be it cheerleading squads or small liberal arts colleges – but it also lays the groundwork for understanding a rather notable schism in Buddhist history: the emergence of the Mahayana (lit. the Great Vehicle), a movement that appeared in India roughly at the beginning of the Common Era and did much to reframe Buddhist discourse in the centuries that followed. However, before launching into an account of Mahayana Buddhism, let's consider the possibility that allowing for such practically invisible internal schisms also might help explain the "life of a schism" in the sense that it may turn out that many religious schisms start "invisibly," with figures within a group gradually pulling together and redrawing lines of legitimacy such that they, within their own mini-group, declare themselves uniquely legitimate vis-à-vis the larger group, even though they have yet to inform the larger group of this coup. Presumably, after this initial phase of minting a new form of legitimacy, the schismatic mini-group could follow one of three paths: (1) renounce its schismatic tendencies and collapse back into the larger group; (2) maintain itself as a dissident group within the larger group, while still laying claim to a kind of hyper-legitimacy; or (3) publicly announce its "self-standing" identity and separate fully from the parent group, moving off to establish itself as the singular repository of tradition. Not surprisingly we will find evidence of all three "paths" in and out of the schismatic moments in Buddhist history.

The place to start this history of schisms in Buddhism is to admit that Buddhism came into being through a schismatic succession during which the Buddha and his initial followers broke away from the complex matrix of Brahmanical and yogic ideas that marked the Buddha's era of the sixth and fifth centuries BCE. Evidence for reading the invention of Buddhism as a schismatic moment comes from the numerous places in early Buddhist texts where one finds substantial sameness admitted between the Buddha's teaching and that of his contemporaries, for instance on the topics of karma, reincarnation, and meditation/trance. Yet despite these shared elements, early Buddhist texts also place great emphasis on the Buddha's uniqueness. In short, Buddhist texts insist that the Buddha was "the best of bipeds" who was "naturally" and categorically above his competitors, since he alone had truth whereas they had, at best, half-truths. Presumably it was due to this need to negotiate this matter of sameness and difference vis-à-vis the competition that one finds many narratives from the Buddha's life that admit that he studied with a range of non-Buddhist teachers but that he then surpassed their teachings and accomplishments. A similar dialectical dependence on non-Buddhist groups is evident when Buddhist narratives go out of their way to explain that the gods, yogis, Brahmans, and all other such high-placed representatives of the non-Buddhist traditions, came, again "naturally," to recognize the Buddha's superiority. In effect, then, Buddhist narratives rely on the spokespersons from the prior matrix of meaning to confirm the "natural" fact of the Buddha's superiority and thereby give the impression that the schismatic succession that gave birth to Buddhism was, in fact, simply a case of the older forms of religious authority recognizing their inferiority vis-à-vis the Buddha.

With this body of myth rationalizing the Buddha's singular superiority and establishing Buddhism as a "self-standing" tradition, basic Buddhist identity was organized in two ways. For laity, Buddhist identity was marked by a simple ritual: one recited three times, "I take refuge in the Buddha, his teachings (dharma), and the community of Buddhists (sangha)." With this enunciation, which is still the formula used today in various Buddhist traditions, the speaker identifies the uniqueness of Buddhist leadership, teaching, and community, and publicly vows to step into the community. In the case of someone wanting to become a "professional" Buddhist – a monk or nun, that is – crossing of the line-of-difference was *much* more involved since it was required that the neophyte first be accepted by an ordained representative of tradition, and then train under him or her for several years as a postulant before finally being presented to ten other representatives of tradition in the hope of winning full ordination. These rituals, along with many other community-building procedures, suggest that the architects of the Buddhist tradition understood the importance of drawing these lines-of-difference and constructed them in such a way that the Buddhist community could maintain itself in the midst of a pluralistic and competitive social milieu. In fact, one would not be wrong in thinking that it was precisely because Buddhism had continually to hold its own against the wider Brahmanical and yogic background, that it developed such a complex institutional framework with nearly endless rules for defining correct Buddhist identity and institutional integrity.[1]

The invention of Buddhism was not without its immediate detractors. For instance, the Buddha's success seems to have enraged his cousin, known to us as Devadatta. Devadatta, for whatever reasons, felt that the Buddha's message was too indulgent and needed to be recast as a recipe for radical asceticism, much more in line with the Jains and other more austere groups of ascetics. Intent on rectifying the Buddha's shortcomings, Devadatta supposedly started his own group of renunciants that appears to have been fairly similar to the Buddhists but with Devadatta at the head of the cult. In fact, Devadatta seems to have won some lasting institutional success for himself since his followers are occasionally mentioned in Buddhist sources. In this light, the Devadatta movement is a fine example of a schism growing out of a schism.

Despite the care with which the Buddhists sought to solidify their religious identity apart from Brahmanism and other yogic movements, it seems that the early phase of the tradition was one in which there was widespread internal dissension. To keep things reasonably simple, and to

[1] It is with this logic in mind that Gregory Schopen argues that the monastic codes on the subcontinent are much more complex than the one that survived on the island of Sri Lanka (the Pali Vinaya), since on the mainland Buddhist jurists had, at nearly every step, to manage complex relations with their Brahmanical competitors. For Schopen's argument, see his "Monastic Law Meets the Real World: A Monk's Continuing Right to Inherit Family Property in Classical India," *History of Religions* 35 (2) (November 1995): 101–23, esp. pp. 120ff.

respect the basic fact that we know very little about this early period, we will have to content ourselves with identifying two centrifugal forces at work in this early phase. The first was more or less "accidental" in the sense that as Buddhists moved around India and took up residence at great distances from one another, they began, presumably unknowingly, to transform Buddhism in different ways. Of course, if we also allow that the Buddha taught a variety of things in his life, or that he might have changed his views along the way, we have all the more reason to imagine that the singular figure of the Buddha produced a range of doctrinal positions with differing practices emphasized in different phases of his career. Then, when these differing teachings and practices were transplanted far from the Gangetic plains where the Buddha roamed, it is not hard to imagine that a variety of different Buddhisms would arise to fit local political and social realities.

In fact, the six surviving recensions of the Vinaya – the large "handbooks" detailing the maintenance of the monasteries – make it clear that the form and content of Buddhist monasticism grew piecemeal in response to very site-specific matters. And, presumably, it was precisely this ability to bricolage the institutional "hardware" of Buddhism that kept the various traditions of Buddhism viable. Thus, one can find interesting stories relating how it came to be that the Buddha supposedly instituted landownership for the Buddhist community of monks and/or nuns, or how funerals and the private ownership of property were to be negotiated and so on. Clearly, these stories were written in a post-facto manner, with the current problem fictively presented to the Buddha (in the narrative), who then offers a binding "opinion" that would henceforth guide institutional practices. Key to remember though is that this on-going bricolage in organizing institutional practices was only possible because Buddhism lacked a Rome-like center. And, even though the surviving Vinayas show a lot of consistency on some matters, they also vary considerably on important points, and cover very different ground, which is to say that there were in fact rather different ways of practicing Buddhism. Put otherwise, the success of the basic Buddhist message – that nirvana could be attained with knowledge of reality won through following the Buddha's teachings – meant that across the Indian subcontinent a broad range of teachings, practices, and institutional procedures took form precisely because there was no center and no overarching disciplining body.

The second centrifugal force leading to schisms in the Buddhist world reflects what people usually associate with the word "schism": the emergence of mutually hostile ways of interpreting religious thought and practice. In time, these differences became so widely known that it was the norm to speak of the Eighteen Schools of Buddhism. With this language of the Eighteen Schools – how historically accurate this number is remains widely debated – it seems that we have schism in the lightest sense of the word, since though there appear to have been clear lines of difference drawn and acknowledged within the larger Buddhist community, it also seems that commitment to some basic idea of being Buddhist was maintained. Thus, the very category of the "Eighteen Schools" functioned as a catch-all, including and "recovering" dissident Buddhist groups under a non-sectarian umbrella. Buddhist historians, throughout the centuries, tried to make sense of this schismatic past by narrating a series of pan-Indian conferences that supposedly brought together large numbers of Buddhist authorities to resolve the various differences in interpretation and practice. Though modern scholarship has voiced considerable reservation regarding the historicity of these councils, it is still the case that the surviving accounts of the councils offer us a glimpse of how various Buddhist groups articulated their experience of schismatic upheaval and sought, at least with narratives, to reunify tradition.[2]

THE MAHAYANA SCHISM – A TEXTUAL REVOLUTION?

Roughly at the beginning of the Common Era a new schismatic movement arose within Buddhism – the Mahayana form of Buddhism. The relationship between the Mahayana and older forms of Buddhism remains very unclear, with some scholars arguing that the Mahayana grew out of one or more of the Eighteen Schools, or as the result of one of the supposedly historical councils; other scholars see little ground for such claims. Given this uncertainty in the field, I will provide the basic evidence that we have, and then offer several frameworks that might explain the interface between Mahayana Buddhism and older forms of being Buddhist.

As for evidence, what remains from the early Mahayana movement is a large number of texts that are remarkably heterogeneous in form and content. Some of these texts survive in what we believe to be their original language – Sanskrit – but a much greater number of Mahayana works

---

[2] For discussion of the sources available for writing a history of Buddhism's early schisms, see Janice J. Nattier and Charles S. Prebish's "Mahasanghika Origins: The Beginnings of Buddhist Sectarianism," *History of Religions* 16 (3) (February 1977): 237–72.

survive in Chinese translations, translations which began in the late second century and continued more or less unabated up through the eighth and ninth centuries. Similarly, Tibetans began translating Mahayana works in the eighth century and continued to do so until Buddhism began to disappear in India in the twelfth and thirteenth centuries. Thus we have, in various languages, a vast body of literature that seems to represent very different styles of being Buddhist and which, in narrative at least, often makes the divide between itself and old-style Buddhism a fundamental aspect of claiming Mahayana identity. In fact, many of these narratives are designed to effect a conversion experience from old-style Buddhism to the Mahayana form of Buddhism.

However, next to all this textual evidence there remains very little else to support the writing of a history of early Mahayana Buddhism. In fact, according to the careful work of Gregory Schopen, until the fifth and sixth centuries one finds almost no evidence of anyone practicing Mahayana Buddhism.[3] Thus, somewhat surprisingly, there is as yet no evidence of specifically Mahayana monasteries or temples for this early period. Nor can we find Mahayana-inspired art forms, or epigraphic evidence. Oddest of all, I think, is that mainstream Buddhism (what is often referred to as "Hinayana Buddhism") barely mentions this supposed Mahayana revolution.[4] In short, we have a body of literary texts that speak of a revolution in the Buddhist world, and prepares, in a literary way, for that revolution in detail, and yet there is no corroborating evidence that such a revolution in Buddhism happened. Equally odd, and again relying on Gregory Schopen's work, when we do start to find evidence of the Mahayana it appears on the fringe of Buddhist India, in out-of-the-way sites that were abandoned by mainstream Buddhists. Thus once the evidence "on the ground" does begin to appear, it suggests that the Mahayanists of fifth- and sixth-century India were not that central or important to tradition – a perception that again does not match what the texts say about themselves or the textbook explanations of the Mahayana that we have generated in the past one hundred years.

With this perplexing profile of evidence before us, two explanations seem possible. First, we could imagine that a small group of dissident monks began writing works that sought to thoroughly redefine Buddhist

---

[3] See his "Mahayana and the Middle Period of Indian Buddhism: Through a Chinese Looking-Glass," *Eastern Buddhist* 32 (2) (2000): 1–26.
[4] Richard Cohen makes this point well in his "Discontented Categories: Hinayana and Mahayana in Indian Buddhist History," *Journal of the American Academy of Religion* 63 (1) (Spring 1995): 1–25, esp. p. 19.

authority, identity, and practice but did so with little fanfare. Instead of directly confronting mainstream Buddhism with protests or debates, they relied on these texts as the medium by which they hoped to infiltrate mainstream Buddhism, and convince readers to shift their alliances to these newly configured forms of tradition in which the worship of these texts was often promoted as the be-all and end-all of tradition. Then, despite their verve for writing these often long and involved works, very few monks were convinced and thus few followed the dissident group. Hence, there languished on the periphery of Buddhism a small but active group of readers and writers who consoled themselves by practicing a form of Buddhism that was based on the cultic worship of these texts that claimed to hold the entirety of tradition within their borders. Such a theory seems plausible, since this form of worshiping the text is quite apparent in many Mahayana sutras, so much so that Schopen coined the term "cult of the text" to explain how this kind of self-referential rhetoric works.[5] Also, in support of this theory, one can point to the occasional places in Mahayana texts where partisans are encouraged to leave the monasteries for a more rigorous life in the forest or in other secluded places. Likewise, one can find passages that explain how one should pass these texts to other Buddhists and thereby come to build something of a Mahayana community around just these texts.

The second scenario is a good bit like the first one except that it doesn't imagine that Mahayana Buddhists left the larger community. In this explanation, these texts were written, copied, and passed around among *some* members of the established Buddhist community who realized that the texts broke the symbolic order of the community but did not allow that rent in their metaphysical horizon to prevent them from continuing to belong to the physical community of traditional Buddhists. Hence, in this scenario we are asked to imagine something like an underground Mahayana movement, which was either largely ignored or tolerated by the official forms of Buddhism, and which thrived as a literary group who shared texts and lines of contact but who, by and large, existed as an invisible imagined community within the older style of Buddhism. And, of course, such an "imagined community" is, according to Benedict Andersen, precisely what could be built with this kind of literature, since

---

[5] For Schopen's position, see his "The Phrase 'sa prthivipradesas caityabhuto bhavet' in the *Vajra-cchedika*: Notes on the Cult of the Book in Mahayana," *Indo-Iranian Journal* 17 (1975): 148–81; for more discussion of how this rhetoric works, see my *Text as Father: Paternal Seductions in Early Mahayana Buddhist Literature* (Berkeley: University of California Press, 2005).

this literature would provide the perfect medium for members to "convene."[6]

As we weigh the evidence – and new evidence may appear – I would suggest that both explanations are probably useful, with one form or the other dominating in a time or place. Thus, it would be hard to imagine that some Mahayana adherents did not break away from the monastery and try to invent a wholly different kind of Buddhism.[7] However, reading these sutras makes clear that the intended audience usually is those readers *already* very familiar with Buddhist thought, ritual, and symbolism. This means that Mahayana Buddhism, at least as it appears in the texts, does not represent a schism that fully broke away from its "mother-ship" but instead continued to live next to it, or even within it. If Mahayana Buddhist authors at this point had fully broken with mainstream Buddhism they presumably would *not* have continued to write texts for a Buddhist audience and would have turned to build rhetorics to convince non-Buddhists to join their cause. One can find this kind of outreach effort here and there in Mahayana literature but it is by far the exception that proves the rule that the target audience for Mahayana conversion was mainstream Buddhists. Consequently, I think we have to conclude that, for this early period, Mahayana Buddhism remained something of an "in-house" supplement to ordinary Buddhism. That is, early Mahayana Buddhism looks like an internal schism within Buddhism that maintained its identity and focus by trafficking in these texts which were enough of institutions-unto-themselves that Mahayana-styles of being Buddhist could exist for centuries as a virtual form of new Buddhism, but only insofar as they continued to coexist with the rest of traditional Buddhism.[8]

There may be some who might think that since it seems that Mahayanists did not physically leave the matrix of old-style Buddhism the Mahayana should not be counted as a full-fledged schism. Against this opinion, I would argue that when one reads these texts it is altogether

---

[6] For Andersen's position about the connection between imagined community and literature, see his *Imagined Communities* (rev. edn, London: Verso, 1991).

[7] Jan Nattier's investigation of one Mahayana text points in this direction; see her *A Few Good Men: The Bodhisattva Path According to The Inquiry of Ugra (Ugrapariprccha)* (Honolulu: University of Hawaii Press, 2003).

[8] As a point of comparison, it is worth thinking about how many university-trained scholars of Christianity are ordained and function within their various denominations but participate in a wider world of textuality that, in many ways, calls into question the solidity of the practiced forms of Christianity that they still participate in, and, in fact, often lead. Thus, imagining Buddhists with a "split screen" view on tradition need not be considered such an unlikely arrangement.

clear that there often is an initiation-like process built into the reading experience that is designed, overtly, to make the reader renounce his former Buddhist identity and accept the new Mahayana form of Buddhist identity. For instance, in the *Lotus Sutra* and other like-minded works, one is asked to believe that all previous forms of Buddhism were nothing more than a clever fraud concocted by the Buddha, and that one could only become a real Buddhist by seeing current Buddhism as degraded and illegitimate.[9] It is this radical denial of the fullness and finality of old-style tradition that leaves us little choice but to see these texts as fully schismatic even if this schismatic conversion was expected to occur in the rarefied world of the reader's imagination.

Before exploring more of the theoretical implications of the Mahayana schisms I need to mention one kind of evidence that might bear on our attempts to reconstitute the social reality of early Mahayana Buddhism. There are several surviving travelogues of Chinese monks – notably Faxian, Yijing, and Xuanzang – who walked to India and then recorded their impressions. These texts date from between 399 and 699 and thus one would think that they offer excellent evidence for this period of Indian Buddhism. However, as recent scholarship has pointed out, it is somewhat problematic to take these accounts in a straightforward manner. For instance, all three of the Chinese monks began their travels with convictions about Indian Buddhism that were derived largely from reading Mahayana accounts of "real" tradition – something that might have rather colored what they saw in India. In fact, in some cases it seems that their textual familiarity with "tradition" very much defined what they saw, so much so that in some cases textual descriptions of tradition totally replaced eye-witness accounts.[10] In short, these travelogues need to be treated with care if we are to use them as evidence for imagining this period of Mahayana Buddhism.

Of special interest for the question of sociality in the Mahayana schism is the claim made by these Chinese pilgrims that old-school monks and Mahayana monks lived together in the same monasteries. In the case of the oldest account, Faxian, writing at the beginning of the fifth century, meticulously reports the number of monks of either persuasion in each monastery that he visits.[11] How he knew which monks were of which

---

[9] For an analysis of how these narratives of conversion were deployed, see my *Text as Father*.
[10] For discussion of one such example, see John S. Strong's *The Legend of King Asoka: A Study and Translation of the Asokavadana* (Princeton: Princeton University Press, 1983), pp. 6–7.
[11] Faxian's travelogue is translated by James Legge in his *A Record of Buddhistic Kingdoms* (reprint edn, 1885, New York: Paragon Book Company, 1965).

"sect" is not clarified in his account. More troubling for those who would assume that Mahayana Buddhism must have been a visible reality thriving at the center of these monasteries is the fact that in his narrative one finds no mention of specifically Mahayana elements of ritual, practice, or art, and thus what Mahayana might have meant to Faxian remains decidedly unclear. On the other hand, Yijing, writing some three hundred years later at the end of the seventh century, identifies being Mahayana as a two-part commitment: worshiping Mahayana versions of the Buddha (which could include a range of bodhisattvas not generally included in old-style Buddhism) and, not surprisingly, reading Mahayana literature.[12] Even allowing for substantial distortion in their observations of Indian Buddhism, these comments from the Chinese travelers suggest that the heady overhaul of tradition, as it was generated in the Mahayana texts written at the beginning of the Common Era, found a place for itself within the monastery such that traditional monks and Mahayanists could coexist and abided by some mutually accepted form of monastic rules, even if they might entertain rather different notions of what tradition was really made of.

Standing back from the example of the Mahayana schism/s, two theoretical points are worth exploring. First, against the assumption that schisms result from social pressures, or newly opening niches in the political economy of religion, here it seems that we have a schism generated by a media invention: the written text. Clearly, without this invention the Mahayana, as we have it, could never have taken off. In fact, Richard Gombrich has argued that writing was the likely cause of the Mahayana.[13] Evidence for the use of writing in India dates back to the early third century BCE, and thus it seems that after some two or three hundred years Buddhist thinkers came to realize the potential that this new media-space offered. More exactly, Buddhists began to realize that one could recreate the world of truth and tradition – via innovative narratives – and then ground those narratives in the physicality of the text, which could be defined as the holiest of holies in a manner that collapsed the physical and spiritual "essence" of tradition into the text itself. Speaking metaphorically, perhaps one could argue that the world of

---

[12] Yijing's comments are discussed in Hubert Durt's "Daijo [Mahayana]" in *Hobogirin: Dictionnaire encyclopédique du bouddhisme d'après les sources chinoises et japonaises*, vol. VII (Paris: Adrien Maisonneuve, 1927), pp. 767–801.

[13] See his "How the Mahayana Began," in Tadeusz Skorupski (ed.), *The Buddhist Forum*, vol. I (London: School of Oriental and African Studies, 1990), pp. 21–30.

text in fact did open up new niches on the field of religion–politics, since this space of the written narrative functioned as a kind of virtual world that could be inhabited in a manner *akin* to real-world spaces.[14]

The second theory point is a bit trickier but needs to be kept in view. What these Mahayana texts clearly require is for the reader to become *ironic* about truth and tradition. That is, the basic agenda in many of these texts is to get the reader to shift his assessment of tradition such that he can see it from another point of view – a view that is supposedly more truthful and more conducive to salvation. In fact, in some texts, simply moving to such a position where one sees tradition objectified as small and limited is tantamount to becoming Mahayana, with no other explicit content offered to define being Mahayana. In short, becoming ironic about tradition is taken to be the essence of (new) tradition which claims to be older and realer than the standard form of tradition, even though, of course, it is built out of post facto commentary on tradition. Thinking about schisms in this way is also, I would argue, useful for reading early Christian literature which likewise requires the reader to see the elements of earlier tradition as small and insufficient but then offers little to replace them other than the promise that trading one's old faith in for the new faith (which is defined as a critique of the old faith) is the essence of tradition. In short, both Buddhism and Christianity have, at times, relied on a kind of irony vis-à-vis tradition that, though working in different ways, still needs to be factored into how we assess the beginning of religious movements. Keeping track of this kind of ironic critique of tradition is important, too, for making sense of their later developments in either tradition when this kind of language is drawn on, again, to recreate tradition.

SCHOLASTIC MAHAYANA BUDDHISM

Trying to make sense of the way that Mahayana schismatic rhetoric might have thrived within the monastic setting of mainstream Buddhism leads on to considering two other critical developments in medieval Buddhism in India. The first is the appearance of a scholastic form of Mahayana Buddhism that begins roughly in the fifth century and then develops

---

[14] In thinking about the role of media in schisms, it is worth pointing out that Christianity only appeared with new styles of writing: the Pauline epistle and the gospel. Arguably both are new inventions in the Greco-Roman world and both represent the possibility of radically repositioning both the essence of tradition and access to it.

quite extensively by the seventh and eighth centuries. This form of the Mahayana, apparently, did not write new sutras for itself, but instead focused on logical debates about the essence of tradition and the various legitimate modes of practice. Despite a certain pro-Mahayana partisan-ship evident in these works, it is also the case that some of these authors sought to synthesize the earlier forms of Buddhism with Mahayana notions of Buddhism. In fact, this was accomplished by arguing that a person's practice should replay, in historic order, the forms of Buddhism. Thus, for instance, in the case of the eighth century exegete Kamalashila we have a long and detailed text called Stages of the Path (*Bhavanakrama*) in which Kamalashila argues that one must first begin Buddhist training focusing on old-school forms of Buddhist thought and then slowly move into Mahayana-styled practices.[15] Thus, the "ontogeny" of the practitioner is organized, in some ways, to replay the "phylogeny" of Buddhism. Of course, in presenting the individual's practice as a recapitulation of Buddhism's fractious past, much had to be simplified and, in particular, the glaring antipathy that many Mahayana texts express for earlier forms of tradition had to be suppressed. Thus, what was earlier understood as schismatic incompatibility is now understood to be nothing more than stages on the path to the goal of nirvana and omniscience.

The second post-Mahayana development is even more interesting. Roughly at the time that scholastic Buddhism was coming into its own, a new form of Buddhism became increasingly popular – tantra. This movement, which seems part of a pan-Indian tantric phase of Indian religious history, vitally redefined the nature of Buddhism – as much or more so than early Mahayana Buddhism did. The historical evidence is again sketchy, but it seems that there were a growing number of Buddhist practitioners who, outside of monastic connections, founded secretive underground groups of practitioners who would meet at select times and practice rather untraditional rites, including drinking alcohol, eating vile substances, initiating each other with sex, and so on.[16] Unlike early Mahayana, which was apparently largely text-based and narrative-driven, tantric Buddhism in its early phases seems to have been the opposite, with a focus on rites and little interest in narrative or cult-of-the-text. In

---

[15] For a translation of this text, see Giuseppe Tucci's *Minor Buddhist Texts* (Rome: Istituto Italiano per il Medio ed Extremo Oriente, 1958).

[16] For an account of tantra's place in the history of Buddhism that supplies good textual details, see David Snellgrove's *Indo-Tibetan Buddhism* (Boston, MA: Shambhala, 1987).

fact, when tantric authors sought to produce textual accounts of their practices, they produced works that read like recipe books and in that sense are not really literature at all. Nonetheless, it is clear in some of these works that tantric innovation was, in part, explained in a manner that mimicked older forms of Mahayana thinking, especially in terms of overcoming older forms of Buddhism by arguing for higher forms of wisdom. That is, while it would be hasty to conclude that the irony imbedded in early Mahayana thought gave birth, directly, to tantric speculations that allowed for tradition to be overcome again, it seems nonetheless true that many tantric authors justified their radicalism with arguments that hark back to the early Mahayana phase.

Equally interesting is the fact that the tantric attempt to overhaul traditional Buddhism appears to have suffered the same fate as the early Mahayana movement. Whatever happened to these various groups of tantric-practitioners with their "twilight language" and crossroad meetings, in time a portion of tantric thought and practice was brought within the purview of mainstream Buddhism and, to a certain extent, codified within monastic practice. Naturally, much of the wildness had to be treated symbolically, with, for instance, the orgiastic alcohol-fueled tantric rites taken as metaphors for internal meditations. However, even in this "sanitized" form, the wilder elements of tantra are still visible and would, at times, still lead on to rather innovative ways to practice Buddhism. In short, tantra, like the early Mahayana, started off as a fully schismatic and subversive "attack" on mainstream Buddhism, but in time was modified, domesticated and brought within the fold of tradition. How this happened is not clear, and it is also the case that it did not happen fully since one can find tantric authors writing screeds against normal Buddhism even after normal Buddhism had adopted many tantric inventions.[17] In sum, it would seem that Indian Buddhism gave rise to a number of major schismatic developments, and yet in time this spectrum of alternative practices and beliefs was brought, with major modifications, into the mainstream monastic system. Though this no doubt would have given the dissident Buddhists a measure of legitimization, it also probably threatened their independent standing outside the Buddhist mainstream since their distinguishing features were no longer so distinguishing.

---

[17] The ninth-century Saraha is just this kind of tantric author who makes fun of institutionalized forms of Tantric Buddhism, and Mahayana Buddhism for that matter. For a translation of one of his lyrical works, see David Snellgrove's "Saraha's Treasury of Songs," in Edward Conze (ed.), *Buddhist Texts Through the Ages* (New York: Harper Torchbooks, 1954), pp. 224–39.

TIBETAN BUDDHISM

As tantric Buddhism was developing in the seventh and eighth centuries in India, Buddhism began its historic movement across the Himalayas into Tibet. It was during this period, and for the following four or five centuries, that Buddhism, in its many-layered forms, would slowly be introduced into Tibetan life. Along the way, not surprisingly, much changed, and would continue to change, as Tibetan Buddhism began to take on a life of its own. While the complexity of the emerging profile of Tibetan Buddhism prohibits in-depth discussion in this chapter, we should note that the history of Tibetan Buddhism is filled with several types of schismatic strife which probably would be of interest to anyone generally concerned with this topic. To bring some order to the variety of religious schisms in Tibet, I would suggest three categories of discussion. First, and most prominent, was the divide of Buddhists into sects, often mutually hostile, based on their allegiance to different ancestral teachers – real or imagined. Thus, one's Buddhist identity was constructed around receiving the teachings and mystical "imprimatur" of a prior master, and this transmitted lineage served to keep one more or less apart from other Buddhists who did not share this "history." The result of organizing legitimacy in this manner was the gradual emergence of four schools: the Nyingmapas, the Kagyupas, the Sakyapas, and the Gelukpas. These schools, though often sharing many ideas and practices, produced their own bodies of literature and tried to keep their adherents from reading works from the other schools.

The two other categories of schism, or proto-schism, focus on smaller groups within the four schools. In the first case, it is worth wondering if several of the large Geluk monasteries in and around Lhasa might not count as schisms of a sort. Though the city-sized monasteries, such as Drepung or Sera, belonged to the Geluk sect, they represented blocks of independent institutional power that on occasion took rather high-profile political action on their own initiative – sometimes against the govern-ment, and even against the ruling (Geluk) Dalai Lamas. Thus, though I do not see this as fully schismatic, it would seem that loyalties to these monasteries were, at times, strong enough to begin to stretch and threaten commitments to the Geluk sect. Lastly, within the four schools there is some evidence of important lines-of-difference being drawn based on one's allegiance to differing deities. In one recent case, a debate over the value of the protector deity Shugden in the Geluk tradition led supporters of Gelsang Gyatso to protest the Dalai Lama's leadership since he criticized the patronage of this deity. This acrimonious debate, dubbed the "Shugden affair," appears to have prepared the ground for the sup- porters of Gelsang Gyatso to completely split off from the Geluk school and found their own religious identity.[18]

SCHISMS IN EAST ASIAN BUDDHISM

Having followed the development of Buddhism in India, and then its spread into Tibet, we need to go back to the second century of the Common Era and pick up another important development in Buddhist history – the migration of Buddhism to East Asia. Of course, a full account of the sectarian and schismatic "life" of Buddhism in China, Japan, Korea, and Vietnam is beyond the scope of this chapter. However, I believe we can recognize three paradigmatic examples that will be of use in thinking about schisms in Buddhism, and which will also bring us into the modern era where a different set of forces generated other patterns of dissent and division.

As Buddhism became part of the fabric of life in China, after its arrival in the second century, we can identify one basic type of schismatic development – the divide between government-sanctioned Buddhists and those who lacked this official recognition. In China, Buddhism had a very close and contentious relationship with the state which, at most turns, sought to control the Buddhist clergy and minimize the economic and political clout of the Buddhist monasteries, which had become very numerous in a short period of time.[19] In fact, early on, the state took it upon itself to license Buddhist monks by requiring that they have a state- issued ordination certificate or risk dire consequences should they con- tinue to function as clergy.

However, outside the sphere of these state-sanctioned monks and monasteries, there regularly appeared a range of Buddhist movements that were considered heretical and even demonic. In fact, these move- ments, usually millenarian in character, began to appear soon after the arrival of Buddhism in China, and represent a fascinating aspect of Chinese history. Often it was the case that a charismatic leader, usually with minimum education and even less contact with mainstream "licensed"

---

[18] For details on this conflict, see Donald S. Lopez's *Prisoners of Shangri-La: Tibetan Buddhism and the West* (Chicago: University of Chicago Press, 1998), pp. 192–6.

[19] For an account of the growth of Buddhist monasteries in China, and the consequent set of state- related problems, see Jacques Gernet's *Buddhism in Chinese Society* (New York: Columbia Uni- versity Press, 1998).

Buddhism, would declare himself a living-Buddha with special powers and then lead a group of faithful peasants in an insurrection against the state. This happened a surprising number of times from the fifth century down to the nineteenth century.[20] Of course, part of what was driving these movements was a deep and abiding set of economic realities; however, this does not take away from the fervent beliefs that motivated the followers. Actually, this pattern of religious revolt generated by the Buddhists in the medieval period probably belongs within a wider category of religious revolts that includes Daoist and, more recently, Christian forms of Chinese millenarianism. Crucial to understand, though, is that the Buddhist version of these millenarian movements were seen not just by the state as altogether threatening; they were also feared by the conventional Buddhists, who felt the status quo of the empire at risk and knew, too, that they might be the target of future anti-Buddhist legislation, once the state squelched the rebellion.

Next to these episodic and often catastrophic movements that were led by Buddhist-inspired figures, we need to consider another kind of schism in China. This is the interface between Buddhism and what is often referred to as "Religious Daoism," which took institutional form, roughly, in the fifth century, and which seems to have borrowed much from Buddhism while also insisting that it represented an independent indigenous tradition. Clarifying the dialectic between medieval Daoism and Buddhism will remain a rich area of research in the decades to come, since it seems undeniable that much was traded back and forth between the two religious groups. Treating this form of Daoism as at least partially formed via a schismatic relationship with Buddhism is worth pursuing, I would argue, because Religious Daoism, on the surface at least, looks a good bit like Buddhism but repackaged to make it more Chinese in form and origin. Thus, important Daoist rites, texts, and monastic institutions seem, in part, to derive from previous Buddhist forms and this raises some interesting questions about the limits of the category "schism." If Religious Daoism is in a certain sense a Buddhist-looking form of "not-Buddhism" that prides itself on being able to point to Chinese origins for Buddhist-looking ideas and practices that were otherwise understood to be imported from India, should we count this as a schismatic relationship or something altogether different? The sticking point is that we have not,

---

[20] For a discussion of Buddhist heterodox traditions, see B. J. ter Harr's *White Lotus Teachings in Chinese Religious History* (Honolulu: University of Hawaii Press, 1999); see also Susan Naquin's *Shantung Rebellion: The Wang Lun Uprising of 1774* (New Haven: Yale University Press, 1989).

as far as I know, worked out a language for discussing how religions generate other religions via mimesis such that alternative religious groups are produced outside the perimeter of a group and yet come to resemble that group which, again in a certain sense, was partly responsible for its birth. Arguably this is schismatic, but in a very different sense in which the engine of reproduction is not internal but external since a new group forms as a partial mirror image of another. Figuring out how to theorize this is doubly important since a similar thing seems to have happened in Tibet with the emergence of the Bon religion, which claims to be a fully indigenous religion and yet looks a lot like imported Buddhism.

Next to the challenge of sorting out the relationship between medieval Buddhism and Daoism, the question of Tang Buddhist "schools" (*zong*) represents an equally complex topic. Contrary to many textbook explanations, the past thirty years of research have shown that the so-called "schools" of Chinese Buddhism during this era were *much* less sectarian than imagined. That is, though we find authors in these centuries preferring particular explanations of Buddhism over others, there is very little evidence that literary, philosophic, and ritual preferences ever manifested in full-scale sectarian divides. Instead, we see an assumed syncretism even among authors whom we had assumed to be sectarian partisans. Thus, it does not make sense to argue that seventh-century writers such as Shendao, who promoted Pure Land practices, or Daoxuan, who was interested in clarifying the Vinaya, represent schism or sects. Quite the contrary – they all got lumped into ever-expanding forms of Chinese Buddhism that incorporated these developments without generating sectarian divides.

However, this inclusive syncretism was threatened by two important developments. The first was a nation-wide movement that appeared at the end of the sixth century – the Sect of the Three Stages (*Sanjiejiao*) – which, led by Xinxing (d. 594), represented a full schismatic break with tradition.[21] Xinxing, in arguing that all other forms of Buddhism were corrupt, and that even reading Buddhist literature was a sure ticket to hell, not only reinvented Buddhist thought and practice, but also began to turn these inventions into institutional realities once he won the right to establish separate cloisters within Buddhist monasteries.[22] Thus along with the odd new invention of the "Inexhaustible Treasury" – a kind of public pawnshop that also had important religious functions – Xinxing

---

[21] For more discussion, see Jamie Hubbard's *Absolute Delusion, Perfect Buddhahood: The Rise and Fall of a Chinese Heresy* (Honolulu: University of Hawaii, 2001).
[22] *Ibid.*, p. 10.

was well on his way to generating a wholly different form of Buddhism. Once Xinxing died, and then lost the political support of the prime minister Gaojiong (deposed in 599), his movement was outlawed in a series of imperial decrees beginning in the early part of the seventh century. In fact, these decrees did not destroy the sect and it continued to exist for the rest of the Tang; thus, though censured for being heritical, and ultimately dissolved, the sect managed to leave behind a large body of writing that was luckily stored in the Dunhuang caves and rediscovered during the early part of the twentieth century.

The second development was less divisive and resulted from the emergence of genealogical claims that argued that the essence of tradition flowed in a direct and historical manner from the Buddha down to certain contemporaneous Chinese masters. Such genealogical claims appear in the seventh century and would, in time, come to dominate most forms of elite Chinese Buddhism. Thus, whether one was a Tiantai partisan claiming descent from the Buddha via Zhiyi (d. 597), or a Chan partisan claiming Buddha ancestry via Bodhidharma (n.d.), the basic contour was the same: some members of the Buddhist community claimed to be categorically more legitimate than everyone else – a fractious claim to be sure. After the Tang period of experimentation with "genealogical warfare," Chinese Buddhist elites came to organize themselves into various "spiritual families" which were largely at odds with one another, and manifested their differences in claiming Tiantai, Chan, or Pure Land affiliations for most of the larger monasteries. And yet, the key to understanding this form of sectarianism is to see that it never broke away from a dependent relationship with the imperial state and thus there never was a full schismatic break since the genealogists wrote their tradition-claiming histories hoping to win the throne's approval, and thus, despite the author–author antagonism, the center held, with the State providing something like an umbrella under which sectarian authors made their various bids for Buddhist authenticity but never broke free of the entire arrangement. In short, the relative stability of the Chinese imperial system, and its close policing of the Buddhist monastic system, encouraged a syncretistic style of Buddhism in which a loose confederation of Buddhist authorities came to accept, at some basic level, a variety of competing claims and thus never splintered into wholly different religious groups.

This relationship between Buddhism and the State played out very differently in Japan. In brief, it seems that in the centuries after Buddhism's arrival in Japan in the sixth and seventh centuries, the so-called "schools"

of Chinese Buddhism – such as Pure Land, Tiantai, and Chan – became
institutionally distinct, and at odds with one another; in fact, in time they
literally were at war with one another. A good example of this kind of
violent sectarianism is the case of Nichiren (1222–82), who believed that all
other Buddhists were hell-bound and that his teachings alone, which
promoted the practice of reciting the title of the *Lotus Sutra*, were the
key to salvation. On different occasions he made these claims in public
and was nearly executed more than once for his exclusionary version of
Buddhist legitimacy. Besides seeing Nichiren's life-and-death struggles
with other Buddhists – and the State, for that matter – as proof of the
intensification of sectarian politics in Japanese Buddhism, we should not
miss, too, that his sectarian position came out of his reading of the *Lotus
Sutra*, suggesting that the polemics of that text lived on in a schism-making
manner long after it was penned roughly at the beginning of the Common
Era. The *Lotus Sutra*'s central role in Nichiren's drama also supports the
wider point above that Mahayana Buddhism, early on, produced a body of
schismatic literature that would, regularly, be brought to bear in new
situations that played in countries far from India and far from the "local
politics" that produced the *Lotus Sutra* and the other early Mahayana texts.

As Japanese Buddhism developed after the Heian Era (794–1185), the
shifting and divisive feudal political arrangements of the shogunates seem
to have heightened Buddhist sectarian violence.[23] In fact, it seems that
under these feudal conditions, the shoguns, or warlords, often formed
bonds with Buddhist groups who then would be institutionally established
in a manner that allowed them to break fully with their co-religionists, and
especially those other Buddhists who might be receiving support from a
different warlord. That is, while Chinese Buddhism remained rather syncretic under the umbrella of various imperial dynasties, Japanese Buddhism
splintered into separate sectarian entities as a consequence of the fractured
feudal situation that held sway for most of post-Heian Japanese history
until the nation was reunified after the Boshin war, the civil war that led to
the establishment of the Meiji Era (1868–1912).

MODERN BUDDHISM

In the wake of colonialism and a growing self-awareness that came in
the nineteenth and twentieth centuries, many Buddhist groups in Asia

---

[23] For one look at the vicissitudes of medieval Japanese Buddhism, see Neil McMullin's *Buddhism
and the State in Sixteenth-Century Japan* (Princeton: Princeton University Press, 1985).

reinvented their "philosophies" and their institutional arrangements. These groups, at times, warrant the title "schism" because they consciously sought to draw lines between themselves and their predecessors and they often occupied distinctly new social "spaces."[24] A good example of this modern "schism" in Buddhism would be the "New Buddhisms" of the Meiji and Taisho eras in Japan. Based on a rhetoric that claimed that it was purifying traditional Buddhism of corruption and superstition, writers such as D. T. Suzuki began to craft a new form of Zen that was little like its more traditional form even as it claimed to be more authentically Buddhist.[25] For instance, unlike traditional Zen, Suzuki's Zen did not exist in the monasteries and instead floated forth into the universities, lay groups, and the popular presses. Of course, too, it came to the Occident, where new Zen groups formed that again appeared little like their traditional predecessors. In some cases, American masters were found, such as Philip Kapleau, and these leaders carried on the reinvention of modern Zen in a manner not only fed by New Buddhists from Japan, but also with an eye to making Buddhism viable in America, Europe, and South America.[26] Thus, not only do we have sectarian divides between traditional Japanese Buddhism and New Buddhism, the American groups also soon began demonstrating schismatic tendencies, questioning each other's legitimacy and, ironically, commitment to "traditional" Zen.[27]

Somewhat similar patterns can be discerned in the modernization of South-East Asian Buddhism. For instance, both Burma and Sri Lanka saw important late nineteenth- and twentieth-century developments that broke rather decisively with traditional patterns of thought, practice, and social arrangement.[28] Too, Western masters were identified and began to

---

[24] For discussion of how to treat these new forms of Buddhism, see Jamie Hubbard's "Embarrassing Superstition, Doctrine, and the Study of New Religious Movements," *Journal of the American Academy of Religion* 66 (1) (Spring 1998): 59–92.

[25] For a discussion of New Buddhism, see Robert Sharf's "The Zen of Japanese Nationalism," *History of Religions* 33 (1) (1993): 1–43; see also Brian Victoria's *Zen at War* (New York: Weatherhill, 1998).

[26] For more details on Kapleau's group, see Robert Sharf's "Sanbokyodan: Zen and the Way of the New Religions," *Japanese Journal of Religious Studies* 22(3–4) (1995): 417–58.

[27] The sectarian pressures on groups like the San Francisco Zen Center are abundantly clear in Michael Downing's *Shoes Outside the Door: Desire, Devotion, and Excess at San Francisco Zen Center* (Washington, DC: Counterpoint, 2001).

[28] For details on this process of reinventing Buddhism, see Michael Carrithers's *The Forest Monks of Sri Lanka: An Anthropological and Historical Study* (Oxford: Oxford University Press, 1986); see also George Bond's *The Buddhist Revival in Sri Lanka: Religious Tradition, Reinterpretation and Response* (Columbia: University of South Carolina Press, 1988); and, Richard Gombrich and

generate even more innovative forms of Buddhism for Westerners, such as the highly successful Joseph Goldstein.[29]

CONCLUSIONS

The history of Buddhism appears to have had many phases of schismatic "growth," and depending on the political climate – and the viability of different supporting institutions – these inventions developed into various long-lasting entities. Clearly, we should not continue to keep Buddhism in that category of being just a philosophy and somehow above these more rough-and-tumble forms of religious life. And, equally important, we should see that the Buddhist material underscores the basic assumption that the content of a religion can never be considered apart from the lines-of-difference that it has had to draw against its various competitors. Moreover, it seems sensible to argue that there is a kind of schismatic force built into a number of Buddhist texts, such as the *Lotus Sutra*, that can be called up to frame and "adjudicate" any pressing social situation in which legitimacy needs to be redefined. In short, given that Buddhist history is well stocked with schisms, and even schismatic violence, we ought to set this material next to the histories of other traditions in order, first, to figure out more clearly which forces – internal and external – drive schismatic developments; and second, to clarify how schismatic developments resolve into new patterns of religious life in dependence on different media and institutional arrangements.

Gananath Obeyesekere's *Buddhism Transformed: Religion Change in Sri Lanka* (Princeton: Princeton University Press, 1988), esp. ch. 6.
[29] For a review of recent publications on American Buddhism/s, see Peter Gregory's "Describing the Elephant: Buddhism in America," *Religion and American Culture* 11 (2) (Summer 2001): 233–63.

CHAPTER 4

Schisms in Japanese new religious movements

Robert Kisala

Although controversial, new religious movements in Japan have an aggregate membership of perhaps 10 to 15 percent of the population, in a country where only 30 percent profess religious belief. They are, therefore, important conveyors of the various religious traditions of Japan to members of contemporary society. They also provide a fertile field for exploring the dynamics of schism in Japanese religion. A look at the dynamics of schisms helps to illustrate some characteristics of Japanese religiosity and Japanese society that contribute to the proliferation of these movements in that society in the modern era.

Three groups are identified as being especially fertile in the spawning of break-off groups: Tenrikyo, Omotokyo, and Reiyukai. Often these schismatic groups in turn spawn their own break-offs, leading to a third or even fourth generation of schismatic groups. Below I present representative groups from these three larger traditions, to illustrate some of the dynamics of schism.

TENRIKYO AND ITS OFFSHOOTS

Tenrikyo, founded in 1838, is generally recognized as one of the oldest of the Japanese new religious movements (NRMs). Its founding is traced back to the possession experience of Nakayama Miki (1798–1887), a farmer's wife living in the area of Nara, the ancient capital. After she had already lost two daughters to disease, a *yamabushi*, or mountain ascetic, was called to cure the injured foot of Miki's son. Since the shamaness, or *miko*, who would normally accompany the *yamabushi* and act as his medium could not come, Miki took her place. After falling into a trance, Miki was possessed by a god who revealed his name as Tsukihi. This incident was followed by numerous other possession episodes, subsequently without the aid of the *yamabushi*. At the direction of Tsukihi, later also called Oyagami, meaning God the Parent,

Miki began to give alms to the poor, to the extent that the Nakayama family, once wealthy landowners, was left destitute. Miki took up sewing to support the family, and from the 1850s began to gain a reputation as a healer and miracle worker, after which time this new faith began to grow.

In 1869, the year following the institution of the new imperial government, Miki, who is said to have been illiterate, took up writing and composed the *Ofudesaki*, the record of Oyagami's revelation, one of Tenrikyo's scriptures. In the *Ofudesaki* the center of the universe is revealed as lying precisely in the Nakayama residence, situated in an area called Yamato, traditionally seen as the birthplace of Japanese civilization.

After her initial possession experience Miki would often fall into a trance spontaneously, and for more than fifteen years, as the family fell further and further into poverty, she was seen as a mad woman, and she made repeated attempts to drown herself. She earned an initial reputation as a healer helpful especially in cases of pregnancy and smallpox, both dangerous situations for the rural population at that time. Once her reputation as a healer began to spread, she was subject to the scrutiny of the authorities. By the 1860s Miki had begun to attract regular followers, calling the attention of the local authorities, and when several followers disrupted a service at a local shrine in 1864 they were arrested, an incident that led many of the early followers to fall away.

Miki herself was arrested seventeen times, the latest shortly before her death at the age of 89. Iburi Izo, a carpenter and one of the early followers, began to deliver divine messages shortly before Miki's death, a role that he continued to play in the group until his own death in 1907. Drawing on the religious elements common to the people of her age and place – the virtues of filial piety, loyalty, generosity; Buddhist beliefs in karma; healing through the intercession of religious specialists; spirit possession – Miki gave voice to a new revelation that identified the Yamato region in Japan as the center of the world, and developed a liturgy that both reenacted God's original creation and contributes towards the realization of the perfect, joyous life that is God's intention for his children. This liturgy, called the Kagura Service, is performed on the 26th of every month, the day on which both the original possession experience (October 26) and Miki's death (January 26) occurred, around a pillar called the *kanrodai*, set up in the center of the main Tenrikyo church, built on the site of the Nakayama residence.

Tenrikyo has a long history of giving birth to other independent movements, some of which have in turn issued in their own set of off-shoots. In the case of Tenrikyo, both structural and doctrinal elements have contributed to the development of derivative movements. We begin with a consideration of these characteristics.

Tenrikyo uses a master–disciple pattern of membership that is also found in some of the other new religious movements in Japan. New converts typically become a member of their recruiter's church, branch, or group, and the recruiter is commonly referred to as the "parent" while the convert is called a "child." In Tenrikyo this is expressed structurally in a system of *daikyokai*, or large churches directly under the Tenrikyo headquarters, and *bunkyokai*, or branch churches, usually under the jurisdiction of one of the *daikyokai*. In order to qualify as a *daikyokai* the church must have at least fifty branch churches under its jurisdiction, and each branch church must have at least sixteen *yoboku*, literally meaning "timber" and in Tenrikyo used to refer to someone who has been qualified to administer *sazuke*, the Tenrikyo healing rite. The rank of *yoboku* is attained by attending a set of nine lectures given at the group's headquarters, a practice that involves some level of commitment but is within the ability of most Tenrikyo believers. As of 1996, there were a total of 159 *daikyokai*, 16,670 *bunkyokai*, and an additional 279 churches outside of Japan.[1]

It is easy to imagine how the master–disciple pattern of membership lends itself to the development of schisms, as particularly charismatic personalities experience success in their church-growth activities and occasionally become authorities in their own right within the church. In the midst of a dispute with the central authority within the group, or in a leadership vacuum, they may decide to separate from the rest of the group, taking their own disciples, or churches and branch churches, with them.

In Tenrikyo, however, this tendency is somewhat abated by the fact that a symbol central to the faith, the *kanrodai*, is identified with the headquarter precincts, thus making it difficult to leave the church without abandoning a central tenet of the faith, that is, the importance of the performance of the Kagura Service around the *kanrodai*. This difficulty can be overcome, however, through reinterpretation of the meaning of the *kanrodai*, as in the case of Onichi Aijiro and the foundation of Honmichi that we will take up below.

---

[1] Foreign churches are directly under the jurisdiction of the Tenrikyo headquarters.

Onishi Aijiro and Honmichi

Other elements in Tenrikyo's doctrine, especially beliefs surrounding the foundress, have positively contributed to the development of derivative groups. In the early church, it was commonly assumed that the foundress would live until the age of 115. This was based on a revelation that, in fact, it was God's plan that all people should live until this age, and as the model (*hinagata*) for humankind Nakayama Miki herself would attain this goal.[2] After she died at the age of 90, in addition to a continuing revelation that God deprived her of twenty-five years precisely to help humankind wake up to its sinful state,[3] her death was also interpreted as a "withdrawal from physical life," and, following another revelation that she continues to live on,[4] that she now lives eternally at her home near the *kanrodai* in the Tenrikyo headquarters. In light of these beliefs regarding the foundress, there was some expectation of a dramatic occurrence involving her around the time when she would have been 115 years old, just at the time of the death of the Meiji Emperor and the beginning of the Taisho period.

This expectation was further heightened by another element of Tenrikyo's faith, that regarding the establishment of a perfect world here on earth. Tenrikyo teaches that humankind was created to enjoy a "joyous life" (*yoki gurashi*), and that ultimately, through the purification of each human being, all will enjoy this life perfectly here on this earth. At the final establishment of this joyous life, nectar will flow from heaven to fill the bowl at the top of the *kanrodai*. While not as strong in Tenrikyo as in some of the other new religious movements, such as Omotokyo, the anticipation of the establishment of this final perfect existence is sometimes accompanied by the expectation that the present order will be wiped away, and this could even happen violently. While repeated criticisms of the "upper people," those who are on the "high mountains," and those who "govern this world" can be found in the *Ofudesaki*,[5] in most references these people will also be brought to repentance through a change of heart rather than through a violent upheaval. However, in God's desire to quickly establish the world as it is meant to be, there are

---

[2] This revelation can be found in the *Ofudesaki*, Part 3: 100.
[3] *Osashizu*, Meiji 20 (1887), February 18.
[4] *Osashizu*, Meiji 20 (1887), January 24.
[5] For references to "upper people" see, for example, *Ofudesaki* 3: 120–2; 4: 111–12; those who are on the "high mountains" can be found in 4: 72, 89, 92, 115; 13: 45, 56; 14: 30, 53; 15: 57–8; the reference to those who "govern this world" is in 4: 104.

occasional references to a possible destruction to be brought about by God's anger.

Eschatological ideas such as these were propounded in the period when Nakayama Miki was herself experiencing persecution at the hands of the local authorities. After her death, and as Tenrikyo embarked on a policy of compromise with the authorities in order to gain recognition as a religious body, these ideas lost much of their force. However, they were resurrected by a Tenrikyo missionary who gradually started his own movement that was eventually called Honmichi, Onishi Aijiro.[6]

Onishi Aijiro (1881–1958) was born the third son of the Kishioka family, farmers in Nara Prefecture, near the Tenrikyo headquarters. Although once a wealthy family, by the end of the nineteenth century the Kishiokas had lost much of their land, and as the third son, without prospects of inheriting any of the remaining land, Aijiro decided to become a teacher, studying at the Nara Prefectural Normal School. It was while he was boarding at this school that he became a believer of Tenrikyo, as a result of the illness of both his older brother and his mother. Although his mother died shortly thereafter, he became convinced that her pain was alleviated through his prayers, and that her death indicated a heavy burden of karma on the Kishioka family that could only be eliminated by devoting his own life to the cause of spreading the Tenrikyo faith.

A member of the Nara branch church, Aijiro left school to become an itinerant missionary for the movement, returning after three years to marry a fellow believer in the Nara church. It was at this time that he was adopted into his wife's family, and he took on the name of Onishi. He was then commissioned by the church to take up missionary responsibilities in Yamaguchi, west of Nara. As a result of administrative responsibilities and the fact that, owing to various circumstances, he was not able to settle down in one area for any period of time, he did not have much success as a missionary. In 1913, after devoting thirteen years to missionary work with little result, he closed himself up in his house for six months, a sign of his disappointment and depression. Finally, on August 15 he became convinced that he was, in fact, the living *kanrodai*, the true leader of Tenrikyo.

The *kanrodai*, as revealed to Nakayama Miki, was to be a hexagonal stone pillar of thirteen tiers, standing about eight feet tall. After the two foundational stones were confiscated by the police as part of their

---

[6] Shimazono (1986) provides details regarding Onishi and Honmichi millenarian thought.

suppression of the group, a wooden model was constructed, and that is what continues to be used at the center of the Tenrikyo headquarters. Reflecting on the revelation presented in the *Ofudesaki* and *Osashizu* (a second volume of sacred scripture in Tenrikyo largely written after the founder's death), Onishi came to believe that Miki would not live forever in her hidden state, but rather that her earthly presence would come to an end when she reached 115 years, the life span appointed by God. Since this would have been 1912, he believed that someone new would be appointed by God to continue her mission, and, finally, that he was the anointed one.

While not directly challenging Tenrikyo authorities at first, he sent a series of messages to leaders of the church expressing his ideas. In response, he was removed from his position and excommunicated from the church, returning in poverty to live with his relatives for a number of years, before finally taking up teaching again in 1920. It was about this time that other Tenrikyo missionaries, familiar with his messages to the church, began to seek him out, and he started to gather a following outside his own immediate family. In 1923 he issued a direct challenge to the church leadership, sending a delegation of followers to the headquarters to persuade them to recognize himself as the true head of the church. The following year he quit his job to devote himself to religious activities once again, and in 1925, when his followers could be numbered in the hundreds, he founded the Tenri Kenkyukai, or Tenri Study Association. As the name indicates, he did not intend to found an independent group, but rather he and his followers still considered themselves believers of Tenrikyo, with the purpose of studying the Tenrikyo scriptures and spreading their own, correct interpretation of the revelation found there.

About this time Onishi also began to concentrate more on the prophecies of an impending disaster found in the scriptures, and became convinced that the time for the renewal of the world was approaching. From September to December of 1927 he worked on a pamphlet called *Kenkyu Shiryo*, or Study Data, where he criticized the imperial government, warned of an imminent disaster for the country, and proclaimed that first Nakayama Miki, and later himself, were anointed as the true leaders of Japan. On March 22 of the following year copies of the *Kenkyu Shiryo* were distributed to government and police officials throughout the country, leading to the arrest of Onishi and hundreds of his followers. After a conviction and appeals that led all the way to the Supreme Court, Onishi was found not guilty by reason of diminished capacity for judgment in 1930.

In the refounding of the group following Onishi's acquittal, it became more of an independent religious body, keeping much of Tenrikyo doctrine but proclaiming itself the "true way," a claim reflected in its new name, Tenri Honmichi. In 1938, however, with his wife near death and once again convinced that a major catastrophe was imminent, Onishi and Honmichi reissued the contents of the *Kenkyu Shiryo*, leading to his arrest and the banning of the group. With his release from prison in 1945 the group was once again reorganized, and all reference to Tenrikyo was dropped from its name in 1950, when the group became known as Honmichi. Currently it has about 300,000 believers.

There have been a number of other mostly small independent groups that have been influenced by Tenrikyo, including Tenrino Meisei Kyodan, founded by Oku Rokubee, a Tenrikyo missionary, in 1888, currently with about 4,000 members, and Shizen Shindo, founded by the head of a Tenrikyo church, Maeshima Reiki, in 1946, with about 7,000 members, including a commune near the foot of Mount Fuji, where the believers practice Maeshima's dietary teachings. In addition, Honmichi itself has influenced a number of other groups, including Shuyodan Hoseikai and Honbushin.

Honbushin

Honbushin was founded in 1962 by Onishi Tama, the second daughter of Aijiro.[7] From her birth, occurring thirty years after Nakayama Miki's death, Tama had been considered by her father as a kind of reincarnation of Miki. For this reason Tama held a role in Honmichi second only to Aijiro himself, and after his death in 1958 she became convinced that she was God's chosen instrument, and gave herself the name of Miroku, a Japanese term used to refer to the Maitreya Boddhisatva, the Buddha who comes to save the world of the future. In 1961 a group recognizing her role called the Tenri Mirokukai formed within Honmichi, and early in 1962 this group split from Honmichi to form a new group called Honbushin in a doctrinal dispute based on Tama's own interpretation of the doctrine. After Tama's death in 1969, Takeda Soshin, the successor appointed in her will, took over as the Kanrodai, the medium of God's will.

While recognizing the teaching of Nakayama Miki as the basis of its belief, Honbushin has added the practice of Naikan, a form of introspection developed by Yoshimoto Ishin, a Buddhist believer of the Jodo

---

[7] On Honbushin, see Yumiyama 1995.

Shinshu sect in Japan, as well as its own form of relaxation therapy. A World Health Center has been set up at the site of the former Honbushin headquarters in Shirojiri, Nagano Prefecture, to promote Oriental medicine and psychological forms of healing. In addition, they advocate the cultivation of a positive attitude in all things through the recital of the *Yukon no kotodama* (Sacred words of the brave spirit).

Primarily through its branch church in Hawaii, Honbushin also promotes work for world peace and the cultivation of health food. In all of these innovations, Honbushin shows evidence of adjustment to the religious environment of the 1960s and 1970s, illustrating common characteristics of many of the new religious groups that emerged or flourished at that time. According to its own reports, it would be the largest of the groups bearing signs of influence from Tenrikyo, with its 900,000 believers rivaling even Tenrikyo itself.

Tama's succession to the charism of her father in taking over the leadership of a splinter group from Honmichi illustrates another common feature of Japanese religiosity – the passing down of the mantle of leadership within the family. Indeed, despite the presence and influence of Iburi Izo, the nominal leadership of Tenrikyo was passed to Miki's grandson, and continues to be held by her descendants. Sometimes the attempt to pass on leadership within the family leads to schisms, as in the case of Sekai Mahikari Bunmei Kyodan, where the attempt by the adopted daughter of the founder Okada Kotama, Okada Keishu, to take over leadership of the group after Kotama's death was opposed by Sekiguchi Sakae, a leading disciple of Kotama, whose claim was eventually supported by the courts: Keishu was forced to leave with her own followers to found Sukyo Mahikari.

Shuyodan Hoseikai

Shuyodan Hoseikai is a relatively small new religious group, comprised of approximately 12,000 members. Although its founder was associated with both Tenrikyo and Tenri Kenkyukai, its faith and practices reflect more broadly the folk religious traditions and popular morality of Japan, as expressed by its founder, Idei Seitaro (1899–1983). Idei was born in a poor farming community north of Tokyo.[8] His father died when Idei was

---

[8] Information on Idei is largely based on Shimazono 1992 and 1999. Reference is also made to a semi-autobiographical account published by Hoseikai under Idei's name (Idei 1965). See also the account on Hoseikai in chapter 5 of my book on new religions and the peace movement (Kisala 1999).

thirteen, and subsequently his mother supported the family by offering classes in soroban, or abacus. Idei had two older brothers, one of whom died in infancy, and an older sister. Popular stories within Hoseikai claim that both his mother and his sister were prone to have mystical experiences, having visions, for example, of Fudo, a Buddhist deity, or Kobo Daishi, the honorary title and popular name of Kukai, the founder of the Japanese Shingon sect of Buddhism.

The already poor soil of the area where Idei was born was made largely unusable because of pollution from local mining operations. Idei was apprenticed to a rice shop in a neighboring town immediately after completing elementary school, and from there he left for Tokyo at the age of sixteen. He spent the next several years doing odd jobs, until he was drafted in 1920. After finishing his compulsory military service he returned briefly to his hometown, and then left once again for Tokyo, arriving in 1923, just before the Great Kanto Earthquake. In the wake of the earthquake, he was pressed into service collecting and disposing of the corpses, an experience that obviously affected him greatly.

Although it is unclear whether Idei first joined Tenrikyo and later Tenri Kenkyukai or directly joined the latter, in either case it was during his first stint in Tokyo, through the influence of an acquaintance he had met while working in the post office. It seems that he had experienced an illness at the time that led him gradually to deeper involvement in the faith. However, it was his experiences in the wake of the earthquake that became formative for his religious life. In his autobiography, for example, he recounts an incident in which a young girl approached his crew just as they were going to dispose of the corpse of the girl's mother, a coincidence that he attributes to the spirit of the mother calling to her daughter, and says he came to believe in the existence of human spirits through this experience (Idei 1965: 73).

Following his experiences in the aftermath of the earthquake, Idei became more deeply involved in either Tenrikyo or Tenri Kenkyukai, becoming a kind of itinerant missionary for the group. In his autobiography he recalls several instances of revelation while on these journeys. Among these revelations he reports hearing a voice tell him that he was the "Pillar of the Nation" – a title appropriated by Nichiren, the founder of another school of Japanese Buddhism. He also reports that he heard the voice of Nichiren himself encouraging perseverance in his missionary work, and finally that through these revelations he came to the realization that he was one with God (Idei 1965: 75–85). Idei's recollections, with their references to Fudo, Kobo Daishi, Nichiren, and other religious figures, indicate how broadly he drew from the popular Japanese religious tradition in forming his own "universe of faith." In fact, in his autobiography there is no mention of affiliation with either Tenrikyo or Tenri Kenkyukai, a curious omission that can perhaps be explained by his involvement in the events leading to Onishi Aijiro's first arrest.

By the latter half of the 1920s Idei was clearly a member of Tenri Kenkyukai, and in 1928 he participated in the distribution of Onishi's *Kenkyu Shiryo*. As a result, he was arrested and convicted of the charge of *lèse-majesté*. Idei was released from prison after about a year, and soon married Imaizumi Kikuno, also a native of the farm country north of Tokyo. He maintained some contact with his former religious companions, but largely ceased his religious activities and found employment in a munitions factory. In 1934, however, he quit his job and returned to religious work, a development that, in his autobiography, is attributed to the fact that he had fallen off a truck at work and had to be hospitalized for a time. Idei says that the accident woke him from his lethargy and reinstilled in him a sense of his mission (Idei 1965: 166–8). This time, however, he did not return to his activities for Tenri Kenkyukai, but instead started acting independently as a kind of miraculous healer and preacher. He had begun to attract a number of followers, apparently mostly former members of Tenri Kenkyukai, when he was arrested again in 1935, also on charges of *lèse-majesté*. It seems that in one of his sermons he offered support to a contemporary theory maintaining that the emperor was merely an organ of the state, a theory that had recently been banned as contrary to the official state doctrine exalting the emperor's position above the state. Idei spent much of the next three years in prison.

Throughout his life, Idei enjoyed the ability to attract the elite of society to himself, a rather surprising development that can only be attributed to his personal charisma, for, as we have already seen, he himself was from the lower ranks of society and had little formal education. He could be quite critical of the status quo, a trait that would not naturally endear him to those who enjoyed an advantageous position in society. In the postwar period Idei first attracted the attention of some officers in the occupying American army, and later some of the major politicians in Japan seemed to take more interest in Idei and Shuyodan Hoseikai than the size of its membership would warrant as a source of votes. This ability to attract powerful people had aided the group from the beginning, since Shuyodan Hoseikai was established as a juridical foundation in 1941 with the help of two retired army and navy officers who had become followers of Idei.

In the above study of Tenrikyo and its off-shoots, we have seen how some elements of the doctrine of the group were reinterpreted to justify the emergence of new leadership, first in Honmichi, and later in Honbushin, as well as how the doctrine and practice have been considerably changed in the latter, third-generation, group. We have also taken a look at Shuyodan Hoseikai, where the influence of Tenrikyo is less obvious, becoming one element in the founder's "universe of belief" that has been passed down in the group. Indeed, it would seem that the founder took some efforts to hide his association with Tenri Kenkyukai as a result of his arrest for collaborating with the group. Or perhaps, in the end, he felt that his participation in the groups was relatively unimportant in light of his own subsequent religious experiences, and therefore felt no need to make explicit mention of it. At any rate, Tenri Kenkyukai's social criticism was taken over by Idei Seitaro and transformed into a national pride in the postwar years that exhorted his followers to the exercise of self-cultivation to live up to the high standards he set for Japanese society. We turn now to a second major grouping within the Japanese new religious movements, Omotokyo and some of the groups it has influenced.

THE INFLUENCE OF OMOTOKYO

Although Omotokyo, with less than 200,000 believers, is not now a major new religious movement, at one time it had a considerably larger following, and its influence on the new religions as a whole bears no correspondence to its current size. Omotokyo was founded in 1898 by Deguchi Nao (1837–1918) and Ueda Kisaburo (1871–1948), who later married into the Deguchi family and took the name Onisaburo.[9] Nao was born to the Kirimura family in a castle town northwest of Kyoto. Although her grandfather had been a carpenter of some rank in the old feudal order, her father was given to drink, and he managed to squander much of the family's wealth before his own death when Nao was nine years old. Unable to care for the family, Nao's mother sent her out to work in one of the local merchant households, and over the course of six years she worked for four different families, earning a reputation for diligence and devotion, even being honored locally as an example of filial piety. At the age of fifteen she returned home to help with the household chores and work summers in a local silk factory. A year later she was

---

[9] On Deguchi Nao and Omotokyo's early development, see Ooms 1993.

adopted into the family of an aunt in the nearby town of Ayabe, Deguchi Yuri, who was childless. When her aunt started pressing her to marry someone from Ayabe, Nao fled back to her own home, for she was apparently already in love with a young man from her own hometown. Desperate for an heir to carry on the family line, after some time Yuri visited Nao and begged her to return to Ayabe. When Nao refused, she cursed Nao and returned home to drown herself in a well.

Nao soon became severely ill, which was attributed to her aunt's curse. Nao thus returned to Ayabe and married the person chosen by her dead aunt, and he was subsequently adopted into the Deguchi family to assuage the spirit of her aunt and continue the Deguchi line. Nao's husband, Masagoro, was ten years her elder, a carefree and cheerful person who contrasted with Nao's rather strict and stern personality. He was a carpenter of some repute, and having inherited considerable property from Nao's aunt the two of them were rather well off in the early years of the marriage. Like Nao's father, Masagoro also enjoyed drinking, however, and as a consequence his work suffered. More and more money was spent on drink, and as a result of unwise financial decisions on the part of Masagoro as well as the oppressive tax system introduced by the Meiji government, Nao and her husband eventually lost all of their property and had to sell their house as well.

Nao largely supported the family now by selling *manju*, a rice and sweet bean cake. Masagoro, whose skills were increasingly impaired by his drinking, fell from a roof where he had been working in 1885, and remained paralyzed until he died two years later. To support her disabled husband as well as her children, Nao was forced to take up rag collecting, which was considered one step above begging.

Five years after her husband's death, Nao had an apparently spontaneous possession experience. One day early in 1892 Nao arrived home shouting, and ordered her sleeping daughters to go pray at the village shrine. When they arrived back home they found Nao dousing herself with cold water from the backyard well. Nao's possession experience continued for thirteen days, during which she ate nothing and continued to perform the cold-water ablutions. Ooms reports that she had powerful physical sensations, and felt as if something were inhabiting her lower abdomen (Ooms 1993: 6). Occasionally she would speak in a deep, harsh voice that was completely unlike her own, and sometimes a conversation would ensue between this other voice and her normal voice

Similar possession experiences continued for about a year, while Nao sought out religious specialists in order to have the spirit exorcised.

Finally, Nao was accused of setting a series of fires in Ayabe, and although someone else later confessed to the crime, she was confined to her home for forty days. It was during this period of confinement that she decided to devote herself to revealing the will of God. It was at this point that she gained control of the possessions, indicated by the fact that she would no longer give voice to God's word, but rather write it down, and the collection of these writings is called the *Ofudesaki*.

Nao began to draw a following as a result of success at healing, exorcism, and divination. She was unable to systematize the teaching and practice, however, or organize a group devoted to the propagation of the revelations. Nao was growing increasingly frustrated in her efforts and impatient that the renewal of the world that was becoming the focus of her teaching be instituted. In 1898 she briefly met Ueda Kisaburo, and, convinced that he could help her in her mission, she asked him to join her the following year, when they founded together the Kinmei Reigakukai.

Kisaburo, who later changed his name to Onisaburo, was born in 1871 to a poor dairy farmer not far from Ayabe. In 1898, at the age of twenty-seven, he had to leave his village as a result of a falling-out with a local gangster, and he took the opportunity to engage in ascetic practices for a week at Mount Takakuma, near his home. At that time he is said to have had experiences of the spirit world, and to have achieved the ability to heal others. Sent on a trip toward Kyoto by a revelation while acting as a medium, he met one of Nao's daughters on the way, and thus began their partnership.

It was not always an easy relationship, as Onisaburo did not completely agree with Nao's apocalyptic teaching, and the two clashed on how to deal with the interference from the police authorities that Nao's teaching was attracting. Following Nao's death, and in the economic and political unrest after the First World War, the group's social criticism began to attract more followers, including members of the economic and military elite, leading to a clamp-down by the authorities, and the arrest of Onisaburo and other leaders of the group in 1921. Consequently the group abandoned its reformist ideas in favor of an emphasis on the spirit world, as Onisaburo wrote the accounts of his experiences while engaged in ascetic practices in the mountains more than twenty years earlier – a collection that is called the *Reikai Monogatari*, or "Tales of the Spirit World." However, as the Japanese military became more aggressive in China in the early 1930s the group began to revert to its apocalyptic teachings and critical stance toward society, leading to a second persecution in 1935 that effectively wiped out the group, until it was reconstituted in the postwar period.

One factor in Omotokyo's success in attracting large numbers of followers from around the 1920s was the use of *chinkon kishin*, a practice that Onisaburo had picked up in the course of his spiritual quest before meeting Nao. Although accounts within Omotokyo attribute Onisaburo's knowledge of the practice to his sojourn at Mount Taka-kuma, it is likely that he was trained in *chinkon kishin* by Nagasawa Katsutate, a disciple of Honda Chikaatsu, the Shinto priest who developed the practice in the late Tokugawa period. Nagasawa was the head of an Inari sect in Suruga, present-day Shizuoka Prefecture, where Onisaburo went after his experience at Mount Takakuma. *Chinkon kishin* is actually the combination of two concepts that can be found in classical works: *chinkon*, which is a method of handling spirits, often for the purpose of healing illness, and *kishin*, or possession by spirits. Onisaburo used it as a method to induce an experience of the spirit world, through breathing and meditative practices. While no longer practiced in Omo-tokyo today – at least in the sense of inducing an experience of the spirit world – the practice was taken up and developed by other groups within the Omoto lineage.

Numerous groups formed around former members of Omotokyo following the persecutions in 1921 and 1935, including Shinrei Kenkyukai (1923), Michi Hiraki (1923), Ishinkai (1928), Seicho no Ie (1930), and Sekai Kyuseikyo (1935). We now turn to the last of those as representative of these groups.

Sekai Kyuseikyo

Sekai Kyuseikyo was founded by Okada Mokichi (1882–1955), a former leader of Omotokyo. The religion has undergone a number of name changes, founded as the Dai Nihon Kannonkai in 1935, and later becoming the Dai Nihon Kenko Kyokai, Nihon Kannon Kyodan, Nihon Miroku Kyokai, and Sekai Meshiyakyo before the present name was adopted in 1957.

Okada Mokichi was sickly from birth, and lived his early years in abject poverty.[10] His family had had a prosperous pawn shop in the late

---

[10] Information on Okada Mokichi is taken from the two-volume biography published by Sekai Kyuseikyo (Sekai Kyusei Kyo 1983 and 1986).

Tokugawa period, but the family fortune had been lost because of poor management before Okada's father was able to take it over. Through the hard work of his parents, Okada was able to enroll in the Tokyo School of Fine Arts at the age of fourteen, in order to fulfill his dream of becoming a painter. He had to withdraw after only a few months, however, as he came down with some kind of eye ailment that did not respond to treatment. Okada was given up for dead on several occasions, suffering from tuberculosis and a variety of other diseases. As a matter of fact, in his biography he is quoted as having said, "Except for women's complaints, I've had it all" (Sekai Kyusei Kyo 1983: 63).

As a result of his father's hard work, and his sister's success in running a banquet hall, there was a modest inheritance for Okada on the death of his father in 1905. He used the money to buy a sundry-goods shop near the fashionable Ginza district in Tokyo, a business he parlayed into a hugely successful wholesale enterprise, selling fashion accessories, some of which were designed by Okada himself. He lost his fortune in 1919, however, owing to unwise investments and mismanagement by one of his employees. At about the same time he lost his wife because of a difficult childbirth. These events led him to turn to religion and, greatly impressed with the prophecies of a reformed and renewed world in the *Ofudesaki* written by Deguchi Nao, he joined Omotokyo in June 1920. This was not the end of his troubles, however, as his efforts to rebuild his business were stymied by the post-World War I depression, and his nephew – raised as a son by Okada after the early death of his sister – died in an accident while swimming near the Omotokyo headquarters in Ayabe. This accident occurred just after Okada had joined the group, and blaming the religion for the death his family insisted that he abandon the group. However, following the Great Kanto Earthquake and the death of his infant son in 1923 (he had remarried shortly after the death of his first wife) he once again took up belief in Omotokyo, but this time it was Omotokyo's spiritism and healing practices that attracted his attention.

His own extensive experience with illness had convinced Okada of the ineffectiveness of modern medicine. After the medical establishment declared his tuberculosis incurable he felt he was able to cure himself with a vegetarian diet. Further, he came to believe that medical practice was not only ineffective but actually harmful. For a long time he had had severe pain in his teeth, and no dental treatment seemed to be able to alleviate the pain. In desperation he turned to a Nichiren faith-healer, and stopped taking the medicine prescribed by his dentists. Almost immediately the pain began to subside, and when he stopped going to the faith-healer but continued to recover he attributed the success to the fact that he was no longer being poisoned by the medicine.

After returning to Omotokyo, Okada became increasingly convinced of his mission to heal others in distress. At first he used the *chinkon kishin* practice taught in Omotokyo for this activity, but as his own experiences with the spirit world began to deepen he began to experiment with different practices – breathing on the sufferer or channeling light energy through the palm of his hand, for example – to see what was most effective in calling out spirits and healing. Later the channeling of light energy through the palm of the hand was called *jorei* – the purification of the spirit – but until shortly before he left Omotokyo in September 1934 he continued to use the word *chinkon* for these healing practices.

While still an Omotokyo missionary, Okada identified his faith more and more with the Buddhist Kannon, the bodhisattva of mercy. This faith came more to the fore after his break with Omotokyo, as we can see in the early names of the group. Because of his connection with Omotokyo, however, he was kept under surveillance by the police, and his healing activities had to be performed under the guise of shiatsu and other traditional therapies. In the postwar period the group increased rapidly as it emphasized the healing practice of *jorei*.

In addition to this healing activity, Sekai Kyuseikyo awaits the establishment of an earthly paradise, and has built several models of this paradise in Japan and Brazil. Okada was himself a collector of art, and the MOA (Mokichi Okada Association) Art Museum was established at the group's Atami compound in 1982, the one-hundredth anniversary of Okada's birth. Sekai Kyuseikyo also promotes the practice of natural farming. The church has been quite successful in attracting people in Brazil, where it claims a following of 300,000. The membership in Japan is reported to be about 800,000. Sekai Kyuseikyo has spawned a number of break-off groups, and especially its healing practices have influenced several other Japanese new religions, including the Mahikari churches mentioned above.

It appears that historical circumstance, namely the persecution of Omotokyo in the early twentieth century, primarily contributed to a flowering of schismatic movements that adapted various elements of Omotokyo's faith in developing their own doctrine and practice. Okada Mokichi's adaptation of *chinkon kishin* as *jorei* has been especially influencial, promoted in the West as well under the name of Reiki. We turn now to a third major group of new religious movements in Japan, Reiyukai and its offshoots.

REIYUKAI AND POSTWAR BUDDHISM

Reiyukai was founded in 1925 by Kubo Kakutaro (1892–1944) and Kotani Kimi (1901–71).[11] Born the fourth son of a small retailer by the name of Matsutaka in the port town of Kominato, outside of Tokyo, Kakutaro lost both parents before the age of fifteen, when he set out for Tokyo to live with a sister who had previously moved there. Having some training as a carpenter already in Kominato, he followed that trade in Tokyo while studying architecture in the evenings. In this way he became involved in the construction of public buildings, and eventually found employment in the Imperial Household Ministry, a prestigious position that brought him in contact with the high-born Kubo family. He was adopted into the Kubo family through marriage in 1919 at the age of twenty-seven. It seems, though, that he was considerably troubled by his step-mother, who was compulsive about cleanliness and suffered from a nervous condition, and she apparently often showed signs of possession at night. Kubo turned to religion for a solution to his problems, and was influenced greatly by two separate strands of the contemporary popular religiosity. One was belief in the *Lotus Sutra*, promoted, in part, by nationalists in the early half of the century. Here Kubo was specifically influenced by the religious thought of Nishida Toshizo, a lay Buddhist who became convinced that it was the modern trend away from veneration of the ancestors that was the cause of personal misfortune and social unrest. He argued that through disregard of such veneration the ancestors have not been able to achieve buddhahood, and thus they cannot protect the individual and the country from harm, which would be the normal state of affairs if the present generation's obligations to the ancestors was being met. Nishida thus advocated that the lay believers practice such veneration, in opposition to customary practices that had left this task to the clergy.

The second influence on Kubo was a spiritualist by the name of Wakatsuki Chise whom he met in 1923. Apparently Wakatsuki was able to help Kubo to identify what spirit was possessing his step-mother, a feat that convinced him of the power of her spiritualist practices. Kubo then sought to train his sister-in-law, Kotani Kimi, as a spiritualist, prescribing harsh ascetic practices in order to attain this goal. With his brother's death in 1924, Kubo and his sister-in-law, now trained as a spiritualist healer, established Reiyukai in 1925.

---

[11] On Reiyukai see Hardacre 1984.

Reiyukai thus combines belief in the *Lotus Sutra* with spiritualist practices, teaching that the believers should undertake the veneration of the ancestors through the recitation of parts of the sutra in their own home morning and evening, in order to promote their own personal happiness as well as the safety of the nation. Nishida's criticism of the Buddhist clergy was taken over by the group, and, with its emphasis on personal spiritual practice and experience, was extended to a more general critique of authority, especially the authority associated with learning and education. Structurally, Reiyukai employed a parent–child organization similar to what we saw in Tenrikyo, with new converts becoming disciples of the missionaries who brought them to the group. Both of these elements contributed to a number of schisms, including Kodokai, Sankai Kyodan, Shinshinkai, and Rissho Koseikai. A series of scandals concerning fund-raising by the group led to a further set of schisms in the early postwar years, schisms that were made easier by the fact that the group continued to employ the parent–child structure of church organization. Postwar schismatic groups include Daijo Kyodan, Reihokai, Myohokai, and Myoshikai. As representative of all of these groups we can take a look at the case of Rissho Koseikai.

Rissho Koseikai

Rissho Koseikai was founded by Niwano Nikkyo (1906–99) and Naganuma Myoko (1889–1957) in March 1938 and continued under their joint leadership until Naganuma's death twenty years later.[12] While Niwano himself experimented with various folk religious practices, some of which were incorporated into Rissho Koseikai's faith, it was Naganuma who possessed certain charismatic powers that allowed her to enjoy considerable influence over the direction of Koseikai's early development. After her death in 1957, authority was concentrated in Niwano's hands, and under his direction Koseikai has become a leader in the movement toward interreligious dialogue and cooperative activities to promote peace.

Niwano was born into a large family in a farming village in northern Japan. He finished his schooling at the age of twelve; proceeding any further would have required living away from home, an expense his family apparently could not bear. After working on the family farm for

---

[12] On Rissho Koseikai, see Dale 1975, or chapter 4 in my book on the peace activities of the Japanese new religions (Kisala 1999). Information on the founder, Niwano Nikkyo, is taken largely from his autobiography (1978).

several years, he left at the age of sixteen to work on a hydroelectric project near his village. The following year, like many of his generation, he left to seek his fortune in Tokyo.

Niwano did not have much time to fulfill his dream on this first trip to Tokyo, however, since he arrived in the city just three days prior to the Great Kanto Earthquake that devastated the city in 1923. Burned out of the retail rice store where he had found employment, Niwano returned to his village to await the city's reconstruction. During the interval at home he suffered his mother's death, and it was not until November of the following year that he was able to return to Tokyo. In his early years there he was engaged in a number of jobs: gardening, coal and charcoal delivery, and a pickled vegetable dealership. It was at this time that he also developed an interest in fortune telling, primarily through one of his employers, and learned several methods of divination.

After a brief stint as a conscript in the navy, Niwano married a cousin from his hometown in Niigata and the two of them settled in Tokyo. By the end of 1931 a daughter had been born, and, borrowing money from his uncle, Niwano set up his own pickled vegetable business. Within a month after his daughter's birth, however, she developed a severe ear infection, and Niwano was told that an operation would have to be performed. As one often sees in the accounts of the founders of the Japanese new religions, it was as a result of this misfortune that Niwano turned to religion in a serious way.

Advised by a friend to try prayers to Tengu Fudo, a mountain spirit worshiped in a form of popular Buddhism, Niwano visited the house of a local shamaness who incorporated worship of the Buddhist Fudo deity with Shugendo practices of strict austerity and faith healing. Visits to pray at the house of this shamaness became part of his daily routine, and following the recovery of his daughter he decided to take up himself the ascetic training, rising to the rank of the shamaness's assistant and performing the healing rites on his own. He was taken aback, however, when the shamaness insisted that he give up his pickle business and work with her full time, and left the group to become involved in yet another form of divination, a form of onomancy based on the number of strokes used in writing the characters comprising a person's name. Niwano says that he found this system more rational, and thus more appealing than the acquisition of mysterious "spiritual abilities" that the leader of the Fudo sect had been encouraging (Niwano 1978: 74).

Niwano's last, and definitive, formative religious experience began in the summer of 1934. At that time he was visited by a missionary of Reiyukai who warned him that if he failed to convert to the group he would shortly suffer some misfortune. His second daughter fell ill with a high fever exactly one week later, convincing him to join Reiyukai at once.

Niwano became a disciple of Arai Sukenobu, a Reiyukai teacher who was apparently well known within the group for his learning and his lectures on the *Lotus Sutra*. Niwano says that his daughter was cured within a week of his joining the group, and he gradually became more and more involved in Reiyukai missionary activities under the direction of Arai, to the extent that his business began to suffer. In order to devote more time to his religious work, Niwano decided to give up the pickle business and took up milk delivery, since he could limit his work to the early morning and evening, devoting the rest of his time to Reiyukai. One of his customers in this new business was a woman by the name of Naganuma Myoko.

Naganuma Myoko was born in Saitama Prefecture, directly north of Tokyo, in December 1889. Losing her mother at the age of six, she had to start work to support the family. Married at the age of sixteen, she divorced her husband, who was famous for his drinking and womanizing, just before she turned forty, following the death of her infant daughter. She then left on her own for Tokyo, where she remarried and opened an ice and sweet potato shop with her husband. Always sickly, Naganuma had sought salvation through several religions, including Tenrikyo. After her meeting with Niwano she was won over to Reiyukai, eventually becoming, along with Niwano, one of Arai's most fervent disciples. She was trained by Arai's wife in the Reiyukai practice of *hatsuon*, or spirit mediumship in a semitrance state. By 1936 both Niwano and Naganuma had become leaders of their own *hoza*, a group of followers that they had recruited themselves.

On March 5, 1938 Niwano and Naganuma jointly started their own religious group, Dai Nippon Rissho Koseikai, joining the growing number of groups that had split off from Reiyukai. In his autobiography Niwano attributes the decision to leave Reiyukai to its anti-intellectualism and its emphasis on attracting new members. About thirty Reiyukai members followed them, and Rissho Koseikai's membership grew steadily, if not overly impressively, to somewhat over one thousand by 1941.

For the first twenty years of Rissho Koseikai's existence, Niwano and Naganuma shared responsibility for its leadership. Naganuma, as the conduit of divine revelations, seems to have had a larger role in guiding the group and directing the training of leaders, including, to a certain extent, her cofounder. Early on, Niwano was directed to devote himself exclusively to the study of the *Lotus Sutra*, and so the reading of extraneous material, including newspapers, was banned. Later on he was allowed to expand his interests to the writings of Nichiren and studies in early Buddhism, and it was through this effort that he was able eventually to take the dominant role in developing Koseikai's doctrine.

Naganuma's influence contributed to a series of conflicts with society, most directly in the first instance, when she and Niwano were briefly arrested in 1943. It seems that Niwano's wife was not entirely in favor of his religious activity, especially after he abandoned his business in order to devote all his energies to the group. Naganuma for her part had been ordering Niwano to give up his family so that he would be undistracted in following his calling, a demand that he had managed to put off. Niwano tells us that his wife, jealous of the influence Naganuma was exerting over their lives, joined with the Fudo shamaness that he had abandoned years earlier to put pressure on the police to have the two arrested for violation of the Peace Preservation Law for disturbing the peace with their missionary activities.

Naganuma died in September 1957, and early in the following year Rissho Koseikai made a dramatic change in direction. From a group marked by divination and prophecy based on Naganuma's leadership it was transformed under Niwano's leadership to a group focusing on the study of the *Lotus Sutra* and early Buddhism, and a player on the international stage through its interreligious engagement. As part of these reforms, in 1959 the group abandoned the parent–child structure that it had inherited from Reiyukai and instead adopted a diocesan structure where local church membership is based on one's residence rather than the person who introduced you to the faith. We can conclude that both of these moves served to enhance the stability of the organization, contributing to the fact that leadership was passed to Niwano's son Nichiko in 1991 without any apparent difficulty.

RELIGIOUS SCHISMS IN JAPAN

In this chapter I have concentrated on the image of the founder in describing the evolution of these groups. Although certainly not the only factor important in explaining the emergence of the hundreds of new religious movements in Japan in the modern era, the founder endures as a central concept of Japanese religion. The image of the founder presented by these groups themselves often emphasizes their poor backgrounds and the difficulties they overcame in realizing their religious or spiritual abilities; the foundations of their spirituality in the various streams of Japanese religiosity; the possession of extraordinary abilities, especially the ability to heal; and the uniqueness of their own private revelation. This strong belief in the founder, or the holy person, is itself one contributing factor to the emergence of schismatic movements in Japan.

Related to this, another common element in the above stories, illustrating another major characteristic of Japanese religiosity, is the development of extraordinary powers, usually powers of healing or prophecy, often as a result of engaging in some kind of severe ascetic practice. Whereas the more common belief in the West would seem to be that certain people are born with such abilities or develop them spontaneously, in Japan there is a rather strong belief, within certain religious circles, that almost anybody can develop these powers if they are willing to put in the time and effort required, as when Niwano devoted himself to the ascetic practices prescribed for him by the Fudo shamaness or when Kubo Kakutaro demanded that his sister-in-law Kotani Kimi engage in these practices in order to develop spiritualist powers. The belief that such powers can be developed leads to a consequent belief in the relatively widespread use of these powers, further contributing to schisms through the authentication of authority by the supposed use of these powers.

Opposed to these ideas of the holy person or charismatic leader possessing extraordinary powers, there is a counter-tendency to pass on leadership of the group within the family. Within Japanese religiosity this is seen most clearly in the case of the Buddhist temples, which are often seen as a kind of family business, owned by the local priest who passes it on to his son, or a priest adopted into the family. As we have seen above, this can be an additional factor that leads to schism within new religious movements in Japan, when the inheritance of leadership is opposed either by a leading disciple of the founder or occasionally by the siblings of the successor.

Another major factor that contributes to religious schisms in Japan is structural, that is, the widespread use of a parent–child type of church organization. The personal relationship with one's "teacher" remains important in Japanese society as a whole, and by carrying over this characteristic into their organizational structure especially Tenrikyo and Reiyukai have made it relatively easy for some of their more successful missionaries to break off and found their own independent movements. The precipitating reason for the split can be doctrinal, as in the case of Onishi Aijiro and his interpretation of the *kanrodai*, or a dispute about priorities and practice, as we saw in Niwano Nikkyo's split with Reiyukai, or social/historical, as in the many movements that emerged out of the persecution of Omotokyo or as a result of the scandals surrounding Reiyukai in the early postwar years.

Finally, it is interesting to point out that nearly all of the groups we have looked at in this chapter emerged before the end of World War II, when the government held tight control over religious groups. While it is undoubtedly true that legal changes in the postwar era making it easier for new groups to be officially recognized contributed to an outpouring of new movements, many of the groups we have focused on here illustrate that the other religious and social factors pointed out above have contributed to religious innovation in Japan throughout the modern period, even when social circumstances did not entirely promote such activity.

REFERENCES

Dale, Kenneth J. 1975. *Circle of Harmony: A Case Study in Popular Japanese Buddhism with Implications for Christian Mission.* Tokyo: Seibunsha.

Hardacre, Helen. 1984. *Lay Buddhism in Contemporary Japan: Reiyukai Kyodan.* Princeton: Princeton University Press.

Idei Seitarō. 1965. *Keireiki.* Tokyo: Heiwakyo Henshubu.

Kisala, Robert. 1999. *Prophets of Peace: Pacifism and Cultural Identity in Japan's New Religions.* Honolulu: University of Hawaii Press.

Niwano Nikkyo. 1978. *Lifetime Beginner: An Autobiography.* Tokyo: Kosei Publishing Co.

Ooms, Emily Groszos. 1993. *Women and Millenarian Protest in Meiji Japan.* Ithaca, NY: Cornell University East Asia Program.

Sekai Kyusei Kyo. 1983. *The Light from the East: Mokichi Okada*, vol. I. Atami: MOA Productions.

1986. *The Light from the East: Mokichi Okada*, vol. II. Atami: MOA Productions.

Shimazono Susumu. 1986. "The Development of Millennialistic Thought in Japan's New Religions: From Tenrikyo to Honmichi." In James A. Beckford, ed., *New Religious Movements and Rapid Social Change*, pp. 55–86. London: Sage Publications.

1992. *Suki to toku: Shinshukyo shinkosha no seikatsu to shiso.* Tokyo: Kobundo.

1999. *Jidai no naka no shinshukyo: Idei Seitarō no sekai 1899–1945.* Tokyo: Kobundo.

Yumiyama Tatsuya. 1995. "Tenrikyo kara Honbushin e." In Araya Shigehiko *et al.*, eds., *Iyashi to wakai*, pp. 15–32. Tokyo: Seikei Daigaku Ajia-Taiheiyo Kenkyu Sentaa.

PART III

Christian traditions

CHAPTER 5

Finishing the Mystery: the Watch Tower and "the 1917 schism"

George D. Chryssides

INTRODUCTION

To the believer, distinctions between orthodox and schismatic, and between the authentic and the inauthentic, seem obvious. To the Jehovah's Witness, there seems an obvious continuity between the Watch Tower Bible and Tract Society, founded by Charles Taze Russell, and the present-day Jehovah's Witnesses, so named in 1931 by their second leader, Joseph Franklin Rutherford. Viewed superficially, a split in a religious organization appears to arise when a subversive leader rises to a position of power, gathers a following that challenges the orthodox teachings of the movement, fails to bring the entire movement to accept his teachings or authority, and subsequently secedes to form his own organization. As is frequently pointed out, however, history tends to be written by the victors, and hence the minority becomes allowed to disappear into relative oblivion.

This chapter focuses on the 1917 split within the Society, with particular reference to the controversies surrounding the Paul Johnson movement, and my aim is to examine the main causes of the schism that surrounded J. F. Rutherford's rise to power. In what follows, I shall argue that the so-called schisms of this period cannot be explained in such a simplistic manner. Indeed, even to refer to it as a "split" is to oversimplify the issues surrounding the dispute. Despite the fact that present-day Jehovah's Witnesses form a coherent unified organization with clear central authority, such a claim could not be made of the Watch Tower organization at the end of Russell's presidency.

Almost inevitably, changes in leadership create tensions within religious organizations. New leaders seldom wish to maintain the status quo, but aim to make their own mark on the movement and take it forward in innovatory ways. Rutherford's innovations caused considerable controversy within the Society. The splits that occurred are often referred to as "the 1917 schism," and are frequently attributed to a power struggle among various potential leaders. As M. James Penton writes, "the Bible Student movement nearly fell apart in 1917 and 1918 because of power struggles among Russell's successors and persecution from secular governments and mobs."[1] Alan Rogerson writes, "There were numerous rival factions within the organization. During Russell's lifetime he had been able to hold them together, but once he was dead there was a fierce struggle for power."[2]

How are we to explain the fragmentation of the Bible Students in the Rutherford period? It would be simplistic to claim that Rutherford rose to office as a result of personal ambition. Ascertaining someone's motives can only be a matter of speculation. In any case, rising to power in a large organization could not be accomplished single-handed, but required the support of other leaders, who favored the changes that Rutherford sought to introduce. True, the ousted directors no doubt harbored some resentment at the treatment they received from Rutherford, but their conflict with Rutherford cannot be disentangled from the fact that the new Watch Tower leader sought to introduce a different type of society from the organization that existed in the Russell era, and which Rutherford's opponents set up on their own subsequent initiative. There were matters of policy at stake, not simply personality clashes.

Sociologists have sometimes attempted to explain the development of religious organizations in terms of institutionalization. According to Max Weber, they take their origins with a charismatic leader and a loosely organized set of followers, and proceed, through "routinization" (a state in which there are clearly defined rules governing members' routine practices), to institutionalization, where members' roles, duties, and responsibilities are clearly defined, and can even be given legal status through formal contracts. As Weber contended, the death of the founder-leader gives impetus to the evolution of a religious organization, since such an event precipitates the issue of hegemonic succession. The new leader, Weber argued, might emerge in one of four ways: an equally charismatic leader may be forthcoming; supernatural revelation may provide a successor; the original leader may have nominated a successor; or the succession may be hereditary.[3]

I have elsewhere attempted to demonstrate the weaknesses of Weber's analysis of charisma and succession, notwithstanding the fact that, like many subsequent sociologists, he was writing about "ideal types," and

---

[1] Penton 1985: 46.   [2] Rogerson 1969: 32.   [3] Weber 1978: 241.

therefore did not expect this theory to fit each case of religious evolution and succession precisely. In the case of the Watch Tower organization, it was already institutionalized during its first leader's lifetime, having become an international organization, legally incorporated in several countries. In terms of Weber's model of hegemonic succession, there is little doubt that Rutherford's succession evidenced the first of Weber's four types. There is no doubt that Rutherford was charismatic, although his personality was quite different from that of Russell. Of the other three modes of possible succession, none was possible. In a fundamentally Bible-based organization, extra-biblical supernatural revelations would be inadmissible, and Russell left no family to assume office.

I have contended that this assessment of the Society's situation in 1917 is superficial. Although commentators frequently refer to "the 1917 schism," numerous splinter groups emerged around that date, and Jerry Bergman (1999)[4] identifies four major divisions that arose, commenting on over forty organizations that emerged from the disputes of this period between 1917 and 1919. Not all of these proved to be significant, of course, and many died out, but the number indicates the scale of the fragmentation.

THE WATCH TOWER SOCIETY BEFORE 1917

In order to examine the salient issues, it is necessary to give a brief history of the Watch Tower organization, and the situation in which it found itself on the death of its founder-leader. The Watch Tower organization was founded by Charles Taze Russell (1852–1916), who was raised a Presbyterian but, in common with a number of Adventist groups with which he subsequently associated, found difficulty in accepting main-stream Christian doctrines such as predestination, eternal torment as a punishment for sin, the Trinity, and the personhood of the Holy Spirit. Russell was also convinced, like other Adventists, that humanity was in its last days, and that Christ's second advent was imminent, but – as several Adventist groups taught – would not be a dramatic descent from the clouds of heaven, but an invisible "second presence" or *parousia*. Present-day Jehovah's Witnesses have often acquired a reputation for end-time calculations and the setting of dates for eschatological events. While it is true that Russell and Rutherford, as well as other leaders, did their share of this, Russell was much more interested in the doctrine of Christ's

[4] Bergman 1999: 287.

ransom sacrifice, atoning for Adam's sin, and this was at the heart of his teaching.

At the age of eighteen, Russell set up his own group of supporters who met together for prayer and Bible study. In 1879 the first edition of *Zion's Watch Tower and Herald of Christ's Presence* was published, and in 1881 Zion's Watch Tower Tract Society was established as an informal organization for the purpose of distributing tracts, becoming legally incorporated in 1884 as Zion's Watch Tower Society. In 1896 its name was changed to the Watch Tower Bible and Tract Society of Pennsylvania Inc., which remains its official name to the present time. The name of its principal organ of communication was changed to *The Watch Tower and Herald of God's Presence* in 1909, finally becoming simply *The Watchtower* – the name with which the public is familiar.

As an aid to understanding scripture, Russell wrote six volumes, entitled *Millennial Dawn*, subsequently renamed *Studies in the Scriptures*. Apparently he had notes for a seventh volume, but did not work the material into publishable form during his lifetime. Russell was also renowned as a preacher, giving Bible talks in various venues in the United States, and later traveling to Europe, where he established the first British branch of Bible Students in 1900. While on one of his preaching tours, Russell became seriously ill, and died on a train at Pampa, Texas, on October 31, 1916.

There had already been some dissent within the Watch Tower Society in 1909, but it was Russell's death that caused more serious creation of factions, resulting in "the 1917 schism." Joseph Franklin Rutherford – sometimes called "Judge Rutherford," since he served as a "special judge" (that is, a deputy judge) in the Fourteenth Judicial District of Missouri – may have seemed an unlikely successor to Russell, since one might have expected William E. Van Amburgh, being vice-president, to take over. Alexander Hugh Macmillan, who was Russell's personal secretary, was another possible candidate. At an early stage, however, both leaders stated that they did not wish to take office.[5] Russell and Rutherford appear to have been quite different personalities. Russell was more scholarly and reflective, and his supporters praised him as someone who was considerate and supportive. Rutherford was flamboyant, blunt, ruthless, and uncompromising. He had no compunctions about publicly reprimanding those whom he believed to have acted inappropriately, or summoning them to his office for a "trimming" – the word used at the

---

[5] Macmillan 1957: 69.

Bethel headquarters for a severe reproof by their leader, which was intended to cut the offender down to size.

PAUL S. L. JOHNSON

Neither Van Amburgh nor Macmillan coveted the office of president, but there was one other contender – Paul S. L. Johnson. Johnson had never been a director, but he had spoken at conventions, and was one of the Society's "pilgrims" – a term used for an itinerant evangelist. Johnson was formally trained in theology; he entered the Capital University of Columbus, Ohio in 1890, where he graduated in 1895 "with high honors," and underwent subsequent training at the theological seminary, Ohio, under the aegis of the Synod of the Lutheran Church, to which he belonged at the time. He graduated in 1898. Like many of those who joined Russell's Bible Students, Johnson had problems in accepting the traditional mainstream Christianity doctrines, particularly the notion of eternal torment. He met Russell in 1903, and became his personal secretary. When Russell died, Johnson was one of the senior leaders who made a speech at his funeral.

In 1916, Russell decided to send Johnson to England as one of the itinerant "pilgrims," with a view to strengthening the Society, as well as reporting back on their progress. Johnson was given plenipotentiary powers, although Watch Tower sources claim that this was merely to ensure that the British authorities would grant him a visa, and that he was instructed not to make personnel changes in the British branch. Initially, his reception was favorable, and members of the London congregation wrote letters to the *Watch Tower* praising his support and encouragement. His talks focused substantially on "Britain's Fallen Heroes – Comfort for the Bereaved," which his listeners found particularly helpful in the midst of World War I. However, at an early stage he clashed with the London leaders – Brothers H. J. Shearn and William Crawford[6] – whom he declared were to be removed from office. He obtained the key of the London headquarters, and took control of some of the funds and possession of all incoming mail.

Meanwhile, Rutherford had become part of the interim executive committee, and had quickly learned of the situation. Rutherford called for the British leaders' reinstatement, and ordered Johnson to return to

---

[6] The term "Brother" was used by Bible Students to designate a baptized male member, and is used as a title. Present-day Jehovah's Witnesses continue to adopt this practice.

the United States. Johnson refused, and in a series of exchanges by cable, he compared himself with biblical characters such as Ezra, Nehemiah, and Mordecai, casting the British leaders in the roles of Sanballat, Tobiah, and Haman. (The allusions become clear if one recalls that Ezra and Nehemiah led the rebuilding of Jerusalem and its Temple after the Babylonian captivity, and were hampered by Sanballat and Tobiah's attacks. Mordecai was the righteous leader in the story of Esther, and Haman the scheming villain who finally was hanged.) Several of the London cables expressed the opinion that Johnson had become mentally ill. He had suffered a nervous breakdown in 1910, and it is possible that his mental problems were experiencing a recurrence. Crawford stated in a cable to Rutherford (April 3, 1917) that Johnson was "either under the influence of spiritism or else has temporarily lost the balance of his mind." Other British leaders were even less charitable: Brother Thomson McCloy stated that he was "off his head." Johnson's response was to refuse to communicate with Rutherford, and instead he corresponded with Ritchie, claiming that Rutherford's leadership of the Society was illegal. Five brothers were sent from Brooklyn to assist with the crisis. The London leaders finally shut him in his bedroom at the London head-quarters, from which he endeavored to escape in the early hours of the morning, by dropping down from the balcony. He finally left the London Bethel on April 4, 1917. Johnson returned to the United States, taking up residence once again at the Brooklyn Bethel, which was the Society's headquarters. Rutherford was minded to send him on a pilgrim mission to Columbus, Ohio – his home city – but Johnson declined, pleading that his health was not up to the journey, and his refusal caused further ill-feeling between himself and Rutherford.

ELECTIONS

The question of succession remained to be formally decided. Russell left a will, in which he gave directions for the continuation of the Society. Until his death, Russell had sole editorial control over the *Watch Tower*, which he was determined should be the sole publication of the Society. His will named five of his supporters, whom he recommended should constitute the new editorial board, "at least three of whom must have read and have approved as TRUTH each and every article appearing in these columns." It was also a requirement that none of them should be associated with any other periodical. The five names that Russell recommended were William E. Page, William E. Van Amburgh, Henry Clay Rockwell,

E. W. Brenneisen, and F. H. Robison, and the Board was to be self-perpetuating, having the sole right to elect new members when the existing ones resigned or died. In the event of these five nominees being unable to assume office, Russell also wrote: "The names of the five whom I suggest as possibly amongst the most suitable from which to fill vacancies in the Editorial Committee are as follows: A. E. Burgess, Robert Hirsh, Isaac Hoskins, Geo. H. Fisher (Scranton), J. F. Rutherford, Dr. John Edgar."[7] For reasons that are not clear, Brenneisen and Page did not take up a place on the panel, and Hirsh and Rutherford were substituted.

A number of points concerning this will are worthy of comment. First, Russell was concerned to make provision for the continuation of the *Watch Tower* magazine, rather than for the Watch Tower Society, thus indicating that his real concern was to publish religious material, rather than to perpetuate a new religious organization. Second, although Rutherford shortly aspired to the presidency, his role as successor does not appear to have been an obvious one: he is merely named as a reserve for the editorial board. Third, Russell mentions "the names of five" to fill vacancies, but, curiously, goes on to list six, prompting one writer to suggest that, "It is certainly possible, but this author has not found it possible to fully confirm or reject this theory, that one name was added to the list after Russell had written it: Rutherford's" (Haugland 2006).

Whatever Russell's intentions, two members of the Board of Directors were appointed to act as an interim Executive Committee – A. I. Ritchie, who was vice-president at the time, and W. E. Van Amburgh, who was secretary-treasurer. Additionally, Rutherford was appointed as the committee's legal adviser. One of Rutherford's first steps was to question the composition of the Board of Directors. Rutherford's legal opinion was that members of the Board had to be elected to office, and that a board could not simply perpetuate itself by assuming exclusive responsibility for replacing deceased and resigning members with their own nominees. Whatever the Society's Charter stated, he argued, this was contrary to Pennsylvanian state law. Elections, he pointed out, had not taken place for twenty years, and hence elections were scheduled for 1918.

What happened next is not totally clear. Rutherford appears to have acted as if he were already the Society's president, notwithstanding his apparent insistence that office-bearers should be properly elected. When

---

[7] Russell, Charles Taze: Last Will and Testament www.pastor-russell.com/legacy/will_doc.html.

it was apparent that there were two different factions among the Board of Directors, Watch Tower sources relate that Rutherford dismissed four members of the Board, including Ritchie, who had been formally appointed to see the Society through this interim period, and replaced them – apparently without election – by A. H. Macmillan, W. E. Spill, J. A. Bohnet, and G. H. Fisher. Although it was the shareholders who had the legal responsibility for electing the office-bearers, it was decided to hold an "advisory election" by the various ecclesias, which were requested to meet and to indicate their preferences. The date of November 1, 1917 was set, and 813 ecclesias returned their recommendations, which were reported in the December 15 issue of the *Watch Tower*. The straw poll overwhelmingly favored Rutherford's supporters, and at the shareholders' meeting on January 5, 1918, Rutherford was elected as president with a very clear majority, with C. H. Anderson as vice-president, Van Amburgh as secretary-treasurer, and Macmillan, Spill, Bohnet, and Fisher taking their places on the newly elected Board. Johnson was one of the candidates who stood for election in 1918, but withdrew at the last moment. According to Watch Tower sources, he claimed succession to the presidency,[8] although he only attracted twenty votes in the advisory elections, against Rutherford's 11,421.

THE FINISHED MYSTERY

During this interim period a further controversy erupted. Russell had published six volumes of *Studies in the Scriptures*; he had left notes for a possible seventh, but never completed it. Rutherford desired to bring it to publication, and he commissioned two leaders – Clayton J. Woodworth and George H. Fisher – to study the notes and prepare the new volume. This appeared the same year, and was entitled *The Finished Mystery* – a commentary on the books of Ezekiel and Revelation, together with a study of the Song of Solomon. The book launch took place on July 17, 1917, when Rutherford ensured that every member of the Bethel received a copy, placed on their lunch table. When the residents arrived and perused their copies, heated controversy broke out, apparently led by Johnson and the ousted directors. According to Watch Tower sources, the shouting and fist-shaking at Rutherford lasted for five hours, with the result that no lunch was served.

[8] *Year Book of Jehovah's Witnesses* 1975, p. 89.

The Finished Mystery is a fairly lengthy piece of writing, almost six hundred pages in all, and it may be asked why it should have proved so controversial, even before the Bethel staff had a chance to study it. There are several features that distinguish it from the other six volumes in Russell's *Studies in the Scriptures*, which would have been apparent, even at a superficial glance. Unlike Russell's previous writings, *The Finished Mystery* was copiously illustrated with a series of cartoons, usually at the expense of mainstream Christendom and its clergy. For example, one cartoon, entitled "Clergy would censure the Bible," depicts a large Bible around which men – presumably clergy – are working with large pairs of scissors, excising the books of Ezekiel and Revelation. Another depicts a clergyman conducting a funeral, pronouncing over the coffin the words, "Our friend is not dead; his soul is hovering near." It is entitled, "Satan's lie perpetuated," and alludes to the prevalent substitution of the doctrine of the immortality of soul from the biblical doctrine of bodily resurrection. By contrast, Russell's six authentic volumes consisted solely of text, without any added artwork. While it might be suggested that the illustrations were a piece of harmless fun, Russell had been affectionately regarded by his followers, and the intrusion of such illustrations would no doubt have been viewed as being too overtly innovative to capture the spirit of Russell's publications, especially in what purported to be a posthumous work.

There were other obvious issues. As Johnson's supporters later pointed out,[9] it is clear that *The Finished Mystery* was not a posthumous publication, at least not in a literal sense. Strictly, a posthumous work is something that an author completed, but which failed to progress to final publication during his or her lifetime. This was patently not the case with *The Finished Mystery*. Although the flyleaf states that the work was "Written in 1886 by Pastor Russell," it had plainly not been kept on ice for nearly twenty years before being issued. Indeed, Russell is referred to throughout in the third person, and the style of the volume is also quite different from the other *Studies in the Scriptures*. The *Mystery* is verse-by-verse, sometimes phrase-by-phrase, commentary on the three books it purports to explain – quite atypical of Russell, whose previous works took a broad theme, such as "Armageddon," which was addressed discursively, drawing on biblical evidence where this was needed.

[9] *Harvest Siftings* www.biblestudents.net/history/harvest_siftings_1917.htm.

There are obvious contradictions, too, between Russell's authentic writings and the "seventh volume." In his end-time calculations in *Thy Kingdom Come* (the third volume of his *Studies in the Scriptures*) Russell identified 1846 as the year of the "cleansing of the sanctuary" (Daniel 8.14). It was, and remains, typical Watch Tower teaching that an invisible heavenly event has some counterpart or visible sign in the physical world, and Russell drew attention to the formation of the Evangelical Alliance in that year as a sign that conservative Christians were coming together to agree on correct teaching, in contrast with those teaching false doctrine – in particular "the papal system" of Roman Catholicism. Although the authors of *The Finished Mystery* stated that they faithfully retained Russell's end-time dates, Russell's explanation of 1846 contrasts blatantly with a two-section cartoon in *The Finished Mystery*, in which the top half depicted the "beast" of Revelation 13:1–3 and was entitled "Papacy as God pictures it"; the bottom half portrays the same beast, but this time bearing the caption "Evangelical Alliance – Church Federation The Image of the 'Beast'." In the body of the text the Alliance is referred to as the "Evangelical-Alliance-Spiritism movement."[10] This marks yet another important contrast between the two early leaders: Russell was non-sectarian, believing that many branches of Protestantism were capable of offering salvation, whereas Rutherford came to view the Watch Tower Society as God's sole vehicle of truth.

The Finished Mystery had repercussions outside the Society as well as inside. It proved controversial for its emphatic anti-war stance, which was particularly unpopular in the wake of the United States' entry into the Great War in 1916. The book was particularly critical of the role of mainstream clergy in the War, to the point of accusing them of responsibility. There are many such accusations in the book, such as the following:

The clergy are the ones directly responsible for the war in Europe. It was not their province to convince the rulers of those countries that their kingdoms are parts of God's Kingdom of peace, holiness, justice, love and truth – monstrous! They are an entirely unauthorized class – except by themselves; a self-perpetuating fraud. They have brought upon their heads the blood of all the nations of the earth in this world war; and God will require it at their hands. In the spring of 1918, and from that time onward forever, it will be as unsafe to tell the lies that have filled Babylon's exchequers as it will to be a king. – Zech. 13:2–6.[11]

---

[10] Russell 1917: 160.   [11] Russell 1917: 228.

One passage in particular riled the Society's opponents:

Nowhere in the New Testament is Patriotism (a narrow-minded hatred of other peoples) encouraged. Everywhere and always murder in its every form is forbidden; and yet, under the guise of Patriotism the civil governments of earth demand of peace-loving men the sacrifice of themselves and their loved ones and the butchery of their fellows, and hail it as a duty demanded by the laws of heaven.[12]

Such remarks were not overlooked by either the civil or the ecclesiastical authorities. Warrants were issued for the arrest of Rutherford, together with W. E. Van Amburgh, F. H. Robison (one of the *Watch Tower*'s editorial committee), A. H. Macmillan, R. J. Martin, Giovanni DeCecca, and of course Clayton and Fisher, who had brought the volume to publication.

The book was banned, first in Canada, and subsequently in the US. Rutherford and his colleagues were tried under the Espionage Act. Extracts from the charges read as follows:

(1, 3) The offense of unlawfully, feloniously and willfully causing and attempting to cause insubordination, disloyalty and refusal of duty in the military and naval forces of the United States of America, in, through and by personal solicitations, letters, public speeches, distribution and public circulation throughout the United States of America of a certain book called "Volume Seven – SCRIPTURES STUDIES – The Finished Mystery"; and distributing and publicly circulating throughout the United States certain articles presented in pamphlets called, "BIBLE STUDENTS MONTHLY," "THE WATCH TOWER," "KINGDOM NEWS" and other pamphlets not named, et cetera;

(2, 4) The offense of unlawfully, feloniously, and willfully obstructing the recruiting and enlistment service of the United States when the United States was at war.[13]

The leaders were sentenced to serve twenty-year prison sentences in Atlanta Penitentiary. (Giovanni DeCecca, one of the arrested leaders, received only ten years, for unexplained reasons.) However, following an appeal by the Watch Tower leaders, all eight leaders were released on March 26, 1919. No doubt the ending of the war reduced public antagonism to Rutherford and his association; nonetheless it is noteworthy that, although these men were in prison while the crucial elections took place, four of them were successfully voted into office. The four directors whom Rutherford removed from office were defeated; no longer having a

[12] Russell 1917: 247.   [13] Quoted in *Year Book of Jehovah's Witnesses* 1975, p. 104.

meaningful role in the Watch Tower Society, the opponents seceded, forming their own separate organizations. The four ousted directors formed the Pastoral Bible Institute in 1918 as soon as their fate in the Watch Tower organization was sealed, while Johnson established the Layman's Home Missionary Movement the following year.

SCHISMATICAL GROUPS

The Pastoral Bible Institute

Some account must now be given of the schismatical organizations.

The Pastoral Bible Institute (PBI) was founded in 1918 by the four ousted Watch Tower directors: I. F. Hoskins, A. N. Pierson, A. I. Ritchie, and J. D. Wright, with around fifty supporters. In common with the Watch Tower Society, the movement was lay-led, without clergy, although in common with Russell's original organization it retained congregational autonomy, with its elders and deacons being voted into office by consecrated (that is, baptized and formally admitted) members. The Bible, of course, was regarded as the fundamental source of authority, and no non-scriptural teachings could be made into articles of faith. The Institute affirmed the main teachings of the Bible relating to creation, sin, and redemption. It affirmed the biblical account of creation: in common with the Watch Tower organization they allowed that the length of a "day" was indeterminate, thus enabling the concession that the Bible allowed for some evolution in animals. However, Adam and Eve were a special independent creation of God's, created perfect, but fell from grace through disobedience, infecting the rest of humanity with sin and its resultant consequence, death. Followers accepted Russell's teaching that there was no eternal torment for the unrepentant, but rather that hell was the grave, where the soul – that is, the life force – simply ceases to exist. The righteous, however, would be resurrected to live eternally in the messiah's future kingdom.

The Institute also endorsed Russell's Christology and soteriology. In contrast with mainstream Christendom, and in common with the Watch Tower Society, it affirmed that Jesus was the Son of God, but not God incarnate, co-equal or co-eternal with God. His birth was miraculous, however: the Bible affirms that he was virgin-born, but not – in contrast with Roman Catholic teaching – that Mary was immaculately conceived or that she remained in a state of perpetual virginity. Jesus, being perfect, was able to attain humankind's salvation by offering himself in substitutionary atonement for Adam's sin: the "ransom theory" of atonement was thus supremely important. Jesus rose from the dead, having sacrificed his physical body, and his resurrection body was a divine body.

Thus far, the doctrines of the Pastoral Bible Institute were congruent with those of Rutherford. The differences lay in their end-time doctrines. The PBI retained the significance of the year 1874, which Russell had defined as the date of the cleansing of the sanctuary, but which the Watch Tower Society had subsequently transferred to 1918.[14] However, both parties accepted Russell's teaching that Christ's second presence was invisible rather than visible. Events in the Middle East were given a role in the divine plan. While Rutherford had seen them as having some significance, the Watch Tower Society was coming to regard human events as confirmation of heavenly ones, rather than happenings that were significant in their own right. The PBI accorded them significance, teaching that Armageddon would be a final conflict in the Middle East, and would herald the return of the ancient patriarchs, who would inhabit a land whose borders would be fully congruent with the ones that God had promised to Abraham. We can therefore see how the Watch Tower Society under Rutherford was moving away from Russell's teachings on a number of matters, and how the PBI wished to retain the authentic teachings of Russell.

The Layman's Home Missionary Movement

Bereft of office in Rutherford's new-style organization, Paul Johnson set up his own movement in 1918. The name "Layman's Home Missionary Movement" had already been used by Russell, although never incorporated, and no doubt this choice of name reflects Johnson's loyalty to Russell rather than Rutherford. In December 1918, Johnson published the journal *The Present Truth and Herald of Christ's Kingdom*, which was followed in 1920 by *The Herald of the Epiphany*, later renamed *The Bible Standard and Herald of Christ's Epiphany*. Its current name has been shortened to *The Bible Standard*, and it is now archived on-line.[15]

---

[14] The Watch Tower Society arrives at the date 1918 by adding a three-and-a-half-year "harvesting period" to the pivotal date of 1914, in which Christ is reckoned to have entered the heavenly sanctuary. The three-and-a-half-year period is a recapitulation of the length of Jesus' ministry, and the year 1918 marks the commencement of the 144,000 anointed ones' entry into the kingdom of heaven.

[15] *The Bible Standard* www.biblestandard.com/.

Johnson was also a prolific writer, and compiled a series of fifteen theological treatises entitled *Epiphany Studies in the Scriptures.*

The use of the word "epiphany" relates to the role ascribed to Johnson as the "epiphany messenger." During his lifetime Russell was typically regarded as having a special role in the fulfillment of biblical prophecy. He was held to be the "faithful and wise servant" mentioned in Matthew 24:45, although he did not in fact claim this title for himself.[16] In Johnson's terminology he was the "*parousia* messenger" – the one who heralded and pointed to Christ's invisible presence. Johnson claimed for himself the complementary role of "epiphany messenger" – the one who is entrusted with proclaiming to the world that the *parousia* has occurred. (It has been alleged that Johnson made more exalted claims for himself, claiming to be the world's great high priest. However, his supporters deny that he ever made such a claim.) The Layman's Home Missionary Movement claims that it is interdenominational. However, in the spirit of Russell, it is non-Trinitarian, and decidedly critical of Roman Catholic doctrine, contending for example that the papacy is the "abomination of desolation" foretold by the prophet Daniel (Daniel 11:31).

The Stand Fast Bible Students

Not all of the emergent schisms disapproved of *The Finished Mystery.* Charles E. Heard, a pilgrim brother and convention speaker, was so enthusiastic about the book that he made arrangements for its distribution throughout one Canadian city. He planned that colporteurs should distribute a copy to each household, returning later to collect a payment of 60 cents from those who wished to keep it. Heard's disagreement with the Watch Tower Society related to Rutherford's recommendation in 1918 that the organization should purchase war bonds as an investment. This, he believed, was contrary to the firm anti-war stance that the Society had thitherto taken. *The Finished Mystery* taught that the end of the Gospel Age "harvest" period was in the spring of 1918. (Russell had divided human history into three broad periods: the Jewish, the Christian, and the Gospel or Millennial periods.) Heard concluded that Rutherford's action completed this harvest period, after which he would provide no sound teaching. It is estimated that Heard gained the support of around 1,200 Bible Students in the North West Area,[17] establishing the Stand Fast Bible Students on December 1, 1918. The name signified not only the

---

[16] Anon. 1916.   [17] Parkinson 2007.

declared need to stand fast in matters relating to war, but also the need to "stand fast in Bible study." The name of their journal, *Old Corn Gems*, is less self-explanatory than the name of the organization: it alluded to a story in the book of Joshua (Joshua 5:11–12), in which it is reported that God ceased to send manna (heavenly bread) to his people after a particular Passover period. Since Passover is in the spring, the story was interpreted as a "type" of the subsequent presumed cessation of "spiritual food" after the Watch Tower's 1918 Memorial.

The Stand Fast Movement soon fragmented, however, with several divisions emerging at its first convention in Seattle in 1919. Of these splinter groups, the best known are the Elijah Voice Society, and the Star Construction Company. The former was organized in 1922 by John A. Hardersen and C. D. McCray, who urged their followers not simply to study the Bible, but actively to witness by preaching Babylon's imminent destruction. The latter was founded by Ian C. Edwards and C. E. Heard in 1923, and moved west to found a commune in Stookie, British Columbia, believing that the faithful would be translated into heaven from that location, commencing in 1924. Their expectations failed to materialize, and the group disbanded in 1927.

THE FOURTH "DIVISION": THE JEHOVAH'S WITNESSES

The fourth division that Bergman identifies is the Jehovah's Witnesses' organization itself. Although the main grounds of the schisms among the Bible Students are attributable to the 1917–18 controversies, Rutherford went on to implement further changes in the Watch Tower organization. Progressively, pressure was increased on elders to undertake the house-to-house work that is so typically associated with present-day Jehovah's Witnesses. By 1927 it was a condition of eldership that house-to-house work should be undertaken. Further standardization of the Society involved the transition from being a federation of ecclesias to a theocratic organization; in 1925 ecclesias were informed that they had either to accept the uniformity of worship prescribed by the Society, or else to withdraw. Although many congregations agreed to conform, this requirement caused many to withdraw from the organization and to continue independently, thus giving rise to further schismatical groups. Further, the year 1927 witnessed the introduction of other radical ideas associated with the Watch Tower Society, such as the abolition of Christmas and birthday celebrations. Significantly, schismatic groups such as Paul Johnson's movement continue to observe these, although the observance of Easter is not emphasized: this is in common with the Adventist tradition from which Bible Students derive, in which emphasis is given to the Memorial, the observance of which the Bible enjoins, not Easter Sunday celebrations. In 1931, at a convention in Columbus, Ohio, Rutherford introduced the new name for his supporters – Jehovah's Witnesses – thus clearly demarcating them from other groups that continued to call their members Bible Students. Finally, in 1938, two *Watchtower* articles entitled "Organization" made it clear that the organization's government must be "theocratic," not democratic, and all congregations were asked to subscribe to the following declaration:

We, the company of God's people taken out for his name, and now at _____ recognize that God's government is a pure theocracy and that Christ Jesus is at the temple and in full charge and control of the visible organization of Jehovah, as well as the invisible, and that "THE SOCIETY" is the visible representative of the Lord on earth, and we therefore request "The Society" to organize this company for service and to appoint the various servants thereof, so that all of us may work together in peace, righteousness, harmony and complete unity. We attach hereto a list of names of persons in this company that to us appear more fully mature and who therefore appear to be best suited to fill the respective positions designated for service.[18]

The Jehovah's Witnesses' congregations now became part of a unified, homogeneous organization, with no room for elections, innovations, or religious creativity. They were Jehovah's instrument on earth, governed by him through their Governing Body.

EXPLAINING THE SCHISMS

Sociologists of religion have developed theories of how religious movements progress, but have offered much less by way of explanation of schism. In the case of the divisions among the Bible Students, it is clear that at least three broad issues came into play: the movement's organization, its requirements, and its doctrines. These cannot be entirely separated: reasons for dissenters objecting to Rutherford's succession included his requirements (such as house-to-house work), as well as his doctrinal innovations. Certainly, concepts such as institutionalization and "power struggle" are weak explanations of events, as is evident from the preceding discussion.

---

[18] Rutherford 1938.

Rutherford's changes were in no way attempts at institutionalization. Rather, he sought to alter the Watch Tower Society in two ways. First, he sought to put the Society on a proper legal footing, with properly conducted elections and appointments. Russell, who was primarily a pastor, a speaker, and a writer, may well have been more interested in proclaiming his message than with the Society's legal affairs, and Rutherford, the lawyer, sought to redress this. Rutherford was uncompromising, and if this meant ousting some of those who were already in office, he did not hold back. Perhaps matters could have been handled more tactfully, but it is significant that no legal challenge was made against Rutherford's changes in office-bearers.

Second, under Russell's leadership, the Watch Tower Society, as its full name implied, was primarily a Bible and Tract Society, its emphasis being on disseminating tracts, books, and Bibles. Groups of Bible Students used Watch Tower publications, or elected not to do so, at their own discretion. Although Russell endeavored to give unity to the organization by holding conventions and issuing invitations to a common Memorial service, the Bible Students were essentially a federation of autonomous ecclesias – congregations who sought to understand the Bible better in whatever way they chose, and who could appoint their own leaders and set their own agendas. Rutherford changed this in two very significant ways: first, he wanted standardization throughout the Society, with the directors having control over the appointment of leaders. Second, under Rutherford's leadership the Society changed from a distributor of literature to Jehovah's own true organization that offered the sole means of salvation – a characteristic that serves to define Jehovah's Witnesses in the present day.

Of the schismatical groups that emerged, some of the differences were theological. Although they preserved several of Russell's key teachings, in common with the emergent Jehovah's Witnesses – notably the two classes of salvation (heavenly and earthly), denial of hell and of the Trinity, and the imminent kingdom of God as the harbinger of everlasting peace on earth – a number of issues separated them from the Watch Tower Society. One such issue was the role of the State of Israel: the Society had come to abandon Russell's view that contemporary events in Palestine had a significant role in the divine purpose. Another issue related to judgment: Russell had taught that all humanity would be judged by God in the last days, but the teaching that emerged in the Watch Tower Society (and continues to prevail among present-day Jehovah's Witnesses) is that God has already judged certain sectors of humanity, for example the pre-diluvians who perished in the flood of Noah's time, and the inhabitants of Sodom and Gomorrah who were destroyed by fire. Such men and women, the Society taught, would not be required to stand judgment for a second time, but were now irretrievably judged, resting in a state of eternal unconsciousness. Several of the dissenting groups questioned this, claiming that Jesus, as the second Adam, must redeem Adam's sin, and offer eternal life to all.

In addition to these doctrinal controversies, the schismatical Bible Students did not accept the emergent new practices of the Watch Tower Society. Their congregations continued to appoint elders by election; they did not accept the centralized uniformity of the Society, allowing methods of preaching to be at the discretion of individual congregations. Methods of evangelism were at the discretion of congregations, and included street witnessing, rallies, and literature distribution. House-to-house ministry was carried out by some congregations, but it was not compulsory, and certainly not the hallmark of the Bible Students, as it is of present-day Jehovah's Witnesses. Individual congregations were permitted to produce their own monthly newsletter, while the Watch Tower Society only disseminated materials that had come from its Brooklyn headquarters, with its seal of approval. In 1924 the Society ceased publication of Russell's writings, and it discontinued their distribution after 1927; most of the schismatical Bible Students endorsed Russell's teachings, rather than Rutherford's innovatory doctrines.

When religious schisms occur, more often than not the schismatical factions present a good case. Although the schismatics are, by definition, the losers in the debates of their times, the inherent worth of their case is often as good, if not better, than that of the faction whose opinion prevails. In the case of the schismatical organizations, there can be little doubt that most were closer to the teachings of Russell than the emergent Jehovah's Witnesses. Bergman writes, "Actually, the Jehovah's Witnesses are as much an offshoot of Russell's movement as are the Standfasters or Layman's Home Missionary Movement."[19] There were two important differences about Rutherford's organization, however: the passage of time proved the Jehovah's Witnesses more successful than their rivals, and Rutherford managed to retain the assets and the legal identity of the Watch Tower organization, which provided a solid foundation for its future growth.

[19] Bergman 1999: 287.

One can understand why so many Bible Students wanted to dissociate themselves from the very radical changes that were happening within the Watch Tower Society. The exact drop-off in allegiance is disputed. Critics such as William J. Schnell contend that Rutherford lost 75 percent of the organization's total membership.[20] Such claims are difficult to substantiate, particularly since systematic records of Memorial attendance and service activity only commenced in 1920. It is documented, however, that 21,274 attended the Memorial in 1917. The figure of 17,961 that is given for 1919, the Watch Tower Society contends, is only a partial figure, since not all countries were able to report. There is little doubt that 1928 marked a low ebb, with only 17,380 Memorial attendees, although the downturn is to a significant degree explained by disillusionment at Rutherford's failed prediction that the Old Testament patriarchs would rise from the dead in 1925. Nonetheless, the downturn of the late 1910s and 1920s was more than recouped during the remainder of Rutherford's period of office, which witnessed a steady and consistent rise during the 1930s and thereafter, reaching a total of 140,450 Memorial attendees in 1942, the year of Rutherford's death.

Rutherford may have been uncompromising, ruthless, and authoritarian, and not all may have welcomed his achievement of a unified, homogeneous theocratic organization with no room for dissenters, individual innovation, or debate. The passage of time demonstrated Rutherford's success, in contrast to that of his opponents: at the time of writing, Jehovah's Witnesses number over 16 million Memorial attendees, well over 6 million active publishers, and around 250,000 new baptismal candidates each year. This contrasts with the dissenting Bible Students, many of whose organizations became defunct, and the strongest of which only continue to attract small handfuls of followers. The Pastoral Bible Institute's circulation of its journal in the early 1990s amounted to a mere 4,000; J. Gordon Melton places the numerical strength of the Layman's Home Missionary Movement at around 10,000, while Bergman suggests that the totality of Bible Students worldwide is no more than that number. The schismatics may well have proved more faithful to the teachings of Charles Taze Russell, but the price of authenticity has proved to be obscurity, and in many cases oblivion.

[20] Schnell 1956: 41.

REFERENCES

Anon. 1916. "Biography." *The Watch Tower and Herald of Christ's Presence*, 37 (23), December 1, 1916, p. 5997.

Bergman, Jerry. 1985. *Jehovah's Witnesses and Kindred Groups: A Historical Compendium and Bibliography*. New York: Garland.

1999. *Jehovah's Witnesses: A Comprehensive and Selectively Annotated Bibliography*. Westport, CT: Greenwood Press.

Harvest Siftings. 2007. www.biblestudents.net/history/harvest_siftings_1917.htm, accessed September 13, 2007.

Haugland, Jan S. 2006. "The Successor Problem: A Focused Biography of Joseph Rutherford, 2nd Leader for the Jehovah's Witnesses, 1916–1942." Master's thesis, University of Bergen, Norway, Fall 2000. *Skepsis* September 2006. Located at www.skepsis.no/articles_in_english/the_successor_problem.html, accessed July 24, 2007.

Macmillan, A. H. 1957. *Faith on the March*. Englewood Cliffs, NJ: Prentice Hall.

Melton, J. Gordon. 1996. *Encyclopedia of American Religions* (5th edn). Detroit: Gale.

Parkinson, James. 2007. *Troubled Years*. www.heraldmag.org/2004_history/04history_6.htm, accessed September 13, 2007.

Penton, M. James. 1985. *Apocalypse Delayed: The Story of Jehovah's Witnesses*. Toronto: University of Toronto Press.

Rogerson, Alan. 1969. *Millions Now Living Will Never Die: A Study of Jehovah's Witnesses*. London: Constable.

Russell, C. T. 1886–1904. *Millennial Dawn*, later renamed *Studies in the Scriptures*, 7 vols., Brooklyn, NY: International Bible Students Association.

1916. Last Will and Testament of Charles Taze Russell. June 29, 1907. Reprinted in *The Watch Tower and Herald of God's Presence* 37 (23), December 1, 1916, pp. 5999–6000. Also located at www.pastor-russell.com/legacy/will_doc.html.

1917. *The Finished Mystery* (completed by Clayton J. Woodworth and George H. Fisher). Brooklyn, NY: International Bible Students Association.

Rutherford, J. F. 1938. "Organization," Part 2. *The Watchtower and Herald of Christ's Presence*, 59 (12), June 15, 1938, pp. 182–3.

Schnell, W. J. 1959. *Thirty Years a Watch Tower Slave: The Confessions of a Converted Jehovah's Witness*. Grand Rapids, MI: Baker Book House.

Weber, Max. 1968/1978. *Economy and Society*. Berkeley: University of California Press.

Yearbook of Jehovah's Witnesses. 1975. Brooklyn, NY: Watch Tower Bible and Tract Society of Pennsylvania.

CHAPTER 6

Challenges to charismatic authority in the Unificationist Movement

David G. Bromley and Rachel S. Bobbitt

One important issue in understanding the emergence and development of new religious movements (NRMs) is the durability and survivability of movement leadership. There is little question that during NRMs' first generation the charismatic authority of the founder/leader is the primary source of movement legitimation and cohesiveness. At the same time, NRM founders also oversee the movement's organizational development. While types of leadership may be divided into the traditional, charismatic, and rational legal ideal types that Weber (1964) has constructed, actual movement leadership is likely to combine these types. In order to understand both the strengths and vulnerabilities of NRM leadership, therefore, both charismatic and organizational leadership must be considered. Further, as movements develop they become more complex entities. NRMs initially tend to form around a charismatic leader based on that individual's revelatory or mystical experience. At this juncture movements mirror the traditional sociological conception of a cult, a loosely organized group with a charismatic leader. As movements develop, they are likely to consist of three major components: the inner circle, which is composed of the founder/leader and a small number of confidants; a set of administrative, economic, and mission-oriented organizations, which increasingly assume a rational-legal, bureaucratic form; and a grassroots membership base, which during the first generation consists exclusively of movement converts (Bromley and Bobbitt 2006; Zald and Berger 1978). In this chapter we argue that each of these three movement segments constitutes a power base, and challenges to charismatic authority may emanate from one or more of these sources. Further, the challenges may be directed either at charismatic authority directly or at organizational control. The result of such challenges may be loss of charismatic authority, loss of organizational control, organizational schism, or movement collapse. Examples from the Unificationist Movement are used to illustrate the nature and process of challenges to charismatic authority.

CHARISMATIC AND ORGANIZATIONAL AUTHORITY

The foundation of authority in NRMs is the construction of a charismatic persona (Bromley forthcoming). NRMs such as Unificationism construct hagiographies (sacred biographies) of founder/leaders that serve as the basis for their charismatic authority. As Katz (1975) points out, charismatic authority rests on the imputation of an inherent state of being (essence), since all that can actually be observed is behavior. At the most general level the imputation is one of moral superiority on some dimension that legitimates both the leader's authority and the follower's submission. One important factor in the solidity of charismatic authority, then, is that the qualities imputed to the leader are understood to be inherent states of being and not simply extraordinary behaviors. The essence of this process in this case is to create a charismatic persona, the Lord of the Second Advent, whose extraordinary qualities transcend those of the actual person, Sun Myung Moon. The socially constructed persona, Lord of the Second Advent, acts through Sun Myung Moon. The successful process of constructing the Lord of the Second Advent, then, has involved establishing the reality of the Lord of the Second Advent who transcends the corporeal Sun Myung Moon. Maintaining this charismatic persona is problematic as followers require ongoing confirmation of the imputed attributes. As Katz (1975: 1382; see also Dawson 2002) observes:

As security for their risky investments in granting extraordinary powers to the charismatic individual, in releasing themselves from proscriptions to heed the call, and in obtaining relief from obligations to mundane others, labelers demand the right to make frequent audits of the status of charisma.

With the support of his inner circle and grassroots followers, Moon has carefully crafted the Lord of the Second Advent persona through his life. For example, according to his hagiography, Moon displayed an extraordinary sense of justice and morality from a young age: "If he saw adults taking advantage of innocent children, he would fling himself on the ground and cry, and beat his arms and legs on the floor. Even though his body was bruised and bleeding, he would not cease until the adults relented" (Kim 1977, vol. 2: 5). Moon is reported to have identified deeply and intimately with the tragic events in Jesus' life. By one account, "Once he wept all night long in his room, and in the morning the people in the house discovered that his flood of tears had soaked through the mat ceiling and formed a puddle on the floor below" (Kim 1977, vol. 2: 6). He possessed tremendous personal energy and commitment to his mission, sleeping only for brief periods each night. The Divine Principle and his subsequent speeches are treated as constituting ongoing revelations of God's purpose for humanity.

Leaders as well as rank-and-file members have contributed to the persona. Members of Moon's inner circle have periodically participated in a ritual in which each assumed the position of the leader of a major religious tradition or nation and paid tribute to Moon (Bromley 1988: 339). In one legend followers have told about him, Moon's dominion over creation was recognized by the animal kingdom, and "whenever he went to the zoo, all the animals would run over to that part of the zoo" (Enroth 1977: 108). Moon was also renowned as a master fisherman. Followers recounted occasions when he threw a baitless hook into the water, whereupon bluefin tuna competed to jump on the messiah's hook. When members achieved personal successes on behalf of the movement, they often attributed it to Moon's "inspiration." Followers have reported that Moon possessed an uncanny ability to discern spiritual compatibility between individuals he chooses as partners for blessing. As one put it, "Hal could have searched for a million years and never have found someone with so many complementary points as Lynda" (Bromley and Shupe 1979b: 111).

In Moon's formulation of his hagiography, his messianic mission began on Easter morning in 1936 when Jesus Christ appeared to him and designated him as the successor to complete his spiritual mission, although Moon did not publicly reveal this vision for several years. However, in the decade following his vision Moon reports that he was continuously at war with Satan, who tried to dissuade him from accepting the messianic assignment. He was also in spiritual communication with God and several great religious figures (Jesus, Moses, Buddha) during this time; the revelations that he received formed the basis of Unificationist theology, the Divine Principle. Moon's unique ability to unlock hidden messages in the Bible also confirms his spiritual status. He asserts that, based on elaborate biblical calculations, the new messiah's birth date was between 1917 and 1930 and that he will come from a nation torn by struggle between godless communism and God-centered democracy, criteria that fit Moon and Korea at the time Moon began his mission.

The identity of the messiah is not predestined, however, as a messianic candidate must complete certain actions to fulfill the requirements for the messianic role. To actually become the messiah, a candidate must become an ideal individual by conquering sin, marrying and creating an ideal family, and assuming leadership for establishing an ideal world. Much of Moon's activity through his lifetime has been devoted to meeting these requirements. For example, Moon's wedding to Hak Jan Han and the couple's bearing of twelve children is interpreted within the Unificationist Movement as the messianic wedding that established the True Family that would serve as the foundation of a new, spiritually pure, God-centered lineage. Likewise the locations and number of his prolific speeches, the innumerable movement projects, and the growing number of blessing ceremonies he conducted were all part of building the Lord of the Second Advent persona (Bromley and Shupe 1979b). A recurring theme in Moon's hagiography is suffering and sacrifice. He reports continuous attempts by Satan to derail his messianic mission, and he has been persecuted by civil authorities who misunderstand or reject his mission. Despite all of these obstacles, in 1992 Moon formally announced that he and his wife together were the True Parents of humanity, the Lord of the Second Advent.

Moon has also sought to become an international figure who could mingle with world leaders and possessed the stature to foster world unification. He has twice addressed members of the US Congress, and his wife has given an address at the United Nations. Moon was invited to the White House by Richard Nixon, to the Kremlin by Mikhail Gorbachev, and to North Korea by Kim Il Sung. At the inauguration of the Uni- ficationists' most recent international organization (The Family Feder- ation for World Peace and Unification International) in 1996, a host of political notables (Gerald Ford, George Bush, Sr., Jack Kemp, Maureen Reagan), religious leaders (Coretta Scott King, Robert Schuller, Gary Bauer, Beverly La Haye, Ralph Reed), and celebrities (Bill Cosby, Pat Boone) were in attendance. When Moon celebrated his eightieth birthday in Seoul in 2000, former US vice president Dan Quayle, former British prime minister Edward Heath, and current Indonesian president Abdurrahman Wahid were present; former president Bill Clinton and current South Korean president Kim Dae-jung sent their congratulations. Scores of noteworthy intellectuals, religious leaders, and Nobel laureates have attended movement-sponsored conferences.

Moon has been skilled in building the Lord of the Second Advent persona. He has created an elaborate hagiography that identifies him specifically as the messianic candidate. He has spent his adult lifetime following the messianic course as he defines it. His followers have contributed ritualistic observances and apocryphal tales that confirm his status. He has avoided some common failings, such as date setting and specific prophecies, that are falsifiable. His marriage and children, visions, speeches, new projects, temporary taskforces, and public events have constituted spiritual victories that have an impact in the spirit world quite independently of any observable changes in the phenomenal realm. At the same time, the construction of a spiritually perfect messianic persona has yielded lofty moral and spiritual expectations and created the potential for numerous types of disconfirmation.

Concurrently with building of the Lord of the Second Advent persona, Moon has established an impressive corporate empire and a network of outreach groups that fund movement growth and further his messianic mission (Bromley 1985). The network of corporate enterprises dates back to the post-Korean War period and capitalized on the resurgence of economic activity in Korea following that conflict and the previous Japanese occupation. When Unificationism spread to Japan, the Japanese wing of the movement proved particularly adept at building businesses and generating revenue for the movement. The arrival of the movement in the United States was accompanied by the establishment of numerous additional business enterprises. Moon also expanded his economic interests into Latin America. The result is a far-flung corporate empire that has generated the economic resources to fund the Unificationist Movement. The economic interests are extremely diverse and include extensive real estate holdings, banks, manufacturing and mining firms, a variety of commercial fishing and seafood related enterprises, media and newspaper publishing companies, and novelty producers. Certainly the best known, although not profitable, of Unificationist businesses is the conservative Washington newspaper the *Washington Times*.

This network of corporations has been the primary economic base of the movement and has served to fund the equally diverse set of movement non-profit organizations that further Moon's messianic mission. Corporate profits are funneled to holding companies that then distribute the funds to the various movement outreach organizations. These organizations and projects have included the Unification Theological Seminary, interfaith and clergy groups, a series of anti-communist organizations, Moon's numerous tours and rallies, student and campus groups, and performing arts companies. Unificationism may be best known for the organizations that have sponsored conferences on world peace, the unity of religion and science, contemporary discussions of God, and academic and cultural exchange. Political, economic, governmental, media, religious, and academic leaders have been invited to these conferences as part of

Moon's mission to unify humanity around his messianic leadership. These outreach groups have been central to Moon's messianic mission and have provided the stage on which he has performed.

Just as in the case of the construction of a charismatic persona, the establishment of the corporate and outreach organization networks created a power base for Moon. Since the movement itself has not developed a substantial membership base, the various outreach groups have provided the movement with visibility and influence well out of proportion to its size. At the same time, the organizational network is spread across several continents and a number of nations. Each organization offers a resource and a power base not only for Moon but also for those who possess operational control of the organization. The organizational network thus constitutes a means of power building within the movement and constraining Moon's control, whether or not Moon's charismatic authority is directly challenged.

INNER-CIRCLE CHALLENGES

Throughout Unificationist history Moon has been adroit at maintaining centralized control over the movement. While he created a far-flung network of movement organizations, control over the movement's major decisions and direction has resided in his small group of inner-circle advisors. Being part of this group has been the litmus test of significant influence within the movement. Members of the inner circle not only provide Moon with advice and set movement policy but also serve as executive leaders of some organizations and members of boards of directors of others. While individual movement organizations typically are legally independent of one another and have their own managerial staff and boards of directors, many of these individuals are merely figureheads who serve at the pleasure of Moon and the inner circle leaders who actually direct those organizations. Moon has several means of controlling the inner circle. For the most part these individuals are longtime, Asian, male disciples with great personal loyalty to Moon. Further, the composition of the inner circle has changed somewhat over time as individuals gained or lost favor with Moon, reducing the likelihood of inner-circle alliances. Finally, Moon has promoted competition within this group. Each of the inner-circle leaders has his own agenda and seeks to increase his own power and influence by bringing proposals to Moon for support and funding. By setting up a competitive system and playing these individuals off against one another, Moon has prevented coalitions forming among this group. Infighting at this level also presumes Moon's status as arbiter and hence has strengthened his authority. With a vested interest in these arrangements, inner-circle leaders have protected Moon against charismatic disconfirmation. For example, when one major public relations event that was anticipated as a great victory for the movement turned into a disaster (Bromley 1988: 341), one of the inner circle assumed responsibility for allowing what was interpreted as a Satanic attack. However, Moon has not been impervious to challenges from the inner circle to his charismatic authority.

Moon has consistently preached that there is an active spirit world from which Unificationists can receive messages. Following the death of his son Heung Jin Nim, as a result of a 1984 automobile accident, "Moon proclaimed that his son had a new mission and that he was free to travel between his spirit world and our physical world" (Beverly 2005: 47). Several Unificationists, including a British woman and an American man, subsequently began to receive messages (Barker 1995: 226). The American man served as Heung Jin Nim's voice box, giving a number of public lectures in New York. However, neither of these individuals challenged Unificationist theology or Moon's charismatic authority. A more serious challenge arose from Cleopus Kundiona, a Zimbabwean convert to Unificationism. Kundiona too claimed to be the voice box of Heung Jin Nim. Moon brought Kundiona to the United States in 1987, asked him questions to which only his son would know the answer, authenticated Kundiona's responses, and initially embraced the messages Kundiona received from the spirit world. Moon's acceptance created instant legitimacy for the messages. Kundiona became a celebrity among Unificationists, moving to the edge of Moon's inner circle for a time. With Moon's blessing, Kundiona headed up a spiritual revival within the movement. Among Kundiona's messages was the revelation that the spiritual discipline of senior members of the church had diminished. Kundiona subsequently began publicly berating, and ultimately physically pummeling, some of the highest-ranking movement leaders, creating a very public humiliation. Inner-circle leader Bo Hi Pak was beaten so severely that he was hospitalized.

Ultimately, however, Kundiona began to presume that his status was independent of Moon's endorsement. He conducted a lecture tour in Europe and began publicly asserting that "he was the Lord of the Second Advent and that Reverend Moon was a precursor to his ministry" (Beverly 2005: 49). At this juncture, Moon simply withdrew his support for Kundiona and ordered him back to Africa, a directive that Kundiona disobeyed. Without Moon's backing, however, Kundiona quickly discovered the strength of Moon's charismatic authority. Mickler (2006: 169) reports that "There was a consensus among Unificationists that Heyng-jin Nim's (Rev. Moon's son) spirit had left the embodiment and an evil spirit had taken over." Kundiona's influence within the movement then plummeted. He ultimately formed his own small, schismatic group in Africa, but this posed no threat to Moon or the larger movement (Barker 1995). In the end, Moon absorbed the challenge and used Kundiona to consolidate his own power by demonstrating to senior leaders that they served at Moon's pleasure.

Moon's claim to be the True Parent of humanity, his theological assertion that sexual indiscretion was the source of original sin, his requirement that members remain celibate before blessing, and his assertion of the importance of the Blessed family as the building block of humanity's spiritual restoration have created extraordinarily high expectations regarding Moon's own sexual and parental conduct. He has therefore been vulnerable to charges of moral lapse. In fact, there is a long history of unsubstantiated sexual impropriety charges against Moon that have produced disillusionment among some Unificationists. As chronicled in *40 Years in America* (Inglis 2000: 540–1), "During the long course of what the movement regarded as misinformation or disinformation campaigns, many members accepted the public's view of reality and fell away." These charges resurfaced in the 1990s with allegations of ritual sexual activity involving Moon by an early disciple, Pak Chong-hwa, who later recanted the allegations. The most public and damaging allegations were made by Nansook Hong, who was married to Moon's son, Hyo Jin Moon. In her book *In the Shadow of the Moons* (1998), Hong casts doubt on the perfection of marriages blessed by Moon as she reveals physical and emotional abuse at the hands of Hyo Jin Moon, who engaged in a lifestyle of heavy drug/alcohol use, promiscuous sexual relations, and gambling. Further, she disdains the image of Moon and his wife as loving True Parents in her portrayal of the Moon household as profligate and imperious in its treatment of members who serve the True Parents at their East Garden estate. Most damaging in light of Moon's mandate that members remain celibate prior to marriage and his sacralization of the marriage relationship was her revelation that, in addition to a failed first marriage, Moon had fathered an illegitimate child earlier in his life. All of this constituted a direct challenge to the Lord of the Second Advent persona, particularly Moon's assertion that misdirected love constituted original sin, his insistence on celibacy, and his representation of himself and his wife as humanity's True Parents and the beginning of a God-connected lineage.

Movement spokespersons issued an ambiguous response to Hong's allegations in which they asserted that Moon had "never violated the Principle nor violated his responsibility as the messianic protector of True Love" (Introvigne 2000: 33). They went on to state that these events represented "three attempts to set up an ideal family" (Goodstein 1997) and that the complicated biblical and providential history precludes Moon being judged by conventional standards. The Moons also acknowledged Hyo Jin Moon's personal problems, but they declared that they were compelled to sacrifice their own family to carry out their messianic mission. The substantial negative publicity aside, the most telling indication of the erosion of Moon's charismatic standing was the defection of a number of long-standing members in response to Hong's portrait of the Moons and life at East Garden (Inglis 2000: 541). As one movement official put it, "Many members have been disappointed . . . It challenges some people's faith" (Lattin 2001).

BUREAUCRATIC INSURGENCY

Moon has encountered two types of bureaucratic challenges. The first is the institutionalization, compromise, and settling effects that bureaucratization represents. As the movement grew in size and complexity, the bureaucracy began to exert influence in that direction. Further, the bureaucracy sought to stabilize the movement by diminishing movement–societal conflict during the period when the Unification Church was regarded as the archetypal cult (Bromley and Shupe 1983). As Mickler (1987: 179) observes:

the idea has been that if the church is to gain a hearing and accomplish its objectives, it must become more reputable. Rhetorically, this has meant "contrition" from PR representatives for past mistakes and expressed willingness to work within the American denominational framework. Substantially, it has meant the emergence of "careerism" both within and outside of the church. The rationale here is that for church membership to have any appeal in the eighties, at least among the "baby-boom generation," it needs to take on a "young urban professional" or yuppie profile.

Moon has persistently combated this type of institutionalization of the Unificationist Movement. It was his inspiration and creativity that energized and directed the movement. With an entire world to be unified, the movement has no shortage of self-defined goals and challenges to meet. One way that Moon has resisted bureaucratization, therefore, has been constant changes of direction and endless new initiatives, a system that has functioned to maintain flexibility and charismatic direction. Further, through much of movement history he created projects and taskforces rather than formal organizations. Once the immediate task was accomplished, which often involved a spiritual rather than an empirical goal, the group was disbanded and members moved on to the next project. As a result, the size of the formal bureaucracy has been kept very limited so that it never has become a powerful entity in its own right. More formally, Moon refused to allow members to become ensconced in bureaucratic positions. He instituted a policy of rotating individuals out of their bureaucratic positions every three years, which effectively eliminated the possibility of bureaucratic careers (Bromley and Shupe 1979b: 135–6).

The second type of bureaucratic challenge became possible as a result of the Unificationist Movement's size, complexity, and geographic dispersion. The movement consists of local, regional, national, and international components as well as corporate, outreach, and administrative units. It has been possible, therefore, for various segments of the movement to achieve substantial self-sufficiency by developing economic and organizational autonomy within a geographic area. This has been a problem for Moon throughout Unificationist history as jealousies and conflicts have arisen within and between various factions of the movement. Going back to the very beginnings of the movement in America, the early missionaries formed independent organizations that cooperated only to a limited degree (Bromley and Shupe 1979b: 76–7). In the United States the East Coast and West Coast wings of the movement constituted the primary geographic divisions. Under the leadership of Mose Durst, the West Coast branch of Unificationism, known as the Oakland Family, moved toward organizational independence and showed signs of independent charismatic authority as well. This division came to constitute a threat to Moon's authority.

The Oakland Family developed a more humanistic version of the Divine Principle that attracted disaffected, countercultural youth. As Bromley and Shupe (1979b: 104) note:

Many elements of the complex maze of numerology, Old Testament history, Satanic threat in the form of international communism, and the need to work off indemnity were either dropped or radically altered. They were replaced by elements of humanistic psychology, reflecting the professional backgrounds of Mose Durst, who studied at the National Training Laboratories in Bethel, Maine, and of Kristina Morrison, his chief assistant, who had completed all but the thesis for her doctorate in psychology. For example, rather than speak of

Satan, Durst in his lectures dwelled on human alienation and failure to lovingly communicate sentiments as true sources of mankind's present dilemmas. Due to faulty socialization, inability to adequately comprehend and cope with the pressures of modern urban life, and a limited vision of what the brotherhood of man could mean, human beings (he claimed) now found their social and personal relationships fragmented and less than satisfying. Without a new principle of reciprocal loving around which people could center their actions and a new model of community based on such loving into which people could organize themselves, there was very little hope for humanity to end its most pressing social problems.

The emphasis was on self-actualization within the communally organized group and emphasis on building loving relationships. Durst (1982: 144) acknowledged this, stating: "I started groups like Project Volunteer and the Creative Community Project in an attempt to apply the wisdom of the world and humanistic psychology (I studied a little with Abraham Maslow) to the depth of *Divine Principle*." There was a pervasive sense in the West Coast wing of the movement that the Oakland Family was spiritually superior to the more doctrinaire East Coast wing. As one member put it, "Of course, it's considered that we in the Oakland Family are living the Principle most fully" (Bromley and Shupe 1979b: 140). It was precisely this attitude that infuriated other wings of the movement, which referred to the Oakland Family as "immature," "irresponsible," and "principalistic."

It was not simply theological differences that produced tension between the Oakland Family and the larger movement. Durst began to assume some of Moon's charismatic persona. Bromley comments that: "Indeed, at one time the Dursts were referred to as the 'True Parents of the West Coast' and many members referred to them as 'Omma' and 'Oppa' (father and mother), paralleling the terminology used to refer to Moon and his wife" (1988: 349). Under Durst's leadership the Oakland Family also developed an independent economic base by starting a string of small businesses, which gave this wing of the movement substantial financial independence from the larger movement. More significantly, the Oakland Family became the recruiting juggernaut of the movement, which increased its power within the movement. A high proportion of all Unificationist recruits came through the Oakland Family during the 1970s. Oakland Family recruitment was very important to the movement because membership turnover rates in Unificationism, as for most NRMs, was very high. (Barker 1988; Galanter 1989). This meant that the movement was dependent for growth on the Oakland Family since high defection rates were offset only by even higher recruitment rates.

Nonetheless, the Oakland Family's successes were a mixed blessing. Members recruited by the Oakland Family tended to be recruited quickly but also to exit quickly and so contributed to movement instability. Further, the encounter group style recruitment tactics employed by the Oakland family were a primary source of brainwashing charges leveled against the movement, creating a major public relations headache for movement leadership. For these reasons there was considerable ambivalence about the Oakland Family's methods.

Moon was obviously concerned by the challenges and problems that Oakland presented. As Bromley (1988: 350) notes, "For several years there was an ongoing battle between Moon and the Oakland Family, which at least publicly centered on theology and recruitment practices. Moon took frequent public slaps at the Dursts' revisionism." In one speech Moon rejected the interpretation of the Divine Principle proffered by Durst and his wife:

The Dursts come and say, "If we are going to do something, we want to do it joyfully." But I say there is no such thing as 100 percent joyfulness. If God is crying or on the verge of tears, how can Unification church members stay joyful? If mankind is on the brink of perishing, can any Unification Church member be cheerful and gleeful? Forget it.

Moon ordered changes in the Oakland Family and the Dursts resisted, asserting that their successes demonstrated the superiority of their methods. At several junctures there were veiled threats intimating that the Oakland Family might secede from the movement. Moon deftly resolved the emerging charismatic challenge, theological revisionism, and schismatic potential by appointing Durst as President of the Unification Church in America, with headquarters located in New York City (Bromley and Shupe 1979b: 97–108). Durst was given a more prestigious position within the movement, the Oakland Family's successes were legitimated, and the leadership group in the Oakland Family was broken up.

GRASSROOTS REBELLION

Unificationism in America grew rapidly through the mid-1970s, but the movement began to shrink in size by the end of the decade as recruitment rates declined while defection rates remained high. By the end of the 1970s the nature of movement membership had begun to change. The core consisted of longer-term members who were at least several years older, had invested a number of years in the movement, had been pledged to celibacy for a number of years while they engaged in movement building activities, and were looking forward to more settled adult family lives. There was also a continuing outflow of members who had joined earlier in the decade and now were exiting with varying degrees of ambivalence about their Unificationist careers.

Two developments were significant in moving those members who remained in the movement toward more settled lives. First, was the formation of the Home-Church; members were encouraged to leave church-organized communities and establish private family residences. Each family was encouraged to accept responsibility for 360 families in the surrounding community by serving their needs. The hope was that building people-to-people relationships would increase acceptance of the movement. Second, Moon began Blessing American couples in marriage. While the first Americans were Blessed in the 1970s, in 1982 the majority of the American membership was married in two Blessings totaling nearly 8,000 couples. At that point most members left full-time status and became married "house church" members with private residences and traditional careers. Blessings that created individual family units and the shift from communal to individual household organization produced more stable lives for individual members but also increased their resistance to returning to the former total-commitment lifestyle.

For those members who remained there were various reasons to chafe under movement leadership. Women were restive under what was essentially a male hierarchy (Barker 1983; James 1983) that offered them very traditional domestic lives and little opportunity for advancement within the movement. Seminarians, who represented the more liberal wing of the movement, banded together to protest leadership authoritarianism. Two grassroots newsletters, *Our Network* and the *Round Table*, became discussion forums for various sources of discontent.

One of the recurrent issues for American members was movement domination by Asian leaders. As Beverly comments (2005: 177):

Most members willingly accepted criticism and denunciations from Rev. Moon. Nevertheless, some felt that tribalization, particularly the universalization of Korean cultural norms, was an internal peril facing the UCM [Unification Church Movement]. The movement's East Asian leadership relied on Western members to interface with officials, and leadership of its major cultural affiliates was largely vested in Western intellectuals or professionals. However, these were strategic concessions that the movement's leadership was convinced they would not have to make once the center of global civilization shifted to the Korean peninsula. Apart from the universalization of Korean cultural patterns, heavy accretions of shamanistic ritual practices, numerology, and cosmic declarations were off-putting for some, especially in the West. . . Many of them concluded that the movement was too deviant, too Korean, or too Japanese.

One member who ultimately defected from the movement listed a number of traits that were particularly frustrating to American members: male superiority, emphasizing loyalty over honesty, a preference for autocratic over democratic rule, emphasizing saving face and following directions (whether right or wrong), making business decisions hastily without adequate research and then blaming failure on lack of faith, a high value on protocol, and disrespect for analytical or critical thinking (Bromley 1988: 347).

Another source of tension was periodic calls to leave settled lives and renew full-time commitments to the movement. Probably the most significant of these was the mobilization of blessed wives which extended for a three-year period and was intended to rejuvenate the UM's anemic recruitment rates. Members were given quotas of "spiritual children" (converts) which had to be achieved before family formation could begin. Another four-month mobilization was declared in 1986 for a CAUSA signature drive. These mobilizations disrupted settled family and work lives and produced considerable controversy and resistance within the movement. Leaders responded to the apathy and resistance by expelling non-complying individuals who still lived in the movement's communal residences in New York. Some of these members countered by simply finding private residences and employment, with the result that they became more distant from and independent of the movement. Among those who did comply with the directive, many found that times had indeed changed. As one member put it (Publius 1986: 2):

the last three years of IOWC's, emergencies and mobilizations have demanded of us that we return to the status of "interchangeable Moon units," ready to be sent anywhere for anything. While we tried to comply out of personal loyalty to Father, many of us found things were very different than the early 70's. The eschatological sense was gone and the hippies in search of spiritual truth had been replaced with a generation of yuppies in search of success. While a number of ministers are "positive" and "concerned about communism" through CAUSA, few if any are leading their churches to accept Father as Messiah.

While some members responded to the movement's directives, many others responded by ignoring the call for mobilization, voluntarily moving to the margins of the movement, accepting marginalization by the movement, locating niches in the movement where their commitments matched movement expectations, or exiting the movement entirely.

This combination of grassroots resistance, non-response, and apathy eroded Moon's capacity to carry out his messianic agenda. There was, however, a more hostile response from some of those who chose to exit the movement. Members who left the movement during the latter years of the 1970s and the early 1980s found a ready audience for "atrocity story" accounts of the experiences in Unificationism (Bromley and Shupe 1979a). Numerous book-length accounts were published with titles such as *Crazy for God* (Edwards 1979), *Hostage to Heaven* (Underwood 1979), *Moonstruck: A Memoir of My Life in a Cult* (Wood 1979), *Heavenly Deception* (Elkins 1980), *Escape from the Moonies* (Swatland and Swatland 1982), and *The Dark Side of the Moonies* (Heftmann 1982). There were many more books and newspaper and magazine articles, mostly appearing in family-oriented publications (Durham 1981; Kemperman 1981). The themes commonly found in these publications were brainwashing, alleging that conversions to Unificationism were manipulated and not authentic; the break-up of family ties and replacement of the natural family by the movement; political-legal violations, alleging that Unificationism was thinly veiled economic or political adventurism. While these allegations did not have a great deal of impact on core movement members, they significantly tarnished Moon's persona as spiritual leader turning wayward youth to a religious path, promoting family values, and committed to spiritual rather than material ends. These attacks virtually eliminated any hope that he would become a respected and unifying religious figure in American society.

CONCLUSIONS

Leadership in NRMs during the first generation typically is founded on charismatic authority but comes to involve organizational leadership as well, as the movement develops. The combination of charismatic and organizational leadership produces highly centralized authority because it incorporates both dimensions. However, each form of authority at once constitutes a power base and a source of vulnerability. The more expansive the development of a charismatic persona and charismatic authority are, the more vulnerable the leader becomes to persona disconfirmation. The more elaborate and differentiated the organizational structure of the movement is, the more opportunities there are for empire building within the movement. Because both charismatic and organizational authority are in the process of being constructed, power relationships at the charismatic leadership, organizational leadership, and grassroots membership levels are constantly being negotiated. Movements are not as monolithic as they appear, and ongoing tension and conflict are the rule rather than the exception.

The Unificationist Movement nicely illustrates this view of NRM development. There is little doubt that Sun Myung Moon is a dominating figure in the movement. At the same time, he has been challenged by inner-circle members, administrative organizations, factions within the movement, grassroots members, and former members. While schisms to date have been minor, Moon has experienced serious challenges to his power, his ability to mobilize members and unilaterally direct the movement, and his charismatic persona. The future may be fraught with even more danger to movement solidity. A clear successor to Moon has not yet been designated. Moon's corporate management skills have allowed the movement to exercise influence well beyond what might be expected from a relatively small movement, and there are significant tensions between the Korean, Japanese, and American wings of the movement. There would appear to be real potential for separation between both the economic and religious components of the movement and the various national wings of the movement. The ultimate test of Moon's visionary leadership, then, is yet to be determined: how successfully he prepares Unificationism for its post-charismatic future.

REFERENCES

Barker, Eileen. 1983. "Doing Love: Tensions in the Ideal Family." In Gene James (ed.), *The Family and the Unification Church* (pp. 35–52). New York: Rose of Sharon Press.

1988. "Defection from the Unification Church: Some Statistics and Distinctions." In David G. Bromley (ed.), *Falling from the Faith: Causes and Consequences of Religious Apostasy* (pp. 166–84). Newbury Park, CA: Sage.

1995. "The Unification Church." In Timothy Miller (ed.), *America's Alternative Religions* (pp. 223–30). Albany: State University of New York Press.

Beverly, James. 2005. "Spirit Revelation and the Unification Church." In James R. Lewis and Jesper Aagaard Petersen (eds.), *Controversial New Religions* (pp. 43–60). New York: Oxford University Press.

Bromley, David G. 1985. "The Economic Structure of the Unificationist Movement." *Journal for the Scientific Study of Religion* 24: 253–74.

1988. "Economic Structure and Charismatic Leadership in the Unification Church." In James T. Richardson (ed.), *Money and Power in the New Religions* (pp. 335–64). Lewiston, NY: Edwin Mellen Press.

Forthcoming. "Making Sense of Scientology: Prophetic Contractual Religion." In James R. Lewis (ed.), *Scientology*. New York: Oxford University Press.

Bromley, David G. and Rachel Bobbitt. 2006. "Challenges to Charismatic Leadership." Paper presented at the annual meeting of the American Academy of Religion, Washington, DC, November.

Bromley, David G. and Anson Shupe. 1979a. "Atrocity Tales, the Unification Church, and the Social Construction of Evil." *Journal of Communication* 29: 42–53.

1979b. *"Moonies" in America: Cult, Church, and Crusade.* Beverley Hills, CA: Sage.

1983. "The Archetypal Cult: Conflict and the Social Construction of Deviance." In Gene James, ed., *The Family and the Unification Church* (pp. 1–22). New York: Rose of Sharon Press.

Dawson, Lorne. 2002. "Crises of Charismatic Legitimacy and Violent Behavior in New Religious Movements." In David G. Bromley and J. Gordon Melton (eds.), *Cults, Religion and Violence* (pp. 80–101). New York: Cambridge University Press.

Durham, Deanna. 1981. *Life among the Moonies: Three Years in the Unification Church.* Plainfield, NJ: Logos International.

Durst, Mose. 1982. "Life in the Northern California Church." In Richard Quebedeaux, ed., *Lifestyle: Conversations with Members of the Unification Church* (pp. 141–62). New York: Rose of Sharon Press.

Edwards, Christopher. 1979. *Crazy for God.* Englewood Cliffs, NJ: Prentice Hall.

Elkins, Chris. 1980. *Heavenly Deception.* Wheaton, IL: Tyndale House.

Enroth, Ronald. 1977. *Youth, Brainwashing and the Extremist Cults.* Kentwood, MI: Zondervan.

Galanter, Marc. 1989. *Cults: Faith, Healing, and Coercion.* New York: Oxford University Press.

Goodstein, Laurie. 1997. "35,000 Couples Are Invited to a Blessing by Rev. Moon." *New York Times,* November 28.

Heftmann, Erica. 1982. *The Dark Side of the Moonies.* Harmondsworth: Penguin.

Hong, Nansook. 1998. *In the Shadow of the Moons: My Life in the Reverend Sun Myung Moon's Family.* Boston: Little Brown.

Inglis, Michael (ed.). 2000. *40 Years in America: An Intimate History of the Unification Movement, 1959–1999.* New York: HSA Publications.

Introvigne, Massimo. 2000. *The Unification Church.* Salt Lake City: Signature Books.

James, Gene (ed.). 1983. *The Family and the Unification Church.* New York: Rose of Sharon Press.

Katz, Jack. 1975. "Essences as Moral Identities: Verifiability and Responsibility in Imputations of Deviance and Charisma." *American Journal of Sociology* 80: 1369–90.

Kemperman, Steve. 1981. *Lord of the Second Advent.* Ventura, CA: Regal Books.

Kim, David. 1977. *Day of Hope,* 2 vols. New York: Unification Church.

Lattin, Don. 2001. "Continuation of the Church Will Fall to Moon's Son." *San Francisco Chronicle,* February 11.

Mickler, Michael. 1987. "Future Prospects of the Unification Church." In David G. Bromley and Phillip Hammond (eds.), *The Future of New Religious Movements* (pp. 175–86). Macon, GA: Mercer University Press.

2006. "The Unification Church/Movement in the United States." In Eugene Gallagher and W. Michael Ashcraft (eds.), *Introduction to New and Alternative Religions in America: Asian Traditions* (vol. IV, pp. 158–84). Westport, CT: Greenwood.

Moon, Sun Myung. 1983. "New Impetus for the Providence in America." *Today's World* 4 (February): 23–5.

Publius. 1986. "Interchangeable Moon Units?" *The Round Table* (March): 2–3.

Swatland, Susan and Anne Swatland. 1982. *Escape from the Moonies*. London: New English Library.

Underwood, Barbara and Betty Underwood. 1979. *Hostage to Heaven*. New York: Clarkson N. Potter.

Weber, Max. 1964. *The Theory of Social and Economic Organization*. Trans. by A. M. Henderson and Talcott Parsons. New York: The Free Press.

Wood, Allen Tate. 1979. *Moonstruck: A Memoir of My Life in a Cult*. New York: William Morrow.

Zald, Mayer and Michael Berger. 1978. "Social Movements in Organizations: Coup d'Etat, Insurgency, and Mass Movements." *American Journal of Sociology* 83: 823–61.

CHAPTER 7

Persecution and schismogenesis: how a penitential crisis over mass apostasy facilitated the triumph of Catholic Christianity in the Roman empire

Joseph M. Bryant

Late in the year 249 CE, an extraordinary imperial directive was despatched throughout the extended domains of the Roman world.[1] Monitored sacrifices to the gods were to be made by the empire's inhabitants, all of whom – excepting the Jews, whose ancestral monotheism enjoyed legal recognition – were to perform this act of devotional loyalty at their local temples. Commissions were empowered to oversee and record the mandated compliance, with census and tax rolls furnishing controls over identity. Specified times were announced for the stipulated observances, and signed certificates were issued to confirm the loyalty of all dutiful subjects. Here, from the preserving sands of Egypt, is one of forty-six surviving papyrus specimens, all of which were composed in a standardized petitionary form:

[*1st Hand*] To those superintending the sacrifices. From Aurelia Charis of the village of Theadelphia. I have always and continuously sacrificed and shown piety to the gods, and now in your presence and in accordance with the orders given, I have poured a libation, made sacrifice, and partaken of the sacred victims. I request you certify this for me. Prosperity to you. [*2nd Hand*] We, Aurelius Serenus and Aurelius Hermas, saw you sacrificing.

[*1st Hand*] The year one of the Emperor Caesar Gaius Messius Quintus Trajanus Decius Pius Felix Augustus, Payni 22 (= June 16, 250).[2]

[1] I would like to thank Roger Beck, Andreas Bendlin, David Frankfurter, and Rod Nelson for helpful commentary on earlier versions of this chapter, and Brent Shaw and Martin Wallraff for clarifying several issues for me in correspondence. Thanks also to Timothy Barnes, who has done much to guide my interest in this fascinating field of inquiry. Prior Fellowship from the Social Sciences and Humanities Research Council of Canada is gratefully acknowledged.
[2] This is *libellus* 26, of the forty-one certificates presented in the original Greek and translated by Knipfing (1923). Five additional *libelli* have since come to light. I have slightly modified the translation for greater literalness.

From its timing and manifest cultural logic, the purpose of this call for empire-wide sacrifice is not difficult to establish. Coming in the midst of a deepening and many-sided crisis in the affairs of empire – barbarian encroachments, Persian advances in the east, declining agricultural productivity and resulting food shortages, mounting fiscal strains and inflation, collapsing discipline within the army, and ensuing political disorders, as a spate of pretenders to the imperial crown sparked regional mutinies and rebellions that drained resources and undermined effective governance – this decree of the emperor Decius (himself a successful usurper) was a desperate bid to restore the privileged "favor of the gods," the *pax deorum* that had sponsored and sustained Rome's *imperium* from its inception. But why had the ancestral deities withdrawn their tutelary support? What was the transgressive source of divine disfavor?[3]

The certificates of compliance appear to provide a transparent disclosure, seeing as the citizenry had been tasked with a comprehensive affirmation of their loyalty. For in addition to the notarized act of compulsory sacrifice, every dutiful subject was required to attest that he or she had "always" (*aei*) and "continuously" (*diatelein*) offered customary devotion in the past. The Decian decree, in other words, was an instrument to draw out, identify, and discipline religious deviants. In light of the pragmatic inclusiveness of Roman polytheism, and the ease with which its expansive sacred canopy provided legitimacy to a wide range of cultic practices, the deviants in question could only have been those who offended the gods willfully, through perverse refusal of their rightful worship. The suspected transgressors in this regard – already known and widely reviled – were members of the Christian *superstitio*, an illegal association comprised of "degenerates" and "traitors" to religion and empire who, as Tacitus famously inferred, were animated by their "hatred of the human race."[4]

---

[3] For an overview on widespread and growing concern that a once stable and prosperous world was now reeling toward collapse and violent anarchy, see Alföldy (1974).

[4] That the Decian edict carried persecutorial intent has been questioned by some scholars, and likewise the inference that Christians were the primary target. But if Decius had simply called for a mass expression of ritual piety in a time of troubles, as these skeptics suggest, why the pointed requirement of establishing an "orthopractic past," through a recorded declaration that devotional loyalty to the gods had been lifelong and continuous? One might usefully recall the inquisitorial formula of the McCarthy hearings: "Are you now, or have you ever been, a member of the Communist Party?" The retrospective reach of the Decian decree is, I submit, decisive for its intended disciplinary objectives. Note, too, that "second arrests" for suspected Christians are attested in the episcopal correspondence, a clear confirmation that detection and apprehension were central to the imperial policy. As for the perceived *odio humani generis* of the Christians, see Tacitus, *Annals* XV.44. A valuable survey on the generally negative and hostile views that greeted the new faith – fully acknowledged by Christians themselves – is offered by Wilken (1984).

Sporadic persecutions of the Christian "depravity" had occurred under previous emperors, often following upon public disturbances or occasional riots by those enraged at the presence of Christian "atheists" within their midst. Decius, a traditionalist in all matters, now resolved on more deliberate measures. Judicial precedent had established that for self-declared Christians, or those denounced as such, opportunity would be granted to either renounce or disprove their adherence in the illegal cult. As Christian "perversity" and "madness" were known to turn on their demonizing denunciation of traditional polytheism and its cultic conventions, a simple act of sacrifice to the gods before a presiding magistrate served as the standard arbitrating mechanism.[5] By extending the application of this "sacrifice test" to the citizenry at large, Decius and his advisors must have anticipated that the edict would strike a debilitating blow against the offending movement. The novel and binding requirement to obtain notarized certificates could be expected to generate immense pressures upon the Christian faithful to offer the mandated sacrifices, thereby fomenting disorders and mass apostasy within the ranks. In turn, the *libelli* system would permit a more targeted and efficient policing action in the apprehension of militant or fanatical recusants, against whom the imperial power could then deploy its punitive arsenal of tortures, confiscations of property, imprisonment, exile, consignments to forced labor or sexual slavery, and, whenever appropriate, the ultimate sanction, whether by summary execution or the staged spectacle of fatal torments in the arena.

As the implementation and enforcement of his decree rolled across the provinces, the emperor must have been greatly pleased. Several prominent leaders of the renegade movement were quickly netted and executed; scores of others were imprisoned. More welcome still would have been incoming reports that vast numbers of Christians had complied with the injunction to sacrifice, thus implicitly abandoning their subversive allegiance to the "crucified criminal" they had hitherto worshiped as a "lord and savior" of their "future kingdom." Martyrdoms were surprisingly few; flight was commonplace. Everywhere the church communities were broken and in disarray. Having mobilized to the task, the Roman state had demonstrated a formidable capacity to create apostates.

How the situation might have unfolded had Decius remained in power – he and his son were killed during a Balkan campaign against

---

[5] The legal aspects and juridical procedures of persecution are authoritatively examined by G. E. M. de Ste. Croix (1963, 2006) and T. D. Barnes (1968).

invading Goths in the summer of 251 – is difficult to specify, though the late emperor had displayed remarkable organizational skills and a firm determination to restore Roman discipline in matters military and religious. How historically ironic, then, that his calculated strike against the Christian cult – so successful in forcing defections and in breaching its most sacred principles of identity and commitment – precipitated a schismatic rupture within the Church that would greatly enhance its prospects for eventual triumph in the reign of Constantine.

SALVATION BELIEFS, BOUNDARY MAINTENANCE, AND PENITENTIAL PRACTICE IN THE EARLY CHURCH

Christian sources are unambiguous in describing the devastation that the Decian persecution wrought upon church communities across the empire, its destructive course extending from Spain, Gaul, Italy, and North Africa in the Latin-speaking west, on through Egypt, Palestine, Syria, Asia Minor, Pontus, Cappadocia, and Armenia in the Greek-speaking east. Notwithstanding that the sin of idolatry was universally regarded as the most serious offense a Christian could commit – a heinous betrayal that forfeited not only membership in the sacred body of God's elect, but salvation in the life to come – massive numbers of fearful Christians made their way to the temples, there to deny their Savior through self-polluting acts of sacrifice, pouring libations to the demons they had been pledged to combat rather than venerate. In some places, bishops led their entire flocks to the smoking and blood-drenched altars, jeered upon and cheered by the pagan crowds who thronged in attendance. Countless others hit upon the ploy of purchasing bogus certificates of compliance from corrupt officials. Flight offered a third option, and here the clerical ranks were notoriously prominent, as scores of bishops, presbyters, and deacons chose discretion over the glorious martyrdom their own pastoral exhortations had repeatedly encouraged.

As the intensity of the persecution began to abate – God's avenging hand having struck down its hell-born sponsor – church leaders confronted the daunting task of rebuilding their shattered communities. Two challenges were to prove immensely difficult, and momentously divisive. Given that so many of the Lord's ministers had fled or openly apostatized, how might clerical order and discipline be restored in the wake of so scandalous a capitulation? And, correspondingly, what disciplinary measures were appropriate to deal with the overwhelming numbers of *lapsi*, those "fallen" or "lapsed" members of the Church who had denied their Savior, through either the abominable act of sacrifice or the damning deceit of procuring the illegal certificates of idolatrous compliance? In working toward a resolution of this crisis, church leaders would find themselves in a bitter struggle over the very meaning of Christian identity and the nature and purpose of the Church as a salvific body.

As new standards and policies were proposed to accommodate the disheartening reality that so many in the *militia Christi* had "broken ranks" under Satan's persecuting assault, familiar lines of internal tension and opposition began to reappear. Founded upon expectations of a pending eschatological deliverance, the nascent Christian movement had experienced recurring disputes over the terms of membership within its self-proclaimed community of the "pure and holy." The salvation promise that keyed the Church's conversionist program provided the cognitive and emotive frames for early Christian identity and self-understanding, which in turn established the parameters of normative practice. As the baptismal ritual of initiation functioned simultaneously as a purification rite, cleansing the convert of all past offenses and bestowing the indwelling gift of God's Holy Spirit, the "reborn" Christian was called to exacting standards of moral probity. Through the miraculous "washing of regeneration" (*loutrou palingenesias*), Christians were spiritually empowered to resist the temptations of Satan and his demonic minions, their continued faith in God's promise freeing them from "sin's dominion" (Romans 6.2; Ephesians 2.1; 1 Peter 2.24). Minor failings and transgressions were more tolerantly recognized – baptism providing only the "first fruits" of the full harvest of salvation to come – and the repentance and forgiveness motifs that figured so prominently in the Gospel message were duly invoked in extending pastoral care to those whose human frailties had issued in renewed sinning. But crucial specificities were still lacking. Where, it was asked, should the line of restorative indulgence be drawn? Were there limits beyond which sinful conduct merited expulsion from the ranks of the saved?

On these questions the leaders of the Christian movement had long disagreed, as laxists, moderates, and rigorists disputed the meaning and intent of the scriptural texts that informed their shared worldview, and invoked differing exemplars of practice from the unfolding history of ecclesiastical governance and lay piety to reinforce their penitential and pastoral preferences. One categorical distinction that commanded widespread agreement from early on, however, marked off lesser or "venial" sins, like dishonesty, drunkenness, greed, or vanity, from the major or "mortal" sins, so-called because these were abominations so heinous that the bestowed Spirit of God departed from the soul of the perpetrator, thus voiding the baptismal redemption and rendering the offender spiritually "dead unto Christ." These unpardonable "sins against the Spirit" were judged to have been authoritatively identified in the famous Jerusalem ruling of 49 CE, as recorded in Luke's Acts of the Apostles (15.28–9), which arose out of controversies entailed in carrying Christ's message to non-Jews. According to the terms of this Apostolic Decree, Gentile converts were to be released from the necessity of circumcision, but strictly held to three minimal requirements: abstention from "meats offered to idols" (idolatry or apostasy), from "blood and things strangled" (a dietary restriction that was also thought to refer to murder), and from "fornication" (any form of sexual intercourse outside the marriage bond).

A more immediately pressing dispute concerned the wider issue of post-baptismal sins generally. Having been once purified and spiritually empowered by the baptismal waters, what were the consequences of subsequent sinning? Should the churches continue to tolerate the polluting presence of recidivist offenders in their midst? Was eternal salvation jeopardized or lost upon the accumulation of transgressions of venial classification? Within most communities, Paul's injunction to shine forth as "a glorious congregation, having neither spot nor wrinkle nor any such thing, but holy and without blemish" (Ephesians 5.27) appears to have remained binding. Wayward members were thus duly excommunicated whenever their tearful confessions before the faithful and attending acts of penitence – prayers, fasting, almsgiving – were rendered nugatory by continued sinning. As adopted "children of God" filled with divine grace (Romans 8.14–17), believers were to regard their own persons as living "temples of Christ," ever mindful of the need to remain "without spot and blameless" in anticipation of the imminent Second Coming of their Savior and the eschatological Day of Judgment (1 Corinthians 3.16–17; 2 Corinthians 6.14; Romans 12.1–2). So even where traditional atonement practices for the lesser category of sins were deemed sufficient for continued communion within the Church, these faults and failings nonetheless placed the offending member in an ambiguous state, seeing as mainstream belief did not yet countenance any restoration to the pristine sanctity that had been bestowed in the baptismal cleansing.

Maintaining virtuoso standards of purity and holiness became increasingly difficult as the ranks of the faithful were augmented by less zealous converts, and as doubts and anxieties were generated by continuing delays in their Redeemer's anticipated return. Early second-century Christian writings disclose signs of mounting internal strains, as "double-minded" believers were accused of taking up anew the worldly vanities and vices they had renounced at conversion, while other tainted members despaired over their possible salvation. To address this discrediting slippage between the baptismal promise and the reality of continued sinning, penitential practices were adjusted accordingly, and a "second remission" of sins was gradually introduced and adopted: initially as a special "jubilee" period of restored grace for all those displaying heartfelt repentance (*c.*130), and then as a formal sacrament of penance (*c.*190), which offered a second, but now final, "back-up" cleansing to remove the venial sins that had accumulated since baptism. Though rigorist factions opposed this lowering of standards, mainstream churches found ways to reconcile the Gospel ideals of personal holiness with a more generous understanding of the Church's powers of forgiveness, citing the many scriptural passages that called for mercy and encouraged repentance and confidence in God's love for his elect.[6]

A more controversial and disruptive penitential reform was to follow. Several prominent bishops, notably Callistus of Rome (217–22) and Agrippinus of Carthage (*fl.*220), chose to modify radically the traditional distinction between venial and mortal sins, through rulings that extended priestly powers of absolution to those who repented of fornication and adultery. This policy deepened existing antagonisms and promptly led to new schismatic ruptures – most famously in Rome, where the learned presbyter Hippolytus (*c.*170–235) was elected counter-bishop. His empassioned denunciation of his laxist rival speaks to the contested transformation underway, as a movement that had been founded on exacting purity demands and promises of spiritual empowerment was now shifting the locus of holiness to the sacramental apparatus of the Church itself:

This imposter [Callistus] . . . established a school in antagonism to the teachings of the Church. He was the first to think up a way of colluding with the sinful pleasures of men, saying to all that he himself would remit their sins . . . And those hearing him, overjoyed with his tenets, continue deluding themselves and many others, and crowds stream into his school. So his followers multiply, and they exult in throngs attending for the sake of pleasures that Christ did not permit. For in contempt of Him, they forbid no kind of sin, alleging that Christ will remit the offenses they have approved of. (*Refutation of All Heresies*, 9.12.20–6)[7]

---

[6] I explore these developments more fully in two earlier publications (1993; 1998).
[7] My translation is based on the critical edition of the original Greek text, edited by Miroslav Marcovich, *Hippolytus: Refutatio Omnium Haeresium* (Berlin: Walter de Gruyter, 1986).

It was against this already fractious and roiling internal conflict over Christian identity and purpose that the Decian persecution would strike, its enforced demand to render sacrifice to the gods providing the catalyst for a historically decisive splitting of the Church into opposing camps, setting puritan traditionalists against pragmatic moderates.

THE CRISIS OF THE LAPSED AND THE ONSET
OF THE NOVATIANIST SCHISM OF THE *KATHAROI*

Put to test by a Roman state now intent on breaking an illegal *superstitio* that had alienated the empire's patron deities, overwhelming numbers of Christians opted to violate their own sacred commandment against idolatry. Convulsed and shattered by apostasy on so staggering a scale – across all provinces and regions, in rural backwaters as well as major cities – the churches of Christ were thrown into a comprehensive crisis, ideological and organizational. For a movement largely defined and driven by its distinctive worldview, the manifest inability of so many believers to uphold the most binding principles of the faith constituted a shameful disconfirmation of the Christian promise of spiritual empowerment. All the many nucleated congregations, hitherto sustained by strong bonds of in-group solidarity and welfare support, along with mutually reinforcing displays of pneumatic enthusiasm and shared assumptions of divine election, were now internally riven by the mass defections that had occurred. Clerics who had apostatized could command no authority, while those who had gone into hiding were assailed for having abandoned their flocks in a time of greatest need. Demoralization ran deep, disorder rampant. Factional alignments were not slow in staking out their positions: a fatefully divisive contest for the future of Christianity had begun.

The drama that was to unfold is best characterized and comprehended in reference to the anthropological concept of *schismogenesis*, which pertains to situations wherein rivalrous groups develop their own identities and objectives through a dialectical process of polarizing opposition and separation.[8] As points of in-group tension become manifest, the emergent factions move increasingly toward disequilibrium, each side defining and valorizing their own respective positions through an intensifying deprecation and negation of the practices and principles espoused by the

---

[8] The concept was first introduced by Gregory Bateson (1935) for purposes of explicating the structural and cultural dynamics of intra-group differentiation and separation.

other – a process Sahlins has instructively styled "deviation amplification" (2000: 340). A schismogenic dynamic, in short, is one that progressively transforms the engaged parties into "structural antitypes," as each side organizes itself as "the inverse of the other" (Sahlins 2004: 69). Having started from a shared or common orientation, the contending factions are inexorably driven into providing principled rationales or justifications for their disagreements; in the course of placing excessive and pointed emphasis on those differences that form the grounds of disputation, contrapositional identity-markers come to the fore. Failing mediation or compromise, the escalating hostilities will issue in fissiparous rupture and the formation of autonomous or independent communities.

The factional rift within Christianity that was precipitated by the Decian persecution would follow a schismogenic pattern to a striking degree, as disagreements over the appropriate pastoral response to the crisis of widespread apostasy became progressively sharper at each stage in the dispute. Remarkably, the arguments in these contested proceedings can be followed quite closely, owing to the survival of a significant portion of the episcopal correspondence and pamphleteering that served as the principal communicative instrument in the formulation of policy and in the making and breaking of alliances. The *Ecclesiastical History* of bishop Eusebius of Caesarea (*c.*260–340) contains excerpts from many of these sources; but the most detailed and revealing evidence is to be found in the extensive corpus of writings associated with one of the key participants in the dispute: the metropolitan bishop of the African Church, Cyprian of Carthage (248–258). In addition to his two treatises on the unfolding crisis, *On the Lapsed* and *On the Unity of the Church*, an invaluable collection of eighty-two epistles has survived under his name, dating from the onset of persecution (early 250) and continuing up to Cyprian's martyrdom during the persecution of Valerian (summer 258). These letters – written to and from major bishops and other clerical leaders across the empire – were not only "history-making" in their consequences; they inscribe the turbulent flow of events in a "real-time" sequence. Disclosed therein is a sociological dialectic of reform and reaction, as the tactical adjustments in policy and practice that were called for by the urgency of circumstance also stoked the in-group factionalism that would issue in schismatic rupture.[9]

---

[9] All quoted materials from the Cyprianic epistolary corpus are from G. W. Clarke's magisterial four-volume set, *The Letters of St. Cyprian of Carthage* (Mahwah, NJ: Paulist Press, 1984–89).

Enforcement of the Decian edict appears to have been effective at the outset. Prominent leaders were arrested and large numbers of Christians, lay and clerical, either complied with the sacrilegious order to sacrifice or found ways to procure the required certificates. Of those who, upon arrest, remained faithful to their salvation pledge, sentences of incarceration typically followed; protracted failure to "come to one's senses" was commonly met by tortures of the mangling, scraping, and burning variety. In some places Christian women were threatened with and sometimes condemned to brothel slavery – perhaps in awareness of the illegal cult's peculiar emphasis on virginity and sexual renunciation. Though Christian idolaters, apostates, and fugitives greatly outnumbered these heroic "confessors," the ranks of the "glorious martyrs" did gain appreciable increase. In the absence of reliable figures, any attempted "body count" can only be impressionistic (in the low hundreds?). But it does appear that the hardships and unsanitary conditions of the prisons and mines claimed more victims, cumulatively, than did the empire's innumerable sporting arenas – the loci of those staged dramas so vividly represented in the many *Acta Martyrum* that Christians dutifully composed, both to encourage the faithful and to commemorate the spiritual victories that heralded the advent of God's promised kingdom.

The opening exchange of communiqués between Rome and Carthage – the two most important sees in the west – allows entry into the shock and despair that struck the churches across the empire upon enactment of the edict. Brethren who have confessed their faith are languishing in dark prisons, subject to ongoing torture and threats of impending execution. Clerical governance has all but collapsed, owing to widespread flight and open apostasy. Congregations everywhere have been broken by the overwhelming numbers of believers who have failed to stand firm, their eternal salvation now forfeited by the polluting sacrifices they have made or the deceits of idolatrous compliance they have faithlessly resorted to. Though some of these "lapsed" have returned to their former lives of pagan corruption, the vast majority are now clamoring for forgiveness and readmission, despite the enormity of their recent crimes. The persecution – viewed in cosmic terms as a struggle between the divine and the demonic – rages on.

From his place of refuge, bishop Cyprian sends letters to his clergy, urging them to provide support and funding for those imprisoned and for all the poor and indigent who have remained faithful. To avoid rousing further hatred and attention, brethren are advised to refrain from attending on the confessors in conspicuous numbers, and priests should minister to them with discretion (*Epistles* 5 and 7, March 250). He sends another letter to the Carthaginian confessors – men, women, and children – exhorting them to persevere for "the crown of martyrdom," thinking not of their present torments but on the immortality they have secured, and the martyr's privilege to pass directly and immediately to heaven, where they will reign and sit with the Lord in pending judgment upon this corrupted world (*Ep.* 6).

A letter arrives for the clergy of Carthage in early summer, sent by the clergy in Rome, now governing collectively following the martyrdom of their pope. The missive is crude in style, brusque in tone; it carries thinly veiled censure of the fugitive bishop of Carthage, while praising the "good shepherds" who courageously tend to his vulnerable flock. The Roman congregations, too, have suffered idolatrous desertions, but there are also loyal brethren now bound in chains giving glory to God. As the contest has only just begun, it is imperative that the fallen everywhere be encouraged to rise again for renewed battle, and to that end the lapsed must be called to repent their sacrilegious crime. In a critical ruling, the Roman clergy enjoin that all the apostates be "exhorted to penance, in the hopes that somehow they may be able to win pardon from Him who is able to bestow it" (*Ep.* 8.2.3). Those who are ill and approaching death – many Christians having braved tortures before apostatizing – should be given the departing comfort of a Eucharistic communion, conditional upon demonstration of heartfelt penitence. Most pointedly, the lapsed must be made to understand that they can yet reclaim their lost salvation, by confessing Christ upon a second arrest. Copies of this missive should be sent far and wide, to instruct and fortify "all who call upon the Lord."

Having thus received a conservative challenge to his authority from abroad, Cyprian is now assailed from within his own church, by laxists who are pressing for a prompt and full reconciliation of the lapsed (*Epp.* 14–20). Acting on the established principle that "those who bear witness to Christ" enjoy intercessory powers with the Lord, large numbers of Christians who have sacrificed are making appeals to the imprisoned confessors for clemency and restoration. To his dismay, Cyprian learns that some of his own presbyters and deacons are leading this "rebellion" against the Church, and that many of the confessors are authorizing blanket "letters of peace" for all the recent apostates, promising to intercede on their behalf and secure forgiveness from God upon their martyrdom. In churches across the region, irresponsible clergy, along with those intimidated by the crowds of sinners pressing for readmission, are already receiving into communion those who have stained their souls with idolatrous sacrifices, profaning thereby the sacred body of the Lord! Under the pretense of mercy, Cyprian charges, these laxists are unwittingly condemning the lapsed to eternal damnation, for it is only through rigorous and lifelong penance that those who have denied Christ can possibly hope to win His compassionate indulgence on the Day of Judgment. Cyprian is adamant that the Eucharist can be offered to remorseful apostates only on their deathbed. For all the others, his episcopal command remains unchanged: the battle is still being fought; those who are genuinely repentant can erase their fatal offenses by seeking a martyr's crown.[10]

Hard-pressed by the growing laxist clamor for full restoration and the chaos occasioned by the wholesale traffic in martyr waivers, Cyprian turns to Rome for support (*Epp.* 20, 27, 28), justifying his earlier decision to withdraw for safety as the most secure way to manage affairs, via envoys and epistles. He attaches copies of the relevant correspondence to demonstrate that he is fully committed – like the brave clergy and confessors of Rome – to enforcing "the unshakeable discipline of the law of the Lord."

In late summer, Cyprian receives the backing he has sought, as the Roman clergy glowingly acclaim his hardline stance (*Ep.* 30). A new presence is manifest in the style and substance of this letter, which conveys an assured and unyielding rigorist spirit from beginning to end. Authored by the learned presbyter Novatian, the text makes repeated mention of the need to uphold "ecclesiastical censure and discipline," to adhere steadfastly to the "ancient faith" and "ancient strictness," and to impose the "just severity of evangelical discipline." Most insistently, Novatian emphasizes the primacy of conscience in assessing the gravity of the sins that have been committed, seeing as "the whole sacred mystery of our faith is contained in confessing the name of Christ" (30.3.1). Those

---

[10] A similar dynamic is underway in Egypt, where the persecution has been marked by considerable popular violence, according to Dionysius, bishop of Alexandria (247–265). Lamenting all the many brethren in the towns and villages who have been "torn asunder by the heathen," and also the great multitude of fugitives who have perished while wandering in the deserts and mountains (the bishop generously credits them with confessions of "election and triumph"), the laxist Dionysius adopts a more conciliatory approach on the matter of the lapsed. Where his Carthaginian colleague registers alarm over easy readmission, Dionysius ratifies the recommendations of his own confessor-martyrs to grant early and reassuring peace to the fallen, by enrolling them among the *consistentes* or "co-standers," the highest order of penitents who, unlike the "mourners" or "hearers," are entitled to full fellowship, though temporarily excluded from communion during their term of penance. The Alexandrian bishop defends this policy on the grounds that "bringing grief to kindness" would not comply with scripture, for God takes pleasure in the repentance, not the death, of a sinner (in Eusebius, *Ecclesiastical History* VI.42).

who have resorted to the "evasive stratagems" of bogus certificates, the *libellatici*, are thus no less guilty of apostasy than those who flocked to the temples and ingested the polluting flesh of the burnt offerings, the *sacrificati*; all alike have suffered "mortal injury to their heart and conscience." The faithful must unite against the laxist clergy and the sacrilegious petitions of peace they are soliciting from the misguided confessors. For while "God is indeed forgiving, He also enforces, and zealously enforces, His own commandments . . . He has prepared heaven, but He has also prepared hell" (30.7.2).

The beleaguered bishop of Carthage has found a powerful ally, and he promptly utilizes this correspondence – supplemented by a similar letter from the imprisoned Roman confessors – in his ongoing contest against the laxist factions in the African Church. A united front between the sees of Rome and Carthage has been established, grounded on the following principles: (i) apostasy remains a mortal sin, regardless of whether actual sacrifices or certificates were involved; (ii) as "a sin against God," this offense cannot be remitted by God's servants, but only by God alone; (iii) lifelong penance might secure divine mercy, and merits Eucharistic consolation for the dying; (iv) martyrdom, as a cleansing "baptism of blood," remains available for those eager to reclaim their lost salvation; and (v) the illicit waivers of the confessor-martyrs and the hasty reconciliations of rebellious clergy must be denounced as false and deadly remedies, for it is only through the diligence of obligatory penitence that sinners can hope to find favor with God and His Church.[11]

By the spring of 251, the storm of persecution has sufficiently weakened that church leaders are preparing to reconvene in regional synods, to formulate policy on matters of governance and discipline. The Africans are first to hold their congress, a body of high-ranking clerics assembling in Carthage in late April. After extended readings of scripture and careful deliberations, this African Council issues the following main rulings: laxist factions that have persisted in sedition against Cyprian are officially excommunicated; lapsed clergy can be admitted to penitence only on condition of a

---

[11] Cyprian would express these views quite forcefully in his treatise *On the Lapsed*, then in composition for the upcoming synod: "Let no man deceive himself, let none be misled. Only the Lord can grant mercy. Sins committed against Him can be cancelled by Him alone who bore our sins and suffered for us, by Him whom God delivered up for our sins. Man cannot be above God, nor can the servant by any indulgence of his own remit or condone the graver sort of crime committed against his Lord" (*On the Lapsed*, 17; from the edition translated by Maurice Bévenot, Mahwah, NJ: Paulist Press, 1957).

permanent loss of clerical status; as the sin of the *libellatici* is a lesser form of apostasy, these lapsed brethren are to be restored to communion following periods of penance individually determined by their bishops; the *sacrificati* must continue with lifelong penance, whereupon they will pass to the Lord with the Church's Eucharistic blessing. Although Cyprian has been forced to abandon his established position that the *libellatici* and *sacrificati* are equally guilty of apostasy, he nonetheless hails the new consensus for its "balance and moderation" (*Ep.* 55.6.1).

Before these conciliar proceedings have concluded, however, news is received that a succession crisis has erupted in Rome, with rival elections to the vacant papacy. The first to have been consecrated was Cornelius, a senior presbyter; the second, Novatian. Envoys from the latter presented themselves before the African synod, where they laid charges that Cornelius' election had been both fraudulent in procedure and sacrilegious, owing to the man's earlier procurement of a self-damning certificate of sacrifice. Acting upon their insistence that a public investigation be held, the African bishops promptly sent delegates to Rome to conduct inquiries. Shortly thereafter, two Italian bishops who had participated in Cornelius' disputed election arrived, denouncing the Novatianist usurpation (*Epp.* 44, 45). The situation was critical. Had Cornelius, a possible *libellaticus*, taken power at the behest of laxist factions? If Novatian's counter-election was merely an act of personal aggrandizement – as Cornelius alleged – why were the glorious Roman confessors supporting his cause?

Letters of justification were sent out by the rival popes, initiating an intense propaganda war. Opinion in the churches divided sharply, and in many places congregations wavered back and forth before splitting along existing fault lines, with laxists and rigorists competing for the moderates whose backing usually decided the local balance of power. A schismogenic dynamic of separation and inversion would develop rapidly following Novatian's excommunication by an Italian synod, convened by Cornelius in early July. The Novatianists respond with a full-scale offensive to garner support for the rigorist cause. Presenting themselves as "defenders of ecclesiastical doctrine," as "vindicators of the Gospel," the Novatianists proceed to establish links of fellowship with like-minded clerics and laity in Christian enclaves across the empire. Communities without suitable leadership will receive bishops and presbyters consecrated in Rome by Pope Novatian himself. With astonishing speed, a Church of the *Katharoi* assumes institutional form and ideological coherence, its ranks filled by all the many traditionalists and puritans who could not consent to remaining in communion with known idolaters and apostates. In laying claim to "purity" status, the Novatianists were signaling their opposition to the penitential reforms being pushed by the moderate and laxist elements in the "Universal" or Catholic Church, whose leaders were now charged with abetting the most sacrilegious of sins and offenses against God. Novatian's call to reaffirm and reconstitute the *ecclesia pura* that Christ and His Apostles had mandated – a Church free from the polluting presence of apostates, fornicators, and adulterers – struck a resonant chord.[12]

Cyprian, having already made accommodative gestures toward the lapsed in the recent African synod, sided with Cornelius. With his own episcopacy under continuous pressure from laxist circles and direct threat by open seditions, any alliance with hardliners now carried too great a risk. Cyprian's own theological ecclesiology had long emphasized that the unity and preservation of the Church rested upon the authority and collegial concord of Christ's earthly representatives, the "bishops of God." Given that Cornelius' papal election had been both prior and legitimate (according to the bishops who consecrated him), Novatian's rash decision to raise a second, "counterfeit altar" constituted an act of schism. Indeed, inasmuch as rending the Church brings about the fall of many, it is a graver sin than any singular failing of idolatry – so reasoned Dionysius of Alexandria, in his epistolary appeal for Novatian to abandon his divisive episcopal claim (in Eusebius, *Ecclesiastical History* VI. 45.1).

What, then, of the scriptural requirement for purity within the Church, and the need to uphold the ancient evangelical discipline? Cyprian was to be challenged on those very points by one of his own African bishops, absent – like many others – from the recent synod, and who expressed unease over its (unrepresentative?) laxist rulings. In his extended reply (*Ep.* 55), expressly composed for wide circulation, Cyprian attempts to justify his own questionable shifts in position while countering the arguments Novatian had been advancing with alarming effectiveness. He concedes that his stance during the recent persecution had been strict and unwavering, but defends this as a tactic necessary in rousing the fallen to return to battle. Now that the Lord has granted respite, Cyprian shares the compassionate views of his episcopal colleagues, "that conditions for reconciliation ought to be made less stringent" (55.3.2). Pastoral requirements

---

[12] The Church of the *Katharoi* wasted little time rejecting the earlier penitential innovation of Callistus, who had extended sacerdotal powers of remission to the sins of adultery and fornication. In his treatise *In Praise of Purity*, Novatian reaffirmed that those guilty of "vices of the flesh" (6) had lost their inheritance in the heavenly kingdom, for these are sins that "bring death to the soul" (14).

accordingly take precedence, and "in the interests of gathering our scattered brethren together and of healing their wounds, I yielded to the urgent needs of the times and considered we ought to make provisions that would bring salvation to the many" (55.7.2). It is a just and "healthy moderation" that those who sacrificed should submit to heavier penitence than those who merely obtained certificates. Novatian's "callous and cruelly overrigid" insistence to the contrary only reveals that he is a follower not of Christ, but of the Stoics, subscribing to their perverse paradox that "all sins are equal" (55.16.1). This pitiless, arrogant man fails to acknowledge that the lapsed are grievously wounded, not dead, and can be "revived into faith" by penitence (55.16.3).[13]

As for Novatian's many calumnies and falsehoods against God's chosen ministers, these emanate from his master, the Devil, who uses heretics and schismatics "to rupture the bonds of Catholic unity" (55.7.2). Allegations that Cornelius has admitted fallen clerics into his fellowship, and has been restoring the *sacrificati* to communion indiscriminately, are vile distortions. Cyprian grants that some of those who have received deathbed reconciliations subsequently recovered; but should we now attempt, he asks, to force their departure by choking or suffocating them? No, their miraculous revival is yet another sign of God's loving-kindness (55.13.1). For Cyprian and his episcopal allies, there are henceforth no limits to Catholic powers of reconciliation: "No one," he sweepingly declares, "ought to be debarred from the fruits of repentance" (55.27.3). On authority of the scriptures, "sinners are to be invited back" and all "lost sheep" restored to their flocks. Given that God is compassionate and forgiving, "reconciliation can be granted through His bishops, to all who implore and call upon the mercy of the Lord" (55.29.1).[14] Dionysius of Alexandria will go so far as to claim that the deathbed offering of the Eucharist actually "blots out the sin," thereby accomplishing what others have more cautiously left to divine discretion (in Eusebius, *Ecclesiastical History* 6.44).

Given the directionality of Catholic pastoral reasoning, additional penitential concessions are not difficult to implement. In 253, the African Council offers a blanket amnesty for all the lapsed, *libellatici* and *sacrificati*

---

[13] Cyprian makes no mention that he himself had deemed apostates "spiritually dead" only months earlier, having written that those who hastened to offer the mandated sacrifices had rushed "to their own deaths," offering themselves up as victims upon Satan's altar (*On the Lapsed*, 8).

[14] Here again Cyprian abandons an earlier position, having insisted in his *Testimonies* that "There is no remission in the Church for one who has sinned against God" (3.28). Under this principle he actually quotes several of the key scriptural passages (Matthew 12.30–32; Mark 3.28; 1 Samuel 2.25) that the Novatianists will subsequently invoke to justify their denial of ecclesiastical absolution for those guilty of mortal sins.

alike. Citing divine "warnings and signs" that herald a pending persecution, Cyprian defends this lifting of all penitential requirements as a measure to prepare the *militia Christi* for the apocalyptic battle that is fast approaching (*Ep.* 57). Reconciling the lapsed permits their restoration to communion, and as there is no protection greater than "the body and blood" of the Redeemer, it is imperative that God's warriors enter the fray fully nourished and fortified by the Eucharist's sacred powers.[15] Cornelius and his successor Lucius duly ratify these rulings for the Italian churches (*Ep.* 68), and a grand eastern synod will convene later in the summer in Antioch, where a majority of attending bishops rule against "the innovation of Novatian" (in Eusebius, *Ecclesiastical History* VII.4). Corresponding separations of Novatianist and Catholic congregations were taking place elsewhere, from Spain and Gaul in the west to Mesopotamia and Arabia in the east.

In the polemical discourse that attends and directs this deepening rift, two competing conceptions of Christianity will find clarifying specification. For those of Catholic persuasion, the Church is increasingly viewed as an instrument for the salvation of its loyal followers, their requisite holiness being produced and restored through expanding ministrations of the sacraments. Continued membership is no longer predicated upon living in protracted righteousness, but upon submitting to routinized penitence under episcopal authority and in preserving Church unity. For the *Katharoi*, in contrast, the salvific powers of the Holy Spirit can only reside in those who uphold their baptismal vows and who remain faithful to the purity commitments established in sacred scripture. As the Church has no power to remit the unpardonable sins against God, communal fellowship must be denied to those guilty of such crimes, lest their polluting presence defile Christ's "betrothed," the "virginal, mystical bride" that is the Church itself.

Having engaged in mutual excommunications at the organizational level, which issued in sundered congregations and parallel priesthoods, the two Christian factions were caught up in a relentless schismogenic

---

[15] Cyprian anticipates Novatianist mockery of this resolution. Seeing as the traditional option of martyrdom remains ever open – and this is the very point Cyprian himself has invoked to block reconciliations of the fallen during the Decian persecution – the granting of this amnesty is superfluous, especially since penitence itself is a mechanism for spiritual recovery. Cyprian's counter is to vest indispensable potency in the ecclesiastical *sacramentum*, arguing that "a man cannot be fit for martyrdom if he is not armed for battle by the Church; his heart fails if it is not fired and fortified by receiving the Eucharist" (4.2).

Table 7.1 *Schismogenic antitypes*

THE CATHOLIC CHURCH	THE CHURCH OF THE *KATHAROI*
Affirmative identity-markers	*Affirmative identity-markers*
Forgiveness and reconciliation for all who are penitent (mortal sins included)	Mortal sins irremissible in the Church
Unity of the Church, founded upon bishops established through apostolic succession	Purity of God's elect
"There is no salvation outside the Church"; the Holy Spirit is exclusively gifted to the Catholic Church	Salvation is predicated upon living a Christian life of holiness; the true Church is a Church of the Spirit
"Healthy moderation" in the assignment of penance – incline to "gentle justice"; the fallen can be restored to grace through "the healing medicines of penance"	"Strict evangelical censure and discipline"; penance for mortal sins is encouraged, but idolaters, apostates, and fornicators must look to God's mercy
Schism the gravest of sins; it is a demonic form of collective apostasy from the Church, for which no expiation is possible – not even through martyrdom, as "there can be no martyrs outside the Church"	Apostasy is the gravest of sins, as it violates the primary obligation to confess Christ
Discrediting identity-markers	*Discrediting identity-markers*
Tolerates the polluting presence of apostates, fornicators, adulterers	Arrogant, prideful exclusion of brethren who are weak, wounded, and in need
"Irreligious laxity," "mistaken compassion," "indulgent advocates of vice"	"Enemies of compassion," "murderers of penance," "destroyers of charity"
Sacraments ministered by sinful clerics are void, as they are lacking in the Spirit	Schismatics and heretics forfeit sacramental grace upon apostatizing from the Church
Deserters from God's army; destroyers of the ancient *fides* and *disciplinae evangelicae*	Followers of the fratricidal heresy of Cain; not Christians, but adherents of the Stoics

dynamic of ideological inversion. Each side was led to affirm principles and practices that the other negated or devalued, resulting in progressively antagonal identities. A distillation of the claims, charges, and sloganeering that sustained and informed their countervailing rhetorics is presented in Table 7.1.

With leaders of the Catholic faction denouncing the *Katharoi* for their "brother-hating" and "inhumane" tenets, and the *Katharoi* reciprocating by mocking their Catholic rivals as *Capitolini* (i.e., those who offer idolatrous worship to Jupiter, Juno, and Minerva, the triad of Roman deities commonly venerated in the main urban temple complex), there was little likelihood this schism would yield to effective mediation. We do hear of "converts" passing from one side to the other – which triggered another bitter dispute, over whether rebaptism was necessary to remove the polluting stain of prior "heretical" affiliation – but the two communities would persist in obdurate opposition for centuries to come. The scriptures selectively cited by each side were, after all, hardly less divided than their partisan advocates, with calls to mercy and forgiveness counterbalanced by stern rulings and demands for holiness. Whether Noah's ark – one of the favored symbols of the early Church – was "a vessel of the saved," or a container of "animals clean and unclean," was very much open to interpretation.

AFTERMATH: THE CATHOLIC–*KATHAROI* SCHISM AND THE REMAKING OF CHRISTIAN IDENTITY

The emperor Valerian initiated a second empire-wide persecution in the summer of 257, which opened with the exiling of bishops and presbyters and a total ban on Christian assemblies and ceremonies. The following year he ordered the execution of all the higher clergy who refused to offer sacrifice, and loss of property and status for any senators, equestrians, and high-ranking officials who refused to end their participation in the illegal *superstitio* (*Ep.* 80). Many prominent clerics attained their martyrdoms – Cyprian and Novatian included – and countless confessors suffered imprisonment, exile, or condemnation to the mines. But as these measures targeted the clerical and social elites of the Christian movement, the great majority of lay devotees passed through unchallenged and unscathed. The emperor's ignominious capture and alleged flaying at the hands of the Persian king Shapur I, in the summer of 260, brought a swift termination to the persecution. Valerian's son Gallienus, beset by usurpers and barbarian onslaughts, promptly signaled de facto toleration for the Church by returning confiscated properties and permitting "unmolested" resumption of Christian religious activities.

Over the next four decades, the Church would operate in an environment largely free from imperial threat or interference, and its membership would grow accordingly. But while this "external peace" was undoubtedly conducive to Christian expansion, the Catholic–*Katharoi* rupture had initiated a reorganization of Christianity's "internal" field of action that would prove correspondingly facilitating. Where laxist, moderate, and rigorist elements had formerly counterbalanced and restrained each other

within a unitary institutional assemblage, post-schism Christianity proceeded along bisected paths, in separate and antagonal Church establish-
ments. The Catholic variant would move to a new axis of equilibrium
centered on laxists and moderates; the Novatianists would ground their
practices and beliefs in the concentrated presence of traditionalists and
puritans. The "before" and "after" sociological configurations are represented in Figures 7.1 and 7.2, respectively.

    With the expulsion/exodus of its hardline constituency, the Catholic
Church was henceforth free to pursue a reformist pastoral strategy better
suited to both preserving and augmenting its membership ranks. For
what was a demographically marginal religious movement at the time
(perhaps 3 percent in a population of some 60 million), Christianity's
possibilities for future development were clearly dependent upon
restoring its lapsed majorities to communion and, thereafter, widening its
appeal to potential new converts. By expanding its sacramental means of

"laxists"	"moderates"	"rigorists"
tolerant & forgiving in discipline	favoring tradition, but open to necessary/pragmatic reforms if scripturally defensible	upholders of tradition; purity demands are binding; strict discipline

Figure 7.1 Distributional pattern of latent factional dispositions within the Church, prior
to the Decian persecution, 250 CE

The Catholic Church	Church of the *Katharoi*
<<--- "laxists" --->> <<--- "moderates"--->>	"rigorists"
a new laxist-to-moderate continuum emerges within Catholic Christianity, as rigorist elements are now predominately located "outside"; a Church fully committed to the preservation and sanctification of all its members via sacramental grace	a concentrated body of traditionalists; holiness is achieved by living in the Spirit; gross sinners excluded

Figure 7.2 Distributional pattern of factional dispositions within the two Churches,
following schismogenic separation of Catholics and *Katharoi*, c.260 CE

bestowing grace and absolution, the Catholic Church addressed both of those concerns, while simultaneously accomplishing a far-reaching redefinition and reorganization of Christian identity and experience around the privileged themes of "divine compassion," "mercy," and "forgiveness."

The Novatianist Church of the *Katharoi*, in contrast, remained focused on the founding Christian principles of baptismal spiritual empowerment and personal holiness; the adopted children of God could not grievously offend against God and retain the pledge of eternal salvation. This traditionalist understanding held a narrower but more intense appeal, and numerous Novatianist congregations were formed in every region across the empire, many of them to persist well into the sixth century. While unlikely to have matched their Catholic rivals in missionary success – the convert pool for puritan causes being typically quite restricted – the *Katharoi* were more intent on preserving the salvation of those who could live a truly Christian life, as scripturally warranted by their Lord's declaration: "Though many are called, few are chosen" (Matthew 22.14).[16]

The conversion of the emperor Constantine in 312 CE would dramatically alter the fortunes of the Christian faith – and, more directly, the Catholic Church he chose to support with lavish patronage, legal safeguards, and occasional persecutions against her enemies. To appreciate the political cogency of his choice (the theological issues being more elusive), and to bring our analysis to a close, a famous anecdote merits consideration. Eager to establish order and concord within the Christian faith, and to secure divine backing for the empire it now served, Constantine convened the first great ecumenical synod, the Council of Nicaea, in 325 CE. Intent upon healing old divisions, the emperor summoned the Novatianist patriarch of Constantinople, and inquired if he would sign the agreed-upon credal statement. Acesius judged the exposition orthodox, whereupon the emperor asked him to explain why his sect refused communion with other Christians. Acesius recounted the history of the schism, and reaffirmed the scriptural ruling that precluded priestly absolution for the mortal "sins unto death." The emperor, clearly exasperated, shot back: "Place your ladder, Acesius, and ascend alone to heaven" (Socrates, *Ecclesiastical History* 1.10).

---

[16] An informative overview on the history of the Novatianist church is offered by Wallraff (1997).

REFERENCES

Alföldy, Géza. 1974. "The Crisis of the Third Century as Seen by Contemporaries." *Greek, Roman, and Byzantine Studies* 15 (1): 89–111.
Barnes, Timothy. 1968. "Legislation against the Christians." *Journal of Roman Studies* 58: 32–50.
Bateson, Gregory. 1935. "Culture Contact and Schismogenesis." *Man* 35: 178–83.
Bryant, Joseph M. 1993. "The Sect–Church Dynamic and Christian Expansion in the Roman Empire." *British Journal of Sociology* 44 (2): 303–39.
       1998. "Wavering Saints, Mass Religiosity, and the Crisis of Post-Baptismal Sin in Early Christianity." *Archives Européennes de Sociologie* 39 (1): 49–77.
Knipfing, John. 1923. "The Libelli of the Decian Persecution." *Harvard Theological Review* 16 (4): 345–90.
Sahlins, Marshall. 2000. *Culture in Practice.* New York: Zone Books.
       2004. *Apologies to Thucydides.* Chicago: University of Chicago Press.
Ste. Croix, G. E. M. de. 1963. "Why Were the Early Christians Persecuted?" *Past and Present* 26: 6–38.
       2006. *Christian Persecution, Martyrdom, and Orthodoxy.* Oxford: Oxford University Press.
Wallraff, Martin. 1997. "Geschichte des Novatianismus seit dem vierten Jahrhundert im Osten." *Zeitschrift für Antikes Christentum* 1: 251–79.
Wilken, Robert. 1984. *The Christians as the Romans Saw Them.* New Haven: Yale University Press.

PART IV

Western esoteric traditions

CHAPTER 8

Church Universal and Triumphant: shelter, succession and schism

Susan J. Palmer and Michael Abravanel

Church Universal and Triumphant (henceforth CUT) is a new religion based in Montana.[1] It flourished between 1973 and 1999 under Elizabeth Clare Prophet, who was guided by "dictations" received from the Ascended Masters. As their chosen "Messenger," her mission was to publish the teachings of the Ascended Masters and to assist them in ushering in the Age of Aquarius, or the Golden Age. For twenty-five-odd years, Elizabeth Clare Prophet (henceforth ECP) presided over a strong, centralized, hierarchical new religious movement (henceforth NRM). She combined the roles of charismatic spiritual teacher (guru) and chief administrator in her person. At its peak CUT may have counted as many as 25,000 members worldwide (Whitsel 2003).[2]

The commencement of ECP's reign was seamless and unchallenged when, in 1973, she assumed the mantle of "Messenger" upon the death of her husband, Mark Prophet. He had been the charismatic founder of the Summit Lighthouse (CUT's predecessor), and had shared his administrative tasks and aspects of spiritual leadership with his young wife since their marriage in 1963. Mark Prophet prepared her in messengership, and it was believed they were "Twin Flames," originating out of the same white-fire core.[3] By the time Mark Prophet "ascended" from his body in Colorado Springs on February 26, 1973, ECP had already been receiving dictations for over a year. Immediately after his death, Mark revealed himself to her as the Ascended Master "Lanello," and began to dictate

---

[1] The author would like to thank Robert Balch for his helpful insights and response to our data.
[2] According to sociologist Robert Balch, who has researched this NRM and visits regularly with his students, an ex-insider told him the actual number of members at its peak was closer to 10,000.
[3] See *Soul Mates and Twin Flames*, 45. (When Susan J. Palmer visited the Royal Teton Ranch in the summer of 1991, she remarked to the CUT minister who was giving her a tour how unusual it was to find a group where the wife of a charismatic prophet assumes the leadership and turns out to be just as strong a leader as her late husband. He replied, "Not if you know who ECP is." Then he explained that she was Mark's "twin flame.")

messages through her. In a CUT historical pamphlet, we are told that during the forty-day period after his ascension, "Lanello gave two private dictations to the staff. As Jesus taught his disciples . . . Lanello offered his staff access to his Causal Body for forty days. Each night at 10:00 p.m. the staff gathered to form a circle and give ascension decrees" (Prophet 1994: 9).

Two months later, Lanello spoke again (via ECP) to the "Easter Class" attended by four hundred Keepers of the Flame, "the largest gathering of Keepers to that date." According to this historical account, "Mark's ascension brought a virtual explosion in the membership of the Summit Lighthouse. That summer one thousand students attended the July Freedom conference, known as the Land of Lanello. It was by far the largest conference held to date" (Prophet 1994: 9).

Here we find an example of a well-planned and perfectly executed succession in an NRM. Funeral and memorial rituals were combined with charismatic displays that established the credentials of the new leader. Messages from beyond the grave set new directions for the movement, and identified Elizabeth closely with Mark, validating her authority. But it is interesting to note that Mark Prophet's own charismatic career was born from a chaotic series of schisms in the esoteric movements that form the legacy of the Church Universal and Triumphant.

CUT's ancestry began with Theosophy, a strikingly fissiparous tradition. In 1929 Guy Ballard, evidently familiar with Madame Blavatsky's thought-world, encountered St. Germain, during a hike on Mount Shasta (Melton 1994; Whitsel 2003). He began to dictate messages from the saint, as well as from other Ascended Masters. Ballard founded I AM, a syncretic system composed of doctrines from Theosophy and the ideas of Emma Curtis Hopkins of New Thought, with an emphasis on "decreeing," a practice similar to Christian Science "affirmations" (Melton 1994: 2–13).

When Guy Ballard died in 1939, I AM entered a "period of turmoil" (Melton 1994: 12). Ballard's wife and various leaders were convicted of mail fraud (the conviction was overturned by the US Supreme Court upon appeal), and the movement splintered into factions. Aside from the problems of external opposition and criticism, the group lacked spiritual leadership. Guy Ballard had bestowed upon his wife and son the mantle of Messenger, but neither Edna nor Donald Ballard chose to exercise *charismata*.[4] Predictably, a schism occurred. It was instigated by Geraldine

---

[4] Edna Ballard finally began to dictate messages, years after the schisms had formed.

Innocente in 1944, who claimed she was the chosen Messenger of El Morya and Maha Chohan. Innocente went on to found the Bridge of Freedom. In the 1950s there was a battle over copyright to the Masters' messages, and Innocente's follower, Frances Ekey (who founded the Lighthouse of Freedom), began to publish one of her student's dictated messages from El Morya, while preserving his anonymity. The student in question was Mark Prophet; he finally revealed his identity when he began publishing his own *Pearls of Wisdom*. By then, he was firmly established in his role as Messenger and he was able to launch the Summit Lighthouse in 1960 (Melton 1994: 2–15).

Despite her brilliant debut in the Summit Lighthouse (renamed Church Universal and Triumphant in 1974), Elizabeth Clare Prophet, in planning her future successorship, did not follow the exemplary model provided by her late husband in training and anointing a new Messenger.[5] Rather, she appointed an administrator to take over the financial and management aspect of her leadership, leaving a spiritual vacuum in her wake. ECP is still alive, but in 1999 she announced her retirement from her leadership position, owing to a debilitating neurological illness, Alzheimer's.

Soon after she stepped down, her chosen administrator was deposed and CUT was beset by internal conflicts over new initiatives and authority claims. A number of schismatic movements or splinter groups formed.[6] These schisms may be classified as "Messenger" or "non-Messenger" groups.

The first type are formed around charismatic CUT leaders who claim to be "Messengers" – chosen by the Ascended Masters to dictate new messages.[7] The second type formed around charismatic CUT ministers or local presidents of regional Teaching Centers who refused to accept orders from an ECP-less headquarters. They evolved into splinter groups, continuing to study and apply the rich body of esoteric teachings believed to derive from the Masters, as transmitted by ECP and her late husband and Twin Flame, Mark Prophet.

---

[5] It is rumored that her daughter, Erin Prophet, was in training to be the next Messenger but she defected and in 2008 published a book with Lyon's Press, *Prophet's Daughter: My Life with Elizabeth Clare Prophet Inside the Church Universal and Triumphant.*

[6] Robert Balch said in 2006 that a spokesperson for CUT claimed there were seventeen schismatic groups.

[7] In CUT's worldview, a Messenger is understood as "one who is trained by an Ascended Master to receive by various methods, the words, concepts, teachings and messages of the Great White Brotherhood" (Prophet and Prophet 2001: 328).

The purpose of this chapter is to describe the endogamous social context of CUT's schismatic movements; to attempt to analyze the structural conditions underlying CUT's propensity toward schism; and (hopefully) to offer fresh insights into the sources of opportunity or conditions facilitating or inhibiting a NRM's tendency to form schisms. In trying to identify these underlying conditions, we will address the following questions:

1 To what extent did the prophetic failure of the "Shelter Cycle" generate schisms and warring factions in the leadership?
2 To what extent were CUT's schisms a reaction to the retirement of ECP and her "social death" brought on by a long-term illness – equivalent to the battle over the succession that frequently ensues after the unexpected death of the charismatic founder?
3 To what extent was this factional conflict the inevitable outcome of ECP's planning for her retirement and her decision to opt for an administrative successor, which left a lacuna in the spiritual leadership?

We will explore these various factors and attempt to analyze CUT's schisms within the framework of theories of charisma, typologies of NRMs, and the body of work on schisms produced by Weber (1968) Wallis (1979) and others.

METHODOLOGY

Much of our information concerning schisms within CUT was gleaned from interviews with former members, Keepers of the Flame, and Communicants in Montreal. Three of them were former presidents of Teaching Centers in Canada, and many of them studied at the Summit University and lived at the Ranch and its outlying community, Glastonbury. Several participated in the millenarian activities of the Shelter Cycle; they built bomb shelters, and went underground in the "Preparedness" drill of March 15, 1990. Our informants continue to revere ECP as a spiritual teacher and Messenger, but are now active members in a splinter group, Spiritual Awareness Fellowship.

In the interests of transparency, it is worth noting that the author had never studied or researched CUT before she was introduced to a group of former CUT members by Michael Abravanel in July 2007. Abravanel is a second-generation member of CUT, who, as an infant, experienced the Shelter Cycle and the March 15, 1990 night in the family fallout shelter, but is currently a member of the Spiritual Awareness Fellowship.

HISTORICAL BACKGROUND

In 1958, Mark L. Prophet founded the Summit Lighthouse, in order to publish the teachings of the Ascended Masters[8] who have mastered time and space through the cycles of reincarnation and reunited with God through the ritual of the ascension. These teachings appeared in weekly letters called *Pearls of Wisdom*, and were received as "dictated" messages from El Morya, and other Ascended Masters. In 1961 Mark Prophet met Elizabeth Clare Wulf (1939–), and he married her in 1963. Under Mark's tutelage, Elizabeth officially became a Messenger in 1964 (Santucci 2006: 283–4). As Messengers, Mark and Elizabeth Clare Prophet were the sole individuals within the Summit Lighthouse who gave dictations – "a message from an Ascended Master, an Archangel or another advanced spiritual being delivered through the agency of the Holy Spirit" (Prophet and Prophet 2001: 320).

In 1974, ECP was called by Jesus to "found his Church." The name "Church Universal and Triumphant" was suggested to her by Ascended Master Pope John XXIII (Prophet 1994: 12). The Summit Lighthouse then became the publishing arm of the Church. The use of affirmations and decrees constitutes important ritual in CUT. Affirmations are "sentences that affirm the individual's attunement to God and the blessing due to the person as a result of that attunement" (Melton 1994: 11) while a decree is a fiat spoken from the awareness as the "Mighty I Am Presence."

CUT's conservative Republican stance is closely aligned with the Ballards' personal political convictions. As Whitsel notes, the Ballards were "firmly opposed to labor strikes, communism, and the New Deal policies of the Roosevelt administration, the superpatriotic group became a vigorous defender of the status quo" (Whitsel 2003: 25). Thus, unlike other occult groups in America, I AM was "espousing powerful nationalistic sentiments . . . and assumed a political character that set it apart." CUT's worldview reflects the Ballards' influence, for it has incorporated an explicit political agenda into its belief structure.

---

[8] The notion of the Ascended Masters can be traced to the Theosophical Society and other schisms within Theosophy. Mark and Elizabeth Clare Prophet considered themselves as part of the lineage of Messengers appointed by the Great White Brotherhood to disseminate the teachings of the Ascended Masters. Some of these more recent Messengers include: Helena Petrovna Blavatsky, Mary Baker Eddy, Guy W. Ballard and Edna Ballard, and Nicholas and Helena Roerich (*The Chela and the Path*, 121–2).

THE APOCALYPTIC AND CONTROVERSIAL NATURE OF CUT

CUT bought land near Yellowstone Park in Montana in 1981, and moved its headquarters there in 1986. The Church generated considerable controversy in Montana, mainly owing to the members' stockpiling of weapons that were purchased illegally through using faked ID. These actions were part of a millenarian project to build nuclear fallout shelters during the two years before April 23, 1990, a date given by Archangel Michael, who referred to astrological portents as a sign of the beginning of a "Dark Cycle," during which a nuclear strike on America by the Soviet Union was likely to occur. As one of our informants noted, "April 23 is a significant day, the Dark Cycle which refers to the accelerated return of mankind's karma which began on April 23, 1969 and ended April 23, 2002. It was also known as the Kali Yuga."

Mark Prophet, as early as 1969, had spoken of the Dark Cycle and the likelihood of accelerated discord before the millennium (Whitsel 2003: 80–3). On November 27, 1986 ECP received a dictation from St. Germain warning the Keepers of the Flame to prepare for a nuclear strike. In December of the same year St. Germain repeated this warning, advising "Preparedness":[9]

On March 15, 1990, around 7,000 CUT members, who had spent considerable money and invested two years in "Preparedness," were told to enter their fallout shelters for the duration of one night. When March and April passed uneventfully, many of these posttribulationists defected (half of the membership, according to one estimate). CUT was plunged into debt.

Other controversial issues contributed to a growing tension between CUT and its neighboring communities in Montana. Whitsel (2003) says that CUT's first serious setback occurred in 1989 when the Internal Revenue Service launched an investigation into the Church's tax status. The next setback happened when the Justice Department became curious about the members' purchase of guns and tanks. After a three-year investigation, CUT's tax exempt status was revoked by the IRS – which demanded $2.5 million in back taxes and penalties.

Michael Homer has explored CUT's legal cases, and found that they range from custody battles, to tax cases and zoning disputes, to environmental conflicts, to deprogramming cases, to grievance suits by ex-members (Homer 1994: 124).

[9] *Beloved St. Germain* 29(75) (December 16, 1986).

De Haas (1994) has identified environmental factors as a major area of contention between CUT and its neighbors. Environmentalists feared CUT as a threat to the ecosystem of Yellowstone National Park (De Haas 1994: 29–31). On April 15, 1990 there was a disastrous environmental incident when the storage tanks that contained fuel for the main bomb shelter were found to be leaking, amounting to a spillage of 21,000 gallons of diesel and 11,500 gallons of gasoline over five days.[10] The locals were also concerned about the influx of wealthy New-Agers from California who were buying up large tracts of land in this rural area. A popular bumper sticker of the time was "Don't Californicate Montana."

ECP'S PLAN FOR THE SUCCESSION

In July 1996, ECP suddenly announced a profound change in the leadership structure of the organization. Like all her decisions, this was done "under the direction of the Ascended Masters." She split the charismatic and administrative role in two, awarding the latter to a Belgian-born French Canadian, Gilbert Cleirbaut.[11] Cleirbaut was not a minister in CUT. As one informant noted, "Gilbert knew how corporations worked. He was a management person. He was hired as a consultant to prepare the Church for growth, expansion."

Cleirbaut's strengths lay in his experience of human resources, as a consultant to companies who wished to downsize, and in his employment record in Alberta government. He left to take a full-time position with the Church. The new mission of Cleirbaut and his executive board was to "start to implement changes in the organization [to bring about] decentralization, more globalization, stronger regional centers that were independent."

One can only speculate as to ECP's reasons for doing this. CUT was beset with problems (De Haas 1994). A major one was a large deficit in the Church finances.

An informant explained: "the Church was going through a financial crisis. The donations and tithes had not kept up with the expenses. Therefore there was a big deficit. She hired Cleirbaut to fix it." A journalist writing for the *Bozeman Chronicle* also makes this point: "when

---

[10] "CUT Fuel Tanks Spill 20,000 Gallons," *Billings Gazette*, April 15, 1990.
[11] "Cut Decentralizing Power," *Religion Watch* November 1996: 3; "Prophet Gives Up Position," *Billings Gazette*, June 11, 1996.

Cleirbaut took over, he found an organization hemorrhaging money, overstaffed, and underworked" (McMillion 1999).

ECP was experiencing personal difficulties. She and her fourth husband, Edward Francis, would announce their divorce[12] in November of that same year. She was suffering from declining health and memory loss. An informant described her gradual decline in health, as follows:

As she started to get sick, it was very gradual. She had epilepsy as a child, occasional seizures and it would weaken her. There was a progressive deterioration of her memories in the late 1980s, it was very gradual. Then, in the 1990s it was worse, in the late 1990s she announced her disease. It wasn't obvious at the time, only she prepared for an orderly transition.

In 1999, ECP made public her affliction with Alzheimer's and formally retired from leadership, leaving her flock without their guru and a living Messenger who could receive and transmit dictations from the Ascended Masters. The spiritual leadership was assumed by the Ministerial Council, who trained the ministers and interpreted the existing Teaching from the Ascended Masters, but provided no fresh dictations. There was a formal mechanism whereby a new Messenger could be chosen, but it was a long, complicated task. According to Robert Balch's source, applicants were required to submit transcripts of dictations to the elders over a period of years. David Lewis started the process, but then defected. There was also a Council of Elders (twenty-four Elders, as in St. John's *Revelations*) who made decisions about policies and new directions in CUT.

The question of why ECP would parachute a newcomer into her intimate circle is an interesting one. In the 1980s, Prophet's daughter Erin and son Sean were trained as Ministers and it appeared ECP was setting up a family succession, a "traditional" type of authority structure, similar to Reverend Moon's.[13] But an informant explained ECP's deliberate change in the authority structure:

Until now ECP had been a one-man show. I went to a talk where ECP said the only person who could make these changes would have to be a new person. Not somebody who was already there. This would free her to fill her spiritual role, without being a hands-on administrator. Gilbert wanted to make the Church more professional.

[12] "Prophet, Francis Announce Divorce," *Livingston Enterprise*, November 25, 1996.
[13] Robert Balch notes that ECP's two older daughters had left the church by the late 1990s, her son Sean was considering leaving, and her youngest daughter wanted a "normal" life.

Cleirbaut set about taking radical steps to pull the Church out of debt. His first move was to downsize ECP's close aides, the staff living at the Ranch. One informant described this process:

Before, the staff were volunteers . . . they basically got room and board. There was a major cutback . . . a tremendous downshift. Gilbert followed Better Business practices. Over 700 staff went down to 200, then to 70. People were told in advance. This happened over two years.

By 1998 Cleirbaut had reduced their numbers by 90 percent. He also raised the salaries of those who remained, as part of his "better business" policy.

Next, the new President closed down businesses that were losing money, putting an end to CUT's utopian dream of cultivating a self-sufficient agricultural community. Cleirbaut told a journalist that what CUT needed was "a bigger store." "We are expanding the aisles, the products [the Teachings] are the same . . . but the packaging is going to change" (Mcmillion, 1999).

But Cleirbaut also had an ideological goal that lent a new twist to ECP's millenarian agenda to usher in the Age of Aquarius, or Golden Age. One informant explained this:

Gilbert had a vision of a paradigm shift that would empower the individual to be the Christ, to manifest your Christhood. We are all meant to become sons or daughters of God, One with the real self. ECP was a Mother to her children. With her we walked the 14 stations of the cross. The first three cycles (12 years each) were ending. It was meant that the Mother and her children walk the path together, and that we publish the Teachings of the Masters to lay the ground-work for the Age of Aquarius.

Next, the Guru must diminish so that the cycle can increase. ECP diminished herself so that her chelas can take on her role, be examples on the Path.

The rapid institutionalization of CUT

The implications of Cleirbaut's new vision were that CUT must undergo, in sociological terms, a transformation from a sect-like organization into a more church-like organization.

Before the arrival of Cleirbaut, CUT was a hierarchical structure, with three pillars supporting ECP: the Board of Directors, in charge of administrative affairs; the Council of Elders, in charge of ritual and theology; and the Ministerial Council, in charge of training ministers and teaching.

The Board of Directors was initially filled by ECP's family: her husband, her oldest daughter Erin, and her son Sean. Her husband had been vice-president, and they all served as spokespersons for CUT. But over the 1990s all ECP's family left. One informant said:

They were relatively inactive. ECP made all the decisions. She came to realize it wasn't working. She had to spend a lot of time on mundane things. And [she] wanted to concentrate on her role as spiritual leader. She brought in Cleirbaut and made him executive leader of all the departments, like a CEO. There was an executive board under him, and their work was to transform the Church, make it viable for the next years, and to fix the financial imbalance.

Part of Cleirbaut's role was to offer an honest criticism of the Church – and even of ECP's role. According to one source:

He had a lot of input, and some of the things he suggested were very negative toward ECP. He recommended she get out of the way if the Church was to grow and expand. We lived in a culture of fear, not love, he said. If you did not do what the Messenger said, you were out of alignment with the Ascended Masters. There were people who tried to imitate ECP, people trying to act like the Guru. Cleirbaut said it would take a lot of engineering if the movement was to move from a culture of Fear to a culture of Love – to empower the individual.

Whitsel (2003) notes that in a January 1, 1999 press release, Cleirbaut had addressed the need for the Keepers of the Flame to prepare for a future leadership structure without Prophet. He downplayed the right-wing political ideology and apocalyptic aspects of the Church, telling the media that "fanaticism and living in fear" were past chapters and that "CUT's mission in the future would be to simply spread the Teachings" (Whitsel 2003).

POWER STRUGGLES AND FACTIONS IN THE ADMINISTRATION

Predictably, this radical change met with resistance from the old administrators, the 700-odd staff at the Ranch who were on the Board of Directors, and who strove for what Weber calls "tenure of office." Gilbert Cleirbaut's reign lasted from July 1996 to 1999, and he was deposed the same year that ECP retired. Without ECP's support, Cleirbaut and his executive board found it increasingly difficult to control the old members of the Board of Directors, who banded against him, blocking his decisions. Our informant describes how he was ousted and how the administrative and spiritual leadership was reorganized in his wake:

Gilbert was a very fine individual with an outgoing personality. [ECP] loved him – but folks [the Staff] disliked his executive. They saw him as usurping the power of the Board [of Directors]. Once [ECP] became less active, they became more active. They said, "the Board of Directors should be the executive!" When he left, the executive board was dissolved. Then the Board became prominent leaders. They appointed first three, then two people to share the presidency. The Council of Elders became reinvigorated. They became the true spiritual foundation . . . They would interpret the Teachings that had been given up to that point.

After Cleirbaut was deposed, the Board started to meet with resistance from the regional leaders. One of our informants, who had been President of the Montreal Teaching Center during Cleirbaut's administration, described how all the Teaching Centers and Study Groups were controlled, their resources depleted by the central headquarters in Montana, in the interests of "Preparedness":

all the money we got we sent to headquarters – and it stayed at the headquarters. They never sent any of it back, so we couldn't grow. I tried to work out a sharing agreement and proposed it before the Board of Directors. It was not accepted . . . we were told it "gave too much power to the groups."

After Cleirbaut arrived on the scene, his changes had a revitalizing effect on the regional centers:

It seemed great! Cleirbaut wanted the Teaching Centers to be independent and run their own affairs, while maintaining their spiritual ties to headquarters . . . When he came up with the re-engineering, we changed *everything* in Montreal. This was a new program[14] to empower ourselves. Someone who worked with Gilbert came every month to help us with Community Building . . . It was an exciting new time . . . there was more power away from the center into local centers.

In a newsletter sent out to the Montreal Keepers of the Flame in 1997, their president, Arie Abravanel, wrote:

Church Universal and Triumphant is going through a major reenergizing process that has already brought about many changes. A natural consequence of this event has been that Teaching Centers and Study Groups have begun their own process . . . The process was begun in August 1997 and has continued throughout this Fall. (*Source*, by Arie Abravanel)

In another letter, entitled *Overview*, Abravanel explained the new organizational changes:

This re-creating ourselves resulted in the setting up of 4 process teams. They are administrations, finance, services, and outreach. Members of the community

---

[14] "Building a New Culture: Handbook for Individual and Organizational Change," 1997 CUT pamphlet.

were encouraged to join one of the teams, this has led to greater participation of our members in the running of our center resulting in greater harmony and unity within the group.

Each team was empowered to do what they thought best within their domains and within the parameters set forth for their team. Projects and changes would have to be brought to the Board of Directors for approval. Community meetings were then used to discuss these proposals. This has resulted in our members feeling that the Montreal Teaching Center is their center and that each individual's input counts. Ideas are encouraged and initiatives are supported as much as possible.

These changes have freed the Board of Directors from doing all the work as in the past. There is no longer the burden of responsibilities and duties. We now have the entire community involved in the running of our center. This has resulted in the Board becoming more of an overseer of the entire operation making sure that everything is running smoothly. Another important change is that the Board is no longer so vulnerable to the sinister force because the opposition has to get through these teams to get to the Board. In other words, our leadership has rings of protection. This has freed our leadership from many of the stresses of the past.

Our sources describe "community building" as an opportunity for open assessment, a kind of T group or "lemon session." One informant described how she participated in group dialogue, confessions, criticisms and that would be followed by more positive expressions of mutual support and gratitude. These sessions are reminiscent of the "Mutual Criticism" ritual of the nineteenth-century Oneida Perfectionists (Foster 1981), and might be classified as "mortification," a Kanterian commitment mechanism (Kanter 1977).

A major conflict between Cleirbaut's administration and the Board of Directors broke out over his mission to globalize the Teachings. This raised the issue of CUT's patriotic ties and loyalty to the American Nation. Guy Ballard's notion of the central role of America in ushering in the Golden Age was at stake. When Ballard had been escorted by the Ascended Masters on a mystical journey, "he was taught about the Brotherhood's special relationship with America, a nation said to play the key role in the divine plan of God" (Whitsel 2003: 26).

Our informants in Montreal described this debate:

We agreed with Cleirbaut's vision, that there was a need to globalize. But the headquarters said "No!" – that the Ascended Masters had said that the US was the *only* country to be spiritually sponsored by them. Therefore, the movement must not shift the power to outside the US. But then, others said that the spiritual path is an *individual* path, so it doesn't *matter* what country you are in.

But they [the Staff] didn't want the power outside the US. They didn't want the headquarters less strong than it was. When you no longer had HER at the center, the Masters speaking through her. . .this no longer made sense.

CLEIRBAUT'S SCHISMATIC MOVEMENT, "LLL"

In a fascinating new development, Cleirbaut, who in 1999 had resigned from the Presidency in a docile manner, explaining to a journalist that his purpose was "to spend more time with my family," suddenly reappeared in 2001 to spearhead a schism.

He had been forced by the Board not only to retire, but to renounce his membership as a Keeper of the Flame. He then returned to Canada, but was unable to find employment, despite his previous distinguished record as a business consultant ("When he would apply for a job, they would do a Google search and find out he had been President of CUT, considered a 'cult' ").

In 2001 Cleirbaut contacted the Teaching Centers in Canada and Sweden, with a new spiritual mission. He announced that he had received messages from Mother Mary, Jesus, and St. Germain and wished to share them. It is interesting to note that Cleirbaut and his Asian wife collaborated in receiving messages. According to one informant, "he and his wife would pray in their room together until she would see Ascended Master, Jesus, St. Germain and Mother Mary, and he would hear them speak."[15]

Cleirbaut called his movement "LLL" (Launching Loving Legacies) and began to set up a strong evangelical mission that emphasized "community building," brotherly love, and giving back to society. Mother Mary proclaims on the LLL website: "Leave your cares, step back into the world and touch as many Lightbearers as you can."

One informant insisted that Cleirbaut never claimed to be a Messenger: "He was a low-key sort of guy. I remember once telling him he should be more assertive in his personality . . . He never presented himself as a spiritual leader. It [LLL] was all about empowerment . . . he wanted people to work together . . . worldwide networking. He wanted people to find their work passion and render a service to humanity."

---

[15] Husband-and-wife charismatic duos feature prominently in CUT's history. These include George and Edna Ballard, Mark and Elizabeth Clare Prophet, and even the schismatic couple Monroe and Carolyn Shearer who founded the Temple of the Presence.

The same person insisted, "LLL was not presented as an alternative to CUT, it was in a very different form, with no religious orientation." Nevertheless, "he began [LLL] by contacting Keepers of the Flame, then expanded out to find new people . . . a lot were former members."

The Teaching Centers in Canada were very receptive to Cleirbaut's new "LLL" vision, partly because they were frustrated with the lack of response to their requests from headquarters. Cleirbaut's initiatives of 1996–99 had benefited the local Teaching Centers, stimulating financial growth, independence, and a new missionary program. This new process of growth had been aborted when the Board of Directors forced Cleirbaut to resign and sought to reestablish the locus of power at CUT's central headquarters.

An informant offered his view of the power struggle:

I had already sent out letters to headquarters explaining the problems. They were not moving. Our Teaching Center had moved ahead, but headquarters had moved backwards. After Gilbert quit (at least that was what we were told), we thought nothing had changed. But when I talked to Gilbert, I found out he had been constantly backstabbed. People there would not let him do his work. ECP and the Masters were supporting him! But people felt they were losing power, so there was a big power struggle! A lot of Ministers looked at this as a pure power struggle. They would not let Gilbert do anything. He could not take it, and left.

As soon as the Board of Directors in Montana got wind of Cleirbaut's "LLL" they sent Directors out to each of the Teaching Centers in Canada to order them not to receive Cleirbaut again "or there would be penalties." Another informant recalls,

he came to the teaching centers in Ottawa, Toronto, Montreal where he was received very well, but as soon as headquarters got wind of him, they sent a director to each center. "He is not to be received!" they said. He was not allowed to give lectures . . . They showed no interest in the dictations he had received. They were hung up on the fact that he was no longer a Keeper of the Flame. They threatened penalties. Afterwards, he was expelled.

Cleirbaut responded defiantly. He sent out an open letter complaining, "It has been two weeks since the Canadian tour was cancelled . . . CUT leaders have managed to put their members, our beloved KOF's to sleep for almost 3 years!" He began to hold meetings in the private homes of Keepers of the Flame, and started a Teaching Center for LLL in a small town in southern Ontario. But, discouraged by his unemployed status, he suddenly disbanded LLL and moved back to Belgium.

After Cleirbaut resigned, the Board of Directors at headquarters in Montana continued to operate under the old authoritative paradigm, which was no longer acceptable for many of the leaders of regional centers. The former President of the Teaching Center in Montreal complained:

> The leadership then tried to go back to the old way – but there *was* no old way. There was no ECP in charge – getting messages from the Masters, and listening to the people below. This new leadership had *no* contact from above and wanted *no input* from below, from the membership.

Our informant described these bodies as "hidebound":

> The 24 Elders – they vote for themselves, they are aligned with each other, they decide everything, in perpetuity. It [the Council] had become a dictatorship with the two Co-Presidents and the Board of Directors (there were 8 or 9). First, three shared the Presidency, then there were two. These were very *average* people.
>   This became a dead church, with no living word. Once ECP retired, they put up a fence.
>   All the people who showed any ability or attainment, any Light, Christ Consciousness – those were the people who couldn't stay. Mediocrity ruled. Heads were chopped off because it made the leaders look bad. They destroyed a movement that the Masters were using to bring about the Golden Age!

The Board of Directors forced several leaders to resign, among them William Malek, Carl Showalter, Andrew Blumenschein, and Arie Abravanel.

William Malek had been traveling around with Cleirbaut, working with him on Community Building. He was very popular among members of the regional Teaching Centers, and was reluctant to stop his work, so the Board asked him to resign.

Carl Showalter was one of the top ministers at CUT and was invited to become the resident minister for the Keepers of the Flame in Chicago ("People liked him very much"). Chicago was one of the largest of CUT's congregations. Our informant explained Showalter's schism as follows:

> But then when the Board decided to reassert its authority, they tried to undo the work Gilbert had done. Carl disagreed with the Board, he exchanged public letters with the headquarters at CUT and then he was fired. This caused a

schism. Some stayed loyal to him, and others stayed loyal to CUT. He began a new movement called Spiritual Awareness Fellowship.

Andrew Blumenschein was in the Council of Elders at CUT headquarters, and on the Board of Directors at one time. He was sent out to the regional centers to lead decreeing sessions and prayers. He was charismatic and dynamic, and his resignation was a blow to many members who enjoyed his meetings.

Arie Abravanel had been the President of Montreal's Teaching Center, who sent out letters and emails supportive of dissident leaders, and critical of the Board's policies in handling the Moscow group. He describes the situation as follows:

The Russia group broke away after they were ordered to do things they knew were counter-productive. I sent out exposés to tell what was going on. It created a major disturbance in the organization. Some were happy to find out, others couldn't understand. So, there were those people who stayed, others who left. Suddenly, we were up in the air. Those individuals who were deemed trouble makers, their membership was terminated.

It appears that the combination of circumstances – Elizabeth Clare Prophet's retirement, the successful coup against her successor, and the interrupted process of decentralization – created a favorable environment for schismatic movements and pretenders to the mantle of Messenger.

MESSENGER GROUPS

Several members left CUT and began dictating messages from an assortment of Ascended Masters, among them David Lewis and Marsha Covington, and a publication-based group led by Kim and Lorraine Michaels. David Lewis created a website to share his dictations (www.heartspace.org). In 2005 a concerned CUT member complained, "There are at least eight people currently claiming the mantle of Messenger" (www.aznewage.com/prophet.htm).

Temple of the Presence. The most successful schism of this type is the Temple of the Presence, founded by a former high-ranking member and his wife. Monroe Shearer was President of the Board of Directors in the late 1980s when, according to our source, he was informed by ECP that she had received a dictation from El Morya that Monroe Shearer needed to expand his "love flame."[16]

---

[16] In CUT's theology, the path of self-mastery comes partly through the balance of the threefold flame of love, wisdom, and power. As our informant explained, "someone like Monroe who had a

Monroe was relieved from his position on the Board and given an assignment in South America where, "according to the teachings, people have a highly developed love flame." When he returned to the USA in the late 1980s, according to our source, "instead of working under the Messenger he decided to be the Messenger. He put Mother down, said judgment calls were not needed, and portrayed himself as a better Messenger . . . He was favorable to Mark Prophet and less favorable to Mother."

In 1996 Monroe and Carolyn Shearer organized an "Ascended Master group" in Redland, CA, and today they preside over the Temple of the Presence in Chelsea, VT. Carolyn Shearer also functions as a Messenger.

The Board in Montana reacted defensively and sent out an open letter on March 3, 2005 saying, "We completely reject the claims of David Lewis and others to messengership . . . Mother and Jesus told us that in the last days there would be many rival prophets in the land who would imitate the voices of the Masters" (MacMillion 2005).

NON-MESSENGER GROUPS

The Moscow Study Group. The Moscow Study Group was the largest group in the world outside America, attracting approximately 135 people for their weekly St. Germain Service. They held annual teaching classes that drew up to 500 people ("Expose the Truth: Please Read the Other Side of the Story," www.victorysvoice.com, August 27, 2007). On August 29, 2003 the Board of Directors of Ranch headquarters removed five of the six Board members from the Moscow Study group during a meeting between the two parties. The firing stemmed from the Russian Board's reluctance to allow ministers from the American Church to give Summit University lessons in Moscow. They feared this activity would attract anti-cult attention and put them in danger of persecution.

The Ranch headquarters president, Lois Drake, wrote in a September 1, 2003 open letter that the "extremely angry behavior [during the meeting] by the Moscow board was so far removed from the acceptable conduct of chelas, and combined with numerous complaints from Moscow Keepers of the Flame, that there was no choice but to ask five of the six members of the Moscow Board to step down." This forced stepping down resulted in the appointing of new members to the Moscow Board by the Ranch.

lot of wisdom and power, but a lot less love, limited his potential, as his power and wisdom can only be expressed through his lowest common denominator."

The five ex-Board directors protested in a September 4, 2003 letter, "We firmly believe the Church leadership wanted our removal because we refuse to invite ministers and the President of the Church to our city, and we refuse to comply with their demands to break the laws of Russia on their behalf."

The old Board in Moscow continues group activities to this date, and most of the Russian Keepers have remained loyal to them. The Ranch leadership (Presidents, Manager, CUT Board) then responded to this burgeoning schism by stating in an open letter on September 26, 2003:

> For the purpose of clarity we want you to know that the study group led by Olga P, Konstantin A, Julia P, Lidia S and Andrew B, is the only official study group sponsored by The Summit Lighthouse in Montana. There is reported confusion about the legitimacy of the group still being led by Ketino and the removed board. Ketino L, Stuart M, Margarita D, Sergey S and Nina K are no longer leaders or official representatives of The Summit Lighthouse.

FACTORS ENHANCING CUT'S PROPENSITY TO SCHISMS

We have described the historical and social context of CUT's schismatic movements, and now we will attempt to analyze the structural conditions that stimulated the schisms. We will follow Roy Wallis's advice by not focusing on personality clashes or power struggles between individuals, but rather we will try to locate the structural conditions that dictate a NRM's propensity toward schism. In trying to identify these underlying conditions, the following questions must be addressed.

Were the schismatic movements a delayed response to the Shelter Cycle's "prophetic failure"?

There is no doubt that, in the aftermath of the Shelter Cycle, defections occurred and the decline in tithing plunged the Church in debt (although the exact statistics are unavailable). Whitsel writes, "CUT lost about one-third of its total membership in the immediate aftermath of the shelter period" (2003: 131). Cleirbaut suggests in an interview with a journalist that the defection rate may have been as high as 50 percent in the years after the expected nuclear strike in 1990.

Dawson and Whitsel (2005: 4) contrast the prosperity of CUT with the Shelter Cycle's aftermath: "All this abruptly changed with the apocalyptic misadventure of March 15, 1990. So what went wrong?" Whitsel (2003: 153), in his discussion of the problems besetting the authority structure of the Church in the wake of ECP's retirement in 1999, claims "the crisis that is presently playing out in the church stemmed directly from the nonevent of March 15, 1990."

Many of those who did not defect, however, interpreted the "nonevent" as a *victory*. Our informants described the Shelter Cycle as a positive and profoundly meaningful experience. Contrary to media reports and conventional wisdom, ECP's dictations from St. Germain and Mother Mary, both before and after March–April 1990, were quite effective in both "rationalizing" (Dawson 2005) and "spiritualizing" (Melton 1985) the fateful event – at least as far as our informants were concerned. One informant who joined CUT four months after the "nonevent" of March 15, 1990 declared:

The Shelter cycle acted as a major cathartic event for people. Some emerged victorious – because war hadn't broken out. Others felt betrayed – because war didn't break out! Some said, "What am I going to do now, I have nothing!" It was a crisis of faith that maybe this thing isn't real after all. The masters foretold there would be war! For the Toronto group, once the dust settled, I heard the talk: "How could this be?" Some just never showed up again. Some were not bitter, but had lost a spark of their faith – a significant number. Mostly people from other countries who came here especially for the shelter cycle.

When I joined people were still reeling from the experience.

Another informant who moved to the Ranch with his family to participate in "Preparedness" went underground on March 15, and shared his experience of the event:

When nothing happened, a lot of people had got into a lot of debt and some thought, "this is a waste of time!" People had invested – given up two years – to something with no demonstrable return. It was a great sacrifice.

I saw it as a major initiation on the Path. It was like the Stations of the Cross, being buried in the ground. It was an initiation where you accept death, are willing to die. By following directions you pass this major test, you are buried in the ground and then you re-emerge – a sort of resurrection! You have conquered aspects of death without having to experience it physically. On the Path, the most important thing is passing your initiations. It can cost a great deal, it requires sacrifice.

Whether or not March 15, 1990 qualifies as "victory" or a "nonevent," it did not immediately result in schism. It is interesting to note that no rival Messengers surfaced during this ambiguous moment with reinterpretations of prophecy from Ascended Masters. But it could be argued that the Shelter Cycle was a contributing factor in the schisms that occurred after 1999.

During the Shelter Cycle the resources of the local centers had been drained in the interests of "Preparedness." ECP had called on her chelas to leave their homes and move to the Royal Teton Ranch and surrounding area. After the crisis of the Dark Cycle passed, many who participated in the Shelter Cycle returned to their local Teaching Centers "on fire," ready to launch a missionary effort and spread the teachings of the Ascended Masters – a predictable response to "failure of prophecy," according to Festinger et al. (1956). Six years later, Cleirbaut made this possible, and a strong trend toward decentralization and local missionary programs began where members and resources flowed away from headquarters and back into the local centers.

On the basis of our findings, we can assert it was not the members' *experience of cognitive dissonance* that provoked the schisms per se, but rather that schisms resulted from a more complex process. First there were the debts incurred from building the fallout shelters that caused operational difficulties. Second, there was the rapid institutionalization of charisma under Cleirbaut. Third, there was a vacuum in the spiritual leadership as ECP became increasingly inactive. Finally, the Board of Directors squelched local spiritual leaders in an effort to gain administrative control. All these factors contributed to the schisms.

Were CUT's schisms the product of Cleirbaut's decentralization initiatives?

In 1996 we observe a rapid decentralization of the movement preparatory to ECP's retirement. ECP facilitated this decentralizing trend by appointing Gilbert Cleirbaut to implement his "new vision." Predictably, this new leadership and restructuring plan met with strong resistance from the core group at CUT's headquarters. After Cleirbaut's forced resignation, new trends toward decentralization, globalization, and local expansion through outreach were aborted. The resulting discord generated a series of schismatic movements, most of them spearheaded by charismatic regional presidents or by itinerant ministers sent out from headquarters, who were leading decrees and prayer vigils in Canada, Sweden, Moscow, and US cities. Schisms resulted from a power struggle between the Montana Board of Directors and the far-flung Teaching Centers that had been flourishing under Cleirbaut's tutelage and were unwilling to relinquish their new-found independence.

In this conflict between local authorities and central authorities we find one of the structural conditions facilitating schisms as described by Roy Wallis: "Informal personal influence and acknowledged leadership at a local level in the absence of clearly acknowledged authority" (Wallis 1979: 188). Thus, while decentralization has been identified as a condition leading to schism, we would argue that it was rather the interruption of this process, the sudden *recentralizing* initiatives of the Board – the "stop and start" divagations – that damaged CUT, and brought on the schisms.

Was CUT's "proneness" to schism due to the retirement of ECP?
ECP's illness was equivalent to a "social death" since she could no longer communicate with her followers. Wallis (1979) and Weber (1968) have both analyzed the battles over the succession that frequently erupt after the unexpected death of the charismatic founder. Wallis (1979: 177) notes that "schisms have a disproportionate tendency to occur on the death of charismatic leaders and more often in decentralized movements."

But in CUT's case, this factional conflict appears to be not so much a direct consequence of her "death" but rather the result of her deliberate but unrealistic preparations for her retirement. She appointed no new Messengers, only an administrative successor, which left a lacuna in the spiritual leadership.

A similar pattern occurred in ISKCON, in Christian Science, and in the Rajneesh (Osho) Foundation after the death of their charismatic founders. Each leader seemed determined to squelch future charismatic prophets who might initiate doctrinal changes and set up a strong administrative institution to succeed them, and to control charismatic currents among the priesthood. On his deathbed Bhagwan Shree Rajneesh (aka Osho) appointed seven disciples to the "Inner Circle" who, according to my source, were told, "Don't mess with the ideas! Just pay the bills and fix the roof!" A series of "Enlightened Ones" rose up, nevertheless, just before and after Rajneesh's demise – mostly New Age avant-garde therapists from the Rajneesh Meditation University, such as Swami Anand Teertha and Paul Lowe. They began to tour the international Osho meditation centers drumming up business. They offered therapy groups, and gave lectures in which their charismatic claims to guruhood were quite apparent.[17]

Swami Praphupada, before his death in 1974, appointed the Governing Body Commission to lead his movement. He had already ordained a group of spiritual leaders, the Initiating Gurus. Rochford (1985) shows

---

[17] SJP attended one of these events when Swami Teertha came to Montreal to give a therapy weekend in which his claims to be an Enlightened Master were made very clear, and watched several sannyasins in the process of defecting from the Osho movement to follow Teertha.

how, after his death, schisms resulted from conflicts between the Commission and various Initiating Gurus over fund-raising methods (book distribution versus "picking"). Several gurus claimed that Swami Praphupada had bestowed upon them the mantle of succession, and formed schismatic movements.

A similar conflict between the administrative and the spiritual leaders arose after Mary Baker Eddy's death. Wallis (1979: 187) writes: "Eddy had established a substantial bureaucratic edifice sometime prior to her death, and the membership had thus long been accustomed to direction from the Board of Directors of the Mother Church in Boston. Despite these careful preparations, however, there was a period of instability on her death as the Board sought to expand its authority to take Mrs. Eddy's place."

The Board's expansion was challenged by Annie Bill, who claimed to inherit Eddy's mantle of Pastor Emeritus, and opposed the Board's changes. She went on to establish the Christian Science Parent Church. Another challenge came from a Mrs. Augusta Stetson, who felt the Church should become purely "spiritual" in conception and objected to the Board's promotion of its "material" form. Wallis (1979: 188) notes, "both Mrs. Bill and Mrs. Stetson based their claims to legitimacy on an appeal to the unique status of the charismatic leader . . . in opposition to the transfer of authority to a bureaucratic apparatus."

Elizabeth Clare Prophet pursued a similar course of action. She split the leadership role into two, creating an administrative leadership while maintaining her own undisputed role as spiritual leader for the next four years, but did not appoint her successor as Messenger. She parachuted in a relatively new member, someone outside her core group as President, and it is hardly surprising that mature members of her charismatic community, long accustomed to a centralized, hierarchical authority structure, regarded Cleirbaut as an upstart and challenged his authority.

Bryan Wilson (1961: 340–1) observes in his study of the Christadelphians that "the absence of hierarchalization and of any institutionalization of charisma has probably assisted the process by stimulating a struggle for leadership possible only in the absence of defined roles and well-defined spheres of competence."[18] It appears that the authority structure in Montana headquarters became blurred and chaotic during the struggle between Cleirbaut and the Board. Meanwhile, local charismatic leaders gained more power. Cleirbaut's "new vision" had

---

[18] Quoted in Wallis 1979: 178.

deliberately fostered "empowerment" at a local level, so that the blossoming charisma of ministers leading prayer vigils and decrees at the Teaching Centers in the US, Canada, and Moscow posed new challenges to the central headquarters. John Wilson (1971: 10–11) argues that organizational centralization is an important "structural determinant of schism." He suggests that schism happens at either end of the continuum – at the *very decentralized* or *overly centralized*. While we do not find schisms happening in CUT under ECP's centralized rule, Wilson's theory applies to CUT's later, decentralized phase. It could also be argued that the destabilization of CUT's authority structure resulted from a *too sudden* transition from a charismatic to a bureaucratic type of leadership. It appeared to be *artificially* engineered, as opposed to the natural, gradual, involuntary process that can be observed in NRM histories.

Greensdale (1953) has argued that schisms result from a rivalry between sees or ecclesiastical jurisdictions. Certainly, we find conflicts or divisions between various levels of CUT's leadership: between spiritual and administrative leadership; between new and old leaders; and between the core group (the Board of Directors) and the regional Teaching Centers and Study Groups. All these conflicts were generated by ECP's choice in setting up a pattern of succession that relied too heavily on administrative leadership, at the expense of charisma. Without a living Messenger, CUT could no longer offer the same quality of spiritual guidance and political relevance and urgency to inspire its Keepers of the Flame.

THE CHARISMATIC FUTURE OF ELIZABETH CLARE PROPHET

Although ECP is still living, her retreat into Alzheimer's has been experienced by her followers as a "social death." Since then, she has lived on at the CUT headquarters in the care of her chelas and her adult children. One may visit her daughter Erin Prophet's website (www.ecprophet.info) to access recent health reports on Guru Ma and view photographs of ECP, her once radiant beauty dimmed by age and ill health. There is no attempt to maintain her charismatic persona. CUT's press releases, as well as Erin Prophet's reports on her mother's illness, are quite ordinary, and strangely secular.

It may appear strange to researchers in NRMs that, under these post-charismatic circumstances, no one has claimed that ECP is continuing to dictate messages from her sickbed. Laurence Moore (1977) has documented how weak, ailing, and tubercular ladies in the Victorian era were considered highly suitable vehicles for spirit communication, *because* of their frailty. Mircea Eliade (1950) notes that many shamans exhibit signs of epilepsy, but have learned to control their sickness and exploit it as an "archaic technique of ecstasy." ECP was diagnosed with epilepsy, and there is no reason why her weakened body and memory loss would disqualify her from continuing on in her role of Messenger. These messages would be very useful in providing direction as CUT faces high levels of ambiguity and rapid change. The reasons why this has not happened are unknown to these researchers.

REFERENCES

Dawson, Lorne L. 2005 "The Role of Prophecy in the Success and Failure of New Religious Movements: The Case of the Church Universal and Triumphant." Paper presented to the SSSR in Rochester, NY, November 4, 2005.

De Haas, Jocelyn H. 1994. "The Mediation of Ideology and Public Image in the Church Universal and Triumphant." In James R. Lewis and J. Gordon Melton (eds.) *Church Universal and Triumphant in Scholarly Perspective* (pp. 21–38). Stanford, CA: Center for Academic Publication.

Eliade, Mircea. 1950. *Shamanism: An Archaic Technique of Ecstasy*. Princeton: Princeton University Press.

Festinger, Leon, Henry W. Riecken and Stanley Schachter. 1956. *When Prophecy Fails: A Social and Psychological Study of a Modern Group that Predicted the End of the World*. Minneapolis: University of Minnesota Press.

Foster, Laurence. 1981. *Religion and Sexuality: Three American Communal Experiments of the Nineteenth Century*. New York: Oxford University Press.

Greenslade, S. L. 1953. *Schism in the Early Church*. London: SCM Press.

Homer, Michael. 1994. "Protection of Religion under the First Amendment: Church Universal and Triumphant." In James R. Lewis and J. Gordon Melton (eds.), *Church Universal and Triumphant in Scholarly Perspective* (pp. 119–38). Stanford, CA: Center for Academic Publication.

Kanter, Rosabeth Moss. 1972. *Commitment and Community: Communes and Utopias in Sociological Perspective*. Boston, MA: Harvard University Press.

Lewis, James R. and J. Gordon Melton (eds.). 1994. *Church Universal and Triumphant in Scholarly Perspective*. Stanford, CA: Center for Academic Publication.

McMillion, S. 1999. "Selling Off the Promised Land," *Bozeman Daily Chronicle*, March 15.

2005. "Selling Off the Promised Land," *Bozeman Daily Chronicle*, March 13.

Melton, Gordon J. 1985. "Spiritualization and Reaffirmation: What Really Happens When Prophecy Fails?" *American Studies* 26: 17–29.

1994. "The Church Universal and Triumphant: Its Heritage and Thoughtworld." In James R. Lewis and J. Gordon Melton (eds.), *Church Universal and Triumphant in Scholarly Perspective* (pp. 1–20). Stanford, CA: Center for Academic Publication.

Moore, Laurence. 1977. *In Search of White Crows: Spiritualism, Parapsychology and American Culture*. New York: Oxford University Press.

Prophet, Elizabeth Clare. 1994. "The Past is Prologue" (CUT pamphlet). Livingston, MT: Church Universal and Triumphant.

1999. *Soul Mates and Twin Flames: The Spiritual Dimension of Love and Relationships*. Corwin Springs, MT: Summit University Press.

Prophet, Erin, 2008. *Prophet's Daughter : My Life with Elizabeth Clare Prophet Inside the Church Universal and Triumphant*. Guildford, CT: Lyon's Press.

Prophet, Mark and Elizabeth Clare Prophet. 2001. *The Masters and the Spiritual Path*. Corwin Springs, MT: The Summit Lighthouse.

Rochford, Burke. 1985. *The Hare Krishna in America*. Brunswick, NJ: Rutgers University Press.

Saint Germain on Prophecy: Coming World Changes. 1986. Corwin Springs, MT: The Summit University Press.

Santucci, James A. 2006. "The Theosophical Society," In James R. Lewis (ed.), *Controversial New Religions* (pp. 259–94). New York: Oxford University Press.

Swihart, Altman. 1931. *Since Mrs. Eddy*. New York: Henry Holt.

Wallis, Roy. 1979. *Salvation and Protest: Studies of Social and Religious Movements*. New York: St. Martin's Press.

Weber, Max. 1968. *Economy and Society*. New York: Bedminster Press.

Whitsel, Brad. 2003. *The Church Universal and Triumphant: Elizabeth Clare Prophet's Apocalyptic Movement*. New York: Syracuse University Press.

Wilson, Bryan. 1961. *Sects and Society*. London: Heinemann.

1967. *Patterns of Sectarianism*. London: Heinemann.

Wilson, John. 1971. "The Sociology of Schism." In Michael Hill (ed.), *A Sociological Yearbook of Religion in Britain*, 4: 1–20.

CHAPTER 9

Schism and consolidation: the case of the theosophical movement

Olav Hammer

INTRODUCTION

Schism, the *Encyclopedia of Religions* informs us, "is the process by which a religious body divides to become two or more distinct, independent bodies. The division takes place because one or each of the bodies has come to see the other as deviant, as too different to be recognized as part of the same religious brotherhood." (Ammerman 1987: 98). Schism is one of the major mechanisms producing religious diversity, and examples of the process are thus ubiquitous.

A religious schism will typically involve three successive phases. First, there is a period of tension between various individuals or factions within a group. There follows the actual break-up between these factions. Finally, a stage of consolidation allows the situation in the mother organization and the seceding body to stabilize. The last of these stages entails issues that the new organization will attempt to tackle. For years, members of a community have accepted to form part of an existing social formation, and have followed the rituals and doctrines as presented by the leading strata of that organization. When a break takes place, the leaders and most prominent members of the new group will need to create a distinct identity for the new community.

Identity politics of this kind involves characteristic dilemmas. Consider one of the most frequent mechanisms involved in doctrinal and ritual innovation. Claude Lévi-Strauss coined the nearly untranslatable term *bricolage* to describe how mythical innovations take place.[1] The *bricoleur* is a handyman who arranges various preexistent elements into a new

---

[1] Claude Lévi-Strauss 1966: 16. Lévi-Strauss defines the concept thus: "The characteristic feature of mythical thought is that it expresses itself by means of a heterogeneous repertoire which, even if extensive, is nevertheless limited. It has to use this repertoire, however, whatever the task in hand because it has nothing else at its disposal. Mythical thought is therefore a kind of intellectual 'bricolage'."

configuration. In the world of religion, *bricolage* is ubiquitous. Few concepts and practices are truly original; much religious innovation adjusts the details of already known traditions, recombines and reinterprets available elements into new combinations, or replaces old interpretations of existing scriptures with new ones. New religions therefore tend to resemble their predecessors, to such an extent that one well-established system of classifying emergent religions relies on the family resemblances that arise as a result of shared origins.[2] An air of familiarity, it has been argued, is in fact crucial for the success of an emergent religious movement (Stark 1987: 13–15). For a schismatic group, however, similarity with its mother organization is also a problematic trait. If the differences between the two organizations were perceived to be negligible, it would presumably be difficult to convince potential members to join the schismatic group. In the consolidation phase, the success of a schismatic group thus depends on striking a balance between continuity with one's predecessors and drawing boundaries against them.

Creating a separate identity is accomplished by branding one's own movement. Merely stressing the doctrinal and ritual innovations of one's group is rarely enough to ensure successful branding. Novel elements may be sufficient identity markers for virtuoso members, who are trained in the theological arcana of the tradition. In order to reach a broader audience, however, successful identity politics typically requires the deployment of more obvious markers of difference.[3] One common element of branding is polemics that normatively ranks the discourses and practices of the competitors as inferior to one's own. Other religious ideologies may be depicted as utterly false, as being lower on the spiritual scale, or less appropriate to prevailing historical conditions than one's own. Other elements of successful branding include fashioning visually striking material artifacts, instituting communally celebrated festivities, creating easily identifiable symbols that designate affiliation, and using iconography and public discourse in order to elevate the schismatic leader to near-mythic status. Although the term *branding* (or its synonym *brand management*) is typically used to denote the conscious efforts by

---

[2] The system is used in such works as Melton's *Encyclopedia of American Religions* (1989) and Partridge's *Encyclopedia of New Religions* (2004).

[3] Indirectly, this can also be acknowledged by members of religious groups. In discussions with members of the Anthroposophical Society in the Netherlands, I have repeatedly come across the complaint voiced by older members that younger anthroposophists had little understanding of Rudolf Steiner's ideas, and were primarily attracted by Waldorf education, biodynamic farming, or anthroposophical complementary medicine.

contemporary firms and organizations to employ marketing strategies in order to influence the impressions others will have of them, the term is here used more broadly. The effects of brand management may arise without any explicit desire to treat one's religious tradition as a commodity to be marketed. Although the cross was obviously not instituted as a conscious strategy to provide Christianity with a religious symbol, the long-term result has been to give Christian denominations an instantly recognizable logo.

In this chapter, I will discuss these issues by means of two particular cases, schisms that took place within the theosophical movement and led to the emergence of the Point Loma theosophists and the Anthroposophical Society. How did each of these groups manage to consolidate and to present itself as a movement with a distinct identity and a more adequate understanding of spiritual matters?

BRIEF HISTORICAL BACKGROUND

The driving force behind the establishment of the Theosophical Society was Helena Blavatsky, born in 1831 as Helena Petrovna von Hahn.[4] Although the details of her early life remain difficult to trace with any certainty, it is known that her interest in spiritualism and occult phenomena led her on several occasions to create organizations dedicated to such pursuits. While earlier efforts, including a Société Spirite founded in Egypt, were short-lived, her lasting achievement was the establishment of the Theosophical Society in 1875. The event was precipitated by a lecture held by George H. Felt on September 7, 1875 on "The Lost Canon of Proportion of the Egyptians." A group of people who attended, including Blavatsky, called for the creation of an organization to pursue such "alternative" topics. After several meetings to discuss practical matters, the society was formally inaugurated on November 17, 1875 by Henry Olcott. Although Olcott was elected chairman of the newly formed society, the ideological impetus of the society was from the very beginning provided by Blavatsky. Her knowledge of Western esoteric traditions and her purported communication with various spiritually evolved beings were the basis of formulating the doctrines of the new movement.

The stated purpose of the society was to investigate "the esoteric philosophies of ancient times" (Campbell 1980: 28). Two large works by Blavatsky, *Isis Unveiled* (1877) and *The Secret Doctrine* (1888), presented

---

[4] For the background facts of theosophical history, see Campbell (1980).

similar but not identical versions of these "esoteric philosophies." In both books, she incorporated a vast range of topics. References abound to Atlantis, mesmerism, Tibet, Paracelsus, magic, alchemy, India, the kabbalah, and a host of other matters. In Blavatsky's earliest texts, the main sources of this ancient wisdom were (a largely imaginary) Egypt, kabbalah, and various Western esoteric currents. Soon after the publication of *Isis Unveiled*, the homeland of hidden wisdom shifted away from Egypt and the occult West, and moved increasingly toward India. Blavatsky's and Olcott's departure for Bombay in 1878 (and later, in 1882, to Adyar near the city of Madras) basically confirmed a doctrinal change that was already well underway. The orientalization of theosophy was finally consolidated in what today stands out as the canonical text of theosophy: *The Secret Doctrine*. Although in most respects compatible with the teachings of her previous magnum opus, the core ideas expounded in *The Secret Doctrine* are attributed to an ancient palm leaf manuscript from the Himalayas, the Stanzas of Dzyan.

From the perspective of the Theosophical Society itself, the contents of the *Secret Doctrine*, purportedly an extended commentary on these Stanzas, are not based on a specifically Indian tradition. Although Sanskrit vocabulary and references to Hinduism and Buddhism abound, the teachings of theosophy are claimed to transcend any local, historically defined religious current, and are said to distil the essence of an ancient and universal wisdom tradition. The universality of the message was guaranteed by the fact that their source was a hierarchy of Masters, beings whose high level of spiritual evolution enabled them to transcend cultural and religious barriers. They could reveal the secret, esoteric meaning underlying the differing exoteric details of the various religions.

The doctrines and practices of theosophy, as enshrined in this and other documents, as well as the conviction that Blavatsky was the prime conduit of the teachings of the Masters, gave the Theosophical Society a distinct corporate identity. Nevertheless, doctrines, practices, and the convictions of members do not by themselves suffice to constitute a viable religion. A religious organization requires ways to manifest its identity and presence, and does so not least by developing a material culture. Doctrinal and other elements that serve to display that identity cannot be disseminated without the requisite infrastructure: publications and the means to print and distribute these; administrative and religious buildings; human and financial resources. The centre established in Adyar toward the end of the nineteenth century still serves as the headquarters of the Theosophical Society, and has over time grown to include a publisher (the Theosophical Publishing House), a printing press (Vasanta Press), a library (the Adyar Library and Research Centre), schools, craft centers, a hostel for visitors, and several religious buildings that in symbolic form recapitulate basic elements of theosophy. A quote from the website of the Theosophical Society at Adyar shows how the society manifests its identity in tangible form:

On entering the hall, one sees in the alcove behind a marble platform a figure in plaster of H. P. Blavatsky modeled from Schmiechen's portrait of her . . . When Colonel Olcott passed away in 1907, a plaster statue of him was placed by the side of Madame Blavatsky and an inscription engraved on the pedestal: "The Founders of the Theosophical Society: Helena Petrovna Blavatsky 1831–1891 – Henry Steel Olcott 1832–1907." Along the walls of the hall are bas-relief symbols and figures: those on the north, east and west represent living religions – Christianity, Buddhism, Hinduism, Zoroastrianism, Islam, Jainism, Judaism, Taoism, Confucianism, Shintoism, and the Baha'i religion. The south wall represents the extinct religions. In the west is a large board on which are inscribed the names of all the Sections of the Theosophical Society with the dates of their formation.[5]

The three iconographic elements that adorn the main building sum up the history and ideology of the movement: the portraits of the two founders, the symbols of the tradition-transcending universalism that is central to the self-understanding of the society, and the signs of its recent, triumphant history.

THEOSOPHY AS A SCHISMATIC MILIEU

The Theosophical Society did not only function as an institutionalized religious movement, but also shared certain crucial characteristics of what sociologist Colin Campbell (1972) called the cultic milieu. Campbell describes this as an environment in which "alternative" or heterodox ideas are able to flourish, and in which differences of interests and opinion are widely tolerated. Although Blavatsky had an unequalled status as (emically speaking) spokesperson for the Masters, and therefore as the main ideologue of the Theosophical Society, the theosophical lodges tended to attract a range of people with different interests, united perhaps more by their attraction for heterodoxy than for their strict adherence to the specific contents of Blavatsky's publications. To recall just one example: although *The Secret Doctrine* evinces little interest in astrology, the

---

[5] From www.ts-adyar.org/headquarters.html#press (all cited websites were accessed on June 5, 2007).

present-day revival of astrological divination is largely due to the efforts of individuals active in British theosophical lodges.[6]

Despite the tolerance of the cultic milieu, it displays considerable centrifugal forces. The Theosophical Society similarly has seen a number of independent-minded, entrepreneurial former members found (or attempt to found) their own organizations.[7] These tendencies existed already in Blavatsky's own time. Anna Kingsford joined the Theosophical Society in 1883, despite the fact that she promoted a form of occultism which was much more inspired by spiritualism and by esoteric interpretations of Christianity than Blavatsky's version was. In 1884, the London Lodge of the theosophists split into two branches, with one following Kingsford and the other, led by Alfred Sinnett, loyal to Blavatsky (Campbell 1980: 86). Kingsford formed her own group, the Hermetic Society.[8] In the mid-1880s conflicts between Blavatsky and Olcott arose, and these were only partly resolved by allowing a considerable amount of independence for various branches and sections of the society. Olcott attempted to hold power over the British Section, a move that Blavatsky vigorously fought (Campbell 1980: 96–8).

The conflicts between Blavatsky and Olcott were finally halted, unresolved, by the death of the former in 1891. The continuing issues of succession and control, however, led to a series of schisms in the ensuing decades, two of which will be of particular concern here. At the time of Blavatsky's death, the most powerful individuals in the Theosophical Society were Olcott, William Q. Judge who was the leader of the American section of the society, and Annie Besant, a political activist who had converted to theosophy only a few years earlier. Judge made vigorous attempts to oust Olcott from power, and finally succeeded in doing so by forging an alliance with Besant. The uneasy partnership between Judge and Besant did not last. A long and complex series of conflicts between them ultimately made the theosophists split into two distinct groups. In

---

[6] For the nineteenth/twentieth-century revival of astrology, and the involvement of British theosophists such as Alan Leo (1860–1917) in this process, see Curry (1992).

[7] Theosophy has traits reminiscent of the cultic milieu in at least two ways. On the one hand, key members were prone to innovate and secede from the Theosophical Society. On the other, the doctrines of theosophy have diffused through a much vaster network of people than that constituted by the theosophical lodges. The latter process has led to the creation of numerous organizations that have no historical affiliation with the Theosophical Society but share important doctrinal elements (the I AM movement, Summit Lighthouse, and others), as well as to the emergence of a widely shared theosophically inspired discourse on spiritual evolution, reincarnation, karma, and so forth in New Age circles. Here, I will only consider the schismatic trend.

[8] On Kingsford's involvement with theosophy and her founding of the Hermetic Society, see Godwin (1994: 333–46).

1895 the American section decided to leave the parent organization. Judge became the President of the Theosophical Society in America, an organization which – under several different names – has continued to exist until the present day. Besant remained the head of the Adyar-based theosophists.[9]

A second schism took place in 1913, when the leader of the German section of the Theosophical Society, Rudolf Steiner, seceded from the movement, and took the majority of the German and Scandinavian members with him. Whereas the name of Judge's organization implies continuity with the past, Steiner named his organization the Anthro-posophical Society, in an attempt to distance himself more clearly from his theosophical involvement.

Although I will restrict myself to these two cases, it should be noted that further schisms followed throughout the ensuing decades, when disaffected members of the Theosophical Society left the mother organ-ization in order to lead their own communities. Some of these groups have continued to attract members up to the present day. In 1909, Robert Crosbie founded the United Lodge of Theosophists, with the aim of returning to Blavatsky's original teachings, which Crosbie felt had been misrepresented by other theosophists. Yet another group is Alice Bailey's Arcane School. In 1915, Bailey came into contact with the Theosophical Society. Beginning in 1922 (with her book *Initiation, Human and Solar*), she wrote a considerable corpus of theosophically inspired works. The year after, in 1923, Alice Bailey founded her own organization. Finally, one can mention the Agni Yoga society, founded by Nicholas and Helena Roerich in the 1920s. After having been members of the Theosophical Society for some years, they increasingly distanced themselves from that society and began to propagate a theosophically inspired teaching to a circle of interested followers.[10]

THE AMERICAN THEOSOPHISTS

When William Q. Judge broke off from the mother organization in April 1895, some 6,000 members voted to join him (Campbell 1980: 11). Judge

[9] A much more detailed presentation of the conflict between Judge and Besant can be found in Campbell (1980: 103–11).
[10] The most damaging break-up to afflict the Theosophical Society is not included here, because strictly speaking it did not constitute a schism. When Jiddu Krishnamurti, who had been raised as future World Teacher, publicly distanced himself from his role in 1929, he explicitly rejected the idea of forming a new organization with himself as leader.

stood at the height of his career as a religious leader, but it was a short-lived triumph. He died less than a year after the split, in March 1896. The details of the succession to Judge's position are not entirely clear.[11] Around 1892 or 1893, the spiritualist and social reformer Katherine Tingley (1847–1929) had joined the Theosophical Society (Greenwalt 1955: 15). Tingley apparently did not hold any high-level posts in the society, but in the last months of his life Judge became close friends with her and apparently became convinced that she provided him with a mediumistic link to the spirit of Blavatsky (Campbell 1980: 133; Greenwalt 1955: 16). In a series of secret meetings immediately after Judge's death, Tingley convinced other high-ranking members that she should be given the influential role of Outer Head of the Esoteric Section. The presidency of the society was, however, at first vested in Edward T. Hargrove, and Tingley continued to keep a low profile. In 1898, however, Tingley assumed full leadership, after what appears to have been a rather tumultuous power struggle at the theosophical congress in Chicago (Roos 1913: 75). To mark the shift, she renamed the society the Universal Brotherhood and Theosophical Society. The turbulence around these matters of leadership once again led to schisms. Hargrove left the American society together with a small group of members, and founded his own theosophical group, the Theosophical Society of America (Hargrove) (Campbell 1980: 135). In the same year, 1898, the Theosophical Society of New York was founded as an independent movement by J. H. Salisbury and Donald Nicholson, and in the following year W. H. Dower and Frances J. Meyers founded the Temple of the People (Melton 1989: 730).

Of the various American theosophical organizations, the group led by Tingley was by far the most successful. Tingley was able to project a distinct identity for her society by the means outlined at the beginning of this chapter: by rejecting competing approaches, and by crafting distinctive material artifacts, rituals and doctrines, festivities, symbols and hagiographic accounts that could mark Tingley's brand of theosophy as a distinct and superior alternative.

Katherine Tingley took over a movement in which leadership was predicated on being a legitimate conduit of the spiritual insight that came from the hidden Masters. Blavatsky's preeminent position over a movement of which formally she was only co-founder, depended on the acceptance by other theosophists of her claims to privileged access to these

---

[11] For an attempt to uncover these details, see Greenwalt (1955: 12–21).

beings. Judge's bid for leadership also involved asserting that the Masters had chosen him. Tingley similarly professed to have contact with the Masters.[12] More important for the future direction of the American branch, however, was the fact that she brought with her into the society a strong personal interest in social reform and utopianism. In her pre-theosophical days, she had operated the Do-Good Mission in one of the slums of New York (Greenwalt 1955: 15). The very first chapter of Tingley's first published work, *Theosophy, the Path of the Mystic* (1922), reveals how she carried this practical perspective with her into her career as a theosophist:[13]

The principles of theosophy are worthless unless carried out in deeds. It is useless to pile up in the library of our intellectual life ideas upon ideas – and nothing more. The world is weighed down with mere intellectualism already. It must have something more, and that something more is the active, practical expression of those ideas, those spiritual principles, in every act of life.

Tingley's main project as leader of the American society was the construction of a utopian community. Together with a number of prominent members of the organization, she launched herself on a global tour in order to publicize her efforts. In June 1896 the group sailed to England, attempting to find support in the very heartland of the Besant-led faction.[14] They continued to visit in rapid succession Ireland, France, Holland, Germany, Austria, Italy, Greece, Egypt, and India. Olcott, who was residing at Adyar, felt that the Americans invaded his territory. The visitors pointedly reminded him that theosophy was born on Tingley's home turf, New York, and that the Americans had, in fact, contributed most of the funds to maintain the Adyar headquarters (Greenwalt 1955: 30).

Tingley had decided that the theosophical utopia should be constructed at Point Loma, on the outskirts of San Diego. What Adyar had become for the original Theosophical Society under Blavatsky and Olcott, the Point Loma community would become for the American branch: a focal rallying point, and a symbol of the movement. With the backing of

---

[12] Relevant passages from Tingley's writings are excerpted on http://www.theosophy-nw.org/theosnw/theos/th-ktkt2.htm.

[13] Tingley's works have been made available on-line by the Theosophical Society (Pasadena). The quote can be found at www.theosociety.org/pasadena/pathmyst/path-1.htm. The suggestion that theosophy is a practical pursuit rather than a set of doctrines or a path toward hidden insights recurs in later publications. To take just one example, the eighth chapter of her second book, *The Wine of Life* (1925) carries the title "Occultism, the Science of Right Living" (www.theosociety.org/pasadena/wine).

[14] For details of the world tour, see Greenwalt (1955: 23–34).

several wealthy members of the society, sufficient finances were secured for procuring the land and beginning the construction work (Greenwalt 1955: 47). As soon as the first few buildings were in place, and visitors could be housed, Tingley began arranging the first of the many cultural events for which Point Loma would become known. Pageantry, drama, and lectures became recurring features of the community.

A number of buildings were erected over the next years. Few of the Point Loma structures have survived to the present, but architecturally the site must at the time have been truly striking. The main buildings were capped by large tinted glass domes. Photographs of the Temple of Peace show an interior adorned by intricate woodwork and painted arabesques. Huge glass spires surrounded the central dome of the Temple, and these were illuminated at night so that they could be seen from far away. As an acknowledgment of the theosophical veneration of a sacred past, the area also comprised a Greek-style theatre building, a Roman gate, and an Egyptian gate.

Once the Point Loma community was in operation, education for children became one of its most important activities. The community included a preschool for three- to five-year-olds, as well as primary and secondary schools. Drama and music were particularly important subjects at all levels. Underlying the program was a theory of education rooted in a theosophical understanding of human nature: heredity could be overcome; an adequate method of teaching could address the higher, inner person. Perhaps somewhat paradoxically for modern sensibilities, the schooling at Point Loma combined an emphasis on artistic development with Spartan ideals. Strict discipline was enforced, meals were served twice a day only, at precise times, and pupils were not allowed off premises without permission. Again, this was grounded in a dualistic model of the self, according to which one's baser nature must be counteracted in order to let the higher self bloom.

In his book *The Point Loma Community*, historian Emmett Greenwalt notes how similar Tingley's system of schooling was to other didactic currents. It shared its basic orientation with F. W. A. Froebel, who emphasized the importance of artistic and practical activities in the education of young children (Greenwalt 1955: 78). Its more Spartan elements were reminiscent both of Victorian attitudes and of Japanese-style schooling (1955: 88). The performances that were set up at Point Loma were designed in such a way that their inner significance should evoke themes common to all theosophical groups, such as initiation into spiritual mysteries, and did so in a way that resembles other turn-of-the-century esoteric conceptions of art (1955: 100–3). Nevertheless, the didactic practices at Point Loma were promoted as a unique path, Raja Yoga, a method created by Tingley and managed under her strict supervision.

Tingley spread the influence of her group by organizing further tours abroad. As a part of her efforts, Raja Yoga schools were planned for Cuba and Sweden. The Swedish case is well documented in contemporary sources, and serves as an instructive example of branding. A theosophical lodge was established in Sweden in 1889.[15] Shortly after the schism between the American and Adyar theosophists, most Swedish theosophists sided with the American society. The primary reasons for this choice seem to have been political, rather than dogmatic. Whereas Besant advocated centralism and insisted that decisions affecting the European lodges be made at meetings in the London headquarters, the American theosophists accepted a much greater degree of local independence. Ironically, this model of distributed authority made the Swedish theosophical milieu one of the focal points of Katherine Tingley's activities. Tingley was elected an honorary member of the Swedish society, now renamed Universella Broderskapet (the Universal Brotherhood). She visited Sweden for the first time in 1899, returned on several occasions, worked to establish a theosophical community on the island of Visingsö, and spent the last weeks of her life there.

The style of her identity politics can be seen from one of her visits. In 1913 Tingley convened a theosophical peace conference on Visingsö. Presumably in a move to divert interest from their competitors, the Adyar theosophists held a large convention in Stockholm at precisely the same time, with Annie Besant present. Tingley took the occasion to polemicize against her main adversary. At one point during the Visingsö peace conference, a local representative of the Church of Sweden protested against her plans for a community on the island. In an interview for the Swedish newspaper *Aftonbladet*, Tingley recalled the incident as follows:

When the priest who had held the most important speech against theosophy had finished, I went up to him and thanked him. He looked at me in amazement. Why should I thank him? "Because you have rejected precisely what I myself wholeheartedly reject. When you attempted to characterize Theosophy, you referred to Mrs. Besant's opinions, which I consider to be of great detriment to

---

[15] The historical background of theosophy in Sweden is summarized by Sanner (1995: 304–30) and Lejon (1997: 124–36), from which the following information is taken.

genuine theosophy. You could not have done me a greater service than through your speech."[16]

The congress itself was followed in detail by representatives of the national Swedish press.[17] The theosophists had chosen the dramatic ruins of the sixteenth-century Visingsborg castle on the eastern side of the island as the site of the theosophical *Festspiele* that inaugurated the proceedings. Rows of raised seats were placed in an amphitheatre, facing an altar. The elderly Katherine Tingley entered, clothed in a white gown, and held the opening speech. After a musical interlude, the audience was presented with a procession of Point Loma residents, who represented various cultural luminaries from the past. Tingley herself participated in the role of the Swedish medieval saint Bridget. Poetry was recited, some of which is difficult to read as anything else than blunt attacks on the rival Adyar organization: "From the East came the deadly serpent, ready to sting," but "[William Q.] Judge stood fast, without faltering, and without hesitation he gave his life in sacrifice." This was followed by a play depicting the philosophical elite of Ancient Greece, which was also performed by members of the Point Loma community. The piece ended with Socrates being carried away in prophetic ecstasy, foretelling the rise of the Point Loma community two and a half thousand years later. Finally, the symbolic founding stone of the projected Raja Yoga school was laid, and Tingley gave another speech in which she proclaimed Visingsö to be the second most beautiful place on Earth (presumably after Point Loma).

Whereas the performance of classics of the theatrical and musical repertoire met positive reactions, attitudes to pieces developed by the Point Loma community itself differed widely, depending on the background of the observer. One critic with theosophical connections praised the level of artistic achievement; a less sympathetic reviewer found the performances embarrassingly tasteless.[18] Whatever the artistic merits or demerits of the project may have been, considered as a piece of religious rhetoric the Point Loma conference made a clear statement. The many

---

[16] Roos 1913: 90–1 (translation mine). Other accounts of Tingley convey a similar impression of recurrent polemics against her rival Besant. Gunilla von Düben's autobiographical narrative of her time as Tingley's secretary (1916: 53) notes that Tingley spoke of the other theosophical faction and its head with "untiring rancour."

[17] The summary of the events and the quotes from the performances are from Roos (1913: 93–8).

[18] Contrast Daniel de Lange's positive review (quoted in Greenwalt 1955: 104–5) with Anna Roos's ironical comments (Roos 1913: 94–7). De Lange's wife was a theosophist; Anna Roos was a Christian with a skeptical attitude toward theosophy.

similarities with other religious options of Tingley's own time, and the close historical and ideological ties with Adyar theosophy, were dramatically deemphasized in favor of a historiography according to which the highest forms of wisdom had passed as a spark of illumination from Greece, via the great mystics of Western civilization – and Sweden's celebrated mystic in particular – to Katherine Tingley and to her school.

If Tingley's strength was branding her movement through striking material artifacts, it was also her weakness. The Point Loma community had never been self-supporting, and was at the time of her death in 1929 in massive debt (Greenwalt 1955: 187). Owing to a lack of funds for adequate maintenance, the facilities were soon in decline. By the early 1940s, most of the Point Loma buildings had closed down. The Raja Yoga school at Visingsö, which had opened in 1924, had by then also ground to a halt (Greenwalt 1955: 152). The movement itself survived in a downsized format by relocating to a considerably more modest location in Corvina, California.

RUDOLF STEINER AND THE ANTHROPOSOPHISTS

The biographical data regarding Rudolf Steiner can be summarized in a few salient points.[19] He was born in 1861 in Donji Kraljevec, a small Croatian town near the Austrian border. As a child, Steiner showed a talent for philosophy. From 1879 to 1883 he studied at the Vienna Technische Hochschule. On the recommendation of one of his teachers, the precocious Steiner was at age twenty-one entrusted with the editorship of Goethe's works of *Naturphilosophie*. In the same year, 1882, his interest in the occult was awakened by a chance encounter with a Felix Kogutzki.

In 1902 Steiner joined the German section of the Theosophical Society, and he rapidly rose to the position of secretary general. Despite his prominent rank, the next several years were marked by recurrent conflicts with Annie Besant. Some disputes arose over doctrinal matters, in particular the place that Christianity should be given in the theosophical worldview. Other differences of opinion concerned organizational matters, not least Annie Besant's centralism. The most intense and most widely publicized controversies were those over Besant's decision to give the young Jiddu Krishnamurti a messianic role in the movement,

---

[19] Most biographies of Steiner are written by anthroposophists, the remainder by outside skeptics. The most authoritative biography by an insider is by Lindenberg, *Rudolf Steiner* (1997).

promoting him to the position of World Teacher. In December 1912 Steiner sent Besant a telegram accusing her of departing from fundamental theosophical principles, and urging her to resign. Besant replied by excluding the German section from her organization. Steiner promptly formed his own organization, the Anthroposophical Society. Most German theosophists joined him, and seceded from Besant's organization. A number of branches of the Theosophical Society in Switzerland, Austria, Italy, Sweden, Norway, and Denmark soon decided to side with Steiner, thereby effectively converting anthroposophy into a major, international movement (Roos 1913: 81).

Once Steiner had completed the break with the theosophical mother organization, we see the same attempts by the newly formed anthroposophists to distinguish themselves as an esoteric current with a clearly separate identity. Steiner moved to Switzerland, where he began to establish headquarters for his movement at Dornach, near the city of Basel. He spent the remaining eleven years of his life converting his form of esotericism into practical activities. Among other pursuits, he founded Waldorf education, anthroposophical medicine, and biodynamic farming, laid the foundations for a political program, and even described the outlines of an anthroposophically inspired banking system. Steiner also traveled extensively, delivering a truly staggering number of lectures. He died on March 30, 1925.

Steiner presented a distinctly different path toward occult insight than the one adopted by the various theosophical movements. Spiritual knowledge, he suggests, comes from the cultivation of one's spiritual senses. Ideally, *anybody* can reach the highest levels of insight.[20] Three aspects of this epistemological claim deserve particular emphasis. First, Steiner's writings stress that the adequately trained individual can go beyond the immediately observable world, and behind the surface appearance of things distinguish a suprasensible reality in a manner that is as precise, objective, and valid as the measurements of the more conventional scientist. Steiner produced a massive corpus of texts documenting the spiritual truths that he professed to perceive. Beside the books he wrote, some 6,000 lectures were transcribed and subsequently published. In all, the results of this purported suprasensible science have

---

[20] See, for example, a statement to this effect at the very beginning of one of Steiner's key works, *Wie erlangt man Erkenntnisse der höheren Welten*: "Es schlummern in *jedem* Menschen Fähigkeiten, durch die er sich Erkenntnisse über höhere Welten erwerben kann" (There are latent powers in *every* person, by which he [*sic*] can obtain knowledge of higher worlds); emphasis in the original.

been collected in more than 350 volumes. The reader of these tomes will come across highly detailed descriptions of the fate of the soul after the death of the physical body, the past incarnations of scores of specific individuals, the technology and climate of Atlantis, the spiritual characteristics of various nations and "races," the occult properties of metals, esoteric interpretations of the life of Christ, and much more. Second, many of these concrete details are embedded in a philosophic-hermeneutic context that would paradoxically seem to undermine a literal reading. Steiner repeatedly qualifies his statements with terms such as *gewissermassen* and *in einem gewissen Sinne*, suggesting that his specific statements are true only "in a sense." Third, just as people have a lesser or greater talent for scientific research, suprasensible insight is an unevenly distributed resource. Steiner is for his followers the person who came furthest in gaining awareness of the hidden dimensions of reality. While anthroposophical literature comprises exercises to develop one's suprasensible faculties, and the anthroposophical lifestyle includes such practices, the corpus of Steiner's writings are by and large the standard against which any personal insights that one might have are measured. We shall later return to these three characteristics.

Besides crafting this doctrinal corpus, Steiner took great pains to convert his esoteric vision into a visible, material entity, i.e. to manage anthroposophy as a brand. Visual representations in particular occupied him throughout his career, since art for Steiner constituted a third vehicle – beside science and religion – for conveying the truths of the suprasensible world. Art, for Steiner, had the particular advantage of representing these truths in a non-intellectualizing manner, the opposite of what he called an "abstract symbolic or wooden, allegoric art" (eine abstrakt symbolische oder eine stroherne allegorische Kunst).[21]

Steiner's career as an architect was part and parcel of his artistic ambitions, set in motion not least by the fact that he had created four esoteric mystery dramas, and lacked an appropriate arena for their performance (Creese 1978: 48). His first project was to direct the work on the site where the theosophical congress of 1907 in Munich was to be held. Over the years, projects included venues for producing mystery dramas, a building for the theosophists of Stuttgart, and a complex of buildings that would form the location of the first Goetheanum (of two). Besides the

---

[21] Steiner 1921: 16. Non-literalism is the general case. There are parts of Steiner's work where precision reigns. One such exception is eurythmy, a dance-like form of art in which the sounds of language and music are expressed in movement by means of a set of quite specific rules.

main Goetheanum building, a considerable number of private homes and utility buildings in the same style were erected. Finally, work on the present-day, second Goetheanum was initiated after the first building with that name burned down on New Year's Eve 1922/3.

Steiner's use of art and architecture is in some ways reminiscent of Tingley's. Just as the Point Loma commune attracted attention through both its artistic program and its architecture, Dornach became the site of a spectacular building used for artistic performances. The Goetheanum building as well as the use to which it has been put embody Steiner's religious and artistic vision. The construction, as we will see, even personifies his leadership style. Together with other visual elements – e.g. Steiner's portrait, a particular selection of colors, and an instantly recognizable font – the building functions as a distinctive logotype of the movement. Quite a few national or local anthroposophical websites incorporate an image of the Goetheanum, and even more sites include a page on Steiner's architecture.[22] Similarly, one of the biographical accounts written by an insider to the movement (Steiner's disciple Johannes Hemleben) carries an image of the building on the front cover.

The attempt to express esoteric religiosity in artistic terms was by no means unique to Steiner. The theosophical movement had attracted a number of painters around the turn of the twentieth century. Vasilij Kandinsky and Piet Mondrian are no doubt the best known, but they represent examples of an entire artistic trend. In the German-speaking theosophical milieu, Steiner had a predecessor in Hugo Höppener (1868–1948), nicknamed "Fidus." In the years around 1900 Höppener attempted to express a theosophically inspired nature religion through painting, and designed a Temple of the Earth (which was never constructed).[23] Nor is the anthroposophical architectural style completely unprecedented. A basic idea behind anthroposophy, one that the movement shares with its sister organizations in the theosophical family, is to provide an alternative to what was perceived as a materialistic culture. Anthroposophical architecture is similarly meant to be organic and alive.[24] Most obviously, this is a style of architecture that distinguished itself sharply from the

---

[22] E.g. the Swiss headquarters at www.goetheanum.org/aag.html, the Finnish site for anthroposophical medicine www.antroposofinenlaaketiede.fi/, the New Zealand organization at www.anthroposophy.org.nz, and many others.

[23] On Höppener and his religious art, see e.g. Bibo 1995.

[24] Schleicher 1987: 7. Steiner's own exegesis of his architecture was presented inter alia in a series of lectures held in 1923; an English-language translation of these has been published as *The Arts and Their Mission*.

functionalism that emerged in the first decades of the twentieth century. While functionalist architects utilized straight lines, cubes, and repetition, and eschewed decorative elements, Steiner's architecture employed rounded contours and irregular shapes. In doing so, the anthroposophical movement developed a visual language that in many ways resembled other anti-functionalist styles: art nouveau, expressionist architecture, and so forth.[25] The Catalan architect Antoni Gaudí (1852–1926) is today arguably the best-known proponent of this kind of architectural language. The early twentieth century saw quite a few attempts at creating sculptural and dramatic styles; among the chief examples in the German-speaking world, one finds Hans Poelzig (1869–1936), Bruno Taut (1880–1938), Hugo Häring (1882–1958), and Erich Mendelsohn (1887–1953). To name just one example, the Einstein Tower that Mendelsohn designed in 1917 and had built in the early 1920s is strikingly similar to some of the Dornach buildings created around the same time.

An outsider to the anthroposophical movement can thus be struck by the ways in which Steiner was part and parcel of his historical context. Like Tingley, Steiner and the anthroposophists faced the problem of branding his schismatic movement: to distance it from this context, present it as the unique and superior creation of its founder, and to impose Steiner's particular vision on the movement. The literature on anthroposophical art and architecture points at the success of the anthroposophists in doing so. Works written by outsiders will readily note the similarities and continuities that I have sketched here. Texts written by insiders present a different picture. Other "organic" architectures, from this perspective, merely have this-worldly characteristics and purposes, whereas anthroposophical architecture has a spiritual dimension. The design of the Goetheanum promotes spiritual insight in those who dwell in the building (Pehnt and Dix 1991: 9). Perceived historical links are relatively unimportant, since Steiner's architectural language constitutes "the creative expression of the great spiritual secrets of mankind and the universe" (Shepherd 1983: 77). Steiner's own view was that "it would of course be possible to juxtapose this style of building with others, but doing so wouldn't really lead you anywhere" (man könnte natürlich diesen Baustil angliedern an andere Baustile, aber damit kommt man doch nicht eigentlich weiter) (Steiner 1921: 20). When

---

[25] For a different assessment, however, see Adams (1992: 183); the author suggests that Steiner's architecture "shows very little outside influence and is not readily classifiable as an example of some already-recognized style or context."

historical links are mentioned, this is done in a selective fashion. As the name Goetheanum suggests, there is a continuity of intent between Rudolf Steiner and Goethe that Steiner himself readily discussed (1921: 9), and which is pursued by later anthroposophical authors such as Åke Fant (Raab, Klingborg and Fant 1992). This link is presumably acceptable because Goethe, from an orthodox anthroposophical perspective, also had insight into hidden spiritual realities. There are also indications that Steiner actively distanced himself from contemporaneous historical currents, perhaps in an attempt to present himself as the recipient of a unique spiritual insight. Mondrian tried to correspond with Steiner, but Steiner apparently never answered Mondrian's letters. In a later lecture, however, he described Mondrian's art as merely an intermediate step toward a truly spiritual means of expression (Ohlenschläger 1999: 29).

The Goetheanum has been put to use in ways that symbolize the anthroposophical movement. The building contains theatre stages, concert halls, and lecture rooms. In that sense, the Goetheanum resembles secular institutions for the fine arts. A distinguishing trait of the programs presented there is that the lectures, plays, and concerts largely reflect Steiner's own taste, or at least the parts of the European repertoire that resonate with Steiner's own oeuvre.[26] The Goetheanum in form as well as function represents a particular form of Western European esoteric high culture.

The links between Steiner's esoteric ideology and his artistic creed run deep. The rise of the mechanistic natural sciences in the seventeenth century had drawn a sharp line between objective and subjective characteristics of objects in the natural world. Galileo was a prominent spokesperson for this dichotomy; for him, mass is a primary, objective trait inherent in any object, while color is secondary, a subjective impression that arises only when an object is perceived by a human consciousness. For Goethe and other exponents of Romantic science, the distinction is fundamentally misguided. Scientific investigation should concern itself with the uniquely human act of consciousness that perceives

---

[26] A list of current events can be found at www.goetheanum.org/vk.html. At the time of writing (June 2007), the calendar did include non-anthroposophical elements (such as concerts with classical music). Many sessions, however, focused on themes such as eurhythmics, organic foods, sessions on the work of anthroposophically inspired artists such as Joseph Beuys, and lectures on Steiner's work. In view of what has been said above regarding Katherine Tingley's emphasis on classical Greek drama, the central place of the Orestes theme in Greek tragedy in the June 2007 schedule of the Goetheanum may be indicative of common interests in the post-theosophical schismatic milieus.

colors as well as other properties in the natural world. Steiner built on this Romantic conception and radicalized it. The three aspects of Steiner's epistemology outlined above – its passion for detail, its anti-literalism, and its portrayal of insight as a scarce resource concentrated in one person – prove to be particularly important in this context. His writings on the elements of spiritual art can be quite specific. Writing on colors, Steiner informs us that purple is the color of mysticism, blue calms the soul, red gives a feeling of festivity, while green is associated with the earthly domain. Furthermore, different colors enable the visionary seeker to see different classes of normally invisible spirit beings (Ohlenschläger 1999: 145). However, it is also stressed that colors and shapes cannot be interpreted as symbolic reflexes of particular occult realities. The first Goetheanum embodied this tension between being the tightly controlled result of Steiner's visionary activities, and the fluidity (not to say vagueness) of his overarching hermeneutic. Every last detail of how the building was to be designed and constructed was supervised by Steiner, since it was the result of his access to levels of insight that others lacked. Although the Goetheanum thereby was the visible manifestation of a transcendent reality, it could not be symbolically decoded: any claim that it could be, would constitute slander (*Verleumdung*) (Steiner 1921: 16–17). The Goetheanum is of course the result of detailed engineering work, but it is also a sacred and ineffable site.

Steiner the builder is very much Steiner the charismatic leader, in control of every aspect of design and construction. Architecture, more than most other forms of art, requires the mobilization of resources. Work on the building was to a considerable extent unremunerated, carried out by those members of the society who had the necessary skills. In keeping with a dominant trend of the times, the details of the building were to be executed in a spirit of craftsmanship, rejecting mass-production and standardized methods. As a programmatic statement, this view was at the time hugely influential owing to the efforts of people such as John Ruskin (1819–1900) and William Morris (1834–94). As a concrete artistic program, the arts and crafts ideal needed to balance its desire for authenticity and unique craftsmanship against the high manufacturing costs that the approach entailed. Steiner's access to nearly free labor gave him a unique opportunity to realize his intentions in the carefully crafted glasswork, painting, and woodwork of the Goetheanum interior.

Every last detail of the project was vetted by Steiner. His followers, who saw Steiner as the pinnacle of spiritual wisdom, seem to have accepted every command by him as a manifestation of his genius. The Swiss poet

Albert Steffen, a member of the close circle around Steiner, affirmed of his every pen-stroke that they were "cures for the soul" (diese Striche waren Seelenkuren).[27] Those who voiced dissenting opinions were removed from the project. The architect Carl Schmid-Curtius, who had been closely involved in several earlier anthroposophical building projects, conceived of the architraves differently than Steiner did, and was promptly fired (Pehnt and Dix 1991: 11).

After the first Goetheanum was burned to the ground by an arsonist, construction of the second building proceeded along much less "purist" principles. The main structure was constructed in concrete, a more durable, albeit far less organic, material. Like its predecessor, the second Goetheanum continues to fulfill its role as a monument to anthroposophy as the unique product of Steiner's spiritual genius, rather than, say, a building characteristic of its period. Steiner died before the second Goetheanum was built. At the time of his death, plans had come no further than to deciding on the form of the empty shell of the building. The present appearance and use of the building is the end result of a series of decisions taken over a period of many years after Steiner's death. The construction project was taken over by successive architects who carried out further work on the building, adding several stairwells, auditoriums, and an entire north wing.[28] The latter was completed as late as 1989. There is hardly any doubt, however, that the building continues to be considered Steiner's work.

CONCLUDING REMARKS

Dissent, it seems, is part of practically all religious movements. Unless there are powerful mechanisms in place to prevent schisms, it is easy for religious entrepreneurs to take their disagreements to the next level: to secede from their mother organizations, and to take with them a number of members of that body. The challenge is to navigate successfully through the consolidation phase.

The history of the theosophical family of movements suggests that there are at least three elements essential to ensuring the viability of one's own movement: striking a balance between the familiar and the novel, keeping tight control over both ideology and resources, and branding one's movement by means of a distinct material culture. By doing so, the

---

[27] Quoted in Ohlenschläger (1990: 140).
[28] http://www.goetheanum.org/136.html?&L=1.

leaders of the schismatic group create something that is sufficiently familiar to attract followers, yet new enough to make the divorce from the parent movement appear necessary and legitimate. Any successful consolidation requires considerable entrepreneurial talent, but in the theosophical schismatic milieu at least, durability appears to be the biggest problem. Several schismatic groups proved very short-lived. Others have endured, but only in organizationally very weak forms. The teachings of Alice Bailey still seem to attract considerable interest, but the readers of her works primarily constitute an audience cult.[29] The experience of the Point Loma theosophists and the Anthroposophical Society suggest that the task of creating a successful movement resembles that of marketing (secular) commodities. Recent studies in marketing have proposed that novel commodities can generate discourse and behavior that verges on the religious.[30] The converse also seems to be true: in the world of religious schism and innovation, astute brand management is at least as important as the creation of original content.

REFERENCES

Adams, David. 1992. "Rudolf Steiner's First Goetheanum as an Illustration of Organic Functionalism." *Journal of the Society of Architectural Historians* 51 (2): 182–204.

Ammerman, Nancy. 1987. "Schism." In Eliade 1987: vol. 13, 98–102.

Bibo, Claudia. 1995. *Naturalismus als Weltanschauung? Biologistische, theosophische und deutsch-völkische Bildlichkeit in der von Fidus illustrierten Lyrik (1893–1902)*. Frankfurt: Lang.

Campbell, Bruce. 1980. *Ancient Wisdom Revived: A History of the Theosophical Movement*. Berkeley: University of California Press.

Campbell, Colin. 1972. "The Cult, the Cultic Milieu, and Secularization." *A Sociological Yearbook of Religion in Britain* 5: 119–36.

Creese, Robb, "Anthroposophical Performance." *Drama Review* 22 (2): 45–74.

Curry, Patrick. 1992. *A Confusion of Prophets: Victorian and Edwardian Astrology*. London: Collins & Brown.

Eliade, Mircea (ed.). 1987. *Encyclopedia of Religions*. New York: Macmillan.

Godwin, Joscelyn. 1994. *The Theosophical Enlightenment*. Albany: State University of New York Press.

Greenwalt, Emmett. 1955. *The Point Loma Community in California 1897–1942: A Theosophical Experiment*. Berkeley and Los Angeles: University of California Press.

---

[29] For this term, see Stark and Bainbridge (1985: 27–8).
[30] See Muñiz and Schau (2005) and literature cited there.

Hemleben, Johannes. 1963. *Rudolf Steiner: in Selbstzeugnissen und Bilddokumenten.* Reinbek bei Hamburg: Rowalt.

Lejon, Håkan. 1997. *Historien om den antroposofiska humanismen: den antroposofiska bildningsidén i idéhistoriskt perspektiv, 1880–1980.* Stockholm: Almqvist & Wiksell.

Lévi-Strauss, Claude. 1966. *The Savage Mind.* Chicago: University of Chicago Press.

Lindenberg, Christoph. 1997. *Rudolf Steiner: eine Biographie,* 2 vols. Stuttgart: Verlag Freies Geistesleben.

Melton, J. Gordon (ed.). 1989. *The Encyclopedia of American Religions.* 3rd edn, Detroit and London: Gale Research.

Muñiz Jr., Albert M. and Hope Jensen Schau. 2005. "Religiosity in the Abandoned Apple Newton Brand Community," *Journal of Consumer Research* 31: 737–47.

Ohlenschläger, Sonja. 1999. *Rudolf Steiner (1861–1925): das architektonische Werk.* Petersberg: Michael Imhof Verlag.

Partridge, Christopher (ed.). 2004. *Encyclopedia of New Religions.* Oxford: Lion.

Pehnt, Wolfgang and Thomas Dix. 1991. *Rudolf Steiner: Goetheanum, Dornach.* Berlin: Ernst & Sohn.

Raab, Rex, Arne Klingborg and Åke Fant. 1992. *Sprechender Beton: wie Rudolf Steiner den Stahlbeton verwendete.* Dornach: Verlag am Goetheanum.

Roos, Anna Maria. 1913. *Teosofi och teosofer.* Stockholm: Norstedt.

Sanner, Inga. 1995. *Att älska sin nästa såsom sig själv: om moraliska utopier under 1800-talet.* Stockholm: Carlsson.

Schleicher, Hans-Jürgen. 1987. *Architektur als Welterfahrung: Rudolf Steiners organischer Baustil und die Architektur der Waldorfschulen.* Frankfurt am Main: Fischer Taschenbuch Verlag.

Shepherd, A. P. 1983. *Rudolf Steiner: Scientist of the Invisible.* Rochester, VT: Inner Traditions International.

Stark, Rodney. 1987. "How New Religions Succeed: A Theoretical Model." In D. G. Bromley and P. E. Hammond (eds.), *The Future of New Religious Movements* (pp. 11–29). Macon: Mercer University Press.

Stark, Rodney and William Bainbridge. 1985. *The Future of Religion: Secularization, Revival and Cult Formation.* Berkeley: University of California Press.

Steiner, Rudolf. [1904/5]. *Wie erlangt man Erkenntnisse der höheren Welten?* Gesamtausgabe 10. Dornach: Verlag am Goetheanum.

[1921]. *Der Baugedanke des Goetheanum.* Gesamtausgabe 289–90. Dornach: Verlag am Goetheanum.

von Düben, Gunilla. 1916. *Drömmen om Point Loma.* Stockholm: Skoglunds Förlag.

CHAPTER 10

Satanists and nuts: the role of schisms in modern Satanism

Jesper Aagaard Petersen

There are no categories of Satanists – there are Satanists and nuts. The Satanic know-it-alls try to fabricate a division.

Anton Szandor LaVey in Barton 1990: 70

Satanism – to many Western readers the connotations of the term bring to mind strife, hate, division and opposition. In a sense, this worldview must be the ultimate schism as it breaks away from all that is considered good, beautiful and just in Christian society. After all, "Satan" is *the* opposition, the accuser and later adversary to God. The dark-robed raving cultist or the suave, often British, but fundamentally evil gentleman are both typical stereotypes of the Satanist of popular culture, sadly brought to life by the moral panics of the Satanism Scare in the 1980s and 1990s that falsely attributed these fictional characters to real life. Even though it would be an important study, I will not attempt to write the history of Satanism as a schismatic movement within Christianity or the use of the allegation "Satanist" in medieval or modern-day religious hysteria.[1] In fact, I consider these interpretations of Satanism to be a subcategory of either theology or the sociology of moral panics and not a critical study of modern religion. There are other real-life Satanists, answering proudly to the term and fighting for their freedom of thought and expression. It is to these individuals and their disagreements we now turn.

Most committed contemporary Satanists share a modern outlook related but not reducible to Humanism, Atheism, Skepticism, the Human Potential movement and the wider New Age phenomenon in the West,

---

[1] On the first, see for example Jeffrey Burton Russell's monumental, but sadly skewed theological history of the Devil (Russell 1977; 1981; 1984; 1986) and Gareth Medway's thoughtful analysis (Medway 2001). On the second, Norman Cohn, Jeffrey Victor and Bill Ellis spring to mind (Cohn 1975; Victor 1993; Ellis 2000).

even though particular participants do not agree on much, as could be expected in a religion or philosophy claiming the Ego as God. Thus Satanism is an important part of the "cultic milieu" of Western culture (Campbell 1972), a sub-milieu, movement or current here dubbed the "Satanic milieu." The only real connection to Christianity is the name and figure of Satan. And even though the interpretations vary from theistic to atheistic, Satan, Set or Sat-Tan is generally used symbolically or didactically as a statement of intent, namely the celebration of the individual – its vital existence, isolate intelligence or Life Force.

This chapter argues that the conflicts, innovations and schisms found within modern organized Satanism are a result of two interrelated dynamics: on the one hand the dual ideal of fruitful self-assertion and continuous non-conformity characterizing Satanism after its initial formulation by Anton Szandor LaVey, and on the other hand the constant renegotiation of the very term "Satanism" to refine and protect salient formulations from the pressure of the Satanic and the wider cultic milieu of which it is a part. Through complex ongoing *negotiations of individuality* simultaneously framed positively as empowerment and self-realization (a "self-religion") and negatively as the *lack* of herd mentality and conformism (an antinomian stance) (Flowers 1997: 4; Harvey 2002; Petersen 2005: 425, 446), individuals and groups claiming authority define "Satanism" and "pseudo-Satanisms" in the milieu as a whole. As such, Satanism thrives on formulations of both positive content and negative *deviance* and *tension* in order to produce a coherent identity on the individual and collective level. In this sense Satanism differs little when compared to other religious trends of this type – innovations and schisms are the norm. They mark important breaking but also crystallization points for new spokespersons, new doctrines, new practices and novel organizations.

One has to be very cautious when the analysis moves from spokespersons, texts and organizations with established authority, doctrines and practices to individual practitioners of Satanism (Dyrendal 2004b: 50, 52). Thus, I have focused this chapter on a general level, a macro-analysis of innovations and schisms within the Satanic milieu through important movement texts and spokespersons (Hammer 2001: 37ff), and not on the microsociological how and what of the individual actor. The analysis of important cleavages is further inspired by Bruce Lincoln's theory of *affinity* and *estrangement* and the constitutive character of discourse in the construction of social borders (Lincoln 1989). As an instrument of social construction, discourse can be thought of as both ideological persuasion and sentiment evocation; a given society or group is thus *a collective* feeling likeness toward each other (affinity) and feeling separate from other groups (estrangement) (1989: 9). The rational and moral instruments are utilized to strengthen these general sentiments. This has several important consequences. First, it is a constructivist view, considering the strategic and tactical uses of discourse in the formation of collectivities. Second, it is an anti-essential position, which implies that borders are artificial and mutating constantly. Third, it is fractal and synthetic, in the sense that *any* collectivity has fault lines within it, thus necessitating a further look at subgroups within the group discussed (or even subgroups within those subgroups):

In practice there always exist potential bases for associating and for disassociating one's self and one's group from others, and the vast majority of social sentiments are ambivalent mixes in which potential sources of affinity are (partially and perhaps temporarily) overlooked or suppressed in the interests of establishing a clear social border or, conversely, potential sources of estrangement are similarly treated in order to effect or preserve a desired level of social integration and solidarity. (Lincoln 1989: 10)

Lincoln suggests that we investigate "segmentary patterns" of "fission and fusion" in order to analyze a social whole, subunits and sub-subunits (1989: 19). As the astute reader has already noticed, this theoretical apparatus is eminently suited to the study of innovations and schisms, especially in a fluid environment such as the cultic milieu. In fact, my concept of a Satanic milieu discussed below is in itself a subgroup within a given whole, and the groups sub-subunits within it.

Before venturing into the dark underworld of the Satanic milieu, a brief discussion of sociological typology is necessary, especially in relation to the concept of schism. When perusing the relevant literature, one cannot fail to notice the blatant disagreement over the definition of two central concepts of new religious movements, namely "cult" and "sect." Although all definitions focus on societal deviance, Rodney Stark and William Bainbridge define the concepts in terms of schismatic birth and thus as absolute terms (Stark and Bainbridge 1985: chs. 2 and 10), while Roy Wallis defines them through legitimation of authority along a continuum (Wallis 1974: 1975). While I do agree with their tripartite division of audience cult, client cult and cult movement, I do *not* agree with Stark and Bainbridge's definition of sect and cult as schismatic and non-schismatic deviant religions (Stark and Bainbridge 1985: 24ff). I would rather use Roy Wallis's definition along a legitimation axis: a sect is a uniquely legitimate, coherent and authoritarian group, while the cult is pluralistically legitimate, eclectic and egalitarian (Wallis 1974: 303–4; 1975: 40ff; Partridge 2004: 24ff). I have several reasons for this.

First of all, Stark and Bainbridge never use Colin Campbell's theory of the cultic milieu, even though they discuss the process of career paths of entrepreneurs and their borrowing from each other (Stark and Bainbridge 1985: 178–83). As will be discussed below, the cultic milieu represents a milestone in the formulation of a coherent theory of contemporary religion, as it functions as the necessary backdrop in the analysis of individual seekership as well as the processes of cult and sect formation when religious movements mutate and evolve. Secondly, Stark and Bainbridge equate the concept of schism with the sect category, as it represents a group that breaks away from "organizational attachment to a 'parent' religion" (1985: 25). The cult, on the other hand, has no organizational ties and should thus be considered an import or innovation (1985: 25–6). While it is true that cults generally represent innovation rather than schism from a previously established religious *organization*, any successful innovation makes use of an available body of rejected material and recombines it through various strategies of appropriation, creating a unique interpretation of it, thus temporarily distancing the creation from the parent material and attracting interested seekers (Hammer 2001). This temporary assemblage could be described as an intellectual rather than a sociological schism – a large unit becomes smaller through new constellations of affinity and estrangement. Even though the general ethos of the cult and the cultic milieu is one of tolerance and eclecticism (Wallis 1975: 41), a cult is *not the same* as the cultic milieu. When it is, it is dead. Consequently, I consider innovation and schism complementary processes of fracture rather than two different kinds. An amicable break and recombination of ideas is still a break from a cultic organization, from a current of thought or even the cultic milieu as a whole.

In this sense, what defines the sect is epistemological authoritarianism, and the schismatic tendency of this category arises from this characteristic, not the other way around. The cult, on the other hand, is epistemologically individualist and based on innovation, and is, in its ideal-typical form of the audience and client cult, a fluid and non-restrictive movement, with little or no doctrinal authority or commitment (Wallis 1974; 1975). But it is still a definable current, a "more or less temporary association of seekers organized around a common interest, or the researches and revelations of an individual" (Wallis 1974: 306). That is exactly why the sect can develop from the cult: spokespersons and leaders try to demarcate the group more strongly. In the following, I will utilize the concepts of *audience cult* and *client cult* to describe the ideal-typical cult in Wallis's model, while the term *cultic movement* represents the middle stage of the centralized cult (Wallis 1974: 325), and *sect* the product of unique processes of legitimation.

First, the chapter will attempt the obligatory circumvention of the field in question, namely modern Satanism, in order to demarcate the potentials of the Satanic milieu and differentiate the manifestations within it. Next, I will examine a concrete case of historical innovation, the early Church of Satan, to understand the selection processes that define rational Satanism but also perpetuate the ambiguity inherent in the milieu. Third, the schism producing the Temple of Set will be related to these ambiguities to understand the process as an activation of alternative potentials within the Church and the cultic milieu. Finally, I will conclude with a summary discussion of themes to transcend the chronological framework and assess the insights gained from the analysis.

MODERN SATANISM: A SHORT INTRODUCTION

As stated above, modern Satanism can be conceived of as a part of the cultic milieu proposed by Colin Campbell in his seminal article "The Cult, the Cultic Milieu and Secularization" (1972). As such, Satanism is a bundle of ideas and practices related to other ideas and practices in the "cultural underground of society" (1972: 122). This heterogeneous but single "assortment of cultural items" is held together by common traits, mainly deviance, syncretism, overlapping communication structures and the ideology of seekership (1972: 122–4). The point is that new religious movements continuously crystallize from this cultural field. It works as both the substantive and functional context for group evolution – it is the cultic milieu and not the individual groups that are permanent (1972: 122).[2]

The cultic milieu is a "fuzzy category" (Taylor 1995: 38ff; Saler 2000: 202ff); in order to have the necessary cohesion (*not* coherence or consistence) without losing its heterogeneous character, its contents are arranged according to the Wittgensteinian notion of *family resemblance*.

---

[2] Christopher Partridge suggests the terms "occultic milieu" and "occulture" to replace Campbell's "cultic milieu" (Partridge 2004: 66), but I find Campbell's term adequate when dealing with the sociological entity producing new religious movements (the functional side of "cult production"). "Occulture" is excellent when speaking broadly of substantial issues (the rejected contents themselves), but when all is said and done the terms are interchangeable.

Nevertheless some streams are more closely related than others, as some concepts, practices or influential formulations work as magnets, making clusters of related items, and these should be categorized as the broad prototypical currents of a *very* complex field of rejected knowledge and communication (Campbell 1972: 124–6; Truzzi 1972: 18; Partridge 2004: 71–84). I would propose to isolate a "Satanic milieu," an important sub-field, current or reservoir alongside for example the neo-Pagan, UFO-related, New Age, Theosophical and Western Esoteric currents, as modern Satanism in its divergent forms is sufficiently distinctive to warrant this accentuation.

The Satanic milieu is in itself a polythetic category with fuzzy borders, and could be conceived of as a cult-producing substance of key terms and practices as well as the reservoir of ideas uniting the broad movement of modern Satanism, mirroring the larger cultic milieu in a fractal sense. Thus the Satanic milieu is a trend in popular culture (Baddeley 2000; Dyrendal 2005), a collective style and identity within Satanic neo-tribes (Hermonen 2002; Smoczynski 2002), and the reference points of the Satanic subcultures that crystallize around distinct interpretations or manifestations of Satanism today (Dyrendal 2004b; Petersen 2005). Even though few modern, self-professed Satanists feel part of a grand movement or clearly definable subculture (and some even attack the very notion of community implied in these words – see for example Barton 1995; Gilmore 1999, 2007: 170ff; Rose 2000), I would certainly state that from a historical and sociological point of view they do belong to a diffuse "occultural" movement and, in the case of organized Satanists, belong to subcultures within it with common identities, histories (both emic and etic), symbols, aesthetics, interpretations and practices; in short: identity, commitment, consistent distinctiveness and autonomy.[3]

Three broad categories or ideal types emerge within the Satanic milieu: Rational, Esoteric and Reactive paradigmatically conform Satanism (Schmidt 1992; Dyrendal 2004b: 48ff; Petersen 2005: 440ff). As they are

---

[3] This is an interpretation of subculture inspired by Paul Hodkinson's analysis of the Goth scene. He suggests "4 indicators of subcultural substance": identity, commitment, consistent distinctiveness and autonomy (Hodkinson 2002: 28–33), and writes: "Rather than these four comprising a definitive blueprint, each of them should be regarded as a contributory feature which, taken cumulatively with the others, increases the appropriateness of the term 'subculture', in the relative degree to which each is applicable. The combination of this degree of malleability with a set of specific criteria should maximize the potential for meaningful use of the concept at the same time as recognizing the greater relevance of alternative terminology – in the form of Maffesoli's notion of neo-tribe perhaps – to describe more fleeting or superficial forms of affiliation" (2002: 29–30). Understood in this way a Satanic subculture is a matter of more-or-less, not either–or.

analytical constructs, they are fuzzy as well; individuals and groups move from one to the other as the Satanic milieu mutates and grows. The categories could be conceived of as points in a triangle, where Rational and Esoteric Satanism occupy a bi-polar scale of organized, mature and systematic worldviews with "reactive paradigmatically conform Satanism" as a catch-all category of popular Satanism, inverted Christianity and symbolic rebellion. Thus reactive paradigmatically conform Satanism is reactive in the sense that it is in opposition to society, but in a way that reiterates central Christian concepts of evil, making it paradigmatically conform to a Christian context. *Satan* is the Devil, and *Satanism* the adolescent or anti-social behavior of transgressing boundaries and "living out" a mythical frame. In the analysis of innovations and schisms in the following, I will only discuss this type of Satanism where it is relevant as a sounding board for the self-religions found in the two next categories.

Rational Satanism is an atheistic, skeptical Epicureanism as formulated by Anton Szandor LaVey in *The Satanic Bible* and other writings (LaVey 1969; 1972; 1992; 1998). It considers *Satan* to be a symbol of rebellion, individuality, carnality and empowerment, and *Satanism* the material philosophy best suited for the "alien elite"; catchwords are indulgence and vital existence. Although ritual practices are described and an ambiguous diabolical anthropomorphism is present from time to time, both are interpreted as metaphorical and pragmatic instruments of self-realization. Science, philosophy and intuition are advocated as authorities, and productive non-conformity the highest goal of the individual. *Esoteric* Satanism is more theistically oriented and uses the esoteric traditions of Paganism, Western Esotericism, Buddhism and Hinduism, among others, to formulate a religion of self-actualization. The understanding of *Satan* is clothed in platonic or mystical terms; although often spoken of as a literal entity, it is not a god to be worshiped, but rather a being or principle to be emulated or understood. *Satanism* is therefore a path to enlightenment in a Left-Hand Path sense of non-union with the universe or true individuality (Flowers 1997). The ritual practices and organizations of this type of Satanism often correspond to other initiation-oriented groups within Western Esotericism, though this may vary considerably.

Finally, it would be useful to summarize by briefly discussing the main traits in a minimum definition of organized Satanism within the Satanic milieu. I would suggest self-religion, antinomianism, the use of certain "S"-words and a formulated ideological genealogy, often in the form of some relation to Anton Szandor LaVey, as the four major factors to be taken into consideration. First of all, self-religion and antinomianism are both ideological core terms. In fact, *self-religion* is shared with many other streams within the cultic milieu as such, and could be a common core for the epistemologically individualist and self-actualizing groups and individuals found within it.[4] Even though the self-annihilating mystic, the goddess-worshiping pagan and the Black Magician have very little in common, they are all focused on the self: "A project to discover, empower and enact our authentic (inner) nature currently contaminated by socialization" (Harvey 2002: 55). Whether it is humanity's animal nature or the isolate intellect, the goal of modern Satanism is found within, not outside, the individual. When it is combined with *antinomian* and elitist interests, we have a project of self-actualization transgressing the moral boundaries of society, setting the self above the conventional expectations and mores. Indeed, as it is contaminated by socialization, the self must confront and dispense with this influence to realize itself (Flowers 1997: 3ff).

A certain self-designation is also important in order to differentiate between prejudice and modern Satanism proper (see Dyrendal 2004b: 48), and to set it apart from other formulations of the cultic milieu. Thus the antinomian self-religion needs to be framed through a use of the words Satan, Satanism, Satanic and Satanist (and related words, of course: Devil, Lucifer, etc.), although the anti-Christian stance of organized Satanism is rooted in an anti-repressive ideology that targets all negative conditioning of the self; these groups are *not* subgroups of Christianity. Rather Christianity is understood as the prime example of a totalitarian, oppressive moral force – other enemies are capitalist society's dictum of consumerism and passive entertainment; "liberal" society's "universal" human rights and bland equality; and the blind obedience and irrationality of the herd in all religions (Flowers 1997: 195–6).

Finally, all individuals and groups construct some sort of genealogy, a time-line of subcultural ancestry. Furthermore, most if not all groups and individuals relate this to the writings of LaVey, especially *The Satanic Bible* (1969). Some relations are positive, others negative, but all have to wrestle with the Beast, so to speak. The interpretations of LaVey range from Black Pope and midwife of the Satanic age to huckster and joke, but they all have an opinion. He is a common denominator of some sort of entry into the Satanic milieu – some stop there and protect his

---

[4] See Heelas 1996 and Partridge 2004; 2005 on self-religion, and Flowers 1997, Harvey 2002, Dyrendal 2004a; forthcoming a and Petersen 2005 on Satanism as a self-religion.

formulation of the Satanic philosophy and others move on and criticize it, but he is necessary as a dark prophet, a vanishing point that plays an important role in all genealogies.

A SCHISMATIC *PASODOBLE*: THE CHURCH OF SATAN AND THE TEMPLE OF SET

In my presentation of modern Satanism (Petersen 2005), I divided the history of the milieu into three distinct phases, primarily modeled on the history of the Church of Satan (CoS). The first phase, from 1966 to 1975, marks the emergence of organized Satanism and the growth and decline of Anton LaVey's creation. The second phase, from 1975 to the mid 1990s, begins with the schism that produces Michael A. Aquino's Temple of Set (ToS) and ends with the introduction of the Internet. The third phase, from the mid 1990s to the present, kicks off with Anton LaVey's death in 1997, which results in a proliferation of new Satanic movements online, battles within CoS over legitimate authority, and fierce struggles both within CoS and in the Satanic milieu in general over the ownership of the term "Satanism." Even though the dust has settled, the development has left CoS an authoritarian movement and the Satanic milieu as visible and diverse as never before (2005: 426ff).

The present diachronic analysis is focused on the early phase between 1966 and 1975, as further studies have shown that important sub-phases can be isolated in order to clarify important reorientations and refor-mulations in CoS and the Satanic milieu. Throughout the analysis, I will engage with relevant theory in order to explicate the strategies and motivations underlying the innovations and schisms, especially the typ-ologies of Wallis and of Stark and Bainbridge discussed above, the concept of syncretism and anti-syncretism proposed by Mikael Rothstein (1996: 18ff), the legitimation strategies of Max Weber (2003: 45–173, 309–357; Lewis 2003: 10–12) and the practical concepts of emic historiography and appropriation systematized by Olav Hammer (2001: 85ff). Taken as a whole, they can conceptualize the ebb and flow of affinity and estrangement in the Satanic milieu.

Cultic innovation: Anton Szandor LaVey and the Church of Satan

The first important fault line in the history of modern Satanism is not a schism in the strict sense but an example of cultic innovation, although the consequence is an analogous *break* with the cultic milieu, as argued above. The establishment of the Church of Satan on April 30, 1966 is a symptom of Anton Szandor LaVey's complete rejection of Christian society and the surfacing of a coherent formulation of thought and practice within the Satanic milieu that is at odds with the reactive paradigmatically conform Satanism and the Christian stereotypes found in Western culture. In this sense, the first major fracture is LaVey's formulation of a specific, new current within the cultic milieu that separates *rational* Satanism from traditional negative interpretations, an antinomian religion of the self, appropriating Satan as a positive symbol:

Is it not more sensible to worship a god that he, himself, has created, in accordance with his own emotional needs – one that best represents the very carnal and physical being that has the idea-power to invent a god *in the first place?* . . . If this is what the Devil represents, and a man lives in the devil's fane, with the sinews of Satan moving his flesh, then he either escapes from the cacklings and carpings of the righteous, or stands proudly in his secret places of the earth and manipulates the folly-ridden masses through his own Satanic might, until that day when he may come forth in splendor proclaiming "I AM A SATANIST! BOW DOWN, FOR I AM THE HIGHEST EMBODIMENT OF HUMAN LIFE!" (LaVey 1969: 44–5)

As such, LaVey can be described as a charismatic spokesperson for a cultic movement with positive relations to the liberal *Zeitgeist* of the late sixties in terms of individuality, freedom, anti-authority, new forms of association and interest in esoteric pursuits, even though the form it takes is somewhat darker than that of the mainstream counterculture. Indeed, LaVey's studies of esoteric lore in the 1950s and 1960s, culminating in the formation of the informal Magic Circle in the mid 1960s, is in fact a perfect parallel to Campbell's ideology of seekership as a "problem-solving perspective" or "quest" (Campbell 1972: 123–4) and the definition of audience cult described earlier. A cursory glance at the official LaVey biography supplied by Blanche Barton's *The Church of Satan* and *The Secret life of a Satanist* (1990; 1992) confirms this picture, even if it is partly fictional, as the biography has been shown to be (Aquino 2002; Dyrendal 2004a).[5] His activities both inwardly and outwardly reflect the common activities of an individual in the cultic milieu: he studies arcane tomes,

---

[5] As Dyrendal shows, schismatic spokespersons such as Michael A. Aquino actively downplay LaVey's knowledge of the occult (Dyrendal forthcoming b: 4). This can be expected, as a thorough understanding of esoteric lore is hard currency in the cultic milieu and an obvious angle of attack. Nevertheless I agree with Dyrendal that the esoteric milieu of the period is fairly small, that LaVey has probably socialized with the esoterically inclined and that his books show a working knowledge of these matters, demythologizing notwithstanding (forthcoming b: 5).

philosophical treatises and scientific expositions, visits fellow seekers, works as a psychic investigator, and later performs rituals and gives lectures and so on.

This is all well and good. In reality, the picture is much more complicated, as LaVey actively utilizes positive and negative syncretism in order to arrive at the specific formulation of Satanism shown above. As Mikael Rothstein states:

> "Syncretism" as a cultural phenomenon corresponds to "no syncretism." By this I imply the fact that religious identity and the construction of religious meaning sometimes are the results of conscious concentration on one tradition in opposition to others. A religious body may well consolidate itself by deliberately disregarding other religious constructions, thus fertilizing what is significant to itself while ignoring foreign religious concepts and social systems. In doing so, however, the officially disregarded religious traditions are in fact being considered. (Rothstein 1996: 18–19)

I agree and would go even further: an entrepreneurial soul might use this tactic to maximize confrontation with and separation from other currents in the cultic milieu, the counterculture and society at large. I consider this, especially embodied in the carnival language and imagery of CoS, the true essence of LaVeyan Satanism. In relation to Anton LaVey, Randall Alfred sums it up quite well: "He spent many years studying various occult subjects in what he now regards as a wandering in the wilderness before stumbling on the true path, the 'Left Hand Path', of Satanism" (Alfred 1976: 186). In the following, I will discuss three major strands of strategic syncretism that are visible in the early CoS and its "true path": the use of the Devil is ambiguous, making the anti-Christian and antinomian aspect highly visible; the use of the cultic milieu is highly critical, focusing on the darker aspects; and the magical and religious aspects of the cultic milieu are in themselves reread through a pragmatic, materialistic, *scientific* lens. Through a negotiation between different positions, CoS constantly reorients itself to capitalize on "respectability" and "outrage" (Alfred 1976: 187; Barton 1990: 16) in its formative period from 1966 to 1970.

The first aspect, the deliberate use of inverted Christianity, including diabolical anthropomorphism and the *enaction* of Devil worship, is most visible in the very early stages of the Church of Satan's existence (in the period 1966–7), although it is also manifest in two important (some would say definitive) movement texts: *The Satanic Bible* and *The Satanic Rituals* (LaVey 1969; 1972). In this strand, CoS is playfully emulating historical cases to shock and gain new recruits – again the carnival springs to mind. As a result, the early CoS confirms most paradigmatic expectations, appealing to the traditional authority of Christian myth. Examples abound: Satan is invoked in black masses, Satanic baptisms, weddings and funerals with nude altars; Satanic strip shows are performed, and the high priest wears a hooded cape and dark robes during rituals (see LaVey 1972: 31ff, 203ff; Alfred 1976: 189; Barton 1990; 1992; the plates in Aquino 2002). In this sense, LaVey's use of the Christian tradition is highly ambiguous, as it is used to distance CoS from competing ideologies, attract a decidedly anti-Christian segment of the cultic milieu, but also "clear the air" of Christian hypocrisy in a cathartic way: "The rituals for the first year were largely intended as cathartic blasphemies against Christianity. Many of the elements were consistent with the reports of Satanic worship from the famous writings of diabolists" (Barton 1990: 16).

The second aspect, interrelated with and growing out of the first, is the highly selective use of rejected knowledge found within the cultic milieu (as the quote above from Alfred 1976 shows quite clearly). Thus, the diabolical imagery is tempered with an appeal to a different type of tradition, namely select parts of the cultic milieu in the construction of a "true Satanism" apart from Christian stereotypes:

LaVey wanted to establish something new, not strict doctrines awash with attitudes of blind faith and worship, but something which would smash all concepts of anything that had come before, something to break apart the ignorance and hypocrisy fostered by the Christian churches. Something, too, that could free people to apply the black magic he and his Magic Circle were using. . . There had always been a Satanic underground, centuries old, but there had never been an organized Satanic religion, practicing openly. LaVey decided it was high time there was. (Barton 1990: 9, 10)

The appeal to a "Satanic underground, centuries old," "black magic" and freedom from "strict doctrines" is indicative of an immersion in the cultic milieu; when constructing an emic historiography (Hammer 2001: 85ff), LaVey is constantly searching for traditionally "evil" aspects to incorporate into a working myth of the "Satanic underground," but also reinterpreting them to fit his self-religion through an appeal to charismatic authority: "something new." The rite of legitimation of the High Priest on Walpurgisnacht 1966 is a case in point:

LaVey shaved his head as part of a formalized founding ritual, in the tradition of medieval executioners, carnival strongmen, and black magicians before him, to gain personal power and enhance the forces surrounding his newly-established

Satanic order . . . Shaving his head is also traditional to the Yezidi devil worshippers as a rite of passage that the emerging adept must perform. (Barton 1990: 11–12)

This is unquestionably a very personal reading of the tradition, but it is also a very common legitimation strategy. Thus, although LaVey is highly critical of most parts of the cultic milieu, perpetually distancing himself from "white witches" and traditional magicians like Gerald Gardner, Sybil Leek, Eliphas Levi and Aleister Crowley (LaVey 1969: 21; 1971; 1992: 146–7; 1998: 166–7f; Fritscher 2004: 10, 24ff), he is also, through reinterpretation, using it to bolster his authority as the Devil's representative.[6] But he is also distancing himself from traditional paradigmatic anti-Christianity and antinomian behavior. This becomes clearer in the phase from 1968–9: "'After that original blast', LaVey remembers, 'there was no need for the ongoing public spectacle and outrage of an inverted Catholic Mass anymore . . . There were plenty of other sacred cows to attack'" (Barton 1990: 29). Indeed there were. LaVey's negative relation to the counterculture is a case in point: he is described as a "law-and-order-man" (Alfred 1976: 7) and as against drugs and compulsive sexuality (LaVey 1969; Truzzi 1972: 28; Alfred 1976: 186–7; Lyons 1988: 118). The pendulum swings toward respectability.

This leads us to the third and later dominant strand in the early CoS: the appeal to science and rational authority to distance Satanism from the supernaturalism of the cultic milieu: "'I realized there was a whole grey area between psychiatry and religion that had been largely untapped,' said LaVey. He saw the potential for group ritual used as a powerful combination of psychodrama and psychic direction" (Barton 1990: 16–17). This is in turn based on a view of human nature as an animal (LaVey 1969: 25, statement 7), thus appropriating natural science as a worldview (Lewis 2003: 106–7) and legitimating an individualistic self-religion with the human being, indulgence and vital existence as its natural center.

Nowhere is the appeal to science more visible than in the rationalization of lesser and greater magic found in *The Satanic Bible*, *The Satanic Rituals* and *The Satanic Witch* (LaVey 1969; 1972; 1989). Although the very use of the word "magic" to describe these psychological techniques is

---

[6] An interesting example is his visit to a Thelemic lodge in Berkeley: "As early as 1951, LaVey's growing convictions about Satan led him to try to seek out a group of 'official' Devil worshippers. He had heard that followers of Crowley were practicing Satanists, but when he visited the Order of Thelema in Berkeley, he was sorely disappointed. He found a gaggle of mush-minded card readers who emphasized the study of Eastern philosophy, Oriental languages, astrology and contemplation to reach an unnamed mystical oneness with the Universe. This wasn't LaVey's idea of Satanism" (Barton 1990: 41).

in itself an indication of the complex conglomeration of diabolism, magic and science through positive and negative syncretism (Dyrendal forthcoming b: 11), and although LaVey is deliberately vague when discussing science and magic (LaVey 1969: 110–13), the trend toward secularization is evident in the scientific terminology used to explain "the change in situations or events in accordance with one's will, which would, using normally accepted methods, be unchangeable" (1969: 110). Lesser magic is manipulation, greater magic emotional release, but both lie between psychiatry and religion (Truzzi 1972: 28). Thus, his understanding of ritual is paradigmatic to his formulation of a *rational* Satanism and in accordance with the scientistic legitimation strategies of the Human Potential movement and the New Age (Hammer 2001: 201ff).

With the appeal to science, the complex relation between LaVey's understanding of the occult on the one hand and the eclecticism, syncretism and pluralism of the cultic milieu (the "many paths to truth" argument) on the other is amply illustrated. In a sense, LaVey takes the epistemological individualism of the milieu to the extreme, as he constructs a pragmatic combination of science, philosophy and religion to suit his needs, while at the same time discarding much traditional material as "baloney." Thus the whole concept of LaVeyan Satanism is a negotiation of individuality over and against the traditional legitimation strategies of the cultic milieu, and a suggestion that each and every Satanist critically exercises his or her faculties when confronted with them. He considers Satanism a pure and, more importantly, *working* distillation of occultism and mystical religion:

Summing up, if you NEED to steep yourselves in occult lore, despite this diatribe, by all means do so. But do it as a ritual in itself, i.e., *objectively towards subjective ends!* Read on, *knowing* that you won't learn a damn thing in principle from Levi, Crowley, Regardie, (or Sybil Leek either!) that isn't extended one-hundred fold in *The Satanic Bible* or *The Compleat Witch, but* that you'll have the spooky fun, ego-food, and *involvement* which invariably accompanies a curriculum concerned more with the gathering of ingredients than the application of principles. (LaVey 1971: 3)

Thus, the early Church of Satan is both steeped in the occult underground and holding it at arm's length. LaVey is effectively creating a centralized cultic movement out of his syncretistic reading of the rejected materials of the cultic milieu, and in the process both *confirming* the general dynamics of cult formation and the available strategies of legitimation, and *rejecting* most of the rejected persons, practices and ideas for

a less pluralistically legitimate reading of the sacred traditions. Consequently, LaVey is constantly restating sentiments of affinity and estrangement to make the most of his creation.

Whether these strands are underlying aspects of LaVey's thought that
are simultaneously present from the start or made up as the Church
moves along is difficult to answer – what is obvious is that they contribute
to the doctrinal and organizational ambivalence that ultimately results in
schism. While they are all effective legitimation strategies in a smaller
circle with easy access to the charismatic glue that is the High Priest
himself, the ambivalence is increasingly problematic in the long run – in
effect, CoS becomes too popular for comfort, attracting a wide variety of
people whose worldviews are mutually exclusive (Barton 1990: 29ff, 119ff;
1992: 125–7). This in turn highlights the conflict between individual
empowerment, and thus individual authority to construct a worldview on
one hand, and Church doctrine on the other.

In the intermediate period between the publication of *The Satanic
Bible* in January 1970 and the formation of the Temple of Set in 1975,
the fluctuation between anti-organization and centralized organization
becomes more apparent. Two aspects are worth discussing before moving
on to the major break ahead. The first is the impact of *The Satanic Bible*,
and the other the experiment with decentralization called the grotto
system.

The Satanic Bible is in many ways *the* central text of the Satanic milieu,
as it holds a privileged place in many Satanists' autobiographies (Lewis
2003: 117) and has a notoriety far exceeding the humble story of its birth
(2003: 112; Aquino 2005: ch. 5). It is thus important not only for the
organization CoS, but also for the milieu as a whole. This is in large part
because the book advocates all strands of Satanism discussed above,
scattered throughout the four books of Satan, Lucifer, Belial and Leviathan.
First, it includes a mission statement from Satan himself, a list of infernal
names and a cookbook of black magic to name but a few paradigmatically
conform items (LaVey 1969: 27ff, 58ff, 107ff). Second, the inclusion of the
Enochian keys (1969: 153ff) is the appeal to a very old tradition within the
cultic milieu, though they are reinterpreted as "Satanic paeans of faith"
(1969: 156) and presented with the true translation (by Anton LaVey
himself, of course). Third, the entire book of Lucifer and the discussion of
Satanic magic touched upon earlier is clothed in rational authority and
secular philosophy (1969: 37–107, 110–14). In the words of Ole Wolf, a
critical ex-member of CoS: "The Satanic Bible thus represents an occult-
nick slam dunk: most readers will agree with certain portions of *The*

Satanic Bible as long as they are either atheists on a rational level, deists with symbolism but no supernatural beliefs, or even theists believing in God and/or Satan but not particularly caring about their sentences in the afterlives" (Wolf 2002: 263). It is therefore an eminent example of the ambiguous style of the early CoS and the potentialities present in both rational Satanism and the wider Satanic milieu.

The second aspect is the grotto system implemented after 1970 (Aquino 2005: 86) and the simultaneous withdrawal from the public of the High Priest and the Central Grotto in San Francisco (Barton 1990: 29, 119) in the early seventies. Though the grottos are conceived of as formal independent lodges within the Church, a cell-structure with responsibility for local activities and authority on a regional level, thus alluding to the increasing number of geographically dispersed members within the organization, some element of control is still in the hands of the High Priest, as the Central Grotto screens members and publishes both the Church newsletter the *Cloven Hoof* and later *The Satanic Bible* and *The Satanic Rituals*. Furthermore, the degree system is elaborated,[7] which functions both as a delegation and maintenance of control, and a *Manual for Grotto Administration* and some *Articles of Protocol* are composed (Aquino 2002: 160, 280). In essence, this structure is a way to continue working as a centralized cultic movement without the publicity and day-to-day micro-management. All in all, the "absolute" power of the High Priest and Priestess is still asserted: "The position held by Anton LaVey as High Priest is monarchial in nature, papal in degree, and absolute in power" (LaVey in the *Cloven Hoof* in 1970, quoted from Flowers 1997: 181).

Nevertheless, the problems start immediately. As documented by Michael A. Aquino in his history of CoS, practically all grottos experience crises of different kinds: personal animosities, criminal acts, etc. (Aquino 2005; see also Lyons 1988: 116ff and Baddeley 2000 for shorter presentations). Splinter groups appear in 1973 and 1974, although all are short-lived (Lyons 1988: 116ff). Thoughts of restructuring the organization are apparently aired by LaVey to Aquino as early as 1972: "I'm sure you haven't forgotten one of the first letters you wrote to me, projecting the hypothesis that as Satanism becomes a reckonable force in the world, so will the formal structure of the Church become increasingly distilled,

---

[7] The system has five degrees: (1) Apprentice or Active member, (2) Warlock/Witch, (3) Priest/Priestess, (4) Magister and (5) Magus (apparently the last two had no female equivalents). The three upper degrees compose the Priesthood of Mendes. In addition, the High Priest (LaVey) and High Priestess (his wife Diane) are rulers for life.

rejecting external organization out of necessity so that the Satanic 'gadfly' may be given freedom to spread and multiply. I reckon that time has come" (Aquino 2005: 191). The distillation is essentially a marketing of "Satanic goodies to low-level gadflies" (2005: 192) and a withdrawal of authority from the grotto system. These thoughts are later reformulated as the implementation of "phase IV" in an overall "master plan" of the Church of Satan:[8]

> When the High Priest accepted the Infernal Mandate to assume his office, a Master Plan for the long-range development of the Church of Satan was instituted. This plan was divided into a series of phases, each characterized by a radical readjustment in the overall composition and posture of the entire Church at a precise moment in time. The success of each phase depends in part upon a general ignorance of its successors. The Nine understand that a new phase must now commence . . . In the strictest Orwellian sense we now enter a phase whereby the cohesiveness of Satanism will be reinforced by its individuality and dispersion. Thus an empire will be forged which can be magnetized and rejoined ten million-fold at a future date. At present, in unity there is chaos; in dispersion there is strength . . . We will no longer huddle together for mutual comfort among those who have demonstrated security by their presence. (Aquino 2005: 793–6)

Writing as John M. Kincaid on behalf of the ruling body, the Council of Nine, Anton LaVey here hypothetically reasserts the top-down hierarchy, creating a "cabalistic underground" (Barton 1990: 29) with coherence on a center-to-individual rather than center-to-group level. It is in effect quite the opposite, namely the creation of an audience cult: "No new member will be placed in contact with another, nor will existing Agents, Grotto leaders, or clergy be notified of new members. Only by this procedure will the potential of each surface . . . All Grottos will be formed through individual initiative, drawing from the **outside** rather than the **inside**" (1990: 29). In reality, this constitutes a major reshuffling of authority and membership affinity, and the solutions offered are indicative of the schism to come.

The major schism: Michael A. Aquino and the Temple of Set

All of these different factors – the ambiguous formulation of rational Satanism, the organizational anarchy, the apparent monopolization of

---

[8] The term is mentioned in Aquino 2005: 117, in a letter from 1971, but is first used by LaVey as a developmental plan from 1974. According to Aquino: "I doubt that an actual master plan ever existed, but it was a suitably impressive and mysterious oracle to invoke, if nothing else" (2005: 357).

power, the ubiquitous master plan, as well as mounting confusion and/or dependence (whether you are reading Aquino or LaVey) – contribute to the chaos that is modern Satanism's "dark reformation" in 1975. What can be determined as fact is that a group of disgruntled members of the Church of Satan – the number varies from twenty-eight (Lyons 1988: 126) to a hundred (Aquino 2005: 869) – led by Michael Aquino, leaves in the summer of 1975 and forms the more esoteric variant of modern Satanism called the Temple of Set. This organization is a cultic movement along much the same lines as CoS around 1970, with "pylons" replacing grottos, Set replacing Satan, and Aquino and his wife Lilith Sinclair acting as High Priest and Priestess, although the High Priest seems to have less power and the focus of the organization is guided self-initiation through the practice of magic.[9] Here I will focus on the narrative strategies surrounding the schism and discuss relevant divergences and similarities between the two organizations in order to understand the fracture.

The why of the schism is narrated in two strategic versions: Anton LaVey claims that he planned it all along according to the master plan, while Michael Aquino calls upon the shift in emphasis from meritocracy to more pecuniary motives in CoS: the selling of Priesthood degrees. Other narratives focus on theological differences: an atheistic or theistic conception of Satan, the distribution of power and intellectual vs. carnal understandings of Satanism (Lyons 1988: 126). What is important in the two spokespersons' narrativization of the event in the light of the preceding discussion is the ideology used to authorize the schism and the rhetorical and practical acts undertaken to substantiate the claims. Let us examine the two major narratives as they are formulated in relevant publications.

Michael Aquino's version is extensively corroborated in his self-published e-book *The Church of Satan* (Aquino 2005), which documents the rise and fall of CoS over 986 pages and 161 appendices. It is composed linearly, leading to the eventual climax that is the schism, and builds up suspense along the way. Certain indicators, such as the aforementioned letter from LaVey to Aquino in 1972 advocating the marketing of CoS goods, the crisis of the Stygian Grotto (Aquino 2005: 190ff) and the enigmatic fourth degree of Magister given to LaVey's personal chauffeur Tony Fazzani (2005: 399–400), are subtle hints of the catastrophe to come. On May 20, 1975, Aquino receives a letter from the LaVeys in his role as editor of the *Cloven Hoof* with a decree from the High Priest

---

[9] On the Temple of Set, see Harvey 1995: 285ff; Flowers 1997: 215ff; Aquino 2006.

stating that "professional services, funds, real estate, objects of value, etc., which contribute to the tangible, worldly success of the Church of Satan are qualification for elevation to both II* and III*" (2005: 407, emphasis deleted). He replies:

let's not "sell" our degrees. The symbolism and image of the degrees are sacred to those who presently hold them, and a price could never be set upon them. To do so would be to lose the lifeblood of the Church as an institution destined to revolutionize human history. We have the ignoble fate of Crowley's organizations as a case in point. (2005: 408)

A conflict ensues – the correspondence is analyzed in chapter 35 and primary documents included as appendices 127ff in *The Church of Satan* – and finally, Aquino replies on June 10 with the schismatic words:

I reaffirm my degree as Magister Templi, and I reaffirm the degrees of all those who have won them and honored them according to the standards Satan himself has upheld since the dawn of human civilization. Since you – Satan's High Priest and High Priestess – have presumed to destroy these standards and replace the true Church of Satan with a "Church of Anton," the Infernal Mandate is hereby withdrawn from the organization known as the "Church of Satan, Inc." and you are no longer empowered to execute your offices. The degrees you scorn are no longer yours to administer, but shall be safeguarded according to the Will of Satan. (2005: 833–4)

The rhetoric is unmistakably religious: "the standards Satan himself has upheld," "Infernal Mandate," "The Will of Satan." This is a far cry from the rational Satanism developed by LaVey and a curious mix of traditional diabolism and esotericism. Thus the authority used to legitimize the claims is a combination of the traditional, "diabolical authority" of the Satanic tradition and the anthropomorphic Satan (the "Infernal Mandate"), and a bureaucratic, rational-legal authority found in the degree system of the now superseded organization ("I reaffirm my degree . . .," "the true Church of Satan"), underscored by an obvious but unstated transferral of charisma. In other words: science is gone and replaced with the Mouth of Satan. In this sense, the entire quote is a speech act, a "hereby"-action transferring authority in the religious as well as the secular sphere, redrawing the boundaries in the Satanic milieu. But this is only the beginning, as the following letter from Aquino to the defectors shows:

When it became evident to me that the Church of Satan was to be destroyed, I sought an explanation via ceremonial invocation. Since the 9th of June I had received a series of indications that the overall situation and my own actions therein were not haphazard. Consultation of *The Book of Thoth* on Friday, June

13th, for example, yielded the following sequence: 2 of Cups, 7 of Disks, 9 of Disks, 2 of Wands, The Devil. But I had not received what I considered to be a conclusive answer to these events . . . It is the right of a Magister Templi to evoke the Prince of Darkness if it is his Will to do so. During the night of June 21–22, year X, therefore, I addressed such an evocation by means of the first Part of the *Word of Set* [as I had since come to understand as the original "Enochian Keys"]. The evocation was effective, and an answer was received. (Aquino 2005: 412)

This answer is the *The Book of Coming Forth by Night*, a book confirming the transferral of the "Infernal Mandate" from LaVey to Aquino (Aquino 1985: 20ff) and reorienting modern Satanism toward the cultic milieu from whence it came. Three aspects stand out: the use of tradition, the revelatory practice and the focus on degrees, all interrelated. With regard to tradition, the influence of Aleister Crowley is not only alluded to by the Egyptian setting and the use of concepts such as Aeon, Magus and Will, but also directly discussed in the text (1985: 14ff.). Thus, Aquino is constructing an emic historiography (Hammer 2001: 85ff), a sacred legitimating timeline from the dawn of time, including Set, Horus, Crowley, LaVey and himself, and connecting the timeless void, the Prince of Darkness, the authority of Crowley and Temple of Set, to aid the transition from the Age of Satan to the Aeon of Set.[10] This indicates an entirely different underlying ideology much closer to the "mainstream" of seekership in the cultic milieu, a procedure utilizing the traditional legitimation of authority through sacred history in comparison to LaVey's more ambiguous and critical approach.

This brings us to the revelatory practice and the transferral of charisma; Aquino is also emulating Crowley, as well as a host of previous schismatic leaders, through the use of prophecy and revelation as legitimating practice (Wallis 1974: 308; 1979: 177). Notice for example the use of the Tarot in the quote above (suitably including the Devil), alluding to Crowley via *The Book of Thoth*, and the reappropriation of the Enochian Keys (also found in *The Satanic Bible*), translated into a Setian frame as LaVey translated them into a Satanic. What is most important, though, is the activation of a more theistic concept of the Prince of Darkness with whom one is able to commune. Even though he later indicates that this process in no way resembles ecstasy or enthusiasm, as there is an equality between the subjective and objective universes (Dyrendal forthcoming b: 17, 19), he nevertheless affirms an intimate connection with and authority from Set. This is used as a powerful weapon of delegitimation against

---

[10] On the connections between Crowley, LaVey and Aquino, see Dyrendal forthcoming b.

LaVey, whom he earlier supported through revelatory books such as the *Diabolicon* and the *Ninth Solstice Message* (both found as appendices in Aquino 1985).

Lastly, the rhetoric and practice are much more doctrinally charged and organizationally motivated than LaVey's. This can be seen in the formulation "the lifeblood of the Church as an institution destined to revolutionize human history" from the first letter, the whole tone of the second letter, where the disappointed bureaucrat "revokes" the High Priest's administrative powers, and the invocation of the "right of the Magister Templi" to call upon the Prince of Darkness himself in the third letter. Aquino is suitably given the degree of Magus by Set (LaVey's degree in CoS) and later assumes the degree of Ipsissimus, the highest degree in ToS and another appropriation from the Hermetic Order of the Golden Dawn and Aleister Crowley (see Flowers 1997: 220). Thus one of Aquino's primary interests is the reinstating of "the true Church of Satan" as a less anarchistic and less "Anton"-oriented religious group. Although I would hesitate to call the Temple of Set a sect, as it is indeed as pluralistically legitimated as any cultic movement, the group reestablishes the true church with a bureaucratic structure of degrees, gets the doctrine and practice back on track, and revitalizes the Satanic milieu with a new formulation of very old and rejected material: organized esoteric Satanism is born, which is a very different amalgamation than its rational counterpart.

As could be expected, LaVey interprets the schism in light of the phase model outlined earlier, which is in effect a spring cleaning of the over-burdened Church, as well as a reinforcement of the rational interpretation already enjoying hegemony. In the letter "Hoisted by his own Patois" (Aquino 2005: 850–1), dated June 20, 1975 and addressed to the recipients of the schismatic second letter quoted above, LaVey states that the diabolical imagery and rhetoric of the Church is "symbolic, not literal," that the organization "is progressing according to plan (including schism)" and that "I am running this outfit." Most importantly, the letter accomplishes two things: first, a redefinition of "Michael Aquino" as an insecure, pompous and very un-Satanic character, regarding both his personality and his doctrinal eclecticism, in whom LaVey has been dissatisfied for a long time, and secondly a clarification of the Church of Satan and consequently true Satanism as "an organization dedicated to rational self-interest, indulgence, and a glorification of material and carnal elements." He continues: "I held these beliefs in the beginning as I do now. If others re-interpret my organization and philosophy into a fundamental kind of supernaturalism, it stems from their needs to do so." In effect, this is a rational-scientific appeal to authority, but also the very beginning of a rational-legal appeal through routinization of charisma ("my organization and philosophy"), later turning into a full-blown tradition to be protected (Lewis 2003).

This is confirmed in "The Church of Satan, Cosmic Joy Buzzer" (LaVey 1976). Here LaVey reveals the master plan earlier alluded to and interprets Church history through a five-phase development plan: emergence, development, qualification, control and application (LaVey 1976 in Barton 1992: 250–1). The development is in effect a pendulum swing from outrage and antinomianism over respectability and self-religion to alienation and elitism. Thus LaVey acknowledges "Phase One Satanism" (outrage and antinomianism) (Barton 1990: 29) as a necessity in the early stages of the Church, the emergent phase, but also the inevitable "phasing out" of these individuals, the isolation of a Satanic "ideal" (Phase four, control, in 1972) and the subsequent stratification of individuals (Barton 1990: 119–23). The schism in 1975 thus coincides with (or rather *is*) Phase five, application, where only the "productive aliens" are left in the "Church of Satan back on track," namely "a forum, a loosely-structured cabal" (Barton 1990: 30). In brief, this is an affirmation of alienation and elitism as the key words for "true" Satanism. The Church of Satan is thus equated with a sociological experiment in group dynamics (Barton 1992: 250).

CONCLUDING DISCUSSION

Summing up, I really do believe the organizational angle, as it is propagated by both spokespersons and in essence encapsulates other salient features of the rupture. In my opinion it is a question of the negotiation of individuality, antinomianism and leadership. LaVey wants to construct an anti-organization that best supports his radical vision of productive alienation and thus his formulation of antinomian self-religion that has taken form from the early 1970s, while retaining as much power as possible with the least amount of work: he wants to be the manager in a Carnival. He also needs to clear the air internally of the ambiguity present from the inception – the diabolical and traditional baggage – and affirm the scientific legitimation strategy: Satan is a symbol, man is an animal. To do so, he needs to clean the Church of both the very committed members and the rebellious anti-Christians. The pecuniary angle is not original, but I think it is safe to say that it is a fitting carnevalesque, even commonsensical way of putting subtle pressure on these unwanted members. When reading Aquino's documentation, I do indeed see a distance forming on exactly the "scam" versus "school" conceptions of the Church from around 1972.

Aquino, on the other hand, wants an organization with clear demarcations of authority, such as degrees and color-graded medallions, comprising the top percent of isolate intelligences out there and giving them freedom to pursue their Satanic studies as they see fit: he wants to be the principal of a university.[11] He too needs to clear the air internally of the ambiguities – but in his case toward an affirmation of the traditional esoteric elements of the cultic milieu and a more theistic conception of Satan as a First Principle. In this respect, LaVey's early diabolism becomes a clear indication of *true* revelation and authority, and his later symbolic reinterpretation a fall from grace – right into Aquino's lap. The Temple of Set *is* the Church of Satan, but with the necessary focus on self-actualization rather than antinomy. To this almost academic understanding of Satanism, money and play is a rather insulting degradation of the serious business of becoming. All in all, personal ambitions, doctrinal differences and organizational ideas coincide to produce the schism, reinforced by nascent sentiments of affinity and estrangement.

The reformed Church of Satan becomes an audience cult that seeks "a few outstanding individuals," but almost disappears into the cultic milieu (Lewis 2003: 111). LaVey retreats into solitude and concentrates on the artificial companions and total environment of his Black House. In practice, LaVeyan Satanism is almost exclusively propagated by *The Satanic Bible* and other works by the High Priest. This leaves the Satanic milieu less ambiguous, perhaps, as both the rational and esoteric types of modern Satanism now have spokespersons, movements texts and visible organizations, but also more divided, as a fault line in the milieu has been activated and reinforced, supported by new variations of doctrinal syncretism, new constellations of authority and new feelings of community. The end result of the schism is a complex array of internal articulations in the Satanic milieu that can be used in a variety of ways in the negotiation of identity, attributing "Satanism" and "pseudo-Satanism" along different lines.

One of these is the formulation of the Satanic worldview itself. First of all, we have the ontological or metaphysical themes of *materialism versus*

---

[11] He is a successful army man, Boy Scout and academic, while LaVey is more of a carnival man (compare the biographies in e.g. Flowers 1997: 175ff and 217ff)

idealism and *atheism versus theism*. The Church of Satan and related rational groups regard more idealistic or theistic conceptions of the world as paradigmatically conform stupidity: they are at best intellectual mistakes and at worst Christian nonsense. Supernaturalism in any form is a "New Age mish-mash of ideas masquerading as philosophy" (Gilmore 1999: 3). True Satanism considers humanity's carnal and Satan's symbolic nature as self-evident. On the other hand, the Temple of Set and other esoteric groups have a broader notion of Satanism corresponding to the more explicit relation to other currents within the cultic milieu. Set is a platonic ideal and a being with an objective existence, Sat-Tan is Being and Becoming (Petersen 2005: 439). The LaVeyan personality cult of the modern Church of Satan is mistaken (Flowers 1997: 179), barring the true self-realization of the individual. When the relation is articulated in a positive way, as in Stephen E. Flower's book on the Left-Hand Path, rational Satanism is viewed as an *immanent* Satanism with a focus on antinomianism in contrast to the *transcendental* Setianism that pursues self-deification (1997: 5), but there is no doubt that the Temple of Set has the more holistic view.[12] Naturally, the theism of these groups never takes the form of a horned Devil with a pitchfork, but is rather a "psyche-centric" (1997: 5) or mystical conception. The Christian Devil is as pseudo-Satanic as LaVey's degrees up for sale.

A related fault line is the appropriation of *science versus religion*. Indeed most groups within the cultic milieu will seek an alliance with science, as Olav Hammer has amply illustrated (Hammer 2001: 201ff), and regard religion as herd mentality of the worst kind. Nevertheless, as I have shown earlier, rational Satanism generally eschews the term "religion" and appropriates science and philosophy as *genuine* Satanism, whereas esoteric Satanism is much more inclined to view certain "spiritual technologies" in a positive light, as resources to be used in the personal project of actualizing the Black Flame within. This difference is less clear-cut and more tactically keyed than other themes, though the swear-word "religion" tastes like Christian Devil worship whether you are rationally or esoterically inclined. In this sense, it is surely one of the defining characteristics of *pseudo*-Satanism, whoever is on the receiving end. The Satanic underground championed by LaVey is also engaged selectively by

---

[12] For example, the Temple of Set concludes the book and is thus the crown jewel in the manifestation of Satanism in the West, and positive contributions of the Church of Satan to the Left Hand Path are restricted to the formative years between 1966 and 1975 (Flowers 1997).

the modern Church of Satan (Gilmore 1999: 4), a sure sign that the ambiguity discussed earlier is alive and well.

Another important cleavage forms around two traits in my minimal definition, namely *self-religion versus antinomianism*. The post-schismatic LaVey and Church of Satan definitely reorient themselves around the concept of the "alien elite," the non-joiners and productive misfits, thus keying true Satanism emphatically to the negative statement of non-conformity, whereas the Temple of Set is more quiet and withdrawn, and considers self-deification the natural occupation of all isolate intellects. But again, not only are the two terms intertwined; they are also employed strategically. As such, they are useful not only as positive articulations of one's own philosophy, but also as negative descriptors for the other groups on the "pseudo-Satanic fringe" (Peter H. Gilmore, quoted in Wolf 2002: 276). *True* individuality and *true* non-conformism is repre-sented by exactly the form of Satanism the speaker is promoting, but it is always more fun to point out that the Temple of Set, for example, is filled with conform joiners and degree-hunters (Gilmore 2005), or that the LaVey-cult of the upper echelons of CoS is in fact a crypto-fascist devotion to the guru "Doctor LaVey" (Wolf 2002).[13] When all is said and done, the antinomian behavior of the reactive paradigmatically conform Satanist, whether it is a Devil-worshiping teenager or a serial killer claiming that he is doing the will of Satan, is condemned as the worst kind of conformism.

If we now turn to the organizational themes prevalent in the negoti-ations of identity within the Satanic milieu, the *legitimation of authority* garners a lot of attention. The complex negotiation between individual worldviews and a Church doctrine suggests that there is a pluralistic doctrinal environment within CoS from the very beginning, as long as one does not criticize the High Priest nor try to make individual syn-cretisms the official party line (Baddeley 2000: 218). The serious enemies are first the hypocritical Christians and later "pseudo-Satanists" in the Temple of Set and other splinter groups. In a very real sense, you can believe almost anything, as long as you don't rock the boat. On the other hand, arguments proposed by LaVey in the wake of the schism in 1975 already point toward a formulation of "orthodox" LaVeyan Satanism,

---

[13] The reason for the title is unclear. Stephen Flowers states that it is the proper address for a Magus (Flowers 1997: 183), while Blanche Barton writes that "[h]is closest associates call him 'Dr. LaVey', 'Doc' or 'Herr Doktor' as, he says, 'a term of affection and respect – much as a circus calliopist or whorehouse pianist was once called 'Professor'" (Barton 1990: 45). Indeed this discrepancy clearly illustrates the organizational differences of ToS and CoS.

although this is a fluid concept; this process is accentuated after 1997, mainly because of the Internet's effect on the Satanic milieu (Petersen 2002) and the death of LaVey that year. What is clear is that LaVey's charismatic authority is routinized into a tradition and a legal bureaucracy (Lewis 2003), clearly demarcating what is authentic Satanism as that which is of the Church – itself quite ambiguous. Thus it is somewhat easier to say what Satanism is *not*: all which is not formulated or sanctioned by LaVey (see for example Anthony 2000 and Gilmore 2000). I agree with Ole Wolf that this complex strategy is in fact an "*enforced* dogmalessness": "if a follower revises his or her view, then the new view is Satanism, too. It is only when the follower does not accept other views as Satanic that the Church of Satan administration typically responds with an explanation that the follower's 'one true way' attitude is not appreciated" (Wolf 2002: 281). Thus the Church continues the fluid strategy devised by LaVey, although his charisma is now routinized (the *Satanic Bunco Sheet* [n.d.] is a good example). This semi-unique legitimation strategy has indeed sprouted new splinter groups and resentment from the Satanic milieu, which unfortunately is beyond the scope of this chapter.

Paradoxically, the Temple of Set is as pluralistically legitimated as other cultic movements: it is definitely not a sect, even though its legitimacy derives from a unique revelation, *The Book of Coming Forth by Night*. This is mainly because Setians regard Aquino as exemplary, not unique. On the whole, ToS is very close to the cultic milieu and esoteric groups with a focus on seekership and individual ambition. Group cohesion is in large part the result of the degree system, Aquino's huge literary output and the creative management of the heritage from the cultic milieu.

The final theme is a Satanic Procrustean Bed: *individuality versus collective*. How can one balance the *individual* right to express a personal view of Satanism (which is obviously *true*) with the just as valid need to debunk *alternative* interpretations as misunderstood? It is not even remotely a problem when you are alone or when other Satanists are invisible – but it is very much so when Satanic subcultures clash on the Internet or in real life. The question of legitimation is a central concern for most Satanic *groups* I have encountered, and it is connected with an articulation of collectivity. In a more philosophical mood, this is a pure manifestation of the problem with relativism. Is the unique interpretation of the self-professed Satanist or the minimum standards of a definition more important? Or on a collective scale: individuality or group cohesion?

This classical problem is solved differently in different formulations of Satanism, but is a constant source of tension within the Satanic milieu and groups born from it. This is part of the inheritance that is the ambiguity of LaVey and the very pluralistic strategies it nurtures.

In conclusion, Gavin Baddeley provides a fitting coda: "The conflict between promoting individuality and presenting a united front plagues every serious Satanic organization. LaVey's solution was typically perverse: an organization dedicated to liberty, but run like a dictatorship. That LaVey's ideal – of a church of productive misfits, a club for non-joiners – hasn't been too contradictory to survive is remarkable in itself" (Baddeley 2000: 218). This is a very perceptive statement, but the only way it *has* survived is by spawning a host of churches and clubs – a natural consequence of the oxymoronic project. On the one hand Satanism is a pure breed of the cultic milieu, confirming many central assumptions; on the other, the very ambiguity of LaVey's construction has a certain bizarre authoritarian effect. Thus modern Satanism, understood as a Satanic milieu comprised of significant themes and their strategic deployment, inspires perpetual negotiations of identity, affinity and estrangement that nevertheless relate to the same constant pool of doctrines, practices and organizational structures.

ACKNOWLEDGMENTS

Thanks to Asbjørn Dyrendal for useful comments, suggestions and inspiring collegial discussions.

REFERENCES

Alfred, Randall. 1976. "The Church of Satan." In Charles Y. Glock and Robert N. Bellah (eds.), *The New Religious Consciousness*. Berkeley: University of California Press, pp. 180–202.
Anthony, K. S. 2000. "To Arms." *The Black Flame* 6 (3–4): 75.
Aquino, Michael. 1985 [1975]. *The Book of Coming Forth by Night*. San Francisco: Temple of Set.
  2002. *The Church of Satan*. 5th edn [Internet]. San Francisco: Temple of Set.
  2006. *The Temple of Set*. 6th edn [Internet]. San Francisco: Temple of Set.
Baddeley, Gavin. 2000. *Lucifer Rising: Sin, Devil Worship and Rock 'n' Roll*. London: Plexus.
Barton, Blanche. 1990. *The Church of Satan*. New York: Hell's Kitchen Productions.
  1992. *The Secret Life of a Satanist*. Los Angeles: Feral House.

Campbell, Colin. 1972. "The Cult, the Cultic Milieu and Secularization." *A Sociological Yearbook of Religion in Britain*, 5: 119–36.
Cohn, Norman. 1975. *Europe's Inner Demons*. London: Paladin.
Dyrendal, Asbjørn. 2004a. "Et satans mannfolk: den autoriserte Anton LaVey." *Din* 2–3: 73–83.
    2004b. "Satanisme – en innføring." *Din* 4: 48–58.
    2005. "Satanisme og populærkultur." *Din* 3–4: 49–59.
    forthcoming a. "Darkness Within: Satanism as a Self-religion." In Jesper Aagaard Petersen (ed.), *Contemporary Religious Satanism: A Critical Anthology*. Oxford: Ashgate.
    forthcoming b. "Satan and the Beast: The Influence of Aleister Crowley on Modern Satanism." In Henrik Bogdan and Martin P. Starr (eds.), *Aleister Crowley and Western Esotericism: An Anthology of Critical Studies*. New York: State University of New York Press.
Ellis, Bill. 2000. *Raising the Devil: Satanism, New Religions and the Media*. Lexington: University Press of Kentucky.
Flowers, Stephen R. 1997. *The Lords of the Left Hand Path*. Smithville, TX: Runa-Raven Press.
Fritscher, Jack. 2004 [1971]. *Popular Witchcraft: Straight from the Witch's Mouth*. 2nd edn. Madison: University of Wisconsin Press.
Gilmore, Peter H. 1999. *A Map for the Misdirected*. Accessed on the Internet July 5, 2007 at www.churchofsatan.com/Pages/Map.html.
    2000. "Towards the Well-Known Region." *The Black Flame* 6 (3–4): 26–7.
    2005. *Pretenders to the Throne: Regarding the Temple of Set*. Accessed on the Internet July 5, 2007 at www.churchofsatan.com/Pages/Pretenders.html.
    2007. *The Satanic Scriptures*. Baltimore, MD: Scapegoat Publishing.
Hammer, Olav. 2001. *Claiming Knowledge: Strategies of Epistemology from Theosophy to the New Age*. Leiden: Brill.
Harvey, Graham. 1995. "Satanism in Britain Today." *Journal of Contemporary Religion* 10 (3): 283–96.
    2002. "Satanism: Performing Alterity and Othering." *Syzygy* 11: 53–68.
Heelas, Paul. 1996. *The New Age Movement*. Oxford: Blackwell.
Hermonen, Merja. 2002. "Rationalistic Satanism: The Individual as a Member of a Countercultural Tribe." *Syzygy* 11: 69–104.
Hodkinson, Paul. 2002. *Goth: Identity, Style and Subculture*. Oxford: Berg.
LaVey, Anton Szandor. 1969. *The Satanic Bible*. New York: Avon Books.
    1971. "On Occultism of the Past." *The Cloven Hoof* 3 (9). Accessed on the Internet July 5, 2007 on www.churchofsatan.com/Pages/LaVeyPastOccultism.html.
    1972. *The Satanic Rituals*. New York: Avon Books.
    1976. "The Church of Satan, Cosmic Joy Buzzer." *The Cloven Hoof* 8 (2): 3–4. Reprinted in Barton 1992: 248–52.
    1989. *The Satanic Witch*. Los Angeles: Feral House.
    1992. *The Devil's Notebook*. Los Angeles: Feral House.

1998. *Satan Speaks!* Los Angeles: Feral House.

Lewis, James R. 2003. *Legitimating New Religions*. New Brunswick, NJ: Rutgers University Press.

Lincoln, Bruce. 1989. *Discourse and the Construction of Society*. Oxford: Oxford University Press.

Lyons, Arthur. 1988. *Satan Wants You: The Cult of Devil Worship in America*. New York: Mysterious Press.

Medway, Gareth J. 2001. *Lure of the Sinister: The Unnatural History of Satanism*. New York: New York University Press.

Partridge, Christopher. 2004. *The Re-enchantment of the West*, vol. I. London: T. & T. Clark.

2005. *The Re-enchantment of the West*, vol. II. London: T. & T. Clark.

Petersen, Jesper Aagaard. 2002. "Binary Satanism: The Construction of Community in a Digital World." *Syzygy* 11: 37–52.

2005. "Modern Satanism: Dark Doctrines and Black Flames." In James R. Lewis & Jesper Aagaard Petersen (eds.), *Controversial New Religions*. New York: Oxford University Press, pp. 423–57.

Rose, Michael. 2000. *Satanic Brotherhood?* Accessed on July 5, 2007 at www.churchofsatan.com/Pages/RoseBrother.html.

Rothstein, Michael. 1996. *Belief Transformations*. Aarhus: Aarhus University Press.

Russell, Jeffrey Burton. 1977. *The Devil: Perceptions of Evil from Antiquity to Primitive Christianity*. Ithaca, NY: Cornell University Press.

1981. *Satan: The Early Christian Tradition*. Ithaca, NY: Cornell University Press.

1984. *Lucifer: The Devil in the Middle Ages*. Ithaca, NY: Cornell University Press.

1986. *Mephistopheles: The Devil in the Modern World*. Ithaca, NY: Cornell University Press.

Saler, Benson. 2000. *Conceptualizing Religion*. New York: Berghahn Books.

Satanic Bunco Sheet. Accessed on the Internet July 5, 2007 at www.churchofsatan.com/Pages/Bunco.html.

Schmidt, Joachim. 1992. *Satanismus: Mythos und Wirklichkeit*. Marburg: Diagonal Verlag.

Smoczynski, Rafal. 2002. "Polish Cyber Satanism: A Group in Statu Nascendi." *Syzygy* 11: 111–18.

Stark, Rodney and William S. Bainbridge. 1985. *The Future of Religion: Secularization, Revival, and Cult Formation*. Berkeley: University of California Press.

Taylor, John. 1995. *Linguistic Categorization*. Oxford: Oxford University Press.

Truzzi, Marcello. 1972. "The Occult Revival as Popular Culture: Some Random Observations on the Old and the Nouveau Witch." *Sociological Quarterly* 13 (winter): 16–36.

Victor, Jeffrey S. 1993. *Satanic Panic: The Creation of a Contemporary Legend*. Chicago: Open Court.

Wallis, Roy. 1974. "Ideology, Authority, and the Development of Cultic Movements." *Social Research* 41 (2): 299–327.

1975. "The Cult and Its Transformation." In Roy Wallis (ed.): *Sectarianism*. London: Peter Owen, pp. 35–49.

1979. *Salvation and Protest: Studies of Social and Religious Movements*. New York: St. Martin's Press.

Weber, Max. 2003. *Udvalgte tekster. Bind 2*. Edited by Heine Andersen, Hans Henrik Bruun and Lars Bo Kaspersen. Copenhagen: Hans Reitzels Forlag.

Wolf, Ole. 2002. "The Emperor's New Religion." *Syzygy* 11: 257–310.

CHAPTER 11

Schism as midwife: how conflict aided the birth of a contemporary Pagan community

Murphy Pizza

Contemporary Paganism – which consists of Wicca and Witchcraft, Druidry, Heathenry, Asatru, Goddess-worshipers, Ethnic Reconstructionists, and many other traditions – is a movement that is still young and establishing its identity. The members of the movement confront a paradox of wanting to grow and unify, but also of wishing to maintain its characteristic diversity of traditions, identities, and rituals. Not surprisingly, the modern Pagan movement has had a restless and schismatic formation period, especially in the United States, running the gamut from splits based on interpersonal conflicts to the equivalent of denominational breaks brought on by theological differences and issues with organizational structures (Adler 1986; Berger 1999; Clifton 2006; Davies and Lynch 2001; Hopman and Bond 1996; Magliocco 2004; Pike 2001; Salomonsen 2002).

In some ways, the nature of contemporary Paganism – polyvalent, syncretic, and innovative – is set up to incorporate the splitting, renaming, and reforming that appears to characterize the movement; Gerald Gardner, the founder of Wicca, made room for and established guidelines of conduct in his tradition for the eventual and inevitable "hiving off" of coven members to form other groups (Adler 1986; Gardner 1954; Hutton 1999). Modern Pagans' ambivalence toward formal institutionalization, rejection of homogeneity, and embracing of a fluid, permeable and diverse identity within their membership can be argued, in some way, to contribute toward frequent schisms, but as time has passed, and definitions of what constitutes Pagan identity, practice, and community have shifted and drifted, hiving and splitting are being perceived less as a problem plaguing a movement, and instead are now accepted more as a necessary process if the fundamental Pagan value of diversity in the community is to be maintained (Magliocco 2004; Pike 2001; Salomonsen 2002).

Arguably, depending on the experiences of the regional community, enough time has passed and enough perspective has been gained for contemporary Pagans of various identifications to begin to consider schisms within their orders and organizations as a potentially beneficial force; specifically, the splitting and fractioning of a community can result in a larger, more broad-ranging community. In some cases, alliances are made and more groups and organizations have the ability to form, most notably around social action and legal protection issues. In addition, more opportunities become available for newcomers to Paganism to find community entry points, and for families to find more spaces for cultivating shared Pagan values within which to receive support and to raise their children in a culturally and morally agreeable environment in tune with Pagan values.

The death of a small group, in short, can result in the growth of a wider and more successful community of alliances. This has been the case in the Pagan community of the Minnesota Twin Cities, otherwise known by members as "Paganistan." "Paganistan" is the nickname, and now proud moniker of self-identification, of the uniquely innovative, eclectic, and feisty Neopagan community of the Twin Cities Metro area of Minnesota. Filled with many different groups – Druid orders, Witch covens, legal Pagan churches, Ethnic Reconstructionist groups, and many more solitaries, interlopers, and poly-affiliated Pagans – the community gained its name from priest Steven Posch, and it has proudly adopted it. In a sense, the name appropriately expresses the community's sense of being a "Pagan Nation" of tribes (Posch 2005). An incredibly active, diverse, and often overlapping alliance of traditions, it is common to encounter Twin Cities Pagans who possess multiple identities and represent various traditions, such as "Heathen Witches," Italian Druids, shamanic Slavic Reconstructionists, or those who tie everything together and give it a new name, and no one bats an eye.

In the midst of all this diversity, there is the tempering influence of a discernible Midwestern and Minnesotan cultural overlay – a self-deprecating humor and a famously detached "niceness" permeates many encounters – as well as the influence of Minnesota's distinctive and dramatic climate and seasonality. Amidst the formidable creativity, Minnesotans are eminently practical – living room rituals make perfect sense during Yule, and the festival campsites beckon with a vengeance during the summer.

This sort of cultural tension – creativity and cross-pollination buffered with a regional sensibility – is, in many ways, what gives Paganistan its distinctive character and its vibrancy. Paganistanis innovate for very practical reasons. And, perhaps because of its regional overculture's influence, despite its believable claim to being the second-largest Pagan community in the United States, Paganistan has been a surprisingly well-kept secret.

The necessary tension kept in Paganistan serves as a convenient example of the process of the success of new religious movements generally; specifically, the concept of "medium tension," and the maintenance of such in the face of dominant social patterns, ethics, and religious thought (Johnson 1963; Stark 2003). With the equilibrium being the middle tension point – not so innovative and strange that society rejects it, but not so familiar that it is no longer an alternative to the dominant forces at work – the growth of a new religion can be marked by periods of dramatic innovation and mainstream negotiation, which lessen over time. Typically, the tempering effect is caused by institutionalization, and the equilibrium leans toward mainstream acceptance as the religion itself solidifies.

Contemporary Paganism breaks from this pattern inasmuch as the equilibrium maintained is the desired medium tension point and, in the absence of institutions, the contributions of the growing membership mitigate the innovation/compromise dynamic. The growing diversity of influences, of cultural and spiritual backgrounds brought to the table and negotiated, is what keeps Paganism from either schisming completely into irrelevancy or slipping into the mainstream – which is precisely what most Pagans will say they wish to avoid (Adler 1986; Hopman and Bond 1996; Magliocco 2004).

With regard to Paganistan, what complicates this tension even more is the community's own admitted history of innovation. Many of the elders of the Twin Cities community whom I have interviewed tell the story of how, in the 1970s, when the East Coast and West Coast Pagan communities were beginning to have countrywide influence, the Midwest was still considered, as put by priestess Robin Reyburn, "flyover country" as far as Neopagan cultural transmission was concerned. Twin Cities Pagans, impatient with waiting for San Francisco and the Eastern seaboard to notice them, mined sources, courtesy of Gnostica books and Llewelyn Publications, and created "bootstrap" traditions and practices in order to get the kind of magical training and education they wanted. Consequently, the Pagans of Paganistan, more than those from other Neopagan communities, are patient with innovations, creative with reconstructions, and very careful to keep a sense of humor about themselves.

Specifically, this chapter documents and analyzes ethnographically a particularly influential schism in the Twin Cities, that of the Wiccan Church of Minnesota's (WiCoM) split and establishment in the 1980s from its parent organization, Minnesota Church of the Wicca (MCoW). This was a rare opportunity to sit and discuss the issues and mechanisms behind the split with respective founders of both churches: the founders of MCoW, known in the community by their ceremonial names, Burtrand and Aura, as well as WiCoM founders Volkhvy, Maggie Sterba, and Robin Reyburn, agreed to sit for interviews with me to reflect on their contributions to the Twin Cities community, the schism, and the effect of it some twenty years later. What came of these interviews was not just an examination of the workings of a modern Pagan schism, but a snapshot of a time when the definition of "Pagan community" began to change.

The schismatic theoretical pattern that best fits contemporary Paganism, as described in chapter 1 of this volume by Finke and Scheitle, is that of niche stretching; modern Paganism was founded as a countercultural response in the US, and has since established its identity as an oppositional culture (Adler 1986; Magliocco 2004; Salomonsen 2002; Vale and Sulak 2001) with many different traditions, orders, and organizations relishing and attempting to maintain their existence on the fringe. That said, the growth of Paganism in the US has been explosive (Lewis 2006); maintaining a sense of shared Pagan identity has been a delicate balance of groups stretching toward the center, and toward the surrounding dominant culture's norms, alongside the need for individuals and groups to break off and stay rooted in the fringe. This process has resulted in a not-so-conscious maintenance of medium tension that retains members and attracts more.

Time, perspective, and a researcher's outsider positionality allow for this sort of analysis; to those who were and are enmeshed in Paganism's frequent schisms, the process can still be fraught with pain and frustration, and be perceived as a failure to "get it together" as a community. The combination of an etic, theoretical perspective with the emic-view contributions of MCoW's and WiCoM's respective founders – which include their own reassessment of the purpose of their schism – can, I argue, shed some light on the benefits of schism for community building, and how tolerance of it and understanding of its factors by members of the community can help reframe and redefine what it means to be part of and involved in maintaining and transmitting Pagan religion, culture, and community.

MINNESOTA CHURCH OF THE WICCA (MCOW)

The story of the emergence of Paganistan is one of "bootstrapping"; rather than descending from the lineage of a teacher or an author, as is the case on either American coast (Salomonsen 2002; Berger 1999; Magliocco 2004), the formation of covens, groves, and organizations of various sorts in the Twin Cities was largely a repeating self-starting process. Rather than wait for a lineage holder to start a tradition, many Pagan organization founders took advantage of visits and classes at local occult and metaphysical stores – most notably, Carl Weschke's Gnostica, which promoted the Gnosticon occult gatherings in the 1970s (Adler 1986) and was the precursor to Llewelyn Publications in S. Paul, Minnesota. Rather than jump into an existing lineage, however, Minnesotans began to search on their own, took teachings or methods that they liked, dispensed with others, and crafted covens and traditions that were innovative and reflective of Minnesota climate and culture.

Paganistan's "bootstrapping" cultural pattern was certainly in place when Burtrand and Aura formed Coven Elysium in 1976. They were not carriers of a particular Wiccan lineage, like Gardnerian or Alexandrian; Burtrand used the phrase "American eclectic" to describe the tradition they helped instigate. Both Burtrand and Aura shared the story of attending the equivalent of a "Wicca 101" class at a local metaphysical bookstore in the 1970s, facilitated by an out-of-state teacher they referred to as "Eli." (They also referred to Eli's apprentices as "Elites.") Sharing that they were intrigued by the content of the class, and that they signed up to learn more right away, Burtrand and Aura also expressed some initial reservations they had about the instructor's version of ritual practice and magical method. Burtrand commented that much of Eli's method was "Quasi-formal magic in the worst sense," and that he and Aura had disagreements with practices like ritual drug use, so they split off to form their own coven and to take students.

"We did what we could," Aura stated, regarding the formation of Coven Elysium. "Information was scarce then." Burtrand and Aura shared that they mined books and magical sources for material and methods, and when new students and members joined up, they would, as Burtrand put it, "draw things from each of the members and weave it together. Others would drop out and we'd learn to weave over them . . . We didn't really weave things from whole cloth, but were instrumental in cutting and sewing it into the suit it became." Aura agreed: "We wanted exposure to other traditions, and to meet others and to share what we knew." So, by 1976, Coven Elysium composed by-laws and a charter, formally registered with the IRS, and became Minnesota Church of the Wicca (MCoW), Minnesota's first public–private coven and legal Pagan church, and the fourth oldest legally recognized Pagan organization in the US.

Much of the creative work and innovation of MCoW in the first decade of its existence brought the Twin Cities community a controversial reputation along the Pagan festival circuit. At a time when many independent Pagan publications were having in-print debates raging about ritual nudity versus robes, whose Wiccan tradition was the most legitimate, and how authentically linked to European folk practice one's ritual magic practices were, Burtrand, Aura, and MCoW were innovating and piecing together what worked and dropping what did not, in what has now become a Minnesota Pagan tradition, rather than entering fractious arguments about what was authentic, right, or proper. Burtrand summed it up thus: "If it will work, we'll do it." MCoW let members decide for themselves if they wished to be robed or skyclad, resulting in mixed circles. Another technique Burtrand shared was of having participants recite their own versions of the Witches' Rune (a ritual invocation) during ritual, regardless of whether or not the rhyme schemes lined up. Burtrand and Aura stated that some versions of the Rune had an AABB rhyme scheme, others ABAB; rather than bicker over which version to let trump the other, everyone simply recited the version that they knew. They discovered that the word order did not matter as much as the magical energy raised from the overlapping voices reciting different versions of the poem.

One tradition that MCoW founded that is still Paganistan's longest-running celebration is the election by lottery of the May Queen and Green Man from church members on the Feast of Beltane, May Day. The May Couple were essentially ceremonial and symbolic "ruling" positions in the church; every year, members would enter their name into a lottery, and a female member was chosen to be May Queen for a year, and a male for the role of Green Man. The practice reinforced the importance of gender polarity as a theological construct in traditional Wicca, but the process of the lottery was a uniquely Twin Cities innovation.

The May Couple lottery is an example of the Twin Cities Pagan community's innovative and adaptive approach. The practice of retooling what is available to circumstances at hand, and to local landscape, climate, and culture, is something that is indicative of immensely practical

Minnesota Paganism; the sorts of issues that cropped up as points of contention in other Pagan communities – legitimacy, lineage, authenticity – were and are not perceived as the most important issues to be entangled in in Paganistan. It allowed for a great deal of freedom and creativity for Twin Cities Pagans during the 1970s and 1980s; it did, however, also foster a good deal of schismatic fodder after some time.

MCoW's structure during its heyday was of a public–private coven, with an open study circle for basic magical training for new members, and an inner experimental working circle for members initiated second degree or higher. While the exchange of techniques and experiences was often productive and exciting, at other times they were, as Burtrand put it, "weird. We got some strange things." But that was the flip side of innovation, and is another Minnesotan Pagan cultural characteristic: a humility based on not really feeling prepared enough or knowledgeable enough with regard to tradition and magical practice. Burtrand mused, "We had no real time, money, or resources to learn what we really needed to do." Despite this feeling, MCoW began a Minnesota cultural tradition of self-study, experimentation, and adaptation that has lasted until today in Paganistan, although it is nowadays expressed differently.

Burtrand and Aura estimated that over the decades they have had probably about a thousand students, lumping together the dedicated members with those who dropped out after a few meetings. But the strain of teaching, and of interpersonal issues that began to foment within the inner circle at MCoW, contributed to what changed the Twin Cities Pagan Community dramatically.

THE SCHISM, 1988

Robin Reyburn, already a long-time practicing ceremonial magician, got involved with MCoW in 1977, Volkhvy in 1980, and Maggie Sterba in 1982. While all three claimed they were never really official members of the church, they nonetheless became part of the inner experimental magic circle, and have subsequently become respected teachers of magic and ritual themselves in the Twin Cities. Their notable contributions while in MCoW included Reyburn receiving her ministerial credentials through the church; Maggie and Volkhvy were selected as MCoW's May Couple in 1982 – and were married a year later, with Reyburn officiating.

By the mid-eighties, MCoW had an unofficial membership of around thirty people. Burtrand shared in his interview that he and Aura were at a point where they wanted to step back from running the church for a while; Volkhvy, in his account, concurred: "Burtrand wanted to step aside for a bit; a group of us were left running MCoW even though we weren't members. The May Couple were who officially held the church." There were some expressions of dissatisfaction with MCoW's operations at this time; Burtrand suggested that there were interpersonal issues that were plaguing the church, but Volkhvy, Reyburn, and Maggie did not entirely agree with that assessment; Maggie shared: "A joke was going around that he [Burtrand] would initiate anyone. The group was dissatisfied with who was getting in." The aforementioned members actually had more pressing concerns regarding the status of the church: namely, did MCoW exist as a legal entity? Did involvement with MCoW afford any sort of legal protection for its members? These questions started a search for the original by-laws and charter of the church, and a check-in with the State of Minnesota. "We tried to find out if the church was legally registered," Volkhvy said. "There was *nothing* on record with that state. Burtrand may have registered with the feds, or possibly incorporated as a 'doing-business-as', but at the state level, MCoW didn't exist." A search for the original documents of the church was turning nothing up.

So Maggie, Volkhvy, Reyburn, and other members at the time did what they felt they needed to do in order to retain the legal protection they wanted: they sat down and composed new by-laws and a new charter for the church. Reyburn recalled long, four-hour meetings in her living room where members met to draft, re-draft, and critique the by-laws as they were being composed "line by line." When the work was complete, the new documents were presented to the thirty church members, and were roundly accepted.

It was not long afterwards that Burtrand and Aura returned, and were stunned by the actions of the members of the church while they were gone. Aura commented, "They'd gone and tried to change the by-laws, and all sorts of things." "I was initially upset about that," Burtrand shared. "The IRS isn't just going to let you do something like that!"

"Burtrand showed back up, and said, 'You can't do that!'" Volkhvy stated. Advised by other MCoW members to wait a few months before pressing the issue, the new charter composers discovered that the original charter and by-laws had resurfaced. But reviewing them brought out a bigger problem, according to Reyburn: "There was no provision in the by-laws for succession after the founders [Burtrand and Aura] go. We thought, we need to provide for succession and protection." It became clear to many in MCoW that something needed to be done. Reyburn continued: "[Burtrand] was right, we couldn't just do that. But now we had this really neat new charter and by-laws." Between that, and the members' genuine desire for a more protective and state-approved legal entity, the wheels were in motion for a schism to occur, and it did, in 1988.

"It went fairly well, even though it took forever," Volkhvy stated. Legally, registering the new church – which founders called the Wiccan Church of Minnesota (WiCoM) – proved not to be difficult. Ministers of MCoW who were interested in joining WiCoM had their status and credentials "grandfathered in": "Robin's credentials were our hook for the feds," Volkhvy commented. "We just said, 'we're schisming', which gave us a leg up as far as the IRS was concerned." Recognition by the State of Minnesota brought no problems; federal recognition took a bit more effort and money, but WiCoM eventually was, and since 1989 has been registered with both the IRS and the State of Minnesota.

Interpersonally, and community-wide, the schism was much more difficult to negotiate. "People were pissed," Maggie shared. WiCoM's founders stated that they were actually surprised at how many MCoW members left the fold to join WiCoM once it was established. Volkhvy and Reyburn speculated that while they had no real interpersonal issues with MCoW, it was clear that many other members did. Reyburn noted: "It was one of the more tumultuous periods . . . There was bad blood for a while on both sides. Some felt misled by Burtrand; some were upset about the schism."

Time and reflection have made both sides philosophical about the 1988 schism. Burtrand commented, "We're a lot less stand-offish than we used to be, but it was upsetting at the time." Separately, Maggie stated, "Now they talk to us, we talk to them . . . Some attempts were made to bring the two back together, but it never really happened." Those attempts, upon closer examination, were less about hurt feelings and interpersonal issues, and more with the change in organizational structure that came with WiCoM's formation. WiCoM was not simply a competing public coven or church; it was something new and completely different.

WICCAN CHURCH OF MINNESOTA (WICOM)

The founders of WiCoM that I interviewed stated that their organization was not simply a competitor with MCoW; WiCoM provided different focus points for members. "It's an umbrella organization that provides legal affiliation. MCoW was a coven; we don't have a high priest and priestess like they did. We have trustees and representatives," Reyburn said.

"WiCoM is a group that's set up to cover as many different groups as possible," Volkhvy added. Despite the name "Wiccan" in its title, WiCoM was established from the beginning to be a legal protection entity for any Pagan tradition – Druid, Witch, Heathen, and others – that was interested. Volkhvy added, "Our organizational structure versus the coven structure aided people in thinking beyond their own path." It is evident that WiCoM's founders were already considering branching out, forming alliances, building wider community, and engaging intra-faith dialogue with other Pagan organizations in the Twin Cities.

The switch to an institutional model, rather than an initiatory, secret society model, and the inclusion of non-Wiccan members opened WiCoM up to innovation. "Room was allowed for much more expression," Reyburn commented. "We've done all different kinds of rituals." In the midst of the innovation, however, was a maintenance of a Twin Cities Pagan tradition: WiCoM has continued the lottery election of the May Queen and Green Man unbroken for thirty-six years. WiCoM members did add an innovative twist, however, in the institution of the election of the Fool along with the May Couple. Many members who did not feel that they fit into the established gender binary of the May Couple – examples being members who self-identified as gay, lesbian, bisexual, or transgendered – voiced their concern about this, and WiCoM decided to add the Fool, a non-gender specific character, as an additional symbolic ruling head, to "keep an eye" on the church and on decisions made by the representatives and trustees.

For the first three years of WiCoM's existence, Volkhvy edited the church's newsletter and was the teachers' representative; Reyburn added, with a laugh, "Haven't we all been the teachers' rep?" Much like their teachers Burtrand and Aura, Volkhvy, Maggie, and Reyburn found that they and other church members became "default elders" in the Pagan community, simply by having put in the time and the effort both in teaching new students and in being instrumental in founding other Pagan organizations in addition to WiCoM. In true Minnesotan style, that situation did not sit well with WiCoM's founders. Regarding ministry and mentorship, Reyburn said humbly, "This was a need that wasn't being met at the time. I agreed to it, but I think there are others who can do the job better."

All three founders have since stepped back from major involvement with the church they helped found; all mention some internal politics stunting the organization as being unappealing enough to make them want to. Maggie stated, "There were some major issues; new people who might be interested are somehow feeling discouraged from getting involved. We can't really determine why." When Volkhvy turned over editorship of the newsletter in 1992, there were seventy-six members on the books; membership since has dropped off considerably. Maggie picked up the newsletter editorship from 1995 to 2000, and she continues to be involved with the mentoring of ministers in the church. Reyburn shared that she was considering retirement from ministerial duties. All three founders do, according to Volkhvy, "show up for ritual from time to time."

WiCoM's founders are also examples of the phenomenon of multiple affiliation in Paganistan. Volkhvy and Reyburn collaborated on the creation of more regionally specific versions of Pagan Witchcraft – named Fourfold and Twyern, respectively (Pizza 2006) – and continuing creative work on her innovative strand of magic keeps Reyburn occupied (Reyburn 2005). Volkhvy and Maggie are also involved with the Minnesota Heathens, a Midwestern organization of northern European ethnic reconstructionist Pagan traditions, including Asatru, Germanic, and Slavic traditionalists. All three are involved with the Mentoring Elders Forum – Volkhvy's self-designed elders' curriculum – and the Earth House Project, which exists to raise funds to buy in-the-Cities property for the establishment of a Pagan community center.

So, while their involvement in the larger Twin Cities Pagan community has remained as strong as ever, their engagement with the organization they founded has settled down somewhat. When asked what might bring their involvement back up, Volkhvy shared that if it looked like WiCoM was starting to fail, he might come in to rescue it, simply because the legal hurdles and expense for reestablishing a new church would be too onerous. That said, he did say that he envisioned it possibly transforming into an even broader umbrella group of Pagan alliances, rather than a specifically named "Wiccan Church," in order to interest more affiliations of Pagans in joining.

Maggie stated, rather surprisingly, that at the next WiCoM elders meeting she was going to suggest that the church "either needs to die or start over" adding with a laugh that WiCoM has come to this point before and bounced back. This did beg the question if perhaps WiCoM was on its way to experiencing a schism. Those interviewed did not think it likely: "There is a season to these things," Reyburn commented. "There are lots of organizations out there now." Volkhvy added, "WiCoM has served its purpose; it's been worthwhile. I don't regret the time or money we invested in it at all. It still affords legal protection for Pagans."

CONCLUSIONS AND REFLECTIONS

It would be tempting to conclude that, since there is a fine line between religious schisms and a religion's natural growth, WiCoM is not really a schismatic phenomenon, but an inevitable growth and continuation of MCoW. However, there are two factors at work in the story of WiCoM's split from MCoW that need to be considered. First, from the time it became clear that MCoW's and WiCoM's goals were at odds, the founders of WiCoM decided to use the word "schism" in both legal documentation and correspondence (Duquette 1998). They discovered that the use of the term "schism" when processing their legal status and registering their documentation actually worked in their favor when dealing with the state government. This account begs the question of whether schisming is an effective method of legitimation for any new religious organization as opposed to whole-cloth creation (Lewis 2003).

What WiCoM's split was also a harbinger for was the explosive growth of Pagan community in Paganistan itself. The reconfiguring of a religious organization from a public–private coven structure to an interweaving of alliances appeared and landed on the pulse of what the Twin Cities was desiring as far as community was concerned: less exclusivity, permeable group and identity boundaries, and the sharing of knowledge and building of alliances. The Twin Cities community claims that there are 10,000 Pagan-identified people in the Metro Area; the community itself has worked tirelessly to hold festivals, meet-ups, classes, and other opportunities for Pagans to find each other, and there are now numerous legally recognized Pagan churches and non-profits that are serving the community and engaged in social activist work. This in-community outreach, while hitting a few obstacles along the way and still a work in progress, began in earnest right about the time that WiCoM announced its existence and its policy of opening up and encouraging the involvement of various affiliated Pagans. It was instrumental in this community structural change, and the change in the definition of what Pagan community means.

"We're all different, you know, and we disagree on things. This happens to everybody. If it didn't, we'd all be the same religion everywhere, and we're not," Aura commented reflectively. Despite this response, when MCoW's founders were asked their opinion on the status of the Twin Cities Pagan community, Burtrand responded sardonically, "What community? . . . Nobody gets together anymore on a regular basis to do the sort of magical work and ritual we used to do. There's so much talent here that's not being used." This statement does shed light on the definition of "community" that was MCoW's focus: a more intimate, exclusive, safe group of similarly believing Pagans and magicians who come together strictly for the purpose of doing ritual together.

That definition – and the subsequent goals for community building – changed dramatically with the schism of WiCoM. Pagans in the Twin Cities wanted more than their specific affiliations with their covens, groves, kindreds, and churches could provide for them, and the work began and continues to break through affiliative boundaries and let membership in Pagan traditions, identities, and organizations overlap. The opportunity arrived for Pagans to realize that, despite their personal and theological differences, they had more in common than they realized, and an active community of alliances, as well as a shared sense of community – "Paganistan" – has been allowed to form, maintaining its diversity while uniting at necessary times for the accomplishment of important legal and social justice goals. The Twin Cities community celebrated its Tenth Annual Pagan Pride Day in 2006, and the diverse representation and high attendance attest to this fact. While conscious of disagreements and issues within Paganistan's borders and along its overlaps, WiCoM's founders shared that they have been pleased with the growth of the community; if dissatisfaction arises, it is that they see the potential for it to be broader, longer in reach, and simultaneously more diverse and unified. The work of community in Paganistan has been groundbreaking and continues to be so; the innovative step of considering a schism as a catalyst for growth and rethinking community rather than a failure of a church was a starting point, and a trusted process in Paganistan's continual solidifying and growth.

REFERENCES

Adler, Margot. 1986. *Drawing Down the Moon: Witches, Druids, Goddess-Worshipers, and Other Pagans in America Today*. 2nd edn. Boston, MA: Beacon Press. Original edition, 1979.

Berger, Helen A. 1999. *A Community of Witches: Contemporary Neo-Paganism and Witchcraft in the United States*. Columbia: University of South Carolina Press.

Clifton, Chas S. 2006. *Her Hidden Children: The Rise of Wicca and Paganism in America*. Lanham, MD: AltaMira Press.

Davies, Morganna and Aradia Lynch. 2001. *Keepers of the Flame: Interviews with Elders of Traditional Witchcraft in America*. Providence, RI: Olympian Press.

Duquette, Paul. 1998. Letter to Bill and Holly (Winnipeg). Official correspondence from the Wiccan Church of Minnesota.

Gardner, Gerald B. 1954. *Witchcraft Today*. London: Rider and Company.

Hopman, Ellen Evert and Lawrence Bond. 1996. *Being a Pagan* (Formerly: *People of the Earth: The New Pagans Speak Out*). Rochester, VT: Destiny Books.

Hutton, Ronald. 1999. *The Triumph of the Moon: A History of Modern Pagan Witchcraft*. Oxford: Oxford University Press.

Johnson, Benton. 1963. "On Church and Sect," *American Sociological Review* 28: 539–49.

Lewis, James R. 2003. *Legitimating New Religions*. New Brunswick, NJ: Rutgers University Press.

2006. "The Pagan Explosion." Paper read at National Meeting for the American Academy of Religion and the Society for Biblical Literature, November 18–21, 2006, at Washington, DC.

Magliocco, Sabina. 2004. *Witching Culture: Folklore and Neopaganism in America*. Philadelphia: University of Pennsylvania Press.

Pike, Sarah M. 2001. *Earthly Bodies, Magical Selves: Contemporary Pagans and the Search for Community*. Berkeley: University of California Press.

Pizza, Murphy. 2006. "The Fourfold Goddess and the Undying God: Anatomies of Minnesotan Bootstrap Witchcraft Traditions." Paper read at National Meeting for the American Academy of Religion and the Society of Biblical Literature, November 18–22, 2006, at Washington, DC.

Posch, Steven. 2005. "Witch City, Pagan Nation." In *Radio Paganistan*. Minneapolis, MN.

Reyburn, Robin. 2005. *Twyern*. Available from http://home.earthlink.net/ ~twyern.

Salomonsen, Jone. 2002. *Enchanted Feminism: The Reclaiming Witches of San Francisco*. New York: Routledge.

Stark, Rodney. 2003. "Why Religious Movements Succeed or Fail: A Revised General Model." In L. L. Dawson (ed.), *Cults and New Religious Movements* (pp. 259–70), Oxford: Blackwell.

Vale, V. and John Sulak (eds.). 2001. *Modern Pagans: An Investigation of Contemporary Pagan Practices*. San Francisco: Re/Search Publications.

PART V

Non-Western/postcolonial traditions

CHAPTER 12

Succession, religious switching, and schism in the Hare Krishna movement

E. Burke Rochford, Jr.

Studies of disengagement from new religions have treated defection largely as an individual experience that involves a breakdown in the ideological and cognitive linkage between a convert's values and beliefs and the religious doctrines and practices of the group. Defection thus becomes an act of "falling from the faith" (Bromley 1988). Yet as new religions develop, internal conflict and factionalism produce mass expulsion, group defection, religious switching, and schism (Chancellor 2000; Ofshe 1980; Rochford 1989; 2007a; Rochford and Bailey 2006; Wallis 1976; 1979; 1982; Wright 1988). Some or all of these outcomes are especially likely upon the death of a charismatic founder, should the departed leader fail to authorize an alternative system of authority (Leatham 2003; Miller 1991; Rochford 1989; 1998a; 2007a; Wallis 1979: 187; Zald and Ash Garner 1987: 136).

Beginning in 1977, the International Society for Krishna Consciousness (ISKCON), more widely known as the Hare Krishna movement, experienced ongoing succession problems after the death of its founder, A. C. Bhaktivedanta Swami Prabhupada. Ideological conflict over the behavior of Prabhupada's successors and the basis of organizational authority caused large numbers of devotees to abandon ISKCON's communities in North America, western Europe, and other locations worldwide. Because, in most cases, those disaffiliating remained committed to their Krishna conscious beliefs, many sought alternative sources of authority to Prabhupada's successors. While some joined related Krishna-based religious organizations, others stood their ground and pushed to change ISKCON's system of religious authority. Thus, as ISKCON evolved from a charismatic to an ideological movement (Wallis 1979), factional splits emerged over questions of legitimate authority. As conflict escalated so too did the potential for schism.[1]

---

[1] The historical roots of the Hare Krishna movement are traced to Bengal, India, in the sixteenth century. The Krishna Consciousness preached by ISKCON's founder is part of the Krishna *bhakti*

This chapter discusses insurgency, religious switching, and schism as responses to ISKCON's ongoing succession crisis. My discussion is divided into three sections. The first describes the succession controversies that arose in the years following the death of ISKCON's founder Prabhupada. The second considers ISKCON members who left the organization and joined the Gaudiya Math, the organization established by Prabhupada's spiritual master in India. The third details the development of the ISKCON Revival Movement, initially an insurgent group seeking to reform ISKCON's system of religious authority, but which ultimately fragmented, spawning a schismatic movement. The chapter concludes with a theoretical discussion of factionalism, religious switching, and schism in light of this case study.

SUCCESSION AND RELIGIOUS AUTHORITY

In November 1977, ISKCON's founding guru died at the age of eighty-two in Vrndavana, India, after a long illness. Prabhupada's death proved a major turning point in ISKCON's worldwide development. Prior to his death, he appointed eleven of his closest disciples to serve as *ritvik* gurus, or "ceremonial priests." In that capacity, they were authorized to initiate new disciples on Prabhupada's behalf. With Prabhupada's passing, however, the appointed *ritvik*s assumed the role of regular gurus, offering *diksa* (first) initiation to aspiring devotees who accepted them – rather than Prabhupada – as their spiritual master. Institutionally, the new gurus were accorded the same reverence and authority as Prabhupada. Having proclaimed themselves *acarya*s (heads of an institution), the new gurus exercised complete political, economic, and spiritual authority within their exclusive geographical areas of the world. This structure of religious

---

movement founded by Caitanya Mahaprabhu (1486–1533). A distinctive feature of the Gaudiya Vaisnava tradition to which ISKCON belongs is that Caitanya is believed to be an incarnation of Krishna. The movement was brought to the United States in 1965 by A. C. Bhaktivedanta Swami Prabhupada, or Srila Prabhupada as he is known by his followers. ISKCON was established as a religious organization in 1966 in New York City. ISKCON is dedicated to spreading Krishna Consciousness and has communities and preaching centers throughout the world. The aim of the Hare Krishna devotee is to become self-realized by chanting Hare Krishna and living an austere lifestyle that requires avoiding meat, intoxicants, illicit sex, and gambling. Today the largest portion of ISKCON's North American membership is comprised of immigrant Indian-Hindus and their families (see Rochford 2007b: 181–200). For a discussion of ISKCON's historical roots in India, see Judah (1974). For discussions of the movement's growth and development in North America and internationally, see Brooks 1989; Judah 1974; Knott (1986); Rochford 1985; 2000; 2006; 2007b; Shinn 1987; Squarcini and Fizzotti (2004).

authority, known as the "zonal *acarya* system," existed for nearly a decade (Rochford 1998a; 2006: 29).

The eleven gurus shared responsibility for governing ISKCON with fourteen other senior devotees. The partnership between guru and non-guru leaders on the Governing Body Commission (GBC) proved tenuous from the beginning, however, as the gurus routinely asserted their independence from the GBC. As one insider concluded, "Indeed, the gurus with their status as sacred persons, a status constantly emphasized by formal deference and ceremonial honors, and their growing numbers of personally devoted followers, *quickly eclipsed the GBC*" (Deadwyler 2004: 162; my emphasis).

Challenges to the new gurus' authority arose after the majority of them became embroiled in controversy and scandal (Rochford 1985: 236–45; 1998a). After two gurus were suspended, and two others were sanctioned in 1980, a group of devotees centered in California circulated mimeographed position papers challenging the qualifications of Prabhupada's successors (Rochford 1985: 241–4; 1989; 1998a). Under growing pressure from the membership, the GBC, in 1981, placed limits on the authority of Prabhupada's successors. It also reaffirmed its position as ISKCON's ultimate source of authority (Rochford 1985: 235–6). Yet these decisions ultimately meant little because the gurus retained control over their respective geographical zones where their authority remained firmly in place.

In the years to follow, still other gurus became involved in scandals that further eroded the authority of the new gurus and the guru institution more generally. In 1982, the guru Jayatirtha broke from ISKCON with his disciples after the GBC refused to recognize one of Prabhupada's Godbrothers in India as an initiating ISKCON guru. Jayatirtha was also known to have been taking illegal drugs (Rochford 1985: 231–2, 249–53). In 1983, another guru, Hansadutta, was expelled from ISKCON for illegal behavior. Between 1985 and 1986 three more gurus were forced to resign their positions because of allegations of sexual misconduct and corruption (Rochford 1998a: 106; 2006: 29–30). In 1987, Kirtanananda, the guru leader of ISKCON's West Virginia farm community New Vrindaban, was excommunicated following state and federal charges that included the murder of a dissident devotee (Rochford and Bailey 2006). Finally, in 1999, an influential guru in Europe, Harikesh, left ISKCON after he openly questioned the movement's sexual policies and began a romantic relationship.

In 2007, only two of Prabhupada's original eleven successors remained as initiating gurus. Moreover, after the number of ISKCON gurus grew to more than eighty following reforms to the guru system in 1986, still other gurus fell from their positions.[2] Of the 104 ISKCON gurus appointed between 1977 and 2004, thirty-four were relieved of their positions. An additional fourteen were sanctioned by the GBC for misbehavior (*Back to Prabhupada* 2005a: 10). Inclusive of Prabhupada disciples, as many as two-thirds of ISKCON's membership became "spiritual 'orphans'" having lost their gurus (Collins 2004: 218). The ongoing crisis of authority produced substantial defection as devotees left ISKCON to avoid what one described as "the nonsense that went on after Srila Prabhupada's passing." Estimates indicate that more than 4,000 of Prabhupada's 5,000 disciples no longer remain active in ISKCON. Moreover, in 2000, only 750–900 devotees continued to reside in ISKCON's forty-five North American communities (Squarcini and Fizzotti 2004: 70).[3] An ISKCON *sannyasi* (renunciate) acknowledged in a 1987 letter to the GBC how the leadership shouldered responsibility for driving large numbers of devotees out of ISKCON.

The GBC, both indirectly by impure acts and directly by confrontation and force, has driven large numbers of Srila Prabhupada's disciples out of their service, out of their homes, and out of ISKCON . . . By allowing, advocating, taking part in, perpetuating, and defending these and other forms of contamination and decay, the members of the GBC have brought the ultimate managing authority of the entire International Society for Krishna Consciousness to a state of disrepute and pollution (Jayadvaita Swami 1987; quoted in *Back to Prabhupada* 2005b: 2).

The actions of the leadership thus played a decisive role in the mass defections suffered by ISKCON during the 1980s and 1990s. Mismanagement and spiritual corruption on the part of the gurus and their

---

[2] In addition to expanding the number of ISKCON gurus, the reform movement successfully eliminated guru claims to exclusive geographical zones, reserved the term *acarya* for ISKCON's founder, and limited guru worship to Prabhupada in ISKCON's temples. The reforms implemented effectively ended the zonal *acarya* system (Rochford 1998a).

[3] It should be noted that ISKCON's financial collapse in the early 1980s resulted in mass expulsions from its North American communities. As revenues from book distribution plummeted in 1980, ISKCON's communities could no longer support married people and their children and the movement's communal structure disintegrated thereafter. Accordingly, large portions of ISKCON's membership moved into the larger society where they worked and often sent their children to local public schools. These developments further intensified the growing mistrust of ISKCON's leadership (Rochford 2007b: 52–73).

GBC supporters convinced many that ISKCON no longer served as a legitimate instrument for realizing Prabhupada's teachings. Disillusioned ISKCON members searched beyond the "sacred fortress" of ISKCON's communities (Squarcini 2000: 256) for new contexts supportive of their commitments to Prabhupada and Krishna. Although the majority of those leaving ISKCON moved into independent living situations where they practiced Krishna Consciousness within their households (Rochford 2007b), a portion sought institutional alternatives to ISKCON. Others joined together to form an insurgent group dedicated to restoring what they considered to be the "true" ISKCON. Because these latter two developments generated conflict and the potential for schism they are my focus in the remainder of the chapter.

RELIGIOUS SWITCHING

The guru controversies led some devotees to renounce ISKCON in favor of Vaisnava leaders associated with the Gaudiya Math, the India-based organization founded by Prabhupada's spiritual master. Most notable have been S. R. Shridara Maharaja and Narayana Maharaja, the latter being a disciple of Prabhupada's Godbrother B. P. Keshava Maharaja. Each was an associate of Prabhupada's both before and after he left India for the United States in 1965.

Following Prabhupada's death, members of the GBC sought the advice of Shridara Maharaja to help clarify a number of philosophical issues (Rochford 1985: 245–53). Most important was the authority of the new gurus and their relationship with the GBC. Shridara stressed that the gurus' authority was beyond GBC control (Rochford 1985: 223). When conflict intensified over the zonal *acarya* system, some ISKCON leaders and senior Prabhupada disciples blamed Shridara. In 1982, ISKCON's leadership severed relations with Shridara and "declared him the enemy" because his "presentation of Krishna consciousness often differs from that of Srila Prabhupada" (Vishnu 2004: 182). But as one former ISKCON member and follower of Shridara Maharaja charged, "A more candid explanation for ostracizing Shridara Goswami . . . is perhaps the fact that many members of the [ISKCON] society began to follow him instead of accepting the dictates of the new gurus" (Vishnu 2004: 183). The growing negativity toward Shridara contributed to ISKCON's first major schism in 1982, when the guru Jayatirtha split from ISKCON with a hundred of his disciples to join forces with Shridara Maharaja in India (Rochford 1985: 251).

A recent and more significant threat to ISKCON has been Narayana Maharaja. Over the course of the 1990s, approximately two hundred ISKCON members became followers of Narayana. Those joining him were both longtime Prabhupada disciples and disciples of Prabhupada's successors. Moreover, an additional hundred followers of the ISKCON guru Goura Govinda accepted Narayana as their *siksa* (instructing) guru following their guru's death in 1996 (Collins 2004: 224). As one prominent ISKCON leader attracted to Narayana commented:

the ISKCON followers of Narayana Maharaja felt they were making tangible spiritual advancement by following his advice and example. They were increasing their chanting, became attached to the sacred places where Krsna had performed His pastimes, and were generally experiencing an overall deepening of their Krsna consciousness. (Goswami 1997: 34)

In many cases, those attracted to Narayana believed that his teachings and association would allow them to better serve Prabhupada. As the ISK-CON leader quoted above went on to say about the devotees drawn to Narayana, "Prabhupada, they believed, was now guiding them in the person of Narayana Maharaja" (Goswami 1997: 34). And Narayana actively sought to legitimate his authority by highlighting the closeness of his relationship with Prabhupada. The following appeared on Narayana Maharaja's website under the title, "Like Two Brothers."

In his last days, Srila Swami Maharaja [Prabhupada] very lovingly and affectionately took Srila Narayana Maharaja's hands in his own hands and made Srila Narayana Maharaja promise to always help his western disciples and followers to understand and follow the deep teachings of the Vaisnava philosophy as presented by his gurudeva, Srila Bhaktisiddhanta Sarasvati Thakura [Prabhupada's spiritual master]. Srila Narayana Maharaja humbly agreed to honor his request, considering him to be one of his worshipable siksa-gurus [instructing gurus]. (narayanamaharaja.com 2005)

Philosophically, Narayana Maharaja encouraged his followers to pursue a path of "spontaneous devotion," or *rasika-bhakti*, meditating on the "conjugal pastimes of Krishna with the gopi cowherd women" (Collins 2004: 223), topics Prabhupada strongly discouraged. Prabhupada had stressed repeatedly to his neophyte followers that the path to liberation was in strictly following the rules and regulations of devotional life (*vaidhi-bhakti*); that only highly advanced devotees could pursue the path of *rasalila-katha*.[4] Of grave concern to the GBC was that several high-profile

---

[4] In 1976, Prabhupada reacted strongly against a group of his disciples in Los Angeles who were meeting surreptitiously to read those portions of the *Caitanya-caritamrta* that described Radha and

leaders – gurus and GBC members – were submitting to a spiritual authority other than Prabhupada. As one former ISKCON devotee and Narayana follower stated, "Any hint that someone could be equal to or greater than the Swami [Prabhupada] was considered heretical and utterly intolerable to the ISKCON orthodoxy, since it was interpreted as over-shadowing Bhaktivedanta Swami's preeminent role as 'the Founder-*Acarya* of ISKCON' " (Collins 2004: 223).

Beginning in 1993, ISKCON's GBC began raising questions about the leaders and other senior Prabhupada disciples taking shelter of Narayana and his teachings. After being reassured that their relationship with Narayana was not a serious one, the GBC backed away from imposing sanctions. Yet concern grew when it became apparent that ISKCON's Krishna Balaram temple in Vrndavana, India, was coming under the influence of Narayana's teachings. Moreover, paintings depicting the intimate relations between Krishna and Radha were becoming popular throughout ISKCON. Lectures and temple classes were also beginning to make mention of *rasalila-katha* (Goswami 1997: 34).

Tensions between Narayana Maharaja and ISKCON came to a head in 1994, following a celebration in India commemorating Prabhupada's taking *sannyasa* (the renounced order) thirty-five years earlier. During the proceedings, Narayana announced that "there were many higher teachings that Prabhupada could have given had his disciples been more advanced" (quoted in Collins 2004: 224). To ISKCON leaders this statement implied that Narayana was demeaning Prabhupada's teachings as elementary. Many believed that Narayana Maharaja was simply positioning himself to provide these "higher teachings" to ISKCON's membership. A 1996 GBC position paper responding to Narayana's threat argued, "The implication of Narayana Maharaja's statements is to set up Narayana Maharaja himself as the next acarya of ISKCON after Prabhupada" (Keeping Faith with Srila Prabhupada 1996: 8).

Of enormous concern to ISKCON authorities was that two ISKCON gurus and GBC members present at the celebration had not only failed to challenge Narayana's comments about Prabhupada and his disciples, but they "used the occasion to praise Narayana Maharaja, recommending his association to all members of ISKCON" (Goswami 1997: 34). Voices of protest against Narayana and his supporters emerged immediately following the event as word spread quickly to ISKCON's worldwide

Krishna's "intimate pastimes" (Goswami 1997: 31–2). When Prabhupada heard about the so-called "*Gopi-bhava* Club" he ordered that it be disbanded, fearing that those involved would be led into illicit sexual activities.

communities. Temple presidents from North America, so instrumental in dismantling the zonal *acarya* system, insisted that the leaders involved with Narayana be stripped of their positions. Many in the movement feared that such a stance would result in a major schism, as the leaders involved with Narayana had large followings of disciples (Collins 2004: 223; Goswami 1997: 34).

At ISKCON's international GBC meetings in 1995, the *rasika-bhakti* controversy was first on the agenda. After a week of discussion and investigation, the leaders associated with Narayana conceded that their involvement had unintentionally challenged Prabhupada's teachings and authority. The wayward leaders tendered their resignations from the GBC, which the governing body refused to accept. To have done so would have likely provoked a schism, something the GBC was eager to avoid. Their resignations rejected, the leaders volunteered to discontinue initiating disciples and to refrain from visiting Vrndavana for a one-year period. They also agreed to permanently dissociate themselves from Narayana and to "correct any misunderstandings" their involvement might have caused to devotees throughout ISKCON. Not entirely convinced of their contrition after one year, however, the GBC continued most of the restrictions placed on the leaders at its 1996 meetings (Goswami 1997: 34–5).

Beyond the formal sanctions imposed against the offending leaders, the GBC also passed a resolution in 1995 that, while not specifically mentioning Narayana by name, nonetheless effectively barred all ISKCON members from associating with him or his teaching. The resolution also allowed for the suspension of any ISKCON member who failed to comply (Collins 2004: 222; Keeping Faith with Srila Prabhupada 1996). A subsequent GBC resolution mandated that ISKCON devotees reinitiated by Narayana would be expelled from the organization.

Although the threat of schism was averted, the flow of current and former ISKCON members to Narayana's camp steadily grew. In defiance of the GBC, Narayana began annual preaching tours, in 1996, targeting ISKCON communities in North America and in other Western countries. Narayana specifically reached out to disillusioned members of ISKCON's congregation, rather than trying to recruit residents of ISKCON's temple communities. As one Narayana follower underscored, Narayana had become a threat to ISKCON:

Over the next few years, hundreds and hundreds of disaffected ISKCON members assembled at these gatherings to hear from Narayana Maharaja, attracted by his charismatic qualities. Many devotees even renounced their ISKCON 'priestlike' gurus . . . and took reinitiation from Narayana Maharaja . . . Narayana thus poses a serious and ongoing threat to ISKCON. (Collins 2004: 225)

To ISKCON leaders, Narayana's recruitment efforts represented little more than stealing (Keeping Faith with Prabhupada 1996). The leadership and ISKCON members worldwide responded accordingly. A 2001 letter signed by 350 ISKCON members in Britain strongly protested a planned visit by Narayana: "Throughout the year, and especially at the times of your visits, this *yatra* [branch of ISKCON] is under siege to convert to your line of thought. Our respected entreaty is that you and your followers stop trying to recruit ISKCON members to your line of thought" (Letter by Shivarama Swami, GBC for the UK, June 14, 2001, quoted in Collins 2004: 225). In its 1996 position paper, the GBC directly responded to Narayana's attempts to recruit among ISKCON's congregation.

We therefore ask Narayana Maharaja and his followers not to disturb ISKCON's efforts to preach according to the dictates of Srila Prabhupada and not to lead ISKCON's adherents away from those dictates. And we ask all those who are part of ISKCON to understand clearly that Narayana Maharaja's policies and practices differ in significant ways from those of Srila Prabhupada. (Keeping Faith with Srila Prabhupada 1996: 14)[5]

The devotees joining Narayana Maharaja saw an opportunity to further their spiritual development under the guidance of an elderly charismatic leader. This required accepting two sources of authority – Prabhupada and Narayana – something many disillusioned ISKCON devotees were unwilling to do given their commitments to Prabhupada and his teachings. For these devotees, alternatives to ISKCON could only be entertained if Prabhupada remained the one and only source of religious authority.

INSURGENCY, REVIVAL, AND SCHISM

The ISKCON Revival Movement (IRM) emerged in the late 1990s, claiming that ISKCON's gurus were neither authorized by Prabhupada,

---

[5] Several ISKCON communities in Australia, England, and the United States took measures that went beyond the GBC resolutions, choosing to ban devotees affiliated with Narayana from temple properties. In several instances, ISKCON members otherwise in good standing were expelled from an ISKCON temple community when it became known they were Narayana followers (Collins 2004: 225–6).

nor qualified to serve in their positions.[6] In essence, supporters of the IRM argued that ISKCON had been hijacked as part of a "great guru hoax" (*Back to Prabhupada* 2005c: 3). The solution rested on restoring Prabhupada's authority as ISKCON's initiating spiritual master, at the exclusion of his guru successors. As indicated in the IRM's mission statement:

Since the physical departure of His Divine Grace A. C. Bhaktivedanta Swami Srila Prabhupada . . . the great movement which he single-handedly founded in 1966, and which is the only hope for humanity, has undergone a massive deterioration in its spiritual purity. This has been due to various deviations from the instructions and standards given by Srila Prabhupada, the chief of which being his displacement as the sole *diksa* Guru for ISKCON. The ISKCON Revival Movement (IRM) seeks to restore ISKCON to its former glory, purity and philosophical chastity through the re-institution of all the instructions and standards that Srila Prabhupada gave, beginning with his role as the sole authority and *diksa* Guru for ISKCON. (*Back to Prabhupada* 2007: 10)

The IRM thus represents an insurgent group whose primary mission is to displace ISKCON's existing structure of religious authority, in favor of restoring Prabhupada's position as ISKCON's only initiating guru. As a movement within a movement, the IRM is determined to "rebuild the original ISKCON, the real Hare Krishna movement, as given to us by Srila Prabhupada" (*Back to Prabhupada* 2005d: 15). Reform and revival, rather than schism, have defined the IRM's objectives. A founder and primary spokesperson for the IRM spelled out the group's goals.

Organizing all our supporters spread all over the world into centers, is a process that will take more time, and is not a priority at this stage. We prefer to concentrate on advancing our arguments philosophically, academically and with the media, rather than just opening a few buildings and starting our own separate movement. Our objective is not to begin a separate group which goes off and does its own thing, but to educate every single person who has some contact with ISKCON regarding Srila Prabhupada's position. Therefore, our focus is very much ISKCON's current and former members. (Krishnakant Desai, pers. comm., 2006)

At issue is the IRM's contention that Prabhupada never appointed any of his disciples to serve as *diksa* (initiating) gurus, but only as *ritvik* gurus, authorized to initiate people on Prabhupada's behalf. The IRM cites a

---

[6] The IRM was originally known as the ISKCON Reform Group (IRG) when it emerged, in 1998, out of an ISKCON temple presidents' meeting in Bangalore, India. After the group expanded numerically and its objectives broadened it took on the character of a revival movement.

July 9, 1977 letter, approved by Prabhupada, wherein he indicates how future initiations should be handled in light of his deteriorating health.

His Divine Grace has so far given a list of eleven disciples who will act in that capacity [as *ritvik* representatives of the *acarya*] . . . Now that Srila Prabhupada has named these representatives, Temple Presidents may henceforward send recommendations for first and second initiation to whichever of these eleven representatives are nearest their temple . . . [T]hese representatives may accept the devotee as an initiated disciple of Srila Prabhupada by giving a spiritual name . . . just as Srila Prabhupada has done. The newly initiated devotees *are disciples of His Divine Grace A. C. Bhaktivedanta Swami Prabhupada*, the above eleven senior devotees acting as His representative. (my emphasis, quoted in Desai, Awatramani and Das 2004: 195)

In the absence of documentation to the contrary, IRM supporters accept the July 9 letter as definitive; Prabhupada fully intended to remain in his role as ISKCON's *acarya* and initiating spiritual master after his death. The IRM refers to this as "The No Change in ISKCON Paradigm," rejecting official ISKCON explanations that Prabhupada intended the appointed *ritvik*s to become *diksa* gurus after his passing (Krishnakant 1996; Desai *et al.* 2004). On this basis, the IRM rejected the very idea that ISKCON's gurus were Prabhupada's rightful successors.

Prior to the emergence of the IRM, the *ritvik* position on initiation found appeal among a wide range of devotees in North America and worldwide (Rochford 1998a; 1998b). In fact, a loosely organized *ritvik* movement set the stage for the IRM. The ongoing controversies surrounding ISKCON's gurus convinced many devotees that Prabhupada never appointed any successors. As one former ISKCON member and IRM supporter stated, "How could Prabhupada have made such a big mistake? He is a person who according to scripture cannot make a mistake. How could he have made such a mistake by appointing such unqualified people? Obviously, the answer is they weren't appointed."

Half of ISKCON's congregational members (49%) and over half of the former ISKCON devotees (56%) responding to the North America Centennial Survey[7] agreed that "Prabhupada wanted the eleven *ritvik*s he appointed to continue as *ritvik*s after his departure."[8] Moreover, two-thirds (64%) of the former members and half (51%) of ISKCON's

---

[7] The Prabhupada Centennial Survey was conducted by the author in 1995 and 1996 in fifty-three countries. Two thousand devotees – full-time ISKCON members, congregational members, and former ISKCON adherents – participated. The findings presented here include respondents from the United States and Canada who were initiated disciples of Prabhupada, or one of his successors. For a discussion of the Prabhupada Centennial Survey and its general findings, see Rochford 1998b.

congregational members agreed that "Disciples of Srila Prabhupada have the right to serve as *ritvik*s, initiating new devotees who would become disciples of Srila Prabhupada." Given this level of support for the *ritvik* philosophy of initiation, the IRM appeared well positioned to mobilize support for its cause. Global interest, if not active support, is suggested by the readership of the IRM's *Back to Prabhupada* magazine. In 2005, it had a reported circulation of 10,000 in over a hundred countries (Krishnakant Desai, pers. comm., 2006). Yet estimates by the founder of the IRM, in 2006, suggest that only hundreds of devotees worldwide are *active* IRM supporters (Krishnakant Desai, pers. comm., 2006).

The inability to convert sympathy for the IRM's ideology into active participation grows out of two factors. First, the IRM has resisted establishing its own temple communities, having only a single temple located in New York City. Instead, it has sought to take over established ISKCON temples sympathetic to the *ritvik* philosophy. Although this strategy has met with some success, it has failed to yield the thirty ISKCON temples IRM leaders believe necessary to pressure the GBC into accepting *ritvik* initiation. Because of this, the IRM has floundered, unable to establish a network of temple communities capable of recruiting new and long-standing devotees to the *ritvik* cause.

In those instances where the IRM has successfully gained control of ISKCON temples, conflict has resulted. In one case where the IRM seized an ISKCON temple in India, a violent confrontation developed when ISKCON members sought to reclaim the temple after legal measures failed to produce a positive result. In April 2001, the IRM's regional headquarters in Calcutta, India, "was stormed by representatives of ISKCON" in an attempt to occupy the temple (Desai *et al.* 2004: 209). Fifteen IRM supporters were physically assaulted when approximately a hundred devotees from ISKCON's nearby Mayapura temple sought to evict them. Police arrested seventy-two ISKCON members involved in the take-over attempt (Bhattacharyya 2001; Desai *et al.* 2004: 209–12).

Legal means also failed when ISKCON authorities attempted to expel the management of the Bangalore, India, ISKCON community, which at the time served as the IRM's unofficial world headquarters. In 2002, the Bangalore High Court ruled that ISKCON Bangalore and its associated properties were legally independent of ISKCON (iskcon.krishna.org 2002a). Realizing the significance of the court's decision, ISKCON

---

[8] Twenty-five percent of ISKCON's full-time members also agreed that Prabhupada wanted the eleven *ritvik*s he appointed to remain in that capacity following his death.

appealed to the Supreme Court of India in an attempt to overturn the ruling. The court, however, refused to entertain the appeal, leaving the Bangalore High Court ruling in place (iskcon.krishna.org 2002b).

In an ongoing legal case in the United States, ISKCON is seeking to reclaim its Long Island, New York, temple after a 2004 IRM take-over. ISKCON leaders have reportedly used aggressive tactics in an attempt to extricate IRM supporters, "threatening with dire consequences, physical take-over attempts, bribery, personal false allegations, and finally, expensive lawsuits" (Dasa, Nimai Pandit 2007a). On two occasions, in 2004 and 2006, devotees loyal to ISKCON disrupted and attempted to physically repossess the temple. These efforts having failed, in 2007 ISKCON filed a lawsuit in Nassau County, New York, meant to oust IRM supporters from the Long Island temple. In response, members of the Long Island temple filed a counterclaim arguing that the GBC had no legal standing and thus no authority to conduct ISKCON's affairs (Dasa, Nimai Pandit 2007a; 2007b).[9]

The second factor that has greatly limited the expansion of the IRM relates to its position on performing initiations. Although *ritvik* initiation is the theological foundation of the IRM, the group's leadership has argued against performing Prabhupada initiations in the absence of authorized *ritvik* gurus. Only a small number of *ritvik* initiations have been conducted, despite reports that hundreds of people are awaiting the opportunity to become Prabhupada disciples (iskcon.krishna.org 2001a; 2001b; Rochford 2007b: 174). In North America only a handful of *ritvik* initiations have been performed by the Prabhupada Sankirtan Society, located in New York City (Rochford 1998a: 112), and by two Prabhupada disciples acting on their own initiative. None of the latter are directly aligned with the IRM. The decision by the IRM to forgo *ritvik* initiations is explained by the IRM's most prominent leader.

The IRM does not offer a formal initiation ceremony at present, since it is trying to adhere to Srila Prabhupada's wishes in this matter, and form a real bonafide GBC first, which can authorize *ritviks* in line with the July 9th directive [1977 letter]. A self-appointed *ritvik* would not be much different to a self-appointed

---

[9] IRM supporters have also met with physical force at the hands of ISKCON members when distributing *Back to Prabhupada* magazines at public events sponsored by ISKCON. In a video clip made available on YouTube, ISKCON members, including a guru and GBC member, are shown assaulting IRM supporters by forcefully taking their magazines and ripping them apart to keep them from being distributed to the crowd. The ISKCON leader involved is shown aggressively trying to take the camera away from the IRM devotee filming the incident.

Guru . . . So the IRM is waiting to formalize this initiation later on, once a bonafide GBC is put in place. (Krishnakant Desai, pers. comm., 2006)

In 2001, the Bangalore, India, temple broke ranks with the IRM and began conducting *ritvik* initiations. In April, fifty Prabhupada initiations were performed, followed by another seventeen in May (iskcon.krishna. org 2001a). Lacking official *ritvik*s to conduct the initiations, devotees essentially initiated themselves after first receiving formal approval from the temple president. Going before Prabhupada's *murti* (image) in the temple, a devotee seeking initiation prays: "Dear Srila Prabhupada, currently your ritvik representatives are not doing their service so I am asking you to please accept me as your disciple and inspire me to select a spiritual name" (iskcon.krishna.org 2001b). As in all ISKCON initiations, the candidate commits to following the four regulative principles (no meat, intoxication, illicit sex, or gambling) and to chanting sixteen rounds of the Hare Krishna mantra daily on a string of 108 *japa* beads. A Bangalore temple leader stressed in a 2007 interview that official *ritviks* will be appointed within the next two to three years when additional temples in India and elsewhere join the Bangalore network of temples. Thereafter, elected representatives from each of the temples will form their own GBC. As he further emphasized, "So only the name giving and the formal acceptance by the *ritvik* are pending. Otherwise, every-thing we can rightly do we will. We are following 99% of Prabhupada's instructions. When a GBC is in place we can follow everything 100% as in the July 9th letter."

In conflict with the leaders of the IRM over conducting Prabhupada initiations, the Bangalore temple and its affiliated temples have with-drawn from the IRM. As one of the devotees who pushed for this decision argued:

You [the IRM] have the audacity to say, "No, Srila Prabhupada. You cannot initiate right now because we have not set up a GBC. We don't have 30 temples. So we can't initiate." But this is complete nonsense. Prabhupada is alive and guiding in every other way but why are we killing him on this issue?[10] Why is he dead on this issue? We must let the world know that Srila Prabhupada is initiating. He is accepting disciples. And we must let people know that this is the real difference between our temples and ISKCON; that *we are the way to Prabhupada*. Prabhupada remains the *acarya* here. He is the guru . . . *We are*

---

[10] Devotees seek Prabhupada's guidance and inspiration by reading his books, listening to his taped lectures, and praying and worshiping. On this basis Prabhupada remains "alive" to his disciples and followers.

Prabhupada's ISKCON. They [ISKCON's leadership] are the deviant ISKCON. They are not Prabhupada's ISKCON. (My emphasis, interview 2006)

As these comments reveal further, internal divisions within the IRM have given rise to a schismatic group. Because the Bangalore temple helped fund many of the IRM's activities, its withdrawal has weakened the IRM, although it continues to publish *Back to Prabhupada* magazine and otherwise promotes the *ritvik* cause through its writings and related publicity efforts. Despite having gained its legal independence from ISKCON, the Bangalore temple continues to identify as an "ISKCON temple." In 2007, leaders of the Bangalore temple and its eight affiliated Indian temples were considering a name change to "ISKCON, the *ritvik* order." As one of those involved in these discussions stated, "This will make it so that we can differentiate ourselves from the regular ISKCON. We are the *ritvik* order" (interview 2007).

Not surprisingly, the *ritvik* challenge has provoked strong opposition from ISKCON. As we have already noted, ISKCON authorities have used the legal system as well as direct confrontation in an effort to reclaim temples lost to the IRM in India and the United States. Yet even before these actions, the GBC had gone on the offensive against the "*ritvik* heresy." Responding to growing support for the *ritvik* movement, in 1990 the GBC passed its first resolution outlawing *ritvikism*. In 1999, the GBC amended and reaffirmed its earlier resolution by placing the following into ISKCON law:

The doctrine that Srila Prabhupada desired to continue to act as diksa guru after his departure from this world and did not want any of his disciples to give diksa in succession after him is a dangerous philosophical deviation. Ritvikism directly goes against the principles of parampara itself (of successive diksa and siksa gurus), which sustains the pure teachings and practices of Krishna consciousness . . . It is utterly erroneous to espouse it, deluding and misguiding to teach it, and blasphemous to attribute it to Srila Prabhupada. No one who espouses, teaches, supports, in any way, or practices ritvikism can be a member in good standing. (GBC Resolutions 1999, ISKCON Law 6.4.7.2)

To derail future attempts by the IRM to use the legal system in North America to seize its temples, the GBC, in 2004, began reworking temple bylaws to ensure greater control over local congregations. Throughout ISKCON's history, its temples have been legally incorporated as independent institutions under local control. This has left the GBC with little legal recourse in its efforts to protect temple properties from IRM takeover. The GBC's purpose in rewriting temple bylaws is to bring all of

ISKCON's North American temples under the legal jurisdiction of the GBC. Critics both in and outside of the IRM have condemned the GBC's centralization plan as an attempt by the GBC to control local temples, something Prabhupada rejected in 1972.[11] An influential ISK-CON leader responded to the controversy by detailing the logic behind the GBC's actions.

When the GBC had attempted to remove a philosophically deviant temple president in India, exercising the responsibility placed on it by Srila Prabhupada, that president used Krishna's money to hire lawyers and go to the civil courts . . . And then it happened right here in North America . . . [A] few temples have already put into place an intermediate form of the bylaws. This is why: For quite some time ritvik leaders have been openly boasting that they would take over ISKCON temples in North America, using the means they developed in India. In other words, they would exploit opportunities they found in our current legal documents. When this actually began to happen in Long Island, we began the concerted effort to repair our documents. Then reliable information reached North American leaders that a plan to take over certain other temples had been put into motion. Events confirmed this intelligence. (Dasa, Ravindra Svarupa 2007: 3)[12]

Although ISKCON authorities have aggressively confronted the "*ritvik* heresy," the movement's system of religious authority has nonetheless changed under the weight of the *ritvik* challenge. As the IRM and the broader *ritvik* movement gained increasing support, and as ISKCON's gurus continued to fall from their positions, the GBC passed a number of resolutions meant to redefine the authority of ISKCON's gurus in rela-tion to Prabhupada. GBC resolutions have referred to Prabhupada as the "foundational siksa [instructing] guru for all ISKCON devotees" (1994), "preeminent siksa guru for every member of the institution" (1999), and "preeminent and compulsory siksa guru for all Vaisnavas (gurus and disciples) in the Society" (1999). A disciple of a guru expelled from ISKCON, in 1986, spoke of Prabhupada's influence on his spiritual life in

---

[11] In a 1972 letter to one of ISKCON's leaders, Prabhupada complained, "Do not centralize any-thing. Each temple must remain independent and self-sufficient. That was my plan from the beginning, why are you thinking otherwise? Once before you wanted to do something centralizing with your GBC meetings, and if I did not interfere the whole thing would have been killed . . . Otherwise, management, everything, should be done locally by local men" (Letter to Karandhara, December 22, 1972, in Prabhupada 1992: 994–5). Also see Goswami (1997: 20–1).

[12] Ironically, the GBC's centralization plan may promote schism. Research by Sutton and Chaves (2004) reveals that schisms frequently emerge in response to denominational consolidation engineered by leaders.

a way that expresses current institutional thinking about ISKCON's founder. "Prabhupada is the absolute authority. He gave us our direct connection to Krishna and the *Parampara* [guru lineage] through his books and instructions. Without the pure devotee, we would have nothing. He gave (and still gives) us everything as individuals and as a society" (Rochford 1998a: 113).

CONCLUSION

Although schism is typically viewed as growing out of conflicts over issues of doctrinal purity, this case study has demonstrated the central role of religious authority. It has also highlighted how the circumstances fostering schism remain complex and unpredictable. In part, this is because religious organizations provide opportunities as well as constraints which together shape the timing and development of insurgency. The analytic task thus becomes one of identifying the factors that transform internal conflict into the founding of a schismatic group.

Research suggests that religious groups with centralized authority structures are less prone to schism because they exercise considerable control over members' lives (Sutton and Chaves 2004; Zald and McCarthy 1987: 183). Because of this, challengers face any number of obstacles in organizing collectively *within* the confines of the group. To the extent that protest does emerge, it takes the shape of "pockets of criticism" (Zald and McCarthy 1987: 183) which have little basis for mobilizing collective action. These barriers leave dissidents with little choice but to withdraw from the group as a prelude to organized protest. Accordingly, for hierarchical and totalistic groups such as many new religious movements, schism appears most likely to occur in the aftermath of widespread defection.

ISKCON members who left the organization during the turmoil of the 1980s and 1990s often moved into enclave communities surrounding ISKCON's temples. These communities became the foundation of ISKCON's emerging congregation and constituted "social movement havens" or "free spaces" (Rochford 2007b: 207–8). By definition, free spaces are removed from hegemonic cultural forms and those who champion them. It is in this sense that social movement havens are sites of oppositional cultural formation (Fantasia and Hirsch 1995: 159). Beyond the control of ISKCON authorities, disillusioned devotees critically discussed the failings of the leadership in the context of informal and loosely organized challenging groups. In time, some of these dissidents became supporters of the IRM while others were targeted for recruitment by Gaudiya Math leaders such as Narayana Maharaja.

Stark and Finke (2000: 121–3) argue that people leaving a religious group for another generally choose one that maximizes the conservation of existing religious capital. This theoretical proposition has received indirect empirical support from Sherkat's research on religious mobility (1997; 2001; Sherkat and Wilson 1995). Specifically, people disaffiliating from a religious group are much more likely to join another that is similar to their original faith. In addition, more disciplined and demanding groups such as religious sects more often retain their members precisely because their unique religious identities limit possibilities for religious switching. This is all the more so for quasi-ethnic new religious groups such as ISKCON. In the North American context, devotees leaving ISKCON had next to no options available for religious switching, given the uniqueness of their religious capital. As a consequence, most devotees defecting from ISKCON decided to practice Krishna Consciousness independently within their households. Not surprisingly, those seeking collective alternatives to ISKCON looked to India for suitable alternatives (i.e. the Gaudiya Math). For devotees fully committed to Prabhupada as a first priority, the IRM represented the only viable alternative. In essence, the absence of suitable options for religious switching helped spawn the birth of a new organization exclusively dedicated to Prabhupada's authority and teachings.[13]

Researchers of social movements have often assumed that defection, factionalism, and schism rob a movement of its energy and vitality. Gamson (1975: 101–3) has gone so far as to argue that factionalism is the major cause of movement failure. Yet this view of failure confuses the conceptual difference between movement organizations and movements. If the fortunes of movements are made equivalent to those of movement organizations, defection, religious switching, and schism readily become signs of decline and failure. If we view social movements as fluid, however, organizational boundaries become less important than the broader contexts in which movements operate (Gusfield 1981: 323). The politics of

---

[13] The lack of options available for religious switching also contributed to another development that I will only briefly mention here. Some former and marginally involved ISKCON members established independent devotee communities operating outside the purview of ISKCON's authorities. These householder communities include Prabhupada's Village in rural North Carolina, the Three Rivers community in central California, and the *Saranagati* community in British Columbia, Canada. In addition, ISKCON's largest North American community located in northern Florida (*New Raman-reti*) has on various occasions challenged the authority of the GBC in favor of overseeing its own affairs (see Rochford 2007b: 175–8).

succession may have pushed ISKCON into decline by the end of the 1980s, but Prabhupada's teachings and authority found life in new settings beyond the institutional borders of the religious organization he established.

REFERENCES

Back to Prabhupada. 2005a. "Proof 4 – One Guru Falls = No Gurus Authorized" (special summary issue).
2005b. "Who Is Really Destroying ISKCON." Issue 9, Autumn.
2005c. "The Great Guru Hoax: Parts 1 and 2." (special summary issue).
2005d. "IRM: The Respected Voice of Reform in ISKCON." (special summary issue).
2007. "IRM Mission Statement." Issue 15, Spring.
Baer, Hans. 1988. *Recreating Utopia in the Desert: A Sectarian Challenge to Modern Mormonism.* Albany: State University of New York Press.
Bhattacharyya, Madhumita. 2001. "Devotees Arrested in Temple Tussle." Vaisnava News Network (VNN) website, April 30. Available at www.vnn. org/world/WD0104/WD30-6719.html.
Bromley, David. 1988. *Falling from the Faith: Causes and Consequences of Religious Apostasy.* Newbury Park, CA: Sage.
Brooks, Charles. 1989. *The Hare Krishnas in India.* Princeton, NJ: Princeton University Press.
Chancellor, James. 2000. *Life in the Family: An Oral History of the Children of God.* Syracuse, NY: Syracuse University Press.
Collins, Irvin. 2004. "The 'Routinization of Charisma' and the Charismatic." In Edwin Bryant and Maria Ekstrand (eds.), *The Hare Krishna Movement: The Postcharismatic Fate of a Religious Transplant* (pp. 214–37). New York: Columbia University Press.
Dasa, Nimai Pandit. 2007a. "New Landmark Lawsuit in Long Island." The Sampradaya Sun website, April 23. Available at www.harekrsna.com/sun/editorials/04-07/editorials1464.htm.
2007b. "Bylaws Adoption – Wait till the NY Supreme Court Decides." The Sampradaya Sun website, June 26. Available at www.harekrsna.com/sun/editorials/06007/editorials1686.htm.
Dasa, Ravindra Svarupa. 2007. "Bylaws and Centralization – The Facts." Dandavats website, May 24. Available at www.dandavats.com/?p=3559.
Deadwyler, William H. (Ravindra Svarupa Dasa). 2004. "Cleaning House and Cleaning Hearts: Reform and Renewal in ISKCON." In Edwin Bryant and Maria Ekstrand (eds.), *The Hare Krishna Movement: The Postcharismatic Fate of a Religious Transplant* (pp. 149–69). New York: Columbia University Press.
Desai, Krishnakant, Sunil Awatramani, and Madhu Pandit Das. 2004. "The No Change in ISKCON Paradigm." In Edwin Bryant and Maria Ekstrand

(eds.), *The Hare Krishna Movement: The Postcharismatic Fate of a Religious Transplant* (pp. 194–213). New York: Columbia University Press.

Fantasia, Rick and Eric L. Hirsch. 1995. "Culture in Rebellion: The Appropriation and Transformation of the Veil in the Algerian Revolution." In Hank Johnson and Bert Klandermans (eds.), *Social Movements and Culture* (pp. 144–59). Minneapolis: University of Minnesota Press.

Gamson. William. 1975. *Strategy of Social Protest.* Homewood, IL: Dorsey.

GBC Resolutions. 1999. ISKCON Law 6.4.7.2. *ISKCON Law Book.*

Goswami, Tamal Krishna. 1997. "The Perils of Succession: Heresies of Authority and Continuity in the Hare Krsna Movement." *ISKCON Communications Journal* 5(1): 13–44.

Gusfield, Joseph. 1981. "Social Movements and Social Change: Perspectives of Linearity and Fluidity." In Louis Kriesberg (ed.), *Research in Social Movements, Conflict and Change* (pp. 317–39). Greenwich, CT: JAI Press.

iskcon.krishna.org. 2001a. "Prabhupada Accepts 67 New Disciples at ISKCON Bangalore." ISKCON, Prabhupada Hare Krishna News Network website, May 9. Available at www.iskcon.krishna.org/Articles/2001/05/00302.html.

2001b. "ISKCON Accepts One Ritvik Temple and IRM Disintegrates." ISKCON, Prabhupada Hare Krishna News Network website, April 6. Available at www.iskcon.krishna.org/Articles/2001/02/00263.html.

2002a. "High Court Declares ISKCON Bangalore Legally Independent." ISKCON, Prabhupada Hare Krishna News Network website, April 27. Available at iskcon.krishna.org/Articles/2002/04/019.html.

2002b. "Supreme Court Throws Out GBC Appeal." ISKCON, Prabhupada Hare Krishna News Network website, September 20. Available at www.iskcon.krishna.org/Articles/2002/05/036.html.

Judah, Stillson. 1974. *Hare Krishna and the Counterculture.* New York: John Wiley and Sons.

Keeping Faith with Srila Prabhupada. 1996. ISKCON Governing Body Commission position paper on Narayana Maharaja. No author indicated.

Knott, Kim. 1986. *My Sweet Lord: Hare Krishna Movement.* San Bernardino, CA: R. Reginald.

Krishnakant (Desai). 1996. *The Final Order: The Legal, Philosophical and Documentary Evidence Supporting Srila Prabhupada's Rightful Position as ISKCON's Initiating Guru.* Bangalore: ISKCON Revival Movement.

Leatham, Miguel C. 2003. "'Shaking Out the Mat': Schism and Organizational Transformation at a Mexican Ark of the Virgin." *Journal for the Social Scientific Study of Religion* 42 (2): 175–87.

Miller, Timothy. 1991. *When Prophets Die: The Postcharismatic Fate of New Religious Movements.* Albany: State University of New York Press.

Narayanamaharaja.com. 2005. "Like Two Brothers." Website of Srila Bhaktivedanta Narayana Maharaja. No longer available. Accessed December 6, 2005. www.narayanamaharaja.com/sbnm/bios/2Brothers/?POSTNUKESTD =d963f9ca9a3d.

Ofshe, Richard. 1980. "The Social Development of the Synanon Cult." *Sociological Analysis* 41 (2): 109–27.

Prabhupada, A. C. Bhaktivedanta Swami. 1992. *Srila Prabhupada Siksmrta: Nectarian Instructions from the Letters of His Divine Grace A. C. Bhaktivedanta Swami Prabhupada*, vol. II. Los Angeles: Bhaktivedanta Book Trust.

Rochford, E. Burke, Jr. 1985. *Hare Krishna in America*. New Brunswick, NJ: Rutgers University Press.

1989. "Factionalism, Group Defection, and Schism in the Hare Krishna Movement." *Journal for the Scientific Study of Religion* 28 (2): 162–79.

1998a. "Reactions of Hare Krishna Devotees to Scandals of Leaders' Misconduct." In Anson Shupe (ed.), *Wolves within the Fold* (pp. 101–17). New Brunswick, NJ: Rutgers University Press.

1998b. "Prabhupada Centennial Survey Report." Submitted to ISKCON's International GBC, November 1998 (unpublished). Summary of the report was published in 1999, "Prabhupada Centennial Survey: A Summary of the Final Report." *ISKCON Communications Journal* 7 (1): 11–26. Available at www.iskcon.com/icj/7_1/71rochford.html.

2000. "Demons, Karmies, and Non-devotees: Culture, Group Boundaries, and the Development of Hare Krishna in North America and Europe." *Social Compass* 47 (2): 169–86.

2006. "The Hare Krishna Movement: Beginnings, Change, and Transformation." In Eugene V. Gallagher and W. Michael Ashcraft (eds.), *Introduction to New and Alternative Religions* (vol. IV, pp. 21–46). Westport, CT: Greenwood Press.

2007a. "Social Building Blocks of New Religious Movements: Organization and Leadership." In David Bromley (ed.), *Teaching New Religious Movements* (pp. 159–85). New York: Oxford University Press.

2007b. *Hare Krishna Transformed*. New York: New York University Press.

Rochford, E. Burke, Jr. and Kendra Bailey. 2006. "Almost Heaven: Leadership, Decline and the Transformation of New Vrindaban." *Nova Religio* 9 (3): 6–23.

Sherkat, Darren. 1997. "Embedding Religious Choices: Integrating Preferences and Social Constraints into Rational Choice Theories of Religious Behavior." In Lawrence A. Young (ed.), *Rational Choice Theory and Religion: Summary and Assessment* (pp. 65–86). New York: Routledge.

2001. "Tracking the Restructuring of American Religion: Religious Affiliation and Patterns of Religious Mobility, 1973–1998." *Social Forces* 79 (4): 1459–93.

Sherkat, Darren and John Wilson. 1995. "Preferences, Constraints, and Choices in Religious Markets: An Examination of Religious Switching and Apostasy." *Social Forces* 73: 993–1026.

Shinn, Larry. 1987. *The Dark Lord: Cult Images and the Hare Krishnas in America*. Philadelphia: Westminster Press.

Squarcini, Federico. 2000. "In Search of Identity within the Hare Krishna Movement: Memory, Oblivion and Thought Style." *Social Compass* 47 (2): 253–71.

Squarcini, Federico and Eugenio Fizzotti. 2004. *Hare Krishna*. Salt Lake City, UT: Signature Books.

Stark, Rodney. 1996. "Why Religious Movements Succeed or Fail: A Revised General Model." *Journal of Contemporary Religion* 11 (2): 133–46.

Stark, Rodney and Roger Finke. 2000. *Acts of Faith: Explaining the Human Side of Religion*. Berkeley: University of California Press.

Sutton, John R. and Mark Chaves. 2004. "Explaining Schism in American Protestant Denominations, 1890–1990." *Journal for the Scientific Study of Religion* 43 (2): 171–90.

Vishnu, Swami Bhakti Bhavana. 2004. "The Guardian of Devotion: Disappearance and Rejection of the Spiritual Master in ISKCON after 1977." In Edwin Bryant and Maria Ekstrand (eds.), *The Hare Krishna Movement: The Postcharismatic Fate of a Religious Transplant* (pp. 170–93). New York: Columbia University Press.

Wallis, Roy. 1976. *The Road to Total Freedom: A Sociological Analysis of Scientology*. New York: Columbia University Press.

1979. *Salvation and Protest: Studies of Social and Religious Movements*. New York: St. Martin's Press.

1982. *Millennialism and Charisma*. Belfast: The Queen's University.

Wright, Stuart. 1988. "Leaving New Religious Movements: Issues, Theory and Research." In David Bromley (ed.), *Falling from the Faith: Causes and Consequences of Apostasy* (pp. 143–65). Newbury Park, CA: Sage.

Zald, Mayer and Roberta Ash Garner. 1987. "Social Movement Organizations: Growth, Decay, and Change." In Mayer Zald and John D. McCarthy (eds.), *Social Movements in an Organizational Society* (pp. 121–41). New Brunswick, NJ: Transaction Books.

CHAPTER 13

Schisms within Hindu guru groups: the Transcendental Meditation movement in North America

Cynthia Ann Humes

The word "guru" by now has become quite familiar to many Americans. Its most basic meaning signifies any qualified teacher, regardless of discipline, in India. However, when the term applies to Hindu worldviews, overtones emerge: the guru is the skilled preceptor and divine saint through whose grace and assistance disciples make the spiritual crossing from the ocean of *saṃsāra*, the endless cycle of birth and death, to the ocean of awareness, from the changing flux of phenomenal reality to insight into the real, *brahman*, the far shore of liberation, from death to immortality (Forsthoefel and Humes 2005).

Maharishi Mahesh Yogi is famous in North America for inaugurating the "Transcendental Meditation" or TM Movement in 1959. Maharishi did not claim the mantle "guru" for himself; he took on instead the honorific "rishi" or seer, and always hearkened back to his own guru, Shankaracharya Swami Brahmananda Saraswati – lovingly called "Guru Dev," or "Divine Guru" – for legitimating the TM technique. (For an updated history of the TM Movement, see Humes 2005.) Years after Saraswati's death, Maharishi had claimed that he had rediscovered his guru's means for directly experiencing *brahman* and thereby attaining ultimacy, thus his unique method is the legitimate, authentic, and genuine heir to an ancient tradition of well-recognized and respected teachers (Lewis 2003: 15). Through TM's ongoing practice, the disciple progressively and naturally experiences improvement and opens up to greater knowledge, which Maharishi interpreted through the lens of Advaita Vedanta, the Hindu philosophy of nondualism. The ultimate goal of human endeavor is to find release (*moksha*) from this bondage to the cycle of rebirth. Knowledge (*jñāna*) of the human being's true nature ends bondage due to ignorance (*avidyā*). Liberation is realizing one's true nature, which is *ātman*, the Cosmic Self, precisely equated with *brahman* or the ultimate abstract absolute. *Brahman* is not realized through mere study of texts; only direct experience of the Cosmic Self, brought about through proper understanding, thereby addresses the predicament of illusion and qualifies as true knowledge. Texts and philosophies discussing the experience are relegated to a lower level of Truth for Advaita Vedanta, and philosophy and theology themselves have only limited value; by their nature they are limited.

Maharishi recognized the limitations of language. All teachers, he believed, must adopt *upaya*, the skillful means of adapting one's message to a particular time and circumstance (Humes 2005). He therefore declared that this resurrected practice, the TM technique, could best be expressed to and understood by a Western audience by translating these traditional Hindu truths into the language of Western science (Mahesh 1955; for other twentieth-century religious movement leaders see Bainbridge 1997: 259). Maharishi trained a cadre of "teachers" who delivered the message about TM and "initiators" who were authorized to dispense appropriate mantras based on specific criteria to those interested. This dual tactic – legitimating TM both by appeal to a "widespread India mystique in the counterculture of the late 1960s" and by assertions that the technique was scientific and that the Maharishi had a background in scientific physics – helped expand the pool of prospective meditators (Bainbridge 1997: 189–91).

Even as he laid the groundwork for providing more advanced Vedic training for his key disciples, that is, practices founded on the traditional knowledge systems explicated in the Sanskrit Hindu texts called *Veda*, Maharishi sought to further explicate his principles via science. In 1971, Maharishi asked his initiators to speak to the public exclusively using the new terminology set forth in a series of thirty-three videotapes called The Science of Creative Intelligence™ (SCI). SCI was an encompassing term for Maharishi's translation of Advaita Vedanta teachings into Western parlance. Enlightenment, he taught, is experienced within the context of the mind and body, and thus contacting the *ātman* through meditation results in measurable effects on a person's physiology. Scientific research in support of TM's health benefits initially helped clinch the movement's new respectability and attracted academics, researchers, and intellectuals. Virtually all scientific study of the Transcendental Meditation technique concerns its effect on physiology and potential health disorders.

Maharishi's stance that TM is the starting point on the path for introduction to all truth and his inclusion of worldly goals along the path together demonstrate a world-affirming approach (Wallis 1984).

Traditional Advaita Vedanta ascribes to the four human goals: education and indoctrination into religion, immersion into society as a contributing citizen and parent, well-defined moral practice and faith, and finally the pursuit of enlightenment. By eliminating this four-step scheme, Maharishi removed meditation from its ordinary context and positioned it as transcultural and perennial.

Maharishi further sought to establish SCI in a typical Western setting. He inaugurated the accredited Maharishi International University (MIU) in Fairfield, Iowa in 1974. MIU functioned as the center of the North American TM movement for nearly a decade. To connect other areas to this center, he established "capitals" of enlightenment throughout North America and appointed "Governors" to lead them. TM crested on the "Merv Wave," or the 1975 spike in popularity marked by when Merv Griffin and other famous Hollywood types spoke openly about the benefits they found from TM. Bainbridge and Jackson noted that nearly 300,000 people were initiated in 1975 (1981: 292). The decline of TM began in 1976, and studies offer various theories for why TM eventually turned to more emphasis on religiosity that most would identify as Hindu (Bainbridge and Jackson 1981; Johnston 1980; Ornstein 1986). Thursby (2005) notes that the position taken by the TM movement publicly was that none of the contended terms "Hindu," "Hinduism," and even "religion," should be applied to them. Nevertheless, in 1977, *Malnak v. Yogi* ruled that the teaching of TM was religious (Spiritual Counterfeits Project 1978).

Elsewhere, I have related some of the most significant historical developments in TM in the wake of the *Malnak v. Yogi* ruling (Humes 2005). My concern here is to discuss examples of three leaders who have to varying degrees split off from TM. Each experienced different levels of success, and their efforts to gain legitimacy and a following underwent different processes as well as appealing to different "pre-existing networks" (Stark and Bainbridge 1985). In the concluding section, I explore not only why they occurred, but also the circumstances, timing, and processual factors in their splits from TM. At least in the case of TM, I am optimistic that major arguments contained within the "new paradigm" can be usefully applied (Sharot 2002). Accordingly, throughout, I will hearken to various "new paradigm" insights to explain TM's history of schismatism.

TM AND THE NORTH AMERICAN GURU

While attending an advanced TM training course in 1976 in Switzerland, Robin Woodsworth Carlsen attained full enlightenment together with a privileged understanding of TM that included the specific steps the movement should take to assert its rightful place in the "marketplace of ideas" in the West (Carlsen 1979).

A TM initiator from Victoria, British Columbia, Carlsen criticized the TM movement because of its inattention to "personal reality." God had biased the West in the direction of individuality and the East in the direction of wholeness (1981: 14). Carlsen urged Maharishi's movement to compete with Western intellectualism, not just Vedic science. "[U]ntil we ourselves can demonstrate we know as much about personal reality as we do about impersonal reality, the personalists who dominate the organs of consciousness in the West – intellectually, culturally, artistically, polit- ically – will continue to ignore us" (1981: 13). By TM's over-emphasis on Vedic concepts of the Self as Absolute, as the Whole, TM had not sufficiently adapted itself to the specificities of the North American context.

Since its earliest formulation, Advaita Vedanta had consistently accepted the reality of personal gods, but they were understood to be more limited and inferior to the truly transcendent nature of unqualified *brahman*, the ultimate ground of Being. Worshiping gods was seen to be a preliminary stage along the path, the necessary crawling and stumbling before individuals were mature enough to graduate to higher steps toward abstraction. In early works such as his 1963 commentary on the *Bhagavad Gita* (1990), Maharishi had mentioned personal gods. In an open letter to Maharishi, Carlsen accused his guru of deliberately holding back the experience of the personal. In public, the gods of Hinduism were not mentioned, and students of TM were discouraged, Carlsen alleged, from publicizing possible links to a Hindu pantheon for two reasons: fear of polluting the "purity of the teaching," that is, Advaitin wisdom, as well as scaring off the public from the supposedly unreligious science of creative intelligence.

Carlsen's World Teacher Movement is particularly fascinating because it shows a distinct evolution over time. Carlsen added deeper cleavage to what was initially a theological and philosophical split by directly criti- cizing the TM movement and MIU hierarchy. On July 9, 1983 Carlsen wrote, "Transcendental Meditation and the TM Movement has had its day; the charm has fled the Movement; the beautiful people have left; the petrification of dogma has set in." Many who were attracted to Carlsen came not because of his personalist theology and new techniques, but because of his efforts to recapture a mood of spirituality some felt absent from the SCI versions of TM and the bureaucracy Maharishi put in place to popularize it. When Carlsen promised to bring back the "heart," he intrigued many seekers. Said one erstwhile follower, "Robin Carlsen offered something exciting, very different. He offered new techniques of meditation, and in our imagination, they were much more powerful, and we were sucked in. In a sense, it was the opposite of the TM movement: something quite alive."

Carlsen insisted that Maharishi had privately acknowledged his attaining cosmic consciousness, but he was not accepted by the TM center in Victoria because he was offering teachings at his residence in an area called Sunnyside beyond what the movement allowed. (Carlsen 1979) As a living voice out of the Absolute, as great Hindu rishis did of old, Carlsen was simply and spontaneously offering the truth – indeed, since he was an enlightened master, he was inherently incapable of going against the purity of the teaching and the "natural law" of the universe.

Prior to joining TM, Carlsen was involved with Werner Erhard, creator of *Erhard Seminar Training* or *est*. *Est* was a sixties and seventies therapy cult in which people were confronted with their hang-ups and put under great mental pressure to "free" them of their psychological problems, or "get it." "Getting it" was described as overcoming whatever was holding him or her back, or causing the problems (Rupert 1992). *Est* subjects were taught that each person individually creates his or her own reality. The key to successful living is to alter your reality so that you are able to succeed or be happy: this is "getting it" (Rupert 1992). Carlsen appreciated Erhard's confrontational methods – although he had ideas for its improvement, too. (1980; n.d.a)

For TMers to clue into their own subjective dimension, they needed a process to accelerate what Carlsen called individuation. Carlsen claimed he (and he alone) could see demonic entities entering and leaving people. Central to Carlsen's innovative process was the attempt to find out what part of a person's personality was divine or demonic. Adopting *est* confrontational techniques, Carlsen's complete vision allowed him to confront the demonic in those attending his seminars. An early follower recounted,

He was always making lots of noises, acting really goofy, intentionally, like Steve Martin. After the confrontation part of the program, Carlsen would then manifest the form and consciousness of masters of the holy tradition, and others on demand. This was like the HBO part of the program; after you were totally frightened to death, then there was entertainment. Robin had had an acting career, and I think this helped him a lot. I remember people asking him to manifest such things as the country of Japan, or Karl Marx, or the Battle of

Hastings. Then he would take on a particular facial expression; the elasticity of his body was like Jim Carrey. He would do spasms, and can that man scream!

At the age of 36 in late 1981, Carlsen – a handsome man whom the *Des Moines Register* would subsequently describe "as sort of a mystical Dick Cavett, buttoned down in a business suit" – moved to Fairfield (Pedersen 1983). Carlsen fancied himself the next "World teacher" as described in Zoroastrianism, and he took pains to study Persian history, ventured in the seventies to Iran to meet the Ayatollah Khomeini, and wrote several tracts about his experiences. Carlsen set up shop, and began to offer his special workshops – and to confront his neighbor, MIU. By the spring of 1982, Fairfield's TM community was abuzz with the controversy.

Maharishi was customarily silent about Carlsen. Carlsen interpreted his guru's silence, and over-interpreted the occasional comments Maharishi did offer, as legitimation that he should keep pushing MIU authorities. He even opined that Maharishi wanted him to do as he did, because, as he put it in one letter, "he wants to make enlightenment relevant to the West." Carlsen's confrontational and entertaining style was not limited to his workshops or writings. Carlsen eventually saw himself as none other than the movement's Martin Luther, intent to speak out and overturn what had become an oppressive church hierarchy, and restoring individual, direct access to the Divine Truth.

In September 1982, Carlsen sent a letter to Greg Wilson at MIU, informing him that he would be willing to cease his critical efforts against MIU if they would produce "an official document" from Maharishi asking that he should. Responses and counter-responses escalated in intensity, eventually drawing in observers. A satirical letter penned by members of the MIU community referred to him as "Robbing Bucksworth Quarrelsome," and lampooned his marketing of himself as the new guru of North America.

In October 1982, a message came to MIU via John Cowhig, Maharishi's personal secretary (whose sister Gemma was the primary supporter in Carlsen's movement, and who would later marry Robin Carlsen). John Cowhig quoted Maharishi as saying, "Tell that stupid man, what is his name? that madman who thinks he's functioning with Maharishi's secret guidance – tell him he is a shame to the movement." Carlsen was quite upset, and he secured Vincent P. McCarthy, a law professor at the University of Bridgeport (Connecticut) who was also a TM initiator, to represent him in a suit against Maharishi and MIU. McCarthy commented in an interview, "Carlsen picked apart the hypocrisy of the movement and its refusal to come to terms with Western civilization. I felt his criticisms were on the mark, and he could bring some common sense to the movement."

Carlsen asked for $43 million on the grounds that Cowhig's reporting of Maharishi's comment injured his reputation, and MIU officials were damaging his seminar business by harassing potential clients. MIU officials acknowledged that they had taken down the names and license numbers of those who attended Carlsen's lectures, and that some meditators may have lost their jobs for becoming Carlsen followers. At the time of his lawsuit against MIU, Carlsen had a core of seventy-five strong followers and another two hundred hangers-on in Fairfield. They agreed with his criticism that MIU was repressive, and they wondered, too, about the efficacy of the TM technique and the promise to teach people to live spontaneously. By 1983, most TM insiders had been meditating regularly for ten to fifteen years – so, Carlsen asked, what had happened to the five- to eight-year plan to becoming enlightened? If TM really did work to free the individual to act according to his or her own nature, why was the movement so dogmatic? Many intelligent TMers wanted answers to the same questions posed by Carlsen.

Carlsen also asked his attorney McCarthy to take the case of Paul Hart against MIU for wrongful academic dismissal from the university. With Ty Gale and Sten Karlstrom, Hart had been dismissed for following Carlsen and learning his techniques in the spring of 1982. In March 1983, District Court Judge Daniel Morrison ordered that Hart be readmitted to MIU pending the outcome of Carlsen's own case. After a four-day hearing, Morrison ruled that MIU had "failed to follow its own rules for academic dismissal." The next month, in April 1983, attorney Edward Kelly filed a lawsuit against MIU on behalf of two more dismissed students, this time asking $25 million in damages. Carlsen offered MIU legal counsel Goldman, Goldstein, and James a chance to settle out of court. In a lengthy letter of April 3, 1983, he proposed that officials and faculty of MIU listen to a three-day "presentation of the ideas and the principles of The World Teacher Seminar" to determine if their ideas were actually heterodox with Maharishi's teachings. He ended his letter by saying, "It is this, or it is a protracted and complex lawsuit." The MIU officials refused these conditions.

Early in July 1983, despite McCarthy's advice to seek a monetary claim and pursue MIU for their anti-trust, anti-competitive practices, Carlsen elected instead to threaten to take the whole case to *Time* magazine unless he heard from Maharishi the answers to four questions: Is Carlsen enlightened? Is he deviating from the purity of the Teaching? Are his techniques incompatible with the TM-Sidhi program? Does Maharishi truly want his followers not to attend World Teacher Seminars? Carlsen settled on these four questions after they were "channeled" from "celestials" who also told him that he would be victorious in his lawsuit. The messages of the celestials confirmed that Robin was posed to become the leader of the Age of Enlightenment, continuing the lineage of Maharishi's master, and that the World Teacher Seminar would be the next unfolding of the age.

In mid-July 1983, Maharishi complied to Carlsen's new demands. A taped message from Maharishi was admitted as evidence to the court. Maharishi asked that the court hear this evidence in private and that it be destroyed once it was played. In an interview, Ty Gale recalled:

During the court date in Ottumwa, Maharishi answered on tape, in extremely negative terms, to all four questions. He answered very harshly, curtly. Robin responded with his head in his hands. Usually he was in an almost manic phase, but during Maharishi's testimony, he looked depressed. Everything Maharishi said was against Carlsen: is he enlightened? No. Is he deviating from the purity of the Teaching? Yes. Are his techniques incompatible with the TM-Sidhi program? Yes. Does Maharishi truly want his followers not to attend World Teacher Seminars? Yes.

Carlsen's lawyer, Vincent McCarthy, verified in an interview that Carlsen was "totally shocked" that he was not vindicated by Maharishi. Indeed, on the day of the trial Carlsen had purchased a dozen roses and brought them with him to celebrate. McCarthy mused:

After the trial, I rode with him in the car. He was shocked and quiet. I thought, what could one expect? If he [Maharishi] answered the four questions in the negative, the entire suit would go away . . . The TM movement was attempting to squash anyone else to prohibit teaching anything else in the Fairfield area. We had them on the run; we had an injunction. We would have clearly won, but Carlsen wanted to be accepted by Yogi, because he believed he was an enlightened follower who had achieved cosmic consciousness.

Carlsen sought merely acceptance of his state of consciousness: and was denied it by Maharishi. The others in the suit were directly affected; Paul Hart, for instance, confided in an interview that Judge Morrison confirmed to him that had the original suit remained, he would have been inclined in Hart's favor and awarded him a substantial sum.

The court ruled that within fifteen days Carlsen must contact all individuals whom he had reason to believe were practicing both his and Maharishi's programs "and inform them that the programs are incompatible." Carlsen obeyed the court dictates by composing an open letter, in which he argued that ultimately Maharishi did not mean what he said. He claimed that Maharishi's answers to his four questions "in tone, in vibration, in substance – were perverse, senseless, bizarre" (Robin Woodsworth Carlsen, July 27, 1983, Letter). Later, he claimed that "Maharishi's response was a complete contradiction of Natural Law," which is why Maharishi asked that the tape be destroyed. (MIU officials claimed, by contrast, that Maharishi simply wished to avoid creating a circus around the whole thing.) Therefore, as any enlightened being could tell, Carlsen explained, Maharishi did not really mean his statements to the court. Indeed, Carlsen claimed Maharishi was actually sending a message that he was supporting Robin by speaking against him. "Maharishi Mahesh Yogi," he says, "has rather interesting ways of supporting an enlightened individual that he has created."

Certainly one would have to agree that if this was Carlsen's understanding of support, it was tough love. That fall, Carlsen taught a one-month World Teacher Seminar Teacher Training Program in which he was forced to explain that his techniques were incompatible with those at MIU, as dictated by the court.

Between December 17, 1983 and January 6, 1984, Maharishi offered a "Taste of Utopia" conference at MIU. To insiders, the course was yet another attempt by TMers to give the world a glimpse of the world that could be, if only the greater culture accepted TM. To outsiders, it appeared to be an attempt by Maharishi to round up his wagons in defense against the confrontational "danger process" Carlsen instigated. In a fitting gesture, Carlsen hired a helicopter to drop leaflets onto the campus during the event. The memos from on high chastised the repressiveness of the movement and claimed Carlsen to be the new World Teacher – and open for business.

THE MAHARISHI BRAND

Far from North America, another split from TM began to emerge in the early 1980s. While he continued to have a place in Maharishi's movement, in 1982 Sri Sri Ravi Shankar held the first Art of Living Healing Breath Workshop modeled on his own techniques. Shankar, a long-time disciple of Maharishi Mahesh Yogi, established his own ashram in Bangalore, India, where he sought to "bring out ancient sciences to suit the present-day life." The marked resemblance of Sri Sri Ravi Shankar's marketing plan to that of Maharishi is obvious; clearly under his teacher's tutelage, Shankar developed the managerial skills necessary to set up and run his own religious firm (Stark and Bainbridge 1985). As his master once did, he traveled around the world, conducting courses in the "Art of Living" – so reminiscent of Maharishi's 1968 book, *Science of Being and Art of Living*. As did Carlsen, he advised North American TM practitioners to stay with TM, but to complement it with his unique techniques. Shankar taught Healing Breath (*Sudarshan Kriya*) to restore harmony to body, mind, and spirit. As Maharishi had, Shankar also designed workshops for business industries, students, health care, and prisoners' rehabilitation.

The cult of personality is perhaps the most obvious difference between Maharishi and Shankar. Although Maharishi was clearly respected, loved, and celebrated on *Guru Purnima* (the festival dedicated to gurus every July), well before the early eighties, Maharishi had asked that disciples refrain from displaying public kinds of emotional attachment common to the guru–disciple bond in Hinduism. Shankar, by contrast, allowed others to fawn over him as Hindus characteristically do to their masters – thereby locating his teachings within a Hindu mode of legitimacy, making him a popular choice of guru for Indians. Expressions of love and attachment to the guru are common in weekly *Satsangs*, "gatherings of holy people" devoted to Sri Sri, where, unlike in TM circles, traditional *bhajans* or hymns are sung.

But other differences exist as well. Shankar offers a devotional stance to supreme reality, but through an Advaitin stance. He incorporates *Bhakti*, the Hindu path of devotion, in the development of an ego-less "Divine Love," for one another, for the guru, and for God. Nor has Shankar packaged his Vedic message in scientific jargon. Shankar is a remarkably traditional guru in many respects, but one whose methods have been invigorated by some of Maharishi's innovations.

As did Carlsen, Shankar has claimed that Maharishi approves of his teaching. Unlike Carlsen, there is supporting historical evidence for Shankar's claim. TM practitioners were initially allowed to take his techniques and attend courses, and no overt action was taken by the TM movement hierarchy in the United States against Shankar's programs until 1993.

In the 1990s, anonymous letters and notices began to be posted in TM venues that denied any linkage between Sri Sri and Maharishi, and warned meditators not to associate with his programs. This message, however, directly conflicted with the well-known fact that Sri Sri was head of the Indian TM movement and also administered Maharishi's school for pandit boys. With no public discussion, the early MIU policy was "don't ask, don't tell." Those who became known Kriya practitioners reported having experienced blacklisting and restricted access to events, as recorded in Fairfield news magazines catering to the TM practitioner.

If one looks across to other developments outside of Fairfield, Iowa, the shift taken against Sri Sri's Art of Living becomes more readily understandable as part of a pattern. The hardline taken against the Art of Living program took place at the precise time Maharishi and the TM movement began to take action against the programs of Deepak Chopra.

At one time, Deepak Chopra was among the elite spokespersons for TM, specializing in Ayurveda and self-consciously indebted to Maharishi (Chopra 1988). In happier days, Maharishi referred to Chopra publicly as "Dhanvantari of Heaven on Earth," a heavily symbolic title: Dhanvantari is the mythological physician of the Gods. With the take-off of his bestseller, Chopra and his operations threatened the well-being of his former guru's business world (Chopra 1993).

Their famous falling out in 1993 led to Chopra's uprooting himself and his herbs from cold-hearted Boston and replanting both in a tiny and elite San Diego suburb. According to Chopra, Maharishi told him, "Everyone tells me you are competing with me." He responded that he would never do that, and offered to leave the movement. Said Chopra, "Maharishi was very sweet then, he said, 'Whatever decision would be best for you'" (Knapp 2003). "Later I got a call from [the Maharishi] in Boston. He told me that I could be a great spiritual leader. That everyone would follow me. He said that he would put me in charge of the whole Movement. But I said, 'I don't want to be a spiritual leader. I am a very regular guy – with a wife and kids. I just have the gift of gab.' He seemed perplexed, but in the end he was very sweet. 'Whatever decision would be best for you'" (Knapp 2003).

The amicable separation did not last long. On July 16, 1993, the "Maharishi National Council of the Age of Enlightenment" wrote to all TM centers in the United States: not only had Deepak Chopra left the movement, but "for the purity of the teaching" Maharishi's followers should avoid Chopra and not promote him. Instead, the "pure and complete knowledge of Maharishi Ayur-Ved will now be available to the whole population in the United States and Canada through the courses Maharishi is preparing." Two weeks later, Dr. Chopra wrote a letter to dispel "rumors and misunderstandings." "I am not really sure what is meant when people ask me if I've left the Movement," he wrote. "I still practice TM and the Sidhis, and will continue to recommend them and refer people to the Centers and Clinics." He said he would be pleased to hear from anyone "who feels the need or desire to contact me." Chopra now provides Ayurvedic procedures through his own seminars and institution (La Jolla's Chopra Center for Well Being), offers his own Primordial Sound Meditation, and sells his own food supplements, "all at former students' requests," and often at considerably lower prices than correlative Maharishi Ayur-Ved products.

Elsewhere, I have discussed how Maharishi's strategies might function as a kind of "product differentiation" – that is, his insistence on only Maharishi-approved products helps his line of wares be perceived as higher quality, even if no real difference exists (Humes 2008). During the 1970s *Malnak v. Yogi* crisis, a two-page memorandum was sent to "All Departments" by Lenny Goldman regarding the "proper use of term: 'Transcendental Meditation'." Goldman described how Maharishi's governing apparatus called the World Plan Executive Council was seeking to register all terms identifying movement activities, such as Transcendental Meditation, Science of Creative Intelligence, TM, and SCI, as service marks. The memo explained that WPEC's success with registration applications depended on their proper use; accordingly, he describes a service mark as "a word, phrase, or design which distinguishes the source of a particular service from other sources." By associating these terms with WPEC's services, he continues, people enrolling in programs can be assured they come from the same source. This recognition, he explains, serves the following important functions: "1) It helps and protects the public; a) by distinguising [*sic*] our services from others so that people make easy and accurate choices; and b) by serving as a guarantee of consistent quality. 2) It helps us to advertise our services" (Goldman n.d.).

Maharishi's companies make explicit claims that only his products are truly superior and can meet the needs of the spiritually savvy consumer. Are competing products – such as the meditative techniques passed down by other disciples of Guru Dev and renegade teachers such as Deepak Chopra and Sri Sri Ravi Shankar, for example – capable of achieving similar effects? Are these measures to assure quality – the purity of the teaching or an Ayurvedic tincture – or is it a marketing ploy to make additional profit selling the goods that are prescribed as necessary components?

Contextually, by the early 1990s, Maharishi was faced with two rival Indian leaders who rose within the ranks of the TM movement but were poised to offer alternative techniques that could endanger the financial situation of TM as well as dethrone Maharishi from serving as the interpreter of his guru Shankaracharya Swami Brahmananda Saraswati. The money being brought into the movement had plummeted with changes in fee structure. Both Chopra and Shankar taught at considerably reduced rates (Bainbridge and Jackson 1981). The potential threat of TMers defecting or spending their money on alternative programs rather than the higher-priced TM programs is clear.

By the 1990s, the infusion of dozens of Hindu new religious groups resulted in processual changes in TM's market (Finke 1996). TM did not have much competition initially, but later, as the market pinched, Maharishi had to lock down on his followers by adverting to the "purity of the teaching" and prohibit members from going off to follow Deepak Chopra and Sri Sri Ravi Shankar. The competition was not simply over selling of products, for as Neitz and Mueser (1996: 112) have observed, in TM, the producers and consumers of TM are to a large degree the same individuals.

Whereas before the mid-seventies "Guru Dev" was on every TMer's lips, the emphasis shifted so that virtually everything Maharishi touched bore his name: it was Maharishi who would determine appropriate goods and services.

CONCLUSION

On February 5, 2008, Maharishi died in Vlodrop, Holland. He was over ninety years old and had been in failing health. He had kept busy to the end; among his pet projects are supporting traditional pandit priest groups in India who perform world-purifying rituals, and holding court with "King Tony Nader Raam." The purpose of the latter, I suspect, was to try to fend off any potential succession disputes upon his impending death. In Hindu guru groups, a juncture at which schisms often occur is the death of a charismatic founder. The post once held by Maharishi's guru, for example, is now disputed by several rival claimants, and Maharishi had taken sides in the matter and attempted to lend his support to one faction. Maharishi clearly did not want to leave his organization in a state of crisis. At risk was his entire empire: he had created, in addition to his spiritual enterprises, multiple lines of consumer goods to be purchased, television programs, a political party (Natural Law Party) that is international in scope, and even a "sovereign" country, replete with its own currency (Humes 2005; 2008).

Maharishi's ambition of Raam Rajya – the idyllic rule of the great mythic god-king Raam, which is the true heritage of India – was finally achieved when on October 7, 2000 Maharishi inaugurated the "Global Country of World Peace." The "sovereign ruler," "King," or "Raja" of this utopia is Anthony Nader, "Dr. Raja Raam Nader," an American physiologist, who had been gifted his weight in gold in 1998 for his scientific discoveries.

Contrary to Deepak Chopra, who took pains not to chain his understanding of Ayurveda to just the Hindu Vedic tradition, Nader resolved to link quantum healing firmly with the Vedas, underscoring Maharishi's system as his own brand of Vedic Science, albeit a system global in application (Nader 1995). In Maharishi Ayur-Veda literature, the primary emphasis continues to be on Transcendental Meditation and the development of consciousness, because ill health is caused by our own "mistake of the intellect" – *Pragya Aparadh* (*prajñāparādha*). By failing to understand our true nature, we become estranged from the ultimate source of universal consciousness and we fall ill (Sharma and Clark 1988; Reddy and Egenes 2002). Thus, Maharishi had pinned his legacy on Nader to preserve his technique, his programs, and his products as uniquely legitimate in contrast to all contenders.

As Wallis has observed, a potential schismatic leader must be able to secure a legitimate claim to followers' allegiance. Accordingly, the schismatic propensity of a group is directly related to the perceived availability of sources of legitimation within a movement (1979: 180–1). At one time, Maharishi taught that knowledge of *brahman* was open to all, that the TM technique was easy, and that truth could be understood in the language of science. Several decades later, Maharishi developed a firm organizational structure to his movement and took steps to lock down against personal revelations by rivals. Maharishi thus successfully transitioned TM from the fold that Wallis has described as a "pluralistically legitimate movement," to a "uniquely legitimate movement" (1979). A pluralistically legitimate group is one that does not completely reject the validity of alternative paths to truth, salvation, or utopia, despite holding its own understanding as greatly superior. In its earliest literature, TM had specifically indicated that it was prepared to cooperate to some extent with others and to work within a set of game rules which require collaboration. By contrast, TM came to be a "uniquely legitimate movement" that defined the boundaries of doctrine and practice quite sharply to distinguish themselves from those beliefs and programs that Maharishi sought to reject.

Through his assertions of his need to "preserve the purity of the teaching" of the prophet Swami Brahmananda Saraswati, Maharishi came to effectively limit the bases of legitimation and thereby reduce the chances of schism. In so doing, his organization has sought to hold "a competitive advantage because it provides an inimitable good or service."

This approach has been variously successful; in the case of Carlsen, it was extremely so. Carlsen's seemingly irrational behavior at the final moments of his lawsuit against MIU is illustrative of this power of Maharishi's competitive advantage: Carlsen preferred to have Maharishi's acknowledgment of his state of enlightenment rather than the millions of dollars his lawyer assured him would be his. For Carlsen, leaving the TM denomination would result in the loss of both legitimacy and a host of unique resources (Wallis 1979). Carlsen's disbelief at Maharishi's answers to the divinely channeled four questions was clearly rooted in his knowledge of its inconsistency with what he had known TM to be: a pluralistically legitimate movement.

Carlsen was self-consciously a rebel. He knew he was perceived to be attempting a schism. He referred to himself as "the anti-Christ of the Movement," "anti-Maharishi," the "devil," and his own writings as "the New Testament for the Western [TM practitioner]" (May 1982). Nevertheless, he was convinced that there was still a place for him in the ultimate TM fold, because he saw TM truth as universal truth.

His own characterization of the then TM hierarchy included describing MIU leaders as "devout Fathers of the Church who still look out from a Ptolemaic universe where the planet of MIU is the center of the universe, where Galileo and World Teachers should be incarcerated – but LIFE AND MAHARISHI MADE ME ENLIGHTENED and by cracky the pharisees at MIU had better discover fast that beautiful innocence that their Teacher put inside them" (July 9, 1983). Sprinkled throughout these letters are comments warning that "*Time* magazine is waiting to do a story on this legal case."

Indeed, as indicated by his 1983 memorandum "Wittenberg Updated or 33 Reasons why I am suing Maharishi International University," Carlsen self-consciously recognized his toying with a schism attempt against MIU (not Maharishi). There he accuses MIU of suffering from a "diseased utopianism," and although "MIU presents itself as the model of an ideal society, as the model for effective functioning for the whole world; it is painfully – even embarrassingly – obvious that such a notion represents an incredible act of self-deception" characterized by a "neo-Hindu mode." Further, "Maharishi is not in position to properly represent the values and impulses of a distinctively Western – as opposed to Vedic – culture/cosmology." The reader is left to understand that Carlsen is properly positioned to do so.

But Maharishi could ill afford Carlsen's effort to split the TM community along national lines. By the 1980s, Maharishi had begun to incorporate into TM Indian cultural habits, "baggage" (Nattier 1997) ranging from dressing in specific colors, speaking in certain ways, reading only accepted books, eluding certain astrological occurrences, and avoiding inauspicious architectural design. Carlsen had railed against such "neo-Hinduism," and also criticized TM's doctrines, liturgy, degrees of strictness, and behavioral norms. To counter this alienation from North American custom, Carlsen dared to hold a ritual during which he was invested as the "Shankaracharya of North America," a poignant title for its allusion to the great philosopher Shankara, who in the eighth century had set up four seats of knowledge where his special teachers (Shankaracharya) would inhabit the thrones of orthodoxy in the four cardinal directions of India. While Carlsen continued to have a small following for several years after the great schism, he eventually ended his career as a World Teacher and disappeared from the limelight.

In stark contrast with Carlsen's plight, Sri Sri Ravi Shankar's creation of an ashram in Bangalore and his own group initially followed the model of a normal guru movement's development, whereby one guru emerges from another and sets up his own shop. The strong emphasis on guru veneration in the Hindu tradition has ensured that Shankar never openly criticizes or speaks against his master Maharishi. But the affection seems to have been mutual: only when the *Art of Living* workshops threatened to become more popular than standard TM fare did Maharishi take action against Sri Sri in North America. After a decade of "don't ask, don't tell," TM adherents were no longer allowed to attend his workshops with impunity. Brand loyalty to Maharishi was insisted upon.

In the 1990s, Maharishi was faced with two rival Indian leaders who rose within the ranks of the TM movement but were teaching alternative techniques. The money being brought into the movement had plummeted with changes in fee structure. Both Chopra and Shankar taught at considerably reduced rates. The threat of TMers defecting or spending their money on alternative programs rather than the higher-priced TM programs is obvious.

Chopra reports being taken by surprise when Maharishi confronted him. Chopra did not seek to separate; rather, the schism was actually forced on him by Maharishi, and thus in a sense was an excommunication. Chopra had not realized he was beginning to be perceived by some as a guru and potential threat to his master. Different times called for different measures: Maharishi recognized that Chopra was a charismatic leader who would be able to garner support from a group sizeable enough to break from the larger group. He preferred to lop Chopra off sooner rather than later risk his disciple's competing with the operation. Based on Chopra's comments, it would appear that part of the impetus to throw Chopra aside was a result of personality conflicts among the leadership in Maharishi's organization who warned Maharishi of Chopra's purported ambitions. Today, Chopra has done quite well on his own, and continues to operate within a "non-competition" zone with Maharishi's programs.

In some sense, the greatest schism is the most dispersed: the vast majority of people who started TM did not continue within the TM movement per se. Yet, in important ways, many voluntary defectors from TM followed a pattern Rochford has described in the case of the ISK-CON movement (1989: 175). Rochford's research has shown that many voluntary defectors from ISKCON joined other religious organizations but retained their primary religious framework, thus evidencing a strategy to avoid reconverting to the conventional secular worldview (1989: 175). Voluntary defectors from TM have shown a similar propensity, especially preferring to become members of other new religions, in a process that they describe as a "conversion career." Based on the many former TM proponents in various Hindu cults, the larger movement of TM's Advaita Vedanta teachings has lived on (Humes 2008).

BIBLIOGRAPHY

Bainbridge, William Sims. 1997. *Sociology of Religious Movements*. New York: Routledge.
Bainbridge, William Sims and Daniel H. Jackson. 1981. "The Rise and Decline of Transcendental Meditation." In Bryan Wilson (ed.), *The Social Impact of New Religious Movements* (pp. 135–58). New York: Rose of Sharon Press.
Carlsen, Robin Woodsworth. 1979. *The Sunnyside Drama: The First Three Years of Enlightenment*. Victoria, BC: Snow Man Press.
  December, 1980. *On First Meeting Werner Erhard and est: A Memoir of Deliberate Affirmation*. Victoria, BC: Snow Man Press.
  1981. *An Open Letter to Maharishi Mahesh Yogi: Wings Beating in the Breast of Creation*. Victoria, BC: Snow Man Press, Open Letter Series.
  n.d.a. *An Open Letter to Werner Erhard, or "Getting It" – With Wings*. Victoria, BC: Snow Man Press, Open Letter Series.
  n.d.b. "Wittenberg Updated or 33 Reasons Why I Am Suing Maharishi International University." Written circa 1983.

Palm Sunday (April 4), 1982. *An Open Letter to the Guardians of Purity at MIU.* Victoria, BC: Snow Man Press, Open Letter Series.

May 1982. *An Open Letter to the Faculty of Maharishi International University.* Victoria, BC: Snow Man Press, Open Letter Series.

1982. "Letter to Greg Wilson." Private collection.

July 9, 1983. *An Open Letter to All Meditators, Sidhas, and Governors.* Victoria, BC: Snow Man Press, Open Letter Series.

July 27, 1983. "An Open Letter to all MIU Students/Faculty, Sidhas, Governors and Meditaters." Private collection.

Carlsen, Robin Woodsworth and Vincent McCarthy. April 10, 1983. "Letter to the Curriculum Committee." Private collection.

Cenkner, William. 1978. *A Tradition of Teachers: Sankara and the Jagadgurus Today.* Delhi: Motilal Banarsidass.

Chopra, Deepak. 1988. *Return of the Rishi: A Doctor's Story of Spiritual Transformation and Ayurvedic Healing.* New York: Houghton Mifflin.

1993. *Ageless Body, Timeless Mind: The Quantum Alternative to Growing Old.* New York: Harmony Books.

Finke, Roger. 1996. "The Consequences of Religious Competition: Supply-side Explanations for Religious Change." In Lawrence A. Young (ed.), *Rational Choice Theory and Religion* (pp. 46–65). New York: Routledge.

Forsthoefel, Thomas A. and Cynthia Ann Humes, 2005. "Introduction: Making Waves." In Thomas A. Forsthoefel and Cynthia Ann Humes (eds.), *Gurus in America* (pp. 1–13). Albany: State University of New York Press.

Goldman, Lenny. n.d. Two page memorandum to "All departments." Private collection.

Humes, Cynthia Ann. 2005. "Maharishi Mahesh Yogi: Beyond the TM Technique." In Thomas A. Forsthoefel and Cynthia Ann Humes (eds.), *Gurus in America* (pp. 55–79). Albany: State University of New York Press.

2008. "Maharishi Ayur-Veda™: Perfect Health™ through Enlightened Marketing in America." In Dagmar Wujastyk and Frederick M. Smith (eds.), *Modern and Global Ayurveda: Pluralism and Paradigms* (pp. 309–31). Albany: State University of New York Press.

Johnston, Hank. 1980. "The Marketed Social Movement: A Case Study of the Rapid Growth of TM," *Pacific Sociological Review* 23: 333–54.

Knapp, John. http://trancenet.org/chopra/interview, accessed December 4, 2003.

Lewis, James R. 2003. *Legitimating New Religions.* New Brunswick, NJ: Rutgers University Press.

"The Maharishi National Council of the Age of Enlightenment." July 16, 1993. Private collection.

Mahesh, Bal Brahmachari. 1955. "The Beacon Light of the Himalayas – The Dawn of the Happy New Era." Kerala: Adhyatmic Vikas Mandal.

Mahesh Yogi, Maharishi. 1968. *Science of Being and Art of Living.* New York: Signet.

1990. *Maharishi Mahesh Yogi on the Bhagavad Gita: A New Translation and Commentary, Chapters 1–6.* London: Penguin and Arkana Press.

Nader, Anthony. 1995. *Human Physiology: Expression of Veda and Vedic Literature*. Vlodrop, The Netherlands: Maharishi Vedic University.

Nattier, Jan. 1997. "Buddhism Comes to Main Street." *Wilson Quarterly*: 72–80.

Neitz, Mary Jo and Peter R. Mueser. 1996. "Economic Man and the Sociology of Religion: A Critique of the Rational Choice Approach." In Lawrence A. Young (eds.), *Rational Choice Theory and Religion* (pp. 105–18). New York: Routledge.

Ornstein, Robert E. 1986. *The Psychology of Consciousness*. New York: Penguin Books (1st edn 1977).

Pedersen, Daniel. April 10, 1983. "Rival TM Leader Brings Lawsuit, Discord to MIU." *Des Moines Sunday Register*.

Reddy, Kumuda and Linda Egenes. 2002. *Conquering Chronic Disease through Maharishi Vedic Medicine*. Schenectady, NY: Samhita Productions.

Rochford, E. Burke. 1989. "Factionalism, Group Defection, and Schism in the Hare Krishna Movement." *Journal for the Scientific Study of Religion* 28 (2): 162–79.

Rupert, Glenn A. 1992. "Employing the New Age: Training Seminars." In James R. Lewis and J. Gordon Melton (eds.), *Perspectives on the New Age* (pp. 127–35). Albany: New York: State University of New York Press.

Sharma, Hari and Christopher Clark. 1988. *Contemporary Ayurveda: Medicine and Research in Maharishi Ayur-Veda*. New York: Churchill Livingstone.

Sharot, S. 2002. "Beyond Christianity: A Critique of Rational Choice Theory of Religion from a Weberian and Comparative Religions Perspective." *Sociology of Religion* 63: 427–54.

Spiritual Counterfeits Project. 1978. *TM in Court*. Berkeley, CA: Spiritual Counterfeits Project.

Stark, Rodney and William Sims Bainbridge. 1985. *The Future of Religion: Secularization, Revival and Cult Formation*. Berkeley: University of California Press.

Thursby, Gene R. 2005. "Hindu Movements since Mid-Century: Yogis in the States." In Timothy S. Miller (ed.), *America's Alternative Religions* (pp. 191–213). Albany: State University of New York Press.

Wallis, Roy. 1979. *Salvation and Protest: Studies of Social and Religious Movements*. New York: St. Martin's Press.

1984. *The Elementary Forms of the New Religious Life*. London: Routledge and Kegan Paul.

Warner, Stephen R. 1997. "Convergence Rational Choice: Framework for the Scientific Study of Religion." In Lawrence A. Young (ed.), *Rational Choice Theory and Religion: Summary and Assessment* (pp. 25–45). New York: Routledge.

CHAPTER 14

Schism in Babylon: colonialism, Afro-Christianity and Rastafari

Christopher Partridge

Jamaica, the third largest island in the West Indies, has more than 2.5 million inhabitants and is commonly known not only as a popular tourist destination, but also for its religion and popular culture – most notably reggae and Rastafarianism. The latter, however, is very much a product of another fact of particular significance that is central to the argument of this chapter. Throughout Jamaica there are place names and large plantation mansions that serve to remind the people that their land was, until 1962, a British colony and, until August 1, 1838, a slave colony. The aim of this chapter is simply to argue that these latter exogenous factors are central to understanding schism in African-Caribbean religion. In other words, schism in Jamaican religion is fundamentally related to the colonial and postcolonial experiences associated with plantation society, or what is sometimes termed "Plantation-America."[1] This is based on the general thesis that, as Leonard Barrett's seminal study of Rastafarianism argues, the very psyche of the Jamaican people is a product of their history.

Jamaicans are by nature some of the most fun loving, hardworking, and gregarious people in the Caribbean. Treated with kindness and respect, they are likely to remain the most confident and dependable friends on earth. But if treated with impunity and disrespect, all the rage of a deep psychic revenge may surface with unpredictable consequences. This calm-and-storm personality of contemporary Jamaicans *is a direct inheritance of that group of Africans who suffered the most frustrating and oppressive slavery ever experienced in a British colony.*[2]

---

[1] The concept of "Plantation-America" was developed to refer to societies which had been molded by the rigidly stratified plantation system within which African slave labor was used to produce mainly sugar cane. Although this model has been critiqued and refined, it does highlight "the importance of both social and racial stratification in the development of modern Jamaican society" (Johnson-Hill 1995: 9.). See Wagley 1957: 3–13; Craton 1978; Burton 1997: 13–46.

[2] Barrett 1997: 29 – emphasis added.

Indeed, it will be argued that schism in Jamaica arises directly out of a culture of resistance which was molded in the fires of slavery and colonial oppression.

AFRO-CHRISTIANITY

By 1838, many Jamaican slaves had become at least nominally Christian as a result of the proselytizing efforts of black Baptist preachers, rather than the activities of their white counterparts who, as Richard Burton comments, "began serious missionary work on the colony only in the 1820s, almost forty years after the first wave of slave converts had been made by black missionaries."[3]

It is worth noting at this point that, even though Christianity significantly shaped African-Jamaican religion, particularly following emancipation in 1838, African culture continued to inform everyday belief and practice. To understand the embedded nature of African-derived religion and culture in Jamaica, it helps first to understand the relationship between the slaves and Christianity. For example, unlike other Caribbean islands, such as Haiti, in Jamaica the slaves were not pressed to become Christians. Indeed, quite the contrary. English planters refused to share their religion with their slaves. As Barrett comments, "the Church of England and its high liturgy was considered too sophisticated for people of a 'lesser breed' and, further, the masters feared that the preachers – in their unguarded inspirational moments – would stretch the equality of humanity before God a little too far."[4] Hence, during these early years, the slave population simply developed what it remembered of the religion as it was practiced in Africa. Indeed, continuity with West African culture is hardly surprising since, as Barrett points out, the Africans who were brought to Jamaica were

not just thousands of black bodies known as slaves but, indeed, were culture bearers from highly developed cultural communities where *religion* was the strongest motivating force . . . Contrary to the *tabula rasa* hypothesis promulgated by slave philosophers and historians of Jamaica . . . the people who became slaves were the "cream" of Africa between the ages of 16 and 30. As such they were important carriers of African culture.[5]

---

[3] Burton 1997: 97.   [4] Barrett 1997: 17, 20.

[5] Barrett 1978: 7. It is worth noting that, up until the mid nineteenth century, it was not unusual for those on the frontiers of the colonial encounter to declare its absence, indigenous beliefs simply being dismissed as "superstition" – the opposite of "religion" according to their definition. This opposition between civilized religion and the superstition of "the other" became a central feature of the colonial project.

More significantly, many of these carriers were religious functionaries. This is important, for there is evidence that, because these priests and priestesses were restricted in their traditional duties and unable to fulfill their roles due to the demands of slave labor, they began practicing ritual aggression against the colonial powers. Hence, central to the slaves' burgeoning culture of resistance was what became known throughout their communities as *obeah* and *myal* (to which we shall return below). The point is that continuity with African religion and culture and the subversive use of the sacred against colonial powers are enduring and important threads that run throughout Jamaican history.[6]

As to the influence of Christianity, following the American Revolution some Loyalists fled to the British colony, taking their slaves with them, some of whom were Baptist preachers. Perhaps the most influential of these early slave preachers was George Liele (sometimes spelled Lisle) who traveled to Jamaica in 1783. His preaching, along with that of other black preachers such as George Lewis and Moses Baker, soon met with success. Indeed, as a result of Liele's work, there emerged a movement known as the Native Baptists. Breaking away from European orthodoxy, they interpreted Christian theology in terms of African-derived religious ideas. This transformed Baptist theology into an empowering liberative force, which focused on freedom in this world, rather than emancipation in the next. The freedom of black people was a command of God. That said, while Liele is generally credited with being the founder of the Native Baptist movement, there is evidence that he was concerned about its interpretation of Christianity in terms of Myalism and consequent schism. Indeed, it was not long before Liele wrote to the London Missionary Society requesting assistance. While, he says, "the grand doctrine of these people was the spirit's teaching," it was not the Holy Spirit. Rather "the spirit was sought in dreams and visions of the night, which thus become the source of their spiritual life."[7] Eventually, white Baptist missionaries arrived in order to stem the flow of Afro-Christian syncretic religion and thus prevent schism. In a colonial context, however, the likelihood of persuading African slaves to accept European theology wholesale was always going to be small. Hence, as Barrett comments, there eventually emerged distinct forms of Afro-Christian sectarianism in Jamaica: "*Pukumina*, which is mostly African in its rituals and beliefs; the Revival cult, which is partly African and partly Christian; and Revival

---

[6] This is also evident in reggae. See King 2002.   [7] Quoted in Chevannes 1998a: 8.

Zion, which is mostly Christian and the least African in its rituals and beliefs."[8]

Central to Jamaican African-derived religion were the techniques of *myal* and *obeah*. Generally speaking, *obeah* was used to curse individuals and to manipulate events malevolently, and *myal* was understood to be the remedy, in that it enabled one to remove hexes and provide immunity to spiritual attack. As noted above, it was attractive to the slave community because it represented a form of resistance to European hegemony. It was believed, for example, that slavery, understood as an evil with origins in white sorcery, could be countered by Myalistic techniques. In effect, the rationale was that white slavers were able to wield such power as a result of some form of *obeah* and that this could be removed by the practice of Myalism.[9] The point is that, when Africans responded to Liele's preaching, they did so within the framework of Myalism.[10] Because this led to a certain instability, in that the Christianity of the missionaries found such religion unacceptable, even demonic, the pressure toward schism was there from the outset. Hence, the point is that Jamaican Christian schism was rooted in an African gaze, an attachment to their land of origin, in that their religious identity was molded by a sense of continuity with African religion and culture, with its myths, value, and rituals: belief in spirits of the dead, dancing, drumming, prophesying, glossolalia, trance, possession, and millennialism. For example, Chevannes notes that "African water rituals resurfaced in Christian baptism and missionaries had to wage theological battle to convince the people that John the Baptist was not greater than Jesus and should not be worshipped."[11]

The terms "Revival" and "Revivalism," which in this context refer to Afro-Christian sectarianism, are taken from the Protestant revivalism which spread from Europe and North America to Jamaica in 1860.[12] That is to say, while, as in their countries of origin, a revival significantly increased the number of heads passing through church doors, it also quickly became apparent that Jamaican Revivalism was becoming a synthesis of Christianity and African ecstatic religion. This was perhaps to be expected: not only was this type of syncretism evident in Jamaica since Liele's preaching, but religious fervor during revival meetings often included expressions of spirit possession, including trance and convulsion, which had much in common with African indigenous

---

[8] Barrett 1997: 22.   [9] See Curtin 1968: 29.   [10] See Burton 1997: 99–101; Chevannes 1998a: 7–8.
[11] Chevannes 1998a: 8.
[12] For a good background history of revivals of the period, see Ward 1992.

religions.[13] Once such syncretism was recognized by the ecclesiastical authorities, again it was denounced. Consequently, Revivalist Christianity began to flourish within slave communities outside colonial ecclesiastical authority. As noted above, this led to the development of schismatic traditions, notably Zion Revival and Pukumina – sometimes emically referred to as the '60 and '61 orders. Chevannes explains:

> As the Revival of 1860 progressed into 1861, as it separated itself from orthodox Christianity, more explicitly African beliefs and practices came to the fore. Both worship the sky-bound spirits, the triune God, angels and archangels, but whereas Zion [the '60 order] worships only the apostles and prophets among the earth-bound spirits, Pukumina [the '61 order] appeases and pays homage to Satanic spirits, such as the fallen angels. The Pukumina variant is seldom practised today.[14]

The overall point, however, is that the years between 1838 and 1865 were marked, as Burton comments, "not merely by a conflict for economic and social survival between ex-slaves and ex-masters but also by a cultural (and by extension social and political) struggle between the white missionaries, on the one hand, and, on the other, the freed community and its black preachers over the *kind* of Christianity that was to hold sway in Jamaica."[15] Hence, in Jamaica, schism was closely linked to colonialism and slavery, which strengthened the sense of continuity with African culture, encouraged the desire to preserve it in the diaspora, and increased the longing for repatriation. Indeed, at a more mundane level, colonial culture, which restricted the education of African-Jamaicans and, as we have seen, was reluctant to fully Christianize them, meant that when the faith was received it was not well understood. As Malcolm Calley has argued, "possibly the most important role of slavery in the West Indies was to hinder the diffusion of a detailed knowledge of Christianity to the slaves, thus stimulating them to *invent their own interpretations and their own sects*."[16] However, we have seen that central to the African gaze and the schismatic impulse was a culture of resistance that had developed within slave communities. Indeed, so developed was it in Jamaica that it produced what might be described as an allied culture of schism. Jamaica had "one of the highest rates of slave revolts and conspiracies in the history of any slave society. It certainly had the highest number in the Anglophone colonies, including the decisive rebellion of 1831–32 which

---

[13] See Lewis 2003.   [14] Chevannes 1998a: 8.   [15] Burton 1997: 97.
[16] Quoted in Cashmore 1983: 16 – emphasis added.

hastened the abolition of slavery by Britain in 1834."[17] As Barrett comments, "in Jamaica, as the record will show, not a year passed between the seventeenth and the nineteenth centuries without a rebellion or at least a threat of one."[18] Consequently, Afro-Christian schism needs to be understood in terms of an explicitly political manifestation of this resistance to colonialism. In developing its own sectarian theologies, Afro-Christianity developed a sacred culture of resistance to European religious hegemony, by maintaining a continuity with traditional African cosmologies that defined social realities in ways quite different from those that their oppressors were seeking to impose upon them.[19] As Ennis Edmonds comments, "even when Africans converted to Christianity, the elements of Christianity to which they showed the greatest affinity were those that reinforced their Afrocentric worldview, informed their struggle for liberation, and promised them eventual freedom from and redress of the evil perpetrated against them by the colonial system."[20] It is not surprising, therefore, that one of the biggest challenges to slavery in Jamaica came under the leadership of a Baptist freed slave by the name of Samuel Sharpe who was not unusual in being both a Baptist preacher and, possibly, a "daddy" (i.e. leader or priest) within West African slave religion. Certainly, while he was a member of the London Baptist Mission, led by British missionaries, there is evidence to suggest that Sharpe was also a member of the Native Baptist church, which, we will see, developed a mixture of African-derived religion and Christianity.[21]

Concerning the latter point, it should be noted that dual membership was common in Jamaica, in that many would belong nominally to a European Christian denomination, whilst being actively involved in Afro-Christian sectarian religion as well. As Chevannes has argued,

dual membership, which has been practised from as long ago as the late-eighteenth century . . . is far-reaching in its significance, for it implies that the native religions mean much more to the people than a mere head count would suggest, and alternatively that formal Christianity has not been as successful in changing

---

[17] Chevannes 1998a: 1. See also Barrett 1997: 29–67; Besson 1998; Campbell 1985; Chevannes 1994: 1–43.
[18] Barrett 1997: 38.   [19] See Barrett 1978: 9–13; Burton 1997: 97–103.   [20] Edmonds 2003: 33.
[21] See Barrett 1997: 38–51. It is important to realize, of course, that this type of syncretism is not unusual in colonial/postcolonial African-Caribbean culture. One only has to think of traditions such as Umbanda, Candomblé, and Santería (La Regla de Ocha), which, broadly speaking, combine Roman Catholicism and indigenous religion, often of West African origin. See, for example: Fernandez-Olmos and Paravisini-Gebert 2003; Clarke 1998; Matibag 1996.

the people's worldview as its long history and its large share of members suggest.[22]

The point, as far as we are concerned, is that, even though people broke away from European denominations, under colonialism they continued as nominal members, often practicing their chosen religion in secret. Over time, however, as colonial power waned, so the chosen religion came to the fore and was practiced openly.

Revivalism consistently attracted a large following up until the early 1920s in Jamaica.[23] However, in the years immediately prior to the emergence of Rastafari, not only were Afro-centric beliefs dominant, but, under the pressure of colonialism, apocalyptic beliefs had become more or less commonplace in schismatic religion. It is not unusual, of course, for oppressed communities to develop apocalyptic eschatologies which provide hope of emancipation and a better life free of suffering.[24] This was certainly the case with Jamaica's most famous Revivalist preacher, Alexander Bedward and, following his movement, Rastafari.[25] As Burton comments, "it took the career of the remarkable Alexander Bedward (ca. 1859–1930) to bring the radical energies of Jamaican Afro-Christianity to their peak, whereafter it was superseded as the main challenge to the colonial order by the newly emergent millennialist cult of Rastafarianism."[26] Not atypical of Jamaican political activists during the period (e.g. Sharpe), in 1895, at the beginning of his career, Bedward was arrested for sedition. He preached that African-Jamaicans should rise up and overthrow their white masters. However, later in his career, when hope of immediate revolution began to fade, his gaze turned to the future and to divine intervention. He prophesied the end times and the rapture of true believers into heaven. That said, it is interesting that, while Bedward was vigorously anti-colonial, he accepted the colonialist theological premise that God was white and also taught that "during the postapocalyptic millennial period of the new heaven and new earth, blacks would become white."[27] Of course, this theology needs to be contextualized, for, perhaps surprisingly, a negative understanding of blackness was not an uncommon view amongst Jamaicans during the colonial period as they reflected on why they might be the oppressed: "Black skin

---

[22] Chevannes (1998a: 9) has argued that Revivalism has continued as a form of neo-Pentecostalism. "In a repetition of history . . . Myalism has once more shed its garb and is now wearing Pentecostal clothes."

[23] Chevannes 1998a: 2.   [24] See Newport and Gribbin 2006; Walliss 2004; Wojcik 1997.

[25] See Hill 1983.   [26] Burton 1997: 116.   [27] Chevannes 1994: 28, 109.

color is a sign of debasement. Not only are there common expressions which assume this – for example, blaming race for the failure of Blacks as an ethnic group to advance – but there are also folk-tales which tell, not without humour, how Blacks came to be black. They all tell of some aberration or weakness of character."[28] Hence, Bedward, conscious that Christianity had been received from whites, was expressing ideas about skin color, sin, and colonial oppression that were familiar to many Jamaicans. Indeed, on meeting the ethnographer Martha Beckwith, he took her hand and declared that his own hand would become as white as hers when he entered heaven.[29] Nevertheless, Bedward's experience of colonialism led him to a theology which insisted that the white people of the world were destined for destruction.[30] Moreover, there is evidence that, in 1920, Bedward himself declared not only that he was the harbinger of their end, but that he would be the instrument of their destruction. There is even evidence that he believed himself to be the returned Christ. As such, he would, like Elijah, ascend to heaven in a flaming chariot (on Friday, December 31, 1920) and, after three days, return for his flock, take them to glory, and then begin the events of the apocalypse and the destruction of the white race. Perhaps needless to say, at the appointed time and date, in front of thousands of followers, no flaming chariot appeared. Following three subsequent predictions, each with the same earthbound result, the cognitive dissonance of his remaining followers was assuaged a little when he declared that God had commanded him to remain on the earth to preach. However, in 1921, following his alleged claim to be Christ and incendiary declarations suggesting the overthrow of the colonial authorities, he was arrested and interned in Kingston Lunatic Asylum, where he died in November 1930, a few weeks after the coronation of Emperor Haile Selassie I in Ethiopia.

Finally, of course, thinking of theories of the causes of schism, it is clear that many Afro-Christian leaders, such as Bedward and Sharpe, were charismatic figures introducing distinctive worldviews. Bedward assumed a prophetic role, declared a change of affairs, sought to overthrow the established order, spoke of imminent divine intervention, and, thereby, elicited devotion and commitment from oppressed, poor communities, whose members warmed to his particular interpretation of Christian eschatology. Similarly, Sam Sharpe was noted for his extraordinary charisma: "I heard him two or three times deliver a brief extemporaneous

---

[28] Chevannes 1998b: 24.   [29] Beckwith 1929: 169–70. Quoted in Chevannes 1998b: 25.
[30] For a short, emic, early history, see Brooks 1917.

address . . . and I was amazed both at the power and freedom with which he spoke, and at the effect which was produced upon his auditory. He appeared to have the feelings and passions of his hearers completely at his command."[31] It is little surprise, therefore, that he was able to motivate numerous men to rebel against the system in what became known as the Sam Sharpe Rebellion or, occasionally, the Baptist War (1831–2). Again, the Morant Bay Rebellion of 1865 was led by two charismatic Native Baptists, William Gordon and Paul Bogle, seeking to overthrow colonial power.

It is also important to understand that they embodied an African-Caribbean hope which was both religious and political. They were African slaves themselves who, having been touched by God, became prophetic figures. Just as, for Rastafari, Marcus Garvey was understood as the Black Moses who would lead his people out of the land of oppression to the promised land, ruled by the black messiah, Haile Selassie, so too these early slave preachers were prophetic figures resisting a culture of oppression. That is to say, their teaching articulated a confluence of the sacred and the secular. Slavery and colonialism were never solely political and economic. They were earthly manifestations of spiritual realities and understood within a dualistic theological framework. Consequently, those who opposed colonialism were close to God and walking a path of righteousness, and those who opposed them and supported colonialism were demonized and heading for destruction. For example, central to the Sam Sharpe Rebellion was the news that, while the slaves' free papers had arrived, the plantation owners were putting pressure on the Governor not to release them. Very quickly, notes Barrett, "this idea of free papers took on eschatological significance similar to the messianic 'day of the Lord' concept among the Jews. The prophet who was in touch with the source of the message – England – was Sam Sharpe."[32] God had delivered the slaves, Sharpe was his messenger, and dark powers were interfering with their salvation.

ETHIOPIANISM, THE RISE OF RASTAFARI,
AND THE STRUGGLE AGAINST BABYLON

"Africanity runs through and colours everything . . . [and] exemplifies what has occurred generally throughout the Caribbean since the colonial

---

[31] Henry Bleby, quoted in Barrett 1997: 42.   [32] Barrett 1997: 43.

period."[33] It is not surprising therefore that there is considerable continuity between Afro-Christianity and later sectarian religion. In particular, the colonial pressures which fomented the culture of schism in Jamaica are central to a correct understanding of the rise of Rastafari. As Rupert Lewis insists, "the connection between Bedwardism, revivalism, and early Rastafari is patently clear."[34] Indeed, Afro-Christian activists such as Bedward, Sharpe, and Bogle are cited by Rastas as inspirational examples in their struggle for justice and against "Babylon."

Babylon–Zion dualism is central to Rastafarianism and can be linked to certain political developments in Jamaica from the late eighteenth century onwards. During this period, Jamaica witnessed the emergence of a back-to-Africa movement that followed a pattern that can be observed within other histories of the oppressed. It is, of course, not uncommon for peoples who have migrated from their homelands, usually as a result of force, to develop religio-political Zionisms. As with other migrant communities, the African diaspora came to understand itself as an exiled people living in a hostile land – "Babylon." This in turn led to an understanding of their homeland as pure and sacred – "Zion."[35] Bearing in mind its Afro-Christian history, it is unsurprising that much of the terminology used to describe such peoples and their experiences is biblical. Indeed, particular use is made of the Hebrew Bible. For example, reinterpreting the story of the Israelites' journey from Egypt to the promised land, as detailed in the Pentateuch, not only did Jamaicans think of Africa in terms of the divinely ordained promised land, but they understood the Atlantic Ocean in terms of the River Jordan which needed to be crossed. Hence, as Dick Hebdige puts it, "the Bible is a central determining force in . . . [the] popular West Indian consciousness in general . . . It is the supremely ambiguous means through which the black community can most readily make sense of its subordinate position within an alien society."[36]

As to the emergence of an identifiable back-to-Africa movement (and of Ethiopianism generally), perhaps the key early influence was Edward Wilmot Blyden (1832–1912) – now considered the pioneer of Pan-Africanism.[37] Born into a middle-class free black family in Charlotte Amalie, St. Thomas, in the United States Virgin Islands, he was conscious that his upbringing was very much the exception for black people. From an early age he was recognized as a talented student, particularly in

---

[33] Matibag 1996: xi. This is evident in Douglas Mack's emic history of Rastafari (1999).
[34] Lewis 1998: 149–50. [35] Barrett 1997: 115–17. [36] Hebdige 1979: 32, 33–4. [37] Lynch 1967.

languages, literature, and oratory. So much so that a white clergyman, John Knox, took him under his wing and encouraged him to become a Christian minister. In May 1850, Blyden traveled to the United States to enroll in Knox's alma mater, Rutgers Theological College. In so doing he realized just how sheltered his upbringing had been, for it was here that he first encountered racism. Despite his obvious academic ability, purely on the grounds of his skin color he was refused admission. Disappointed, but not deterred, he applied to two further theological seminaries, both of which turned him down for the same reason. He was now feeling the pressure of "Babylon," a pressure which was about to be increased with the passage of the Fugitive Slave Law in September 1850. The effects of this law were that free black people could be mistaken for fugitive slaves and thus arrested and sold into slavery.

It was around this time that he encountered the American Colonization Society,[38] which, as part of their repatriation program, offered to finance his passage to Liberia, the oldest republic in West Africa and one of only two African countries never colonized by a European power – the other being Ethiopia.[39] Indeed, Liberia's modern political foundations rest on the work of freed slaves who sailed there in the early nineteenth century. Blyden's interest in both the offer and the project was immediate. Within a couple of months, in December 1850, he traveled to Liberia's capital, Monrovia. He enrolled at the city's Alexander High School and by 1858 had become its Principal. Also during this time, he was ordained into the Presbyterian Church, he served as editor of the *Liberian Herald*, and he published the first of his many pamphlets, *A Vindication of the Negro Race* (1857), in which he stridently attacked theories of black inferiority. In 1861 he made the first of seven journeys back to the United States in order to encourage more blacks to return to Africa, arguing that racial supremacy was so much part of the white

---

[38] Founded by a group of Presbyterian ministers in Washington, DC, on December 28, 1916, as the American Society for the Colonizing of Free People of Color in the United States, the American Colonization Society promoted the emigration and colonization of free African-Americans to West Africa. Essentially, the organization understood their *raison d'être* missiologically. African-Americans should take this opportunity to return to their homeland in order to encourage education and Christianity. To southern whites, concerned that the growing number of freed Africans would destabilize their system of slavery, the plan was portrayed as a solution to the problem. Consequently, many blacks believed it to be a proslavery, racist organization. That said, many black leaders, while rejecting the American Colonization Society, did support the notion of a return to Africa. As the society grew, so did the number of influential supporters, including Abraham Lincoln, James Madison, James Monroe, and the United States Supreme Court Justice, Bushrod Washington, the society's first president.

[39] See Grierson & Munro-Hay 1999; Mack 1999: 141.

psyche that it was doubtful that blacks would ever progress beyond being second-class citizens in Western societies.

Blyden's obvious intelligence, his forthright and articulate critiques of European and American cultures, and his promotion of the virtues of his new country led to a steady progression through Liberian corridors of power: President of Liberia College; Secretary of the State of Liberia; Liberian Commissioner to Britain and the United States; Liberian Ambassador to the British Court of St James; Minister of the Interior.

His position within Presbyterianism, however, took a quite different turn. In 1886 he resigned from Presbyterianism and a year later published a pamphlet that essentially detailed his reasons for so doing. Again, reflecting the rationale for schism evident within Jamaican Christianity, in *Christianity, Islam, and the Negro Race* he argued that Africans had suffered far more under Christianity than they had under Islam, and that therefore the Christian faith per se was problematic for blacks. As was implicitly articulated within Afro-Christian teaching and would become explicit within Rastafari, he claimed that Western Christianity had hindered the development of the African personality. Although not all his ideas were well received – such as his defence of polygamy – by the time of his death in 1912 his influence was beginning to be felt. Not only had the first Pan-African conference – which was, to a large extent, shaped by his thinking – been held in London in 1900, but his ideas on black identity began to take hold as the twentieth century progressed. In particular, he argued a thesis that can be traced from Afro-Christian thought through into Rastafari, namely that Ethiopia represents the pinnacle of civilization and learning. Indeed, even before Blydon developed the idea, it was being preached in Jamaica by Liele.

That said, Ethiopia and the celebration of its supremacy represented more than the country itself, becoming identified with Africa per se. That is to say, for many within the African diaspora, Ethiopia became a signifier for the entire African continent; it was the heart of Africa; it was a powerful symbol of a free, sovereign, and sacred Africa; it was, therefore, as Neil Savishinsky has argued, "a potent source of inspiration for African nationalist leaders, many of whom chose the 'pan-African' colours of the Ethiopian flag as a symbol for their emerging political parties and newly independent states."[40] In short, Ethiopianism articulated an expectation of African liberation and the emergence of an Ethiopian empire.

[40] Savishinsky 1998: 135.

It should be noted, however, that, in developing Ethiopianism – and thereby laying the intellectual foundations for back-to-Africa political and religious thought – Blyden was actually developing an idea, the embryo of which was already present in Jamaican culture. Indeed, significantly, as noted above, Liele had himself adopted the idea, and in 1784 founded in Jamaica what he initially called the Ethiopian Baptist Church. As Barrett comments,

> by the time of the emergence of the Black churches, Africa (as a geographical entity) was just about obliterated from their minds. Their only vision of a homeland was the biblical Ethiopia. It was the vision of a golden past – and the promise that Ethiopia should once more stretch forth its hands to God – that revitalized the hope of an oppressed people. Ethiopia to the Blacks in America was like Zion or Jerusalem to the Jews.[41]

As has been noted, for many African-Jamaican colonial subjects it became a focal point on the eschatological horizon, the Zion to which they were being called to return. It was this emergent Ethiopianism that Blyden developed from a Pan-Africanist perspective.[42] Drawing on classical sources, he argued that, rather than being the barbaric, dark continent described by white Christians and, perhaps most eloquently and influentially, in Joseph Conrad's 1902 novel *Heart of Darkness*, Africa was actually the cradle of civilization.

Ethiopianism, however, did not develop into the culture of resistance in America that Blyden and many others hoped it would. Nevertheless, although disappointed, he was optimistic and looked forward to the day when a "black Moses" would lead the dispersed peoples of African origin back to their homeland. Drawing again on imagery from the Hebrew Bible, but interpreting it from a distinctly Afro-Christian, anti-colonial sectarian perspective, he prophesied the following: "The Negro leader of the Exodus who will succeed will be a Negro of the Negroes, like Moses was a Hebrew of the Hebrews – even if brought up in Pharaoh's palace [i.e. at the heart of the land of oppression] he will be found. No half Hebrew and half Egyptian will do the work . . . for this work heart, soul and faith are needed."[43] If, at this time, there was little sign of Blyden's hope coming to fruition in North America, this was not the case in

---

[41] Barrett 1997: 75.
[42] Pan-Africanism is complex, but at a fundamental level it is a political movement dedicated to the unification of all Africans to a single African state to which those in the African diaspora can return. More broadly and amorphously, Pan-Africanism seeks culturally to unite Africans in Africa and in the diaspora through literary and artistic projects.
[43] Quoted in Lynch 1967: 121.

Jamaica. Largely because of its particular history of resistance, the embers of radical religio-political Ethiopianism were smoldering and simply needed someone to fan them. That person was Marcus Garvey. He would be the "Negro of the Negroes." As Barrett argues, "the movement that was to embody the Ethiopian ideology par excellence was the Back-to-Africa Movement of Marcus Garvey. It was in Garvey – the prophet of African redemption – that the spirit of Ethiopianism came into full blossom."[44] He would draw Jamaica's Afro-Christian religio-political threads together.

Marcus Mosiah Garvey (1887–1940), born in St. Ann's Bay, Jamaica, was the leader of the first genuine large-scale black movement and, with reference to Blyden's "prophecy," was popularly referred to during his lifetime as "Black Moses" – his middle name, of course, greatly assisting this perception. On July 20, 1914 he founded the Universal Negro Improvement Association (UNIA) in Kingston. From this point on Garveyism became influential and international, being the movement for African repatriation and self-government that many oppressed Africans had, since Blyden, been longing for. As Peter Clarke points out, "The Garvey movement, like the Rastafarian movement, was born perhaps as much from despair of ending injustice and discrimination . . . as it was from a vision of Africa as a "Land without Evil"."[45]

Resistance to colonialism and the development of an African utopianism – so central to Afro-Christian sectarianism and the distrust of European and American Christian orthodoxy and, of course, also to Blyden's thought – lay at the heart of Garvey's teaching and that of the UNIA. Consequently, the burden of his teaching was the return of Africans to Africa, the only place, he believed, where black people would truly be at home and be respected as a race. Indeed, like Blyden, Garvey can be understood to have actively encouraged schism in his call for Africans to consider returning to Africa, to lay the foundations for a new superior African civilization, to correct the prejudiced white histories of Africa, to recognize African civilization as the world's first and greatest, and, most significantly, to worship a black God "through the spectacles of Ethiopia":

We, as Negroes, have found a new ideal. Whilst our God has no colour, yet it is human to see everything through one's own spectacles, and since the white people have seen their God through white spectacles, we have only now started

---

[44] Barrett 1997: 76.   [45] Clarke 1994: 37.

out (late though it be) to see our God through our own spectacles. The God of Isaac and the God of Jacob let him exist for the race that believe in the God of Isaac and the God of Jacob. We Negroes believe in the God of Ethiopia, the everlasting God – God the Son, God the Holy Ghost, the one God of all ages. That is the God in whom we believe, but we shall worship him through the spectacles of Ethiopia.[46]

Perhaps surprisingly, Garvey himself never visited Africa, his vision of Africa being based less on actual knowledge of the continent and more on the Bible. Nevertheless, while his dream of physical repatriation was not realized, he did succeed in focusing the minds of Africans on issues which were to become central to the Rastafarian movement. Indeed, we will see that, for many contemporary Rastas, this very focusing of the mind can be understood in terms of a return to Africa and thus as Garvey's fulfillment of his Mosaic calling. Psychologically, emotionally, culturally, and spiritually, Garvey has led his people back to the promised land.

Of particular importance, however, were Garvey's comments concerning an African redeemer, which, while maintaining a continuity with Afro-Christian culture and, indeed, reminding one of Bedward's claims, would lead to the emergence of a distinct Jamaican tradition. For example, he interpreted Psalm 68:31 as follows: "We go from the white man to the yellow man, and see the same unenviable characteristics in the Japanese. Therefore, we must believe that the Psalmist had great hopes of the race of ours when he prophesied 'Princes shall come out of Egypt and Ethiopia shall stretch forth his [sic] hands to God'."[47] Indeed, while there is little evidence for the claim, many Jamaicans also believe him to have prophesied the following: "Look to Africa for the crowning of a Black King; he shall be the Redeemer"[48] or "Look to Africa when a black king shall be crowned for the day of deliverance is near."[49] Who would this royal redeemer be? The answer, for Garvey and for many Jamaican Garveyites, came on November 2, 1930, when Ras (meaning "Prince") Tafari Makonnen (1892–1975), the great-grandson of King Saheka Selassie of Shoa, was crowned Negus of Ethiopia. Several days after the coronation, on November 8, 1930, Garvey published an article in his

---

[46] Garvey 1986: 34.   [47] Garvey 1986: 61.   [48] Barrett 1997: 81.
[49] Clarke 1994: 36. While the Garvey scholar Robert Hill argues that "no evidence has so far been found or cited to show that Garvey ever made this assertion," he does draw attention to a comment made in September 1924 by James Morris Webb, a black clergyman, concerning the advent of a "universal black king" as the fulfillment of biblical prophecy (Hill 1983: 25). Others have argued a similar thesis to Edmonds, namely that, although no documentation has been found, "it is likely that Garvey made some oral declaration . . . and that it was kept alive in the memory of people steeped in oral tradition" (Edmonds 2003: 147).

Jamaican newspaper *The Blackman*, which referred back to his earlier comments:

The Psalmist prophesied that Princes would come out of Egypt and Ethiopia would stretch forth her hands unto God. We have no doubt that the time has now come. Ethiopia is now really stretching forth her hands. This great kingdom of the East has been hidden for many centuries, but gradually she is rising to take a leading place in the world and it is for us of the Negro race to assist in every way to hold up the hand of the Emperor Ras Tafari.[50]

Declaring himself to be in the line of King Solomon and taking the name Haile Selassie I (Might of the Trinity), as well as "King of Kings" and "Lion of the Tribe of Judah" – which are important biblical references – it is not surprising that when he was crowned in St. George's Cathedral in Addis Ababa in front of representatives from many nations, those who had been inspired by Garvey's teaching saw more than the accession of another Ethiopian ruler. In Haile Selassie I/Ras Tafari many saw the Messiah, the fulfillment of biblical prophecy, even God incarnate.[51] This interpretation of the events was explicitly informed by Ethiopianism and earlier Jamaican Afro-Christianity. It is also a form of Selassie-oriented theology that was particularly taught by Leonard Howell, who, with Joseph Hibbert, Archibald Dunkley, and Robert Hinds, was one of the principal architects of Rastafarian religio-political thought.[52] However, the scholarly consensus would seem to be that it was Howell who first taught the divinity of Haile Selassie, which was to become a central tenet of much (not all)[53] Rastafarian theology.[54] We have seen that the deification of prominent leaders was not novel in Jamaican religious history.

At this point it is worth noting that the history of Rastafari in Jamaica provides an insight into just how a schism that has been created under the pressure of colonialism can, if kept under that pressure over several generations, generate a cultic milieu within which distinct and perhaps

---

[50] The full text of the article can be found in Lewis 1998: 145–6.   [51] Wint 1998.

[52] Hill 1983; Spencer 1998.

[53] The Twelve Tribes of Israel sect, for example, seem not to insist on the doctrine of the divinity of Haile Selassie, though many do accept it (Rubenstein and Suarez 1994: 3–4). For example, when I raised this belief with a member of the Twelve Tribes of Israel in Manchester, UK, he was adamant that, while Haile Selassie is enormously important in salvation history, he is not literally divine. Indeed, apart from the obvious Rastafarian elements, his beliefs, which we discussed at some length, have much in common with those of orthodox Evangelical Christianity. He even described himself as "a born again Christian."

[54] Campbell 1985: 71, 144; Cashmore 1983: 22; Chevannes 1994: 121; Hill 1983: 28; Smith, Augier, and Nettleford 1960: 6; Spencer 1998: 361.

more extreme new religions are germinated. More specifically, schism within a particular oppressed community can develop ideas which then contribute to an occulture.[55] That is to say, over time, they create a culture within which a range of ideas operate, an environment within which even obscure or taboo ideas cease to become exotic and enter mainstream thinking. The term "occult" should not be thought of in the narrow, popular sense, but rather as that which is "hidden," esoteric, paranormal, or spiritual – which, of course, includes a range of ideas from UFOs and fairies to Ethiopianism and *obeah*. Occulture is, therefore, a reservoir of ideas and practices that can be drawn on by those developing new worldviews. While I have developed this in terms of contemporary Western culture, I suggest that, on a smaller scale and as a direct result of earlier schisms, colonialism, slavery, and the development of African-derived religion, Jamaican occulture contributed to the rise of Rastafarianism. For example, not only was Howell's preaching of the deity of Selassie informed by Afro-Christian occulture, but there is evidence that the Rastafarian movement might be the eclectic product of several independent charismatic personalities preaching similar doctrines drawn from Jamaican occulture.[56] For example, in the same period Hibbert began preaching almost the same theology in rural Jamaica. Having returned from Costa Rica in 1931 – to which he had migrated at the age of 17 and where he had been a member of a Masonic Lodge called the Ancient Mystic Order of Ethiopia – he began preaching a form of Christian millenarian Ethiopianism. Following Selassie's accession, he quickly became convinced that Ras Tafari was indeed the divine coming deliverer. After moving to Kingston and making contact with Howell, and drawing on several occultural sources, Hibbert eventually established the Ethiopian Coptic Church, which was influenced very much by his former involvement with the Ancient Mystic Order of Ethiopia. Similarly, having worked as a seaman for the United Fruit Company, Dunkley, like Howell and Hibbert, returned to Jamaica in the early 1930s with very definite ideas about the significance of events in Ethiopia. Also like Howell and Hibbert, his Rastafarian preaching quickly found a following within the cultic milieu of Jamaica. However, the main point to note is that, regardless of who was the first to proclaim his divinity, largely as a result of the occulture that had evolved in Jamaica since the first slaves arrived, within perhaps three years of his coronation, devotion to

---

[55] For a far more detailed discussion of "occulture," see Partridge 2005.
[56] See Edmonds 2003: 36, 147.

Ras Tafari as the Ethiopian messiah had taken root. The seeds of Rastafarianism had been planted and were beginning to grow rapidly in their native Jamaican soil.

To return to Howell, it is perhaps not surprising that he has been singled out as the earliest exponent of the deity of Ras Tafari, for while it is difficult to assess the impact of each early Rastafarian preacher, it does seem clear that he was the most influential. That said, as is often the case in occultures to some extent, a mist of mythology (some being of Howell's own devising) obscures our understanding of his early history. For example, it is quite widely claimed (even amongst scholars) that, in 1896, he served in the Ashanti Wars[57] and learned several African languages.[58] However, others, most notably the historian Robert Hill, have argued that he was born on June 16, 1898.[59] What does seem to be clear though is that he was born at May Crawle in the Bull Head Mountain district of upper Clarendon, Jamaica, that he traveled to Colon, Panama, and the United States, that he enlisted in the US Army Transport Service as a cook, and that he arrived in New York on October 28, 1918. In May 1924 he signed his first papers for US citizenship. Following his time in the army, he worked as a construction worker in New York, where it is very likely that he encountered the Trinidadian American Communist Party Leader George Padmore, who seems to have had a formative impact on his thinking and with whom he later corresponded from Jamaica (1938–9). In the early 1930s, shortly after the accession of Haile Selassie I – which some claim Howell attended – he returned to Jamaica and began preaching Rastafari. Other significant influences on his thought at this time were Garvey (whom he had also encountered in New York) and, more enigmatically, a book published in 1924 by Robert Athlyi Rogers called *The Holy Piby*. The founder of the Afro Athlican Constructive Church, Rogers argued that Ethiopians were the chosen people of God and that Garvey was his apostle. Indeed, it would seem that Howell's own influential pamphlet, *The Promised Key*[60] – written under the pseudonym G. G. Maragh and claiming to have been published in Ghana – simply plagiarized significant parts of both *The Holy Piby* and another Jamaican

---

[57] The Ashanti had, for some years, been popular in Jamaica, the Maroons having "a special affinity for Ashanti slaves liberated by the British navy and domiciled in Sierra Leone. One author has written: "when a group of Ashanti was liberated the Maroons welcomed them as countrymen, took them into their homes, and taught them trades. Eventually, they were given lots in the Maroon town" . . . Ashanti . . . cultural influence was very strong among the Leeward Maroons during their eighty-five years of rebellion against the British in Jamaica" (Schafer 1981: 208).

[58] Edwards 1999: 645. [59] Hill 1983: 28.

[60] Reproduced with commentary in Spencer 1998: 364–86.

work by Fitz Balintine Pettersburgh, *The Royal Parchment Scroll of Black Supremacy*.[61] However, whatever its value as an original work, there is little doubt that *The Promised Key* occupies a significant place in Rastafarian history as a summary of the key themes preached by Howell.[62]

Again, this all testifies to what might be understood as an occulturally informed culture of schism, in which new churches, sects, and movements break away from older ones and contribute new ideas to the formation of newer ones. Under Howell's leadership Rastafari developed several of its central beliefs and practices drawn from a range of sources. For example, as indicated above, he appears to have assumed the title "Gangungu Maragh"[63] – a non-African, possibly Hindi-derived neologism, which he possibly picked up from Indian laborers in Jamaica. Whatever the etymology, Howell understood it to indicate something of his mystical status, as well as his role as a great leader and teacher of wisdom and virtue.[64] Also, possibly as a result of Indian influence, he promoted the sacramental use of ganga (cannabis), a practice which has since become a significant component of much (but not all) Rastafarian religious practice.[65] He also developed a strongly immanentist theology, in which the divine was understood to be present within all people. It is, it seems to me, important to grasp the implications of this immanentism, since it may account for his often misunderstood declarations that he was himself Haile Selassie. That is to say, although we have seen that such a claim would not have been novel in Jamaica, in actual fact Howell's thesis makes some theological sense in the context of a spirituality which claims both the divinity of Haile Selassie and the presence of the divine within each person. Indeed, it may have been the logical outworking of this theology that led him to the same fate as Bedward. In 1960 he was committed to a psychiatric hospital for reportedly insisting on his own divinity.[66] His son, however, has always insisted that he "didn't think he was God, and the people didn't think of him as God."[67] Nevertheless, this form of theological immanentism has since become important within mainstream Rastafarian thought.

By the 1950s it became clear to observers that Rastafarianism in Jamaica was a religio-cultural force to be reckoned with. It had begun to grow

---

[61] See Spencer 1998: 362; Hill 1983: 27; Clarke 1994: 46.   [62] Spencer 1998: 385.

[63] This, it would appear, was the pseudonym he used for *The Promised Key* – i.e. G. G. Maragh.

[64] See Hill 1983: 35–6; Spencer 1998: 386; Mansingh and Mansingh 1985: 109. This interpretation of "Gangungu Maragh" accords well with similar terms used in Indian religion and culture: "Mahārāja," meaning great king, and sometimes guru; "guru," meaning religious guide or teacher.

[65] Barrett 1997: 128.   [66] Spencer 1998: 361.   [67] Quoted in Foehr 2000: 28.

rapidly, particularly amongst the poor and disaffected who were inspired by its Ethiopianist teachings, its emphasis on black superiority, its commitment to the overthrow of white colonial oppression, and its millenarianism, which taught the apocalyptic end of the present era, the judgment of "Babylon," and the dawning of a new age of peace and love in which Africa would receive its rightful palace of eminence among the nations. That beating within this new Jamaican religion was a millenarian heart is hardly surprising, bearing in mind the Afro-Christian apocalyptic milieu in which it emerged and the occultural well from which it drank. Indeed, as noted above, it can be argued that schismatic millenarianism has been a key force in the shaping of the Jamaican religio-political psyche, particularly that of the poor and oppressed, who longed for liberation and an end to the current world order. However, the point to note here is simply that the history from which it emerged and the consequent apocalyptic critique of the current world order led many Rastas to be distrustful of the colonial authorities, particularly those in law enforcement. Very aware of their African roots and colonial past and influenced by Afro-Christian theology and Garveyite Ethiopianism, they understood themselves to be living in Babylon.[68] Hence, as Clarke points out, "the police and the law enforcement agencies in general became a special object of hatred as members began to be jailed in increasing numbers for ganga (marijuana) offences and, in particular, members of the Nyabinghi section of the movement, for resorting to violence as a means of resolving poverty and discrimination."[69] Indeed, while some Rastas could be described as politically quietist, others sought to stimulate the process of change by engagement in political struggle. As with their ancestors, they wanted change in their current conditions, rather than waiting for liberation in the hereafter. Hence, as the movement expanded and evolved, particularly during the 1960s, it became more political, and thus, inevitably, attracted the attention of "Babylon." Its strident critiques of established religion, the government, the professional classes, and indeed any form of authority which maintained the status quo and thus effectively supported Babylon, "the system," led to a common perception that it was dangerous. And, as noted above, sometimes this perception was not mistaken, in that there were militant Rastafarian factions which instigated significant social unease and violent confrontation with the police.[70]

---

[68] See Johnson 1976: 397ff.   [69] Clarke 1994: 49.   [70] Cashmore 1983: 29–33.

As the 1960s progressed, the complexity of the movement increased, with its appeal broadening. Gradually more privileged social groups, including particularly students, joined the movement. This broadening of appeal led to an evolution of thinking. The students and the more privileged, while committed to notions of black power and Pan-Africanism, were also relatively comfortable and thus not particularly concerned to return to Africa. Indeed, some became openly hostile to the idea of physical repatriation. As in much Pan-Africanism and Rastafarianism today, although some (including a white Rasta I have spoken to) maintained the hope that they would one day relocate to Africa, many began to think in terms simply of a return to African consciousness. In other words, the rhetoric shifted toward a focus on "mental decolonization, a process of deconversion, of turning away from the ethos, mores, and values of colonial society and a reconversion to the African view and way of life."[71] In short, the literalism of earlier schismatic religion, shaped by colonialism and slavery, softened in the postcolonial period. Rather than literal repatriation, some Rastas spoke of the mind of Babylon needing to be replaced by an Ethiopian mind. This, in many ways, was an important theological and ideological shift, that has had significant practical implications. Rastas were not now thinking in eschatological terms of leaving their corrupt, postcolonial societies for a better life in the promised land. Moreover, if they were going to stay where they were, the life here and now needed to be improved. Hence, along with the nurturing of an African consciousness, the oppressed were politicized. Increasingly, the true Rasta felt it a duty to challenge the social, spiritual, and intellectual structures of Babylon from within.

Finally, it is worth noting that, because we have seen that Rastafarianism emerged within the Jamaican culture of schism, it is perhaps not surprising that it has itself been subject to schism. Perhaps the most important Rastafarian sect, the Twelve Tribes of Israel, was founded in 1968, in Jamaica, by Vernon Carrington (known to members as "Prophet Gad" or simply "Gadman"). In many ways, this schism returned Rastafari closer to its Afro-Christian roots. Carrington's principal message was straightforward and simple: read a chapter of the Bible everyday. Indeed, apart from the photographs and sayings of Haile Selassie on the wall, the first thing I noticed when I first visited the house of a member was a well-thumbed Bible on the table. And one of the first points made clear to me was the importance of reading a chapter a day. That said, in keeping with

---

[71] Clarke 1994: 51.

traditional Garveyite and Howellite thinking, the focus on Africa is explicit. For example, central to the work of the Twelve Tribes of Israel is the collection of money for physical repatriation. Indeed, Haile Selassie gave Rastafarians a small area of land in the south of Ethiopia called Shashamane, which the Rastafarian I spoke to has visited with his partner, their aim being to set up a project to help youths in the small Rastafarian community that lives there. However, as Hannah Rubenstein and Chris Suarez comment, "members do not wish to pack their belongings and leave immediately. They stress the importance of getting prepared and organizing before they go. Only in this way and by living the word of Jah do they believe that they will reach the Promised Land."[72]

CONCLUDING COMMENTS

In analyzing schism one needs to understand the various levels of impact of exogenous pressure upon a community. Without rehearsing the various points made above, the overall argument has been that the transportation of African slaves and colonialism are central to an understanding of the dynamics of schism and the subsequent evolution of religion in Jamaica. In short, schism in Jamaica arose directly out of a culture of resistance to colonial oppression, which both strengthened the sense of religious and cultural continuity with Africa and, in turn, elevated and sacralized "Ethiopia" in the Jamaican imagination. Emerging out of African-derived slave religion and developed in the various Afro-Christian schismatic groups, this tradition matured into Rastafari, which, in turn, can be understood as the postcolonial product of a culture of schism.

Stuart Hall's discussion of hybridity and diaspora identity is of some help in understanding these developments. He describes the postcolonial African-Caribbean "diaspora identity" not in terms of "essence or purity," but rather in terms of "the recognition of a necessary heterogeneity and diversity; by a conception of 'identity' which lives with and through, not despite, difference; by hybridity."[73] He continues, "diaspora identities are those which are constantly producing and reproducing themselves anew, through transformation and difference."[74] While this syncretic culture, with its penchant for *bricolage*, is most evident in the music of the island – most notably dub reggae – within Jamaican religion there is what I have referred to as an occultural dynamic, which is particularly conducive to this hybridizing bias, which deconstructs and "creolizes" dominant codes

---

[72] Rubenstein and Suarez 1994: 4.   [73] Hall 1990: 235.   [74] Hall 1990: 235.

and practices, giving received signs new emphasis and meaning. The point is that, bearing this in mind, schism should perhaps be understood less in terms of a "split," a disruptive event – "the breaking away of one group of erstwhile supporters of a social or religious movement"[75] – and more in terms of a process, in this case a process shaped by transportation, slavery, and oppression. Indeed, it is difficult to think in terms of a "parent religion" from which a rebellious offspring emerges, since, first, such a perception arguably betrays a colonial Christian bias, rather than reflecting the actual perception of the slave communities, for which African-derived religion and culture were dominant. Secondly, such religion needs to be understood in terms of a process of synthesis and erasure, a series of modifications.[76] Is the dominant tradition Christianity or is it African-derived belief? The answer, of course, is not the same for all Jamaican sectarian belief and is ambiguous in some cases. Put bluntly, schism and syncretism sometimes overlap and problematize easy definition. Hence, the interesting case of Jamaican religion highlights the need to take a broader and longer view of the formation of schisms. More specifically, while little could be done in this chapter to fill the gap in theoretical analysis, I suggest that postcolonial theory has much to offer the scholar of schism.

REFERENCES

Appiah, Kwame Anthony and Henry Louis Gates (eds.). 1999. *Africana: An Encyclopedia of the African and African American Experience*. New York: Basic *Civitas* Books.

Barrett, Leonard E. 1978. "African Roots in Jamaican Indigenous Religion." *Journal of Religious Thought* 35: 7–26.

1997 [1988]. *The Rastafarians*. Boston: Beacon Press.

Beckwith, Martha. 1929. *Black Roadways: A Study of Jamaican Folk Life* (Chapel Hill: University of North Carolina Press).

Besson, Jean. 1994. "Religion as Resistance in Jamaican Peasant Life: The Baptist Church, Revival Worldview and Rastafari Movement." In Chevannes 1998c: 43–76.

Blyden, Edward Wilmot. 1967 [1887]. *Christianity, Islam, and the Negro Race*. Edinburgh: Edinburgh University Press.

Brooks, A.A. 1917. *History of Bedwardism*. Kingston: The Gleaner & Co. Available at www.kobek.com/bedwardism.pdf, accessed July 1, 2007.

Burton, Richard. 1997. *Afro-Creole: Power, Opposition, and Play in the Caribbean*. Ithaca, NY: Cornell University Press.

---

[75] Wallis 1979: 174.   [76] See Stewart and Shaw 1994.

Campbell, Horace. 1985. *Rasta and Resistance: From Marcus Garvey to Walter Rodney*. St. Johns, Antigua: Hansib Publishing.

Cashmore, Ernest. 1983. *Rastaman: The Rastafarian Movement in England*. London: Unwin Paperbacks.

Chevannes, Barry. 1994. *Rastafari: Roots and Ideology*. Syracuse, NY: Syracuse University Press.

1998a. "Introducing the Native Religions of Jamaica," In Chevannes 1998c: 1–19.

1998b. "New Approach to Rastafari." In Chevannes 1998c: 20–42.

(ed.). 1998c. *Rastafari and Other African-Caribbean Worldviews*. New Brunswick, NJ: Rutgers University Press.

Clarke, Peter B. 1994. *Black Paradise: The Rastafarian Movement*. Black Political Studies 5. San Bernardino: Borgo Press.

(ed.). 1998. *New Trends and Developments in African Religions*. Westport, CT: Greenwood Press.

Conrad, Joseph. 1994. *Heart of Darkness*. Harmondworth: Penguin.

Craton, Michael. 1978. *Searching for the Invisible Man: Slaves and Plantation Life in Jamaica*. Cambridge, MA: Harvard University Press.

Curtin, Philip D. 1968. *Two Jamaicas: The Role of Ideas in a Tropical Colony 1830–1865*. New York: Greenwood Press.

Edmonds, Ennis B. 2003. *Rastafari: From Outcasts to Culture Bearers*. New York: Oxford University Press.

Edwards, Roanne. 1999. "Early Rastafarian Leaders." In Appiah and Gates 1999: 645.

Fernandez-Olmos, Margarite and Lizabeth Paravisini-Gebert. 2003. *Creole Religions of the Caribbean: An Introduction from Vodou and Santeria to Obeah and Espiritismo*. New York: New York University Press.

Foehr, Stephen. 2000. *Jamaican Warriors: Reggae, Roots and Culture*. London: Sanctuary.

Garvey, Marcus M. 1986. *The Philosophy and Opinions of Marcus Garvey*, ed. A. J. Garvey. Dover: Majority Press.

Grierson, Roderick and Stuart Munro-Hay. 1999. "Ethiopia." In Appiah and Gates 1999: 693–9.

Hall, Stuart. 1990. "Culture, Identity and Diaspora." In Rutherford 1990: 222–37.

Hebdige, Dick. 1979. *Subculture: The Meaning of Style*. London: Methuen.

Hill, Robert. 1983. "Leonard P. Howell and the Millenarian Visions in Early Rastafari," *Jamaica Journal* 16(1): 24–39.

Johnson, Linton Kwesi. 1976. "Jamaican Rebel Music." *Race and Class* 17(4): 397–412.

Johnson-Hill, Jack A. 1995. *I-Sight: The World of Rastafari: An Interpretive Sociological Account of Rastafarian Ethics*. Lanham, MD: The Scarecrow Press.

King, Stephen A. 2002. *Reggae, Rastafari, and the Rhetoric of Social Control*. Jackson: University Press of Mississippi.

Lewis, I. M. 2003. *Ecstatic Religion: A Study of Shamanism and Spirit Possession* (3rd edn). London: Routledge.

Lewis, Rupert. 1998. "Marcus Garvey and the Early Rastafarians: Continuity and Discontinuity." In Murrell, Spencer, and McFarlane 1998: 145–58.

Lynch, Hollis Ralph. 1967. *Edward Wilmott Blyden: Pan Negro Patriot 1832–1912.* Oxford: Oxford University Press.

Mack, Douglas. 1999. *From Babylon to Rastafari: Origin and History of the Rastafarian Movement.* Chicago: Research Associates School Times Publications and Frontline Distribution International Inc.

MacKinnon, Angus and Linton Kwesi Johnson. 1979. "Forces of Reality." *New Musical Express*, April 21, 7–8, 52.

Mansingh, Ajai and Laxmi Mansingh. 1985. "Hindu Influences on Rastafarianism." In Nettleford 1985: 96–115.

Matibag, Eugenio. 1996. *Afro-Cuban Religious Experience: Cultural Reflections in Narrative.* Gainsville: University Press of Florida.

Murrell, Nathanial, William Spencer and Adrian McFarlane (eds.). 1998. *Chanting Down Babylon: The Rastafari Reader.* Philadelphia: Temple University Press.

Nettleford, Rex (ed.). 1985. *Rastafari.* Kingston, Jamaica: Caribbean Quarterly, University of the West Indies.

Newport, Kenneth G. C. and Crawford Gribbin (eds.). 2006. *Expecting the End: Millennialism in Social and Historical Context.* Waco: Baylor University Press.

Partridge, Christopher. 2005. *The Re-enchantment of the West: Alternative Spiritualities, Sacralization, Popular Culture and Occulture*, 2 vols. London: T. & T. Clark International.

Pratt, Mary Louise. 1992. *Imperial Eyes: Travel Writing and Transculturation.* London: Routledge.

Rogers, Robert Athlyi. 2000. *The Holy Piby.* Kingston: Headstart; Chicago: Research Associates School Times Publication. Also online: www.sacred-texts.com/afr/piby/ (Accessed: April 6, 2005).

Rubenstein, Hannah and Chris Suarez. 1994. "The Twelve Tribes of Israel: An Explorative Field Study." *Religion Today* 9(2): 1–6.

Rutherford, Jonathon (ed.). 1990. *Identity, Community, Culture, Difference.* London: Lawrence & Wishart.

Savishinsky, Neil. 1998. "African Dimensions of the Jamaican Rastafarian Movement." In Murrell, Spencer, and McFarlane 1998: 125–44.

Schafer, Daniel Lee. 1981. *The Maroons of Jamaica: African Slave Rebels in the Caribbean.* Ann Arbor: University Microfilms International.

Smith, M. G., Roy Augier, and Rex Nettleford. 1960. *The Rastafari Movement in Kingston, Jamaica.* Mona: Institute for Social and Economic Research, University College of the West Indies.

Spencer, William David. 1998. "The First Chant: Leonard Howell's *The Promised Key*." In Murrell, Spencer, and McFarlane 1998: 361–89.

Stewart, Charles and Rosalind Shaw (eds.). 1994. *Syncretism/Anti-Syncretism: The Politics of Religious Synthesis.* London: Routledge.

Tafari, I. Jubulani. 1985. "The Rastafari – Successors of Marcus Garvey." In Nettleford 1985: 1–12.

Taylor, Patrick. 1991. "Rastafari, the Other, and Exodus Politics: EATUP." *Journal of Religious Thought* 17: 1–2, 95–107.

Wagley, Charles. 1957. "Plantation-America: A Cultural Sphere." In V. Rubin (ed.), *Caribbean Studies: A Symposium* (pp. 3–13). Seattle: University of Washington Press.

Wallis, Roy. 1979. *Salvation and Protest: Studies of Social and Religious Movements*. New York: St. Martin's Press.

Walliss, John. 2004. *Apocalyptic Trajectories: Millenarianism and Violence in the Contemporary World*. Berne: Peter Lang.

Ward, William R. 1992. *The Protestant Evangelical Awakening*. Cambridge: Cambridge University Press.

Wint, Eleanor, in consultation with members of the Nyabinghi Order. 1998. "Who Is Haile Selassie? His Imperial Majesty in Rasta Voices." In Murrell, Spencer, and McFarlane 1998: 159–65.

Wojcik, Daniel. 1997. *The End of the World As We Know It: Faith, Fatalism, and Apocalypse in America*. New York: New York University Press.

Index